IN MEMORIAM

OF

GALVESTON'S

DEAD

SEPTEMBER 8TH
1900

RICHARD SPILLANE

EDITOR OF THE "GALVESTON TRIBUNE" AND ASSOCIATED PRESS COR-
RESPONDENT, WHO WAS CHOSEN BY THE MAYOR AND CITIZENS'
COMMITTEE TO SEIZE ANY VESSEL IN THE HARBOR AND CONVEY
TO THE OUTSIDE WORLD THE NEWS OF THE GREAT DISASTER

THE GREAT GALVESTON DISASTER

CONTAINING A

Full and Thrilling Account of the Most Appalling Calamity of Modern Times

INCLUDING

VIVID DESCRIPTIONS OF THE HURRICANE AND TERRIBLE
RUSH OF WATERS; IMMENSE DESTRUCTION OF DWELL-
INGS, BUSINESS HOUSES, CHURCHES, AND LOSS
OF THOUSANDS OF HUMAN LIVES;

THRILLING TALES OF HEROIC DEEDS; PANIC-STRICKEN MUL-
TITUDES AND HEART-RENDING SCENES OF AGONY;
FRANTIC EFFORTS TO ESCAPE A HORRIBLE
FATE; SEPARATION OF LOVED ONES, ETC.

Narrow Escapes from the Jaws of Death

TERRIBLE SUFFERINGS OF THE SURVIVORS; VANDALS
PLUNDERING BODIES OF THE DEAD; WONDERFUL EXHIBITIONS OF
POPULAR SYMPATHY; MILLIONS OF DOLLARS SENT FOR THE RELIEF
OF THE STRICKEN SUFFERERS

BY PAUL LESTER

Author of "Life in the South-West, Etc., Etc.

With an Introduction by
RICHARD SPILLANE
Editor "Galveston Tribune" and Associated Press Correspondent

**PROFUSELY EMBELLISHED WITH PHOTOGRAPHS
TAKEN IMMEDIATELY AFTER THE DISASTER**

PELICAN PUBLISHING COMPANY
Gretna 2000

Published in paperback by Pelican Publishing Company, Inc., 2000

*The word "Pelican" and the depiction of a pelican are trademarks
of Pelican Publishing Company, Inc., and are registered in the
U.S. Patent and Trademark Office.*

Printed in Canada

Published by Pelican Publishing Company, Inc.
1000 Burmaster Street, Gretna, Louisiana 70053

PREFACE.

THOUSANDS of men, women and children swept to sudden death. Millions of dollars worth of property destroyed. Scenes of suffering and desolation that beggar description. Heroic efforts to save human life. The world shocked by the appalling news. Such is the thrilling story of the Galveston flood, and in this volume it is told with wonderful power and effect.

There have been many disasters by storm and flood in modern times, but none to equal this. In the brief space of twelve hours more persons lost their lives than were killed during a year of the war between the British and the Boers or during a year and a half of our war in the Philippines.

The calamity came suddenly. Galveston was not aware of its impending fate. News of an approaching cyclone produced no alarm. Suddenly word was sent that the hurricane was bending from its usual course and might strike the city. Even then there was no sudden fear, no hurrying to escape, no thought of swift destruction. In a moment, in the twinkling of an eye, the city waked up to the awful fact that it was to be engulfed by a tidal wave, and buried in the flood of waters.

The news of the overwhelming disaster came as a shock to people everywhere. Bulletin boards in all our cities were surrounded by eager crowds to obtain the latest reports. Many who had friends in the stricken city were kept in suspense respecting their fate. With bated breath was the terrible calamity talked about, and in every part of our country committees of relief were immediately formed. The magnitude of the disaster grew from day to day. Every fresh report added to the intelligence already received, and it was made clear that a large part of the city of Galveston, with its inhabitants, had been swept out of existence.

This work furnishes a striking description of a great city of the dead. It depicts the terrible scenes that followed the calamity,

the fate that overtook the victims, and the agony of the living.   It
tells of the heroic efforts of the survivors to save their homes and
families, and recover from the terrible blow.

It tells of a thousand of the dead towed out and buried at sea
and of many hundreds cremated on shore; of the vandals who
rushed in to strip lifeless bodies, unterrified by the scenes of horror on every hand; of United States soldiers shooting the robbers
on sight and putting an end to their horrible sacrilege.

The story of the appalling horror, the oncoming of the
cyclone, the rising waters threatening the city, the inhabitants
overtaken by the flood and cut off from escape, thousands hurried
to death, chaos everywhere, recovery of bodies ravaged by thieves,
all this is vividly told in this volume.

The work contains thrilling stories by eye-witnesses.   In this
volume the survivors speak for themselves.   They tell of the sudden danger that paralyzed thousands and made them helpless
against the onslaught of the tempest.

They tell of separation from those who were attempting to
afford relief and how futile all efforts were against the fury of the
waves.   They tell how their homes and places of business, their hospitals, school-houses and churches were swept away as in a moment.

There were splendid examples of courage and heroism.   The
graphic description of the great disaster contained in this book
thrills the reader.   Amidst the alarm, the threatening death, the
overwhelming flood, he sees how nobly men struggled to save their
families and their fortunes.   He seems to ride on the crest of the
waves and witness with his own eyes the terrible tragedy.

Our Government at Washington was quick to come to the
rescue.   It ordered tents to be provided and issued rations by the
tens of thousands for the survivors.   The chords of sympathy
which make all men akin vibrated through every part of the civilized world.

Thousands of helping hands were stretched out toward Galveston.   Millions of dollars were given for the relief of the sufferers.   This volume is a complete and authentic account of the
great calamity told by the survivors.

Introduction

BY RICHARD SPILLANE.

[RICHARD SPILLANE, editor of the "Galveston Tribune," was chosen by the Mayor and Citizens' Committee to seize any vessel in the harbor and make his way as best he could to such point as he could reach, so as to get in touch with the outside world, tell the story of the tragedy and appeal to mankind for help. He crossed the bay during a squall, the little boat in which he sailed being in imminent danger of swamping, having been stove in during the hurricane. He reached Texas City after a perilous trip, then made his way over the flooded prairie to Lamarque, where he found a rail road hand-car. With this hand-car he managed to reach League City, where he met a train coming from Houston to learn what fate had befallen Galveston. On this train he reached Houston, where after sending messages to President McKinley and Governor Sayers, he gave the news in detail to the newspapers of the nation.]

IN THE world's great tragedies, that of Galveston stands remarkable. In no other case in history was a disaster met with such courage and fortitude ; in no other case in history were the people of the whole world so responsive to the call for help for the helpless.

There prevails a belief that Galveston is subject to severe storms. That is a mistake. There have been heavy blows, and there have been times when the waters of the bay and the Gulf met in the city's streets, but the storm of September 8, 1900, is without parallel. The best proof of this statement is furnished by the old Spanish charts of three hundred years ago. They contain as landmarks of Galveston Island the sign of three great trees—oaks—that stood three hundred years ago in what is known as Lafitte's grove, twelve miles down Galveston Island from the city. These oaks withstood the storms of three centuries. They were felled by the fury of the storm of September 8.

The storm of September 8th did not, as has been supposed, come upon the city without warning. The same storm, less ferocious perhaps, had swept along the South Atlantic coast several days before. It had its origin in that breeding place of hurricanes, the West Indies, and, after swirling along the Florida and Carolina shores, doubled on its tracks, entered the Gulf, came racing westward and developing greater strength with each hour, and centered all its energies upon the Texas coast near Galveston.

On September 7th there was official warning of the approach of a severe storm, but no one expected such a tempest as was destined to devastate the city. Such warning as was given was rather addressed to mariners about to go to sea than to those living on shore.

Simultaneously with the approach of the hurricane was a great wind from the north, known locally as a "Norther." This developed at Galveston about 2 A. M., on September 8th. The approaching hurricane from the east and southeast had been driving a great wall of water toward the shore at Galveston. The tremendous wind storm from the north acted as a counter force or check to the hurricane element.

The north wind blew the water from Galveston Bay on the one side of the city and the storm in the Gulf hurled its battalions of waves upon the beach side of the city.

Early in the day the battle between these two contending forces offered a magnificent spectacle to a student of scenery of nature. As long as the north wind held strong the city was safe. While the winds dashed great volumes of water over the wharves and flooded some streets in the business portion of the city and the waters of the Gulf on the other side of the city encroached upon the streets near the beach there was no particular fear of serious consequences, but about noon the barometer, which had been very low, suddenly began to drop at a rate that presaged a storm of tremendous violence.

Following this came the warning that the wind would, before many hours, change from the north to the southeast and to the fury of the wall of water being driven upon Galveston by the approaching hurricane would be added all the tremendous force of the wind that had previously acted as a partial check to the Gulf storm.

To those who previously had no fear, the certainty that the wind would change came as the first real note of warning. With the first shifting of the wind the waters of the Gulf swept over the city. Houses near the beach began to crumble and collapse, their timbers being picked up by the wind and waves and thrown in a long line of battering rams against the structures. Men, women and children fled from their homes and sought safety in higher portions of the city, or in buildings more strongly built. Some were taken out in boats, some in wagons, some waded through the waters, but the flood rose so rapidly that the approach of night found many hundreds battling in the waters, unable to reach places of safety. The air was full of missiles.

The wind tore slates from roofs and carried them along like wafers. A person struck by one of these, driven with the fearful violence of the storm, was certain to be maimed, if not killed outright. The waves, with each succeeding sweep of the in-rushing tide, brought a greater volume of wreckage as house after house toppled and fell into the waters. So tremendous was the roar of the storm that all other sounds were dwarfed and drowned. During the eight hours from 4 P. M. until midnight, the hurricane raged with a fury greater than words can describe. What height the winds reached will never be known. The wind gauge at the weather bureau recorded an average of 84 miles an hour for five consecutive minutes, and then the instruments were carried away. That was before the storm had become really serious. The belief, as expressed by the observer, that the wind averaged between 110 and 120 miles an hour, is as good information as is obtainable.

Nothing so exemplified the impotency of man as the storm. Massive buildings were crushed like egg shells, great timbers were carried through the air as though they were of no weight, and the winds and the waves swept everything before them until their appetite for destruction was satiated and their force spent.

A remarkable feature about the storm is the disparity in the depth of water in different portions of the city, and the undoubted fact that the waters subsided on the north side of the city hours before they did on the south side.

These peculiarities are explained by the topography of the island. Broadway, which marks the center, or middle of the city proper, is on the ridge, from which the land slopes on one side, toward the bay and on the other, toward the Gulf. The waters from the Gulf passed over this ridge and swept on toward the bay during the most furious stages of the storm, but the full energies of wind and water were directed upon that portion of the city between the Gulf and the Broadway Ridge. Of the lives lost in the city, 90 per cent. were in the district named.

How many lives were sacrificed to the Storm King will never be known. The census taken in June showed that Galveston had a population of 38,000. Outside the city limits on Galveston Island there were 1,600 persons living. The dead in the city exceeded 5000. Of the 1600 living outside the city limits, 1200 were lost. This frightful mortality—75 per cent.—outside the city is explained by the fact that most of the people there lived in frail structures and had no places of comparative safety to take refuge in. In the mainland district swept by the storm, at least 100 persons perished. It is safe, therefore, to state that at 'east 7000 lives were lost.

Of the property damage no estimate can be considered accurate. The estimates range from $25,000,000 to $50,000,000.

Of marvelous escapes from death, of acts of supreme heroism, of devotion and courage beyond parallel, the storm developed many instances. In some cases whole families were blotted out, in others the strong perished and the weak survived. Of the various branches of one family, 42 were killed, while in one household 13 out of a total of 15 were lost.

Such a scene of desolation as met the eyes of the people of Galveston when day dawned Sunday, September 9, has rarely been witnessed on earth. Fifteen hundred acres of the city had been swept clear of every habitation. Every street was choked with ruins, while the sea, not content with tearing away a great strip along the beach front, had piled the wreckage in one great long mass from city end to city end. Beneath these masses of broken buildings, in the streets, in the yards, in fence corners, in cisterns, in the bay, far out across the waters on the mainland shores, everywhere, in fact, were corpses. Galveston was a veritable charnel-house. To bury the dead was a physical impossibility. Added to the horror of so many corpses was the presence of carcasses of thousands of horses, cattle, dogs and other domestic animals.

To a people upon whom such a terrible calamity had been visited, now devolved a duty the like of which a civilized people had never been called to perform. To protect the living the dead had to be gotten rid of with all speed, for with corpses on every side, with carcasses by the thousands, and with a severe tropic sun to hasten decomposition, pestilence in its most terrible form threatened the living if the dead were not removed.

The tumbrels that rumbled over Paris streets with the gruesome burdens that came from Robespierre's abattoir had little work compared with the carts and wagons of Galveston in the days that followed the awful storm. It was at first determined to bury the dead at sea, but the procession of the dead seemed never-ending, and the cargoes that were taken to the deep and cast upon the waters came back with the tides and littered the shores. Then it was decided to burn the dead.

Ye who know not the horror of those days, who took no part in the saddest spectacle that man ever witnessed, may well shed tears of sympathy for those whose human tenement blazed on the funeral pyre in street or avenue, or whose requiem was sung by the waves that had brought death—but shed tears, too, for the brave men who faced this most gruesome duty with a Spartan courage the world has never known before.

The dead past has buried its dead.

For a week Galveston was under martial law. There was no disorder. There was some robbing of the dead by ghouls. This was checked by a punishment swift and sure.

The city rose from its ruins as if by magic. Street after street was cleared of debris. A small army of men worked from early morn until the shadows of night descended, to lift the city from its burden of wreckage. Then, when danger of epidemic seemed passed, attention was turned to commerce. The bay was strewn with stranded vessels. Monster ocean steamers weighing thousands of tons had been picked up like toys, driven across the lowlands, and thrown far from their moorings. One big steamship was hurled through three bridges, another, weighing 4,000 tons, was carried twenty-two miles from deep water, and dashed against a bayou bluff in another county.

The great wharves and warehouses along the bay front were a mass of splintered, broken timbers.

But the mighty energy of man worked wonders. Marvelous to say, under such conditions, a bridge 2⅛ miles long was built across the bay within seven days and Galveston, which had been cut off from the world, was once more in active touch with all the marts of trade and commerce. An undaunted people strove as only an indomitable people can strive, to rehabilitate the city.

The signs of the cripple are still upon the city, but every hour brings nearer the day when the crutches will be thrown away and Galveston, which by nature and by man was chosen as the entreport for the great West, will rise to a loftier destiny and a more enduring commercial prosperity than seemed possible before she was tried in the crucible of disaster. Longfellow says :

> Our lot is the common lot of all.
> Into each life some rain must fall,
> Some days must be dark and dreary.

The dark and dreary days were crowded into Galveston's life with horror unspeakable. It is an inexorable law of nature that after the storm comes the radiance of a glorious sunshine.

CONTENTS.

CHAPTER VII.

CHAPTER VIII.

CHAPTER IX.

CHAPTER X.

CHAPTER XI.

CHAPTER XII.

CHAPTER XIII.

CONTENTS. xiii

CHAPTER XXI.

CHAPTER XXII.

CHAPTER XXIII.

CHAPTER XXIV.

CHAPTER XXV.

HOTEL GRAND AND ITS ENVIRONS—GALVESTON

BRINGING THE INJURED TO THE HOSPITAL FOR TREATMENT

CHAPTER I.

First News of the Great Calamity — Galveston Almost Totally Destroyed by Winds and Waves. Thousands Swept to Instant Death.

THE first news of the appalling calamity that fell like a thunderbolt on Galveston came in the following despatch from the Governor of Texas :

"Information has just reached me that about 3000 lives have been lost in Galveston, with enormous destruction of property. No information from other points.

"JOSEPH D. SAYRES, Governor."

This despatch was dated at Austin, Texas, September 9th. Further intelligence was awaited with great anxiety in all parts of the country. The worst was feared, and all the fears were more than realized. Later intelligence showed that the West Indian storm which reached the Gulf coast on the morning of September 8th, wrought awful havoc in Texas. Reports were conflicting, but it was known that an appalling disaster had befallen the city of Galveston, where, it was reported, a thousand or more lives had been blotted out and a tremendous property damage incurred. Meagre reports from Sabine Pass and Port Arthur also indicated a heavy loss of life.

Among those who brought tidings from the sticken city of Galveston was James C. Timmins, who resides in Houston, and who is the General Superintendent of the National Compress Company. After Mr. Spillane he was one of the first to reach Houston with news of the great disaster which had befallen that city, and after all he reported it was evident that the magnitude of the disaster remained to be told.

After remaining through the hurricane on Saturday, the 8th, he departed from Galveston on a schooner and came across the bay to Morgan's Point, where he caught a train for Houston. The hurricane, Mr. Timmins said, was the worst ever known.

The estimate made by citizens of Galveston was that four thousand houses, most of them residences, were destroyed, and that at least one thousand people had been drowned, killed or were missing. Business houses were also destroyed. These estimates, it was learned afterward, were far below the actual facts.

The city, Mr. Timmins averred, was a complete wreck, so far as he could see from the water front and from the Tremont Hotel. Water was blown over the island by the hurricane, the wind blowing at the rate of eighty miles an hour straight from the Gulf and forcing the sea water before it in big waves. The gale was a steady one, the heart of it striking the city about 5 o'clock in the evening and continuing without intermission until midnight, when it abated somewhat, although it continued to blow all night.

WORST HURRICANE EVER KNOWN.

The water extended across the island. Mr. Timmins said it was three feet deep in the rotunda of the Tremont Hotel, and was six feet deep in Market street. Along the water front the damage was very great. The roofs had been blown from all the elevators, and the sheds along the wharves were either wrecked or had lost their sides and were of no protection to the contents.

Most of the small sailing craft were wrecked, and were either piled up on the wharves or floating bottom side up in the bay. There was a small steamship ashore three miles north of Pelican Island, but Mr. Timmins could not distinguish her name. She was flying a British flag. Another big vessel had been driven ashore at Virginia Point, and still another was aground at Texas City. At the south point of Houston Island an unknown ship lay in a helpless condition.

The lightship that marks Galveston bar was hard and fast aground at Bolivar Point. Mr. Timmins and the men with him on the schooner rescued two sailors from the Middle Bay who had been many hours in the water. These men were foreigners, and he could gain no information from them.

A wreck of a vessel which looked like a large steam tug was

observed just before the party landed. In the bay the carcasses of nearly two hundred horses and mules were seen, but no human body was visible.

The scenes during the storm could not be described. Women and children were crowded into the Tremont Hotel, where he was seeking shelter, and all night these unfortunates were bemoaning their losses of kindred and fortune. They were grouped about the stairways and in the galleries and rooms of the hotel. What was occurring in other parts of the city could only be conjectured.

The city of Galveston was|now entirely submerged and cut off from communication. The boats were gone, the railroads could not be operated, and the water was so high people could not walk out by way of the bridge across the bay, even were the bridge standing.

Provisions were badly needed, as a great majority of the people lost all they had. The water works' power house was wrecked, and a water famine was threatened, as the cisterns were all ruined by the overflow of salt water. This was regarded as the most serious problem to be faced. The city was in darkness, the electric plant having been ruined.

BODIES FLOATING IN THE BAY.

There was no way of estimating the property damage. The east end portion of the city, which was the residence district was practically wiped out of existence. On the west end, which faces the gulf on another portion of the island, much havoc was done. The beach was swept clean, the bath-houses were destroyed, and many of the residences were total wrecks.

Among the passengers who arrived at Houston on a relief train from Galveston was Ben Dew, an attache of the Southern Pacific. Dew had been at Virginia Point for several hours, and said that he saw 100 to 150 dead bodies floating out on the beach at that place.

Conductor Powers reported that twenty-five corpses had been recovered by the life-saving crew, many of them women ; that the crew had reported that many bodies were floating, and that they were using every endeavor to get them all out of the water. The water swept across the island, and it is presumed that most of these were Galveston people, though none of them had been identified.

LOST WIFE AND SIX CHILDREN.

One of the refugees who came in on the relief train and who had a sad experience was S. W. Clinton, an engineer at the fertilizing plant at the Galveston stock yards. Mr. Clinton's family consisted of his wife and six children. When his house was washed away he managed to get two of his little boys safely to a raft, and with them he drifted helplessly about. His raft collided with wreckage of every description and was split in two, and he was forced to witness the drowning of his sons, being unable to help them in any way. Mr. Clinton says parts of the city were seething masses of water.

From an eye-witness of the vast devastation we are able to give the following graphic account :

"The storm that raged along the coast of Texas was the most disastrous that has ever visited this section. The wires are down, and there is no way of finding out just what has happened, but enough is known to make it certain that there has been great loss of life and destruction of property all along the coast and for a hundred miles inland. Every town that is reached reports one or more dead, and the property damage is so great that there is no way of computing it accurately.

"Galveston remains isolated. The Houston Post and the Associated Press made efforts to get special trains and tugs today with which to reach the island city. The railroad companies declined to risk their locomotives.

"It is known that the railroad bridges across the bay at Galveston are either wrecked or are likely to be destroyed with the weight of a train on them ; the approaches to the wagon bridge are gone and it is rendered useless. The bridge of the Galveston, Houston and Northern Railroad is standing, but the drawbridges over Clear creek and at Edgewater are gone, and the road cannot get trains through to utilize the bridge across the bay.

"Sabine Pass has not been heard from to-day (September 9th). The last news was received from there yesterday morning, and at that time the water was surrounding the old town at the pass, and the wind was rising and the waves coming high. From the new town, which is some distance back, the water had reached the depot and was running through the streets. The people were leaving for the high country, known as the Black Ridge, and it is believed that all escaped. Two bodies have been brought in from Seabrooke, on Galveston Bay, and seventeen persons are missing there.

"In Houston the property damage is great, a conservative estimate placing it at $250,000. The Merchants' and Planters' Oil Mill was wrecked, entailing a loss of $40,000. The Dickson Car Wheel Works suffered to the extent of $16,000. The big Masonic Temple, which is the property of the Grand Lodge of the State, was partly wrecked. Nearly every church in the city was damaged. The First Baptist, Southern Methodist and Trinity Methodist, the latter a negro church, will have to be rebuilt before they can be used again. Many business houses were unroofed.

MANY TOWNS DEMOLISHED.

"The residence portion of the town presents a dilapidated appearance, but the damage in this part of the city has not been so great as in some others. The streets are almost impassable because of the litter of shade trees, fences, telephone wires and poles. Much damage was done to window glass and furniture. Many narrow escapes are recorded.

"Another train has left here for Galveston, making the third to-day. The two preceding ones have not been heard from, as all wires are prostrated.

"Meagre reports are arriving here from the country between Houston and Galveston, along the line of the Santa Fe Railroad. The tornado was the most destructive in the history of the State.

"The town of Alvin was practically demolished. Hitchcock suffered severely from the storm, while the little town of Alta Loma is reported without a house standing. The town of Pearl has lost one-half of its buildings.

"L. B. Carlton, the president of the Business League of Alvin, and a prominent merchant there, reports that not a building is left standing in the town, either residence or business. Stocks of goods and house furniture are ruined, and crops are a total loss. Alvin is a town of about 1200 inhabitants.

SANTA FE TRAIN BLOWN FROM THE TRACK.

"The Santa Fe train which left here at 7.55 Saturday night, the 8th, was wrecked at a point about two miles north of Alvin. The train was running slowly when it encountered the heavy storm. It is reported that the train was literally lifted from the track."

A thrilling story was told by two men who floated across from Galveston to the mainland. It came in the form of a telegram received at Dallas from Houston :

"Relief train just returned. They could not get closer than six miles of Virginia Point, where the prairie was covered with lumber, debris, pianos, trunks, and dead bodies. Two hundred corpses were counted from the train. A large steamer is stranded two miles this side of Virginia Point, as though thrown up by a tidal wave. Nothing can be seen of Galveston.

"Two men were picked up who floated across to the mainland, who say they estimate the loss of life up to the time they left at 2000."

The above message was addressed to Superintendent Felton, Dallas, and comes from Mr. Vaughn, manager of the Western Union office at Houston. The Missouri, Kansas and Texas north bound "flyer" was reported wrecked near Sayers.

The office of the Western Union Telegraph Company at St. Louis was besieged with thousands of inquiries as to the extent and result of the terrible storm that cut off Galveston from communication with the rest of the world. Rumors of the most direful nature come from that part of Texas, some of them even intimating that Galveston had been entirely wrecked and that the bay was covered with the dead bodies of its residents.   Nothing definite, however, could be learned, as the Gulf city was entirely isolated, not even railroad trains being able to reach it.   All the telegraph wires to Galveston were gone south of Houston, and to accentuate the serious condition of affairs the cable lines between Galveston and Tampico and Coatzacoalcos, Mexico, were severed; at least no communication over them was possible.

The Western Union had a large number of telegraph operators and linemen waiting at Houston to go to Galveston, but it was impossible to get them there.   San Antonio was being reached by El Paso, in the extreme southwestern portion of the State, a procedure made necessary by the prevailing storm.

WATER BLOWN COMPLETELY OVER THE CITY.

Mr. Joyce, another refugee from Galveston, made the following statement:

"The wind was blowing Saturday afternoon and night at about seventy-five miles an hour, blowing the water in the Gulf and completely covering the city.   The people of Galveston did not think it was much at first and kept within their homes. consequently when the wind began blowing as it did and the water dashed against the houses, completely demolishing them, many lives were lost.   I have no idea how many were killed, but think there will be several thousand deaths reported, besides many people whom we will know nothing about.

"I was in the storm which struck Galveston in 1875, but that one, bad as it was, was nothing in comparison with Saturday's."

The following account of Galveston will be of interest to readers in connection with the great disaster that has ruined that once prosperous and thriving city.

Galveston is situated on an island extending east and west for twenty seven miles, and is seven miles in its greatest width north and south.   No city could be in greater danger from such a horrible visitation as has now come to Galveston.   In no part of the city, with its former 38,000 population, is it more than six feet above the sea level.

The flat condition not only points to the desperate situation of the people at such a time as this, but their danger may be considered emphasized when it is known that exactly where the city is built the island is only one and one-quarter miles wide.

On the bay, or north side of the city, is the commercial section, with wharves stretching along for nearly two miles, lined with sheds and large storage houses. Then, in that portion of Galveston, there are three elevators, one of 1,500,000 bushels capacity, one of 1,000,000 and the third of 750,000..

A BRIDGE TWO MILES LONG.

The island from the north side is connected with the mainland by railroad bridges and the longest wagon bridge in the world, the latter nearly two miles in length. In 1872 the entire east end of the city was swept away by the tidal wave that followed a terrific storm that swept the Gulf coast for three days. Then the eastern land, on which buildings stood, was literally torn away. The work of replacing it has since been going on, and Fort Point, that guards the entrance to the harbor, has since been built, and on its parapets are mounted some of the heaviest coast defense ordnance used by the government. By the force of the storm of 1872 six entire blocks of the city were swept away.

It is on the south side of the city, beginning within fifty yards of the medium Gulf tide, that the wealthy residence portion of the city is located, and which was the first part of Galveston to be stricken by the full force of the storm and flood. All of the eastern end of the city was washed away, and in this quarter, between Broadway and I street, some of the handsomest and most expensive residence establishments are located. There was located there one home, which alone cost the owner over $1,000,000. Most of the residences are of frame, but there are many of stone and brick. In the extreme eastern end of the city there are many of what we call raised cottages. They are built on piling, and stand from eight to ten feet from the ground as a precar tion against floods, it being possible for the water to sweep under them.

Any protection that has ever been provided for the Gulf side of the city has been two stone breakwaters, but many times, with ordinary storms coming in from the Gulf, the high tidewater has been hurled over the low stone walls right to the very doors of the residences. From Virginia Point, six miles from Galveston, in ordinary conditions of the atmosphere, the city can be plainly seen. If it is true that Galveston cannot be now seen from the Point, then the conditions of the people in the city must be indescribably horrible. In short, a large part of the city is obliterated and has disappeared.

VAST AMOUNT OF MONEY INVESTED.

Many millions of dollars are invested in the wholesale and retail business of the city. On Strand street alone there are ten blocks of business establishments that represent an invested capital of $127,000,000. Market street is the heavy retail street, and there, in the heart of the flooded district, the losses cannot but reach away into the millions. The fact, as indicated by the despatches, that water is standing six feet deep in the Tremont Hotel, furnishes startling evidence to me that Galveston has been, indeed, dreadfully visited. The hotel is in almost exactly the centre of the city. Two years ago Galveston did the heaviest shipping business in cotton and grain of any Southern city. When I was at home two shiploads of cattle were leaving the port on an average every week.

Dr. H. C. Frankenfeld, forecast official of the Weather Bureau, gave an account of the West India hurricane that travelled through Texas. The first sign of the storm was noticed August 30 near the Windward Islands, about latitude 15 degrees north, longitude 63 degrees west. On the morning of August 31 it was still in the same latitude, but had moved westward to about longitude 67 degrees, or about 200 miles south of the island of Porto Rico. At that time, however, it had not assumed a very definite storm formation. It was central in the Caribbean Sea on the morning of September 1st, evidently about two hundred miles south of Santo Domingo City.

It had reached a point somewhere to the southwest, and not very far from Jamaica, by September 2d. The morning of September 3d found it about 175 miles south of the middle of Cuba. It had moved northwestward to latitude 21 degrees and longitude 81 degrees by September 4th. Up to this time the storm had not developed any destructive force but had caused heavy rains, particularly at Santiago, Cuba, where 12.58 inches of rain fell in twenty-four hours.

OMINOUS PROGRESS OF THE STORM.

On the morning of the fifth, the storm centre had passed over Cuba and had become central between Havana and Key West. High winds occurred over Cuba during the night of the fourth. By the morning of the sixth the storm centre was a short distance northwest of Key West, Fla., and the high winds had commenced over Southern Florida, forty-eight miles an hour from the east being reported from Jupiter, and forty miles from the N. E. from Key West. At this time it became a question as to whether the storm would recurve and pass up along the Atlantic coast, a most natural presumption judging from the barometric conditions over the eastern portion of the United States, or whether it would continue northwesterly over the Gulf of Mexico.

Advisory messages were sent as early as September 1st to Key West and the Bahama Islands, giving warning of the approach of the storm and advising caution to all shipping. The warnings were supplemented by others on the second, third, and fourth, giving more detailed information, and were gradually extended along the Gulf coast as far as Galveston and the Atlantic coast to Norfolk.

On the afternoon of the fourth the first storm warnings were issued to all ports in Florida from Cedar Keys to Jupiter. On the fifth they were extended to Hatteras, and advisory messages issued along the coast as far as Boston. Hurricane warnings were also ordered displayed on the night of the fifth from Cedar Keys to

Savannah. On the fifth storm warnings were also ordered displayed on the Gulf coast from Pensacola, Fla., to Port Eads, La. During the sixth barometric conditions over the eastern portion of the United States so far changed as to prevent the movement of the storm along the Atlantic coast, and it therefore continued northwest over the Gulf of Mexico.

On the morning of the seventh it was apparently central south of the Louisiana coast, about longitude 28, latitude 89. At this time storm signals were ordered up on the North Texas coast, and during the day were extended along the entire coast. On the morning of the eighth the storm was nearing the Texas coast, and was apparently central at about latitude 28, longitude 94. The last report received from Galveston, dated 3.40 P. M., September 8, showed a barometric pressure of 29.22 inches, with a wind of forty-two miles an hour, northeast, indicating that the centre of the storm was quite close to that city.

ALWAYS IN DANGER DURING A HURRICANE.

At this time the heavy sea from the southeast was constantly rising and already covered the streets of about half the city. Up to Sunday morning no reports were received from southern Texas, but the barometer at Fort Worth gave some indications that the storm was passing into the southern portion of the State. An observation taken at San Antonio at 11 o'clock, but not received until half-past five, indicated that the centre of the storm had passed a short distance east of the place, and had then turned in the northward.

Situated as Galveston is, with much of the shore but a few feet above the mean high water, there is so scant a margin of safety that, as was the case on the South Carolina Sea Islands on August 27, 1893, and among the bayous of Louisiana in October of the same year, any abnormal tide means death and destruction. Sabine Pass is a mere sand spit, and Galveston Island itself is but a few feet above the ocean level at the best, and is but three feet above high tide in many places. As the great storm wave raised by the cyclonic winds of the average hurricane

may easily have a crest of from eight to nine feet, for a city such
as Galveston this would be most ominous.

Such a fate as an inundation during the prevalence of a hurricane has been forecast for the island city, whose population
according to the new census is 37,789, many of whom live under
conditions that invite loss of life in case of a tidal overflow. And
,yet, though such a disaster has been foreseen and forecast, the
inertia of one's adherance to normal life and duties is such that
even in the face of specific warning it is not likely any number
would flee to the mainland. On September 8th, for instance, the
Weather Bureau, which had not lost track of the storm, very correctly pointed out that the hurricane was moving northwestward
slowly, towards the Texas coast, Port Eads, La., giving a wind
velocity of fifty-six miles an hour. Storm warnings were ordered
for the eastern Texas and middle Gulf region, and high winds
were specifically forecast for the coast of eastern Texas. More
the Bureau could not do, but it looks as if its warnings were in
vain.

THE FATEFUL WINDS GATHERING FORCE.

Unfortunately for Galveston, the slow movement of the hurricane was an additional menace, since this meant the longer pounding of the vertical winds of high velocities. As most readers
know, the hurricane is a storm which has two entirely distinct
motions. It is a great cyclonic whirl in which the winds blow
into and about the centre at great velocities, while its motion along
its track may be comparatively slow.

In the present case it took the hurricane four days to cross
the Gulf from Key West to Galveston, which was at a rate of
about twelve and one-half miles an hour. Its rotary winds, however, even a hundred miles from the centre on Friday, were raging
at a rate of over fifty miles, and as the vortex passed directly and
slowly over Galveston, the buffeting of the winds beginning on
Friday evening and continuing far into Saturday, must have been
terrific. Moreover, as the whole of Galveston is built up of frame
houses without cellars on uncertain foundations, the evil possibilities must be obvious.

CHAPTER II.

The Tale of Destruction Grows—A Night of Horrors—Sufferings of the Survivors—Relief Measures by the National Government.

THE following graphic account of the terrible disaster is from the pen of an eye-witness, written within twenty-four hours after the city was struck by the hurricane : "No direct wire communication has been established between Dallas and Galveston, and such a connection is not likely to be established earlier than to-morrow. The gulf coast, back for a distance of approximately twenty miles, is one vast marsh, and in many places the water is from three to ten feet deep, making progress toward the stricken city slow and unremunerative in the matter of direct news.

' Although Dallas is 300 miles from Galveston, all efforts for direct communication centre here, as it is the headquarters of the telegraph and telephone systems of the State. Hundreds of linemen were hurried to the front on Saturday night and Sunday morning from this city to try to put wire affairs in workable order.

WIND STORM OF GIANT FORCE.

" Less than half a dozen out of approximately half a hundred wires between Dallas and Houston have thus far been gotten into operation. This is because the wind storm extended inland with terrific force for a distance of 100 miles, and destroyed telegraphic, telephonic and railroad connections to such an extent as nearly to paralyze these channels of communication. With the best of weather conditions, it will require several weeks to restore these systems to anything like their normal state.

" Nothing like definite and tangible information is likely to be received from Galveston earlier than Wednesday or Thursday. All reliable information that has been received up to this hour comes from the advance guard of the relief forces and the linemen sent out by the railroad, telegraph and telephone companies.

" None of these reports place the number of dead at Galveston at less than 2000; some of them predict that 5000 will be nearer the mark.   No one places the property loss at Galveston at less $10,000,000, while Manager Vaughn, of the Western Union office at Houston, wires Manager Baker at Dallas: 'Galveston as a business place is practically destroyed.'   When the waters shall have receded it is feared Manager Vaughn will be found to be a wise prophet.   Along the coast for 100 miles either way from Galveston is a district that is nearly as completely isolated as is Galveston itself.   In this territory are not less than 100 cities, villages and hamlets.   Each of these as far as heard from reports from two to twenty dead persons.

OVER SEVEN HUNDRED CORPSES FOUND.

"In a radius of approximately twenty miles from Virginia Point, the centre of railroad relief operations, up to late this afternoon more than 700 corpses had been washed ashore or picked up from the main land.   Hitchcock, Clear Creek, Texas City, Virginia Point, Seabrook, Alvin, Dickinson and half a dozen other points midway between Houston and Galveston compose one vast morgue.

"Down along the coast toward Corpus Christi and Rockport all is silence.   Not a word had come from there up to this evening. The first news from that section is likely to come from San Antonio, as that is the most directly connected point with that section of the Gulf.   An awful calamity, it is feared, will be chronicled when the report does come.

"Telegraphic communication was opened late this afternoon with Beaumont and Orange on the other extreme end of the Gulf to the eastward of Galveston.   The joyful news was contained that those two towns and Port Arthur were safe, but in the territory adjacent, forty miles wide and 100 miles long, many lives are believed to have been lost and immense property damage sustained.

"Conservative estimates of the property losses, including commercial and other material interests at Galveston and Houston, put the total at from $40,000,000 to $50,000,000 for the State. This includes the damage to cotton, which is placed at 250,000 bales. John Clay, one of the foremost men in the cotton trade at Dallas, addressed wire inquiries to all accessible points in the cotton growing districts of Texas concerning crop losses. He states they will reach ten per cent. of the State's crop. Spot cotton sold at ten cents per pound on the market, an advance of half a cent a pound over Saturday's best figures.

RELIEF WORK STARTED.

"Relief work for the Galveston sufferers started in Dallas vigorously on receipt of an appeal from Governor Sayers. The City Council appropriated $500. A mass meeting of citizens appointed soliciting committees, as did also the Odd Fellows and Knights of Pythias. Fully $10,000 in cash had been subscribed by night.

"A special train was started for Houston over the Houston and Texas Central Railroad carrying committees of Odd Fellows, Knights of Pythias and citizens to render aid and distribute relief in the storm districts. At the request of many persons in Dallas a telegram was sent to Governor Sayers by J. C. McNealus, Secretary of the Dallas County Democratic Executive Committee, asking the Governor his idea as to calling an extra session of the Legislature. Governor Sayers this evening replied as follows:

"'Telegram received. I will do nothing until I can hear directly and authoritatively from Galveston except to call upon the people to render assistance.'

"As there is approximately a surplus of $2,000,000 cash in the State Treasury, it is reasoned that the citizens of Texas would endorse the Governor's action should he conclude to call a special session to furnish public relief to the stricken sections of the State.

"A bulletin received at the Houston and Texas Central headquarters from the headquarters of the company in Houston stated that a courier from the relief force had just arrived. He stated that signal reports from men sent forward to Galveston Island to the relief parties on the main land read:

"'Sixty dead bodies in one block. Six hundred corpses recovered and 400 more reported. People dying from injuries and sickness and for want of fresh water. Survivors threatened with starvation and disease. Doctors, nurses and fresh water needed at once.'

"The telegraph offices at Dallas have been besieged all day with men and women anxious to hear from friends who were in Galveston when the hurricane came on. Messages of inquiry have poured in from all parts of the United States. More than 10,000 messages were piled up in the Dallas offices to-day from local and outside parties, and every telegraph operator has been kept busy as long as he could work. The offices have uniformly had to inform the customers : ' We can't reach Galveston ; can only promise to forward from Houston by boat as early as possible.' Notwithstanding discouragements of this kind, the customers have almost invariably insisted on having their messages sent. Some of the scenes at the local telegraph offices have been very pathetic.

"A telegram was received from E. H. R. Green, son of Hetty Green, dated at Rockport, stating that Rockport had not been damaged by the storm, and that the visitors at the Tarpon Club House, on St. Joseph's Island, were safe. This news lessens the fear felt for the safety of the people living along the coast in the vicinity of Rockport and Corpus Christi.

"Houston and Texas Central Railroad officials at noon received bulletins from their general offices in Houston that the loss of life will reach 3000 in Galveston. The Missouri, Kansas and Texas relief forces near Galveston and along the coast telegraphed at noon that the loss of life will not be less than 5000 and may reach 10,000."

THE CITY IN RUINS.

Richard Spillane, a well-known Galveston newspaper man and day correspondent of the Associated Press in that city, who reached Houston September 10th, after a terrible experience, gives the following account of the disaster at Galveston :

"One of the most awful tragedies of modern times has visited Galveston. The city is in ruins, and the dead will number many thousands : I am just from the city, having been commissioned by

POST OFFICE STREET, SHOWING HARMONY CLUB BUILDING AND
MASONIC TEMPLE

DESTRUCTION AT AVENUE I BETWEEN EIGHTEENTH AND NINETEENTH STREETS

WRECKAGE ON THE WHARF, PIER 20—SPANISH STEAMER IN THE BACKGROUND

SCENE AT AVENUE K AND SIXTEENTH STREET—HOUSE OVERTURNED BY THE WIND

the Mayor and Citizens' Committee to get in touch with the out-side world and appeal for help. Houston was the nearest point at which working telegraph instruments could be found, the wires as well as nearly all the buildings between here and the Gulf of Mexico being wrecked.

"When I left Galveston the people were organizing for the prompt burial of the dead, distribution of food and all necessary work after a period of disaster.

CITY TURNED INTO A RAGING SEA.

"The wreck of Galveston was brought about by a tempest so terrible that no words can adequately describe its intensity, and by a flood which turned the city into a raging sea. The Weather Bureau records show that the wind attained a velocity of eighty-four miles an hour when the measuring instrument blew away, so it is impossible to tell what was the maximum.

"The storm began at 2 o'clock Saturday morning. Previous to that a great storm had been raging in the Gulf, and the tide was very high. The wind at first came from the north, and was in direct opposition to the force from the Gulf. Where the storm in the Gulf piled the water up on the beach side of the city, the north wind piled the water from the bay onto the bay part of the city.

"About noon it became evident that the city was going to be visited with disaster. Hundreds of residences along the beach front were hurridly abandoned, the families fleeing to dwellings in higher portions of the city. Every home was opened to the refugees, black or white. The winds were rising constantly, and it rained in torrents. The wind was so fierce that the rain cut like a knife.

"By 3 o'clock the waters of the Gulf and bay met, and by dark the entire city was submerged. The flooding of the electric light plant and the gas plants left the city in darkness. To go upon the streets was to court death. The wind was then at cyclonic velocity, roofs, cisterns, portions of buildings, telegraph poles and walls were falling, and the noise of the wind and the crashing of buildings were terrifying in the extreme. The wind and waters

3

rose steadily from dark until 1.45 o'clock Sunday morning. During all this time the people of Galveston were like rats in a trap. The highest portion of the city was four to five feet under water, while in the great majority of cases the streets were submerged to a depth of ten feet. To leave a house was to drown. To remain was to court death in the wreckage.

"Such a night of agony has seldom been equaled. Without apparent reason the waters suddenly began to subside at 1.45 A. M. Within twenty minutes they had gone down two feet, and before daylight the streets were practically freed of the flood-waters. In the meantime the wind had veered to the southeast.

VERY FEW BUILDINGS ESCAPED.

"Very few if any buildings escaped injury. There is hardly a habitable dry house in the city. When the people who had escaped death went out at daylight to view the work of the tempest and floods they saw the most horrible sights imaginable. In the three blocks from Avenue N to Avenue P, in Tremont street, I saw eight bodies. Four corpses were in one yard.

"The whole of the business front for three blocks in from the Gulf was stripped of every vestige of habitation, the dwellings, the great bathing establishments, the Olympia and every structure having been either carried out to sea or its ruins piled in a pyramid far into the town, according to the vagaries of the tempest. The first hurried glance over the city showed that the largest structures, supposed to be the most substantially built, suffered the greatest.

"The Orphans' Home, Twenty-first street and Avenue M, fell like a house of cards. How many dead children and refugees are in the ruins could not be ascertained. Of the sick in St. Mary's Infirmary, together with the attendants, only eight are understood to have been saved. The Old Woman's Home, on Roosenburg avenue, collapsed, and the Roosenburg School-house is a mass of wreckage. The Ball High School is but an empty shell, crushed and broken. Every church in the city, with possibly one or two exceptions, is in ruins.

"At the forts nearly all the soldiers are reported dead, they having been in temporary quarters, which gave them no protection against the tempest or flood. No report has been received from the Catholic Orphan Asylum down the island, but it seems impossible that it could have withstood the hurricane. If it fell, all the inmates were, no doubt, lost, for there was no aid within a mile.

"The bay front from end to end is in ruins. Nothing but piling and the wreck of great warehouses remain. The elevators lost all their superworks, and their stocks are damaged by water. The life-saving station at Fort Point was carried away, the crew being swept across the bay fourteen miles to Texas City. I saw Captain Haynes, and he told me that his wife and one of his crew were drowned.

WRECKAGE SWEPT ACROSS THE BAY.

"The shore at Texas City contains enough wreckage to rebuild a city. Eight persons who were swept across the bay during the storm were picked up there alive. Five corpses were also picked up. There were three fatalities in Texas City. In addition to the living and the dead which the storm cast up at Texas City, caskets and coffins from one of the cemeteries at Galveston were being fished out of the water there yesterday. In the business portion of the city two large brick buildings, one occupied by Knapp Brothers and the other by the Cotton Exchange saloon, collapsed. In the Cotton Exchange saloon there were about fifteen persons. Most of them escaped.

"The cotton mills, the bagging factory, the gas works, the electric light works and nearly all the industrial establishments of the city are either wrecked or crippled. The flood left a slime about one inch deep over the whole city, and unless fast progress is made in burying corpses and carcasses of animals there is danger of pestilence. Some of the stories of the escapes are miraculous. William Nisbett, a cotton man, was buried in the ruins of the Cotton Exchange saloon, and when dug out in the morning had no further injury than a few bruised fingers.

"Dr. S. O. Young, Secretary of the Cotton Exchange, was knocked senseless when his house collapsed, but was revived by the water, and was carried ten blocks by the hurricane. A woman who had just given birth to a child was carried from her home to a house a block distant, the men who were carrying her having to hold her high above heads, as the water was five feet deep when she was moved.

" Many stories were current of houses falling and inmates escaping. Clarence N. Ousley, editor of the Evening Tribune, had his family and the families of two neighbors in his house when the lower half crumbled and the upper part slipped down into the water. No one in the house was hurt.

" The Mistrot House, in the West End, was turned into a hospital. All of the regular hospitals of the city were unavailable. Of the new Southern Pacific Works little remains but the piling. Half a million feet of lumber was carried away, and Engineer Boschke says, as far as the company is concerned, it might as well start over again.

EIGHT OCEAN STEAMERS STRANDED.

" Eight ocean steamers were torn from their moorings and stranded in the bay. The Kendall Castle was carried over the flats at Thirty-third street wharf to Texas City, and lies in the wreckage of the Inman pier. The Norwegian steamer Gyller is stranded between Texas City and Virginia Point. An ocean liner was swirled around through the west bay, crashed through the bay bridges, and is now lying in a few feet of water near the wreckage of the railroad bridges.

" The steamship Taunton was carried across Pelican Point and is stranded about ten miles up the east bay. The Mallory steamer Alamo was torn from her wharf and dashed upon Pelican flats, and against the bow of the British steamer Red Cross, which had previously been hurled there. The stern of the Alamo is stove in and the bow of the Red Cross is crushed. Down the channel to the jetties two other ocean steamships lie grounded. Some schooners, barges and smaller craft are strewn bottom side up along the slips of the piers. The tug Louise, of the Houston Direct Navigation Company, is also a wreck.

"It will take a week to tabulate the dead and the missing and to get anything near an approximate idea of the monetary loss. It is safe to assume that one-half the property of the city is wiped out, and that one-half of the residents have to face absolute poverty.

"At Texas City three of the residents were drowned. One man stepped into a well by a mischance and his corpse was found there. Two other men ventured along the bay front during the height of the storm and were killed. There are but few buildings at Texas City that do not tell the story of the storm. The hotel is a complete ruin. The office of the Texas City Company was almost entirely destroyed. Nothing remains of the piers except the piling.

"The wreckage from Galveston litters the shore for miles and is a hundred yards wide. For ten miles inland from the shore it is a common sight to see small craft, such as steam launches, schooners and oyster sloops. The life boat of the life-saving station was carried half a mile inland, while a vessel that was anchored in Moses Bayou lies high and dry five miles up from La Marquet.

MULTITUDES SWEPT OUT TO SEA.

"From Virginia Point north and south along the bay front, at such places as Texas City, Dickinson, Hitchcock, Seabrook, Alvin and a dozen small intermediate points, the number of dead bodies gathered up by rescue trains and sailing craft had reached at noon more than 700. This is only a small scope of the country devastated, and it is feared the death list from the storm will ultimately show not less than 5000 victims. Hundreds have been swept out to sea who will never be accounted for. Two mass meetings were held at Dallas, and many thousands of dollars were subscribed for the relief of the Texas Gulf coast storm sufferers."

The towns of Sabine Pass and Port Arthur, news from which was anxiously awaited, passed through the terrific storm virtually unscathed. At Port Arthur the water spread over the town, but it did not reach a depth sufficient to destroy buildings. The town pleasure pier was washed away completely, as was also the pier in front of the Gales and Elwood Homes. The dredge Florida, property of the New York Dredging Company, which cut the Port Arthur Channel, sunk at the mouth of Taylor Bayou. No other property of consequence was injured.

At Sabine Pass the water reached a depth of about three feet, but nothing except small buildings near the water-front were washed away. Several mud-scows and sloops were washed ashore. The Southern Pacific wharves and warehouses were not damaged in the least. The railroad between Beaumont and Sabine Pass was under water for a distance of twelve miles, but not more than four miles were washed out. The life-saving station of Sabine Pass was washed from its blocks, but the light tower was not damaged. There was considerable damage at Sabine Pass by water rising into the streets.

ARMY TENTS AND RATIONS FOR THE SUFFERERS.

The officers of the National Government took steps at once to render all possible aid and assistance to the flood-sufferers of Texas. The President sent telegrams of sympathy to the Governor of the State and the Mayor of Galveston, and promised to render all possible relief. Adjutant-General Corbin also telegraphed instructions to General McKibbin, commanding the Department of Texas at San Antonio, to proceed to Galveston and investigate the character and extent of the damage caused by the hurricane, and to report to the Secretary of War what steps were necessary to alleviate the sufferings of the people and improve the situation.

Battery O, First Artillery, which garrisoned Fort San Jacinto, was commanded by Captain William C. Rafferty. First Lieutenant Lassiter was on detail duty at West Point, but the Second Lieutenant, J. C. Nichols, was with his company during the storm. Acting Secretary of the Treasury Spalding ordered two revenue cutters, one at Norfolk and one at Wilmington, N. C., to proceed at once to Mobile, Ala., and there await orders. They were needed in supplying food and tents to the storm-sufferers.

Governor Sayers, of Texas, applied to the War Department for 10,000 tents and 50,000 rations for immediate use for the sufferers. Acting Secretary Meiklejohn issued an order granting the request. The tents were sent from San Antonio and Jefferson Barracks, Missouri. A large portion of the rations was procured at San Antonio.

AN APPEAL FROM HOUSTON.

The following telegrams passed between the White House and Texas :

"Houston, Texas, September 10.—William McKinley, President of the United States, Washington, D. C.: I have been deputized by the Mayor and Citizens' Committee of Galveston to inform you that the city of Galveston is in ruins, and certainly many hundreds, if not a thousand, are dead. The tragedy is one of the most frightful in recent times. Help must be given by the State and Nation or the suffering will be appalling. Food, clothing and money will be needed at once. The whole south side of the city for three blocks in from the Gulf is swept clear of every building, the whole wharf front is a wreck and but few houses in the city are really habitable. The water supply is cut off and the food stock damaged by salt water. All bridges are washed away, and stranded steamers litter the bay. When I left this moring the search for bodies had begun. Corpses were everywhere. Tempest blew eighty-four miles an hour, and then carried Government instruments away. At same time waters of Gulf were over whole city, having risen twelve feet. Water has now subsided, and the survivors are left helpless among the wreckage, cut off from the world except by boat. RICHARD SPILLANE."

"Washington, September 10.—Hon. J. D. Sayers, Governor of Texas, Austin, Texas: The reports of the great calamity which has befallen Galveston and other points on the coast of Texas excite my profound sympathy for the sufferers, as they will stir the hearts of the whole country. Whatever help it is possible to give shall be gladly extended. Have directed the Secretary of War to supply rations and tents upon your request.

"WILLIAM MCKINLEY."

A copy of this telegram was sent to the Mayor of Galveston as well as to Governor Sayers.

"Austin, Texas, September 10.—The President, Washington : Very many thanks for your telegram. Your action will be greatly appreciated and gratefully remembered by the people of Texas. I have this day requested the Secretary of War to forward rations and tents to Galveston.   JOSPEPH D. SAYERS,
                                                         "Governor of Texas."

CLARA BARTON READY FOR RELIEF WORK.

Miss Clara Barton issued the following appeal in behalf of the Texas sufferers :

"The American National Red Cross, at Washington, D. C., is appealed to on all sides for help and for the privilege to help in the terrible disaster which has befallen Southern and Central Texas. It remembers the floods of the Ohio and Mississippi, of Johnstown, and of Port Royal, with their thousands of dead and months of suffering and needed relief, and turns confidently to the people of the United States, whose sympathy has never failed to help provide the relief that is asked of it now. Nineteen years of experience on nearly as many fields renders the obligations of the Red Cross all the greater. The people have long learned its work, and it must again open its accustomed avenues for their charities. It does not beseech them to give, for their sympathies are as deep and their humanity as great as its own, but it pledges to them faithful old-time Red Cross relief work among the stricken victims of these terrible fields of suffering and death.

"He gives twice who gives quickly.

"Contributions may be wired or sent by mail to our Treasurer, William J. Flather, Assistant Cashier Riggs National Bank, Washington, D. C. ; also to the local Red Cross committees of the Red Cross India Famine Fund, at 156 Fifth avenue, New York City, and the Louisiana Red Cross of New Orleans, both of whom will report all donations for immediate acknowledgment by us.
                                                 "CLARA BARTON,
                              "President National American Red Cross."

Miss Barton telegraphed Governor Sayers, at Austin, Tex., as follows:

"Do you need the Red Cross in Texas? We are ready."

THE DESTRUCTION INLAND.

Later details show that from Red River on the north to the Gulf on the south and throughout the central part of the State, Texas was storm-swept by a hurricane which laid waste property, caused large loss of life, and effectually blocked all telegraphic and telephonic communication south, while the operation of trains was seriously handicapped.

Starting with the hurricane which visited Galveston and the Gulf coast Saturday noon, and which was still prevailing there to such an extent that no communication could be had with the island to ascertain what the loss to life and property was, the storm made rapid inroads into the centre of the State, stopping long enough at Houston to damage over half of the buildings of that city.

Advancing inland, the storm swept into Hempstead, fifty miles above Houston, thence to Chappell Hill, twenty miles further; thence to Brenham, thirty miles further, wrecking all three towns. Several persons were killed.

The Brazos bottom suffered a large share of damage at the hands of the hurricane, and was swept for fully 100 miles of its length, everything being turned topsy-turvy by the high winds, and much destruction resulting to crops as well as farm-house property. The winds were accompanied by a heavy rainfall, which served to add to the horror of midnight. The telegraph and telephone companies have large forces of men trying to rig up wires to Galveston. The storm seems to have swept all the tableland clear of everything on it, razing houses to the ground and tearing up trees by the roots. It also swept into the mountain gorges and there inflicted the worst damage, and considerable loss of life was reported from that section. From Southwest Texas and points along the Gulf to the city of Galveston the reports were alarming. A number of parties summering at various points along the coast were not heard from. The cotton was nearly ruined, as the storm swept the cotton-belt.

CHAPTER III.

Incidents of the Awful Hurricane—Unparalleled Atrocities by Lawless Hordes—Earnest Appeals for Help.

ON September 11th, the Mayor of Galveston forwarded the following address to the people of the United States:

"It is my opinion, based on personal information, that 5000 people have lost their lives here. Approximately one-third of the residence portion of the city has been swept away.

"There are several thousand people who are homeless and destitute. How many, there is no way of finding out. Arrangements are now being made to have the women and children sent to Houston and other places, but the means of transportation are limited. Thousands are still to be cared for here. We appeal to you for immediate aid. WALTER C. JONES."

On the same date the following statement of conditions at Galveston and appeal for aid was issued by the local relief committee:

"A conservative estimate of the loss of life is that it will reach at least 5,000, and at least that number of families are shelterless and wholly destitute. The entire remainder of the population is suffering in a greater or less degree. Not a single church, school or charitable institution, of which Galveston had so many, is left intact. Not a building escaped damage, and half the whole number were entirely obliterated. There is immediate need for food, clothing and household goods of all kinds. If nearby cities will open asylums for women and children, the situation will be greatly relieved. Coast cities should send us water, as well as provisions, including kerosene, oil, gasoline and candles.

"W. C. Jones, mayor; M. Lasker, president Island City Saving Bank; J. D. Skinner, president Cotton Exchange; C. H. McMaster, for Chamber of Commerce; R. G. Lowe, manager

42

Galveston News· Clarence Owsley, manager Galveston Tribune."

The white cotton screw men's organization held a meeting and tendered their services, that of 500 able bodied men, to the public committee to clear the streets of debris. Big forces went to work, and the situation was much improved so far as the passage of vessels was concerned. The city was patrolled by regular soldiers and citizen soldiery. No one was allowed on the streets without a pass. Several negroes were shot for not halting when ordered.

The steamer Lawrence arrived here early on the morning of the 11th, from Houston, with water and provisions. A committee of one hundred citizens were aboard, among them being doctors and cooks. W. G. Van Vleck, General Manager of the Southern Pacific Railroad, arrived at the same time. He thought it would be possible to establish mail service from Houston to Texas City by night, with transfer boats to Galveston.

BODIES BEING BURIED IN TRENCHES.

It was found to be impossible to send bodies to sea for burial. The water receded so far, however, that it was possible to dig trenches, and bodies were being buried where found. Debris covering bodies was being burned where it could be done safely.

Work on the water works was rushed, and it was hoped to be able to turn a supply on in the afternoon.

Outside of Galveston smaller towns were beginning to send in reports as telegraphic communication improved, and many additions to the list of the dead and property losses were received. Richmond and Hitchcock each reported sixteen lives lost. Alto Loma, Arcadia, Velasco, Seabrooke, Belleville, Arcola and many other towns had from one to eight dead. In most of these places many houses were totally destroyed and thousands of head of live stock killed.

The railroads alone suffered millions of dollars in actual damage, to say nothing of the loss from stoppage of business. The International and Great Northern and Santa Fe had miles of track washed out, and the bridges connecting Galveston with the mainland must be entirely rebuilt.

The following is the description of an eye-witness on September 11: "Galveston is almost wiped off the earth. Fifteen thousand persons are homeless. The loss of life will reach into the thousands. Bodies are piled everywhere.

"When daylight broke over the expanse of floating bodies, rubbish heaps and ruins were all that remained of the prosperous city. A few leading citizens assembled in several feet of water at a street corner and called a meeting at the Tremont Hall, to which they adjourned. A committee of Public Safety of fifteen leading citizens was formed, and Colonel J. H. Hawley, one of the best known men in Texas, was made chairman. He, with Mayor Walter C. Jones and Chief of Police Edward Ketchum, formed a triumvirate, with absolute power, and declared the city under martial law.

MILITARY FORCES AND SPECIAL POLICE.

"They issued a commission to Major L. R. D. Fayling, which made him commander-in-chief of all military forces and special deputies of police, and only subject to the orders of the Mayor and the Chief of Police. Mayor Fayling was authorized to requisition any men or property he may require for his force, and his receipt will be honored by the city of Galveston and any such property paid for by the city.

"As soon as Major Fayling received his authority he collected a handful of half-naked, barefooted soldiers, clothed them, supplied them with food and put them under command of Captain Edward Rogers. Around this nucleus of a force he has built up to meet the necessities of the situation his present force of three full companies of volunteer soldiers and a troop of cavalry.

"A horde of negroes and whites—even white women—were in the ruins of the city. They were robbing the dead and dying, killing those who resisted, cutting off fingers to obtain rings and ears to obtain earrings. Drunken men reeled about the streets intimidating citizens.

" Chief of Police Ketchum ordered the sale of liquor stopped, and began to swear in hundreds of special policemen to rescue the wounded, feed the living and convey the dead to a hundred different morgues.   He worked for thirty-six hours without going home to inquire about his family's fate, which was in doubt.   When told he should do so he replied, characteristically, 'God will be good to me and mine, for I am going to be good to others.'

THE STENCH UNBEARABLE.

" The stench from the dead by Monday morning was unbearable.   The triumvirate ruling the city pressed citizens into service to take the dead out in barges and bury them in the Gulf.   The soldiers impressed into service, at the point of the bayonet, every wagon that came along and every negro to assist in throwing the dead into the sea.   It was impossible to give other burial.

" From the stench which pervades the city it is apparent that hundreds of bodies yet lie under the ruins.   The sun is hotter than in July.   The regular soldiers, who had been working for two days with bloody feet, were utterly exhausted by Monday evening, and were assembled by Captain Rafferty and put in a hastily extemporized hospital, which was formerly a church. Their places were filled by Major Fayling with new recruits, whom he drafted on the streets and supplied with arms and equipment from the local armory.

"Every part of the city was patrolled by 6 o'clock in the evening.   Among many other incidents of last night was the besieging of the squad guarding St. Mary's Hospital.   They were surrounded by a horde of armed negro thieves.   Several hundred shots were exchanged.   Sergeant Camp killed four negroes with his rifle, and about ten or twelve were killed by the squad.   The soldiers have since been picketing the city, doing fourteen hours' duty without rest.   Every hour during the night a fresh negro shooting was reported at headquarters.

"The tug 'Juno' and the propeller 'Lawrence' brought 2000 gallons of water here from Houston but the supply is not enough to go around, and half the population is without any water.   Break fast at the $4 per day hotel Tremont was served to a fortunate few to-day, and consisted of a small piece of bacon and a single cup of coffee. The hotel was untenable yesterday, and guests were refused. It is jammed to-day with local citizens who have been made homeless."

G. W. Ware, teacher of penmanship in a Dallas educational institution, was in Galveston during the hurricane, He reached Dallas on Tuesday, the 11th, and made the following statement :

WORK OF HEARTLESS CRIMINALS.

"It was a godsend, the placing of the city under martial law. The criminal element began looting the dead, and the cold blooded commercial element began looting the living. The criminals were stealing anything they could with safety lay hands on, and the mercenary commercial pirates began a harvest of extortion. The price of bacon was pushed up to 50 cents a pound, bread 60 cents a loaf, and owners of small schooners and other sailing craft formed a trust, and charged $8 a passenger for transportation across the bay from the island to the mainland.

"Mayor Jones and other men of conscience were shocked at these proceedings, and the Mayor decided that the only protection for the citizens would be to declare martial law, confiscate all foodstuffs and other necessities for the common good, and thus stop the lootings and holdups.

"The price of bread was reduced to 10 cents a loaf, bacon was placed at 15 cents a pound, and the price of a voyage across the bay was set at $1.50 a passenger. A book account is being kept of all sales of foodstuffs, and other transactions and settlements will be made at the scheduled rates."

Mr. Quinlan, General Manager of the Houston and Texas Central Railroad, said :

"It is in such cases as this Galveston disaster that the barbarity in some men is seen. I have seen enough in the last two days to convince me that a large element of civilized mankind are veneered savages. My policy would be to take nobody into Galveston except such persons as are absolutely needed to administer to the distressed. Thousands of residents of Galveston ought to be brought out of there as fast as boats can bring them to the mainland, and establish them in charity or detention camps on high ground, where they can get pure air and water and receive attention which cannot be given to them on the island.

"I hope Governor Sayres will find authority to enforce some such policy. This relief work is going to be an all-winter task. Persons who have lost homes and places of business must be taken charge of until they can properly take care of themselves."

THE FINANCIAL OUTCOME.

The effect that Galveston's disaster may have upon the financial obligations of that city was an interesting topic among local financiers. Whether the bonds will be paid when due or whether interest default will result when coupons are presented is a mooted question in certain circles. J. B. Adone, banker, of Dallas, and former member of the old banking firm of Flippin, Adone & Lobit, of Galveston, said concerning these points :

"Galveston's bond and interest obligations will be promptly met, I feel sure. If left to their own resources in the face of the present calamity, the people of Galveston and their public officials would be probably temporarily embarrassed, but there will be no repudiation or defalcation. The people of Texas will respond to the needs of Galveston in her present terrible affliction, and out of the moneys contributed the city's financial credit will be protected if this course should be found necessary."

Pursuant to the proclamation of Mayor Brashear, issued Sunday night, a citizens' meeting was held in the city council chamber at Houston and an organization effected for the relief of the victims of the storm. The following telegram was received by the Mayor from Governor Sayres:

"Austin, Texas, Sept. 10.—I have taken the liberty of directing that all supplies of food and clothing for Galveston be shipped to you. Will you undertake to forward them when received to Galveston for distribution? Answer quick.

"JOSEPH D. SAYRES, Governor."

Mayor Brashear immediately replied that all supplies would be distributed where mostly needed. A telegram from Arcola was received, and there were twenty-five persons there, mostly women and children, in urgent need of relief.

TENTS AND RATIONS SENT.

Orders were issued by the War Department at Washington for the immediate shipment to Galveston of 855 tents and 50,000 rations. These stores and supplies were divided between St. Louis and San Antonio. This represented about all such supplies as the Government had on hand at the places named, but it was stated at the Department that the order could be duplicated in a day.

Mayor Van Wyck, of New York, issued an appeal to the citizens of New York, on the 11th, for help for the sufferers of Galveston, heading the appeal with a $500 subscription.

The Mayor also sent the following telegram to Mayor Brashear, of Houston, Texas:

"Hon. S. E. Brashear, Mayor, Houston, Texas.—In response to your telegram I have issued a call to the people of the city of New York to contribute to the relief of those afflicted by the disaster at Galveston. Please express to the Mayor of Galveston the profound sympathy of the people of New York for the people of Galveston in this hour of their distress.

"ROBERT A. VAN WYCK, Mayor."

Ten doctors and twenty nurses from Bellevue Hospital, New York, volunteered to go to Galveston and help care for the injured and sick. They left New York by special train in the evening.

The following cablegram was received by the American representative of Sir Thomas Lipton :

"Very grieved to see press reports here regarding fearful calamity befallen Galveston. Sufferers have my deepest and most heartfelt sympathy. If getting up public subscription will be glad to give $1000.

"LIPTON."

FIRST BAPTIST CHURCH, GALVESTON, AFTER THE STORM

VOLUNTEERS REMOVING DEBRIS ON TWENTY-FIRST STREET, LOOKING SOUTH

This was a graceful act of sympathy from the gallant yachts-man who made the spirited attempt to capture the cup from the New York Yacht Club, and although failing, became a universal favorite in this country.

Official reports from Galveston to Governor Sayres at Austin, on the 11th, were that 400 bodies had been identified, 200 more were in an improvised morgue awaiting identification, and many more were thought to have drifted out to sea, and their identity will never be known.

CONDITIONS THAT BEGGAR DESCRIPTION.

A telegram from Adjutant General Scurry, who was at Galveston, to the Governor, was as follows:

" Have just returned from Texas City with several Galveston parties, who assure me that conditions there beggar description. Accounts have not been exaggerated. While a portion of the provisions has been destroyed by water sufficient on hand to relieve immediate necessities. The citizens seem to have the situation well in hand. United States troops and Company C., volunteer guard, with citizens, patrol the streets to prevent looting.

" I requested W. B. Wortham to go to Galveston from Texas City for the purpose of advising me of the city's most urgent needs, and I returned here to report and ask for further instructions. I respectfully suggest that the distress is too great for the people of Galveston, even with the assistance of Houston, to stand, and that a general appeal for help would be welcomed. The estimate of 10,000 destitute does not seem to be excessive.

" From reports reaching the Governor this morning it will be necessary to co-operate with the Federal troops to place all the mainland opposite Galveston, as well as the island, under martial law.

" Thieves have begun to enter the city for the purpose of pilfering the bodies of the dead. The Governor has been informed that the commander of the Texas troops has been ordered to Galveston by the Federal authorities, and the Governor will lend him

4

every assistance possible with State militia to keep vandalism down.   There is only one road operating to the coast from Houston, and that will be placed under military supervision temporarily.

"Governor Sayres was in receipt of a telegram from Miss Barton, of the Red Cross Society, offering the assistance of that association if necessary, and he replied that he would call on the society if he found that its help was needed.

"A large number of State militia tents were shipped from Austin to Galveston for temporary use on the island.

MONEY BEGINNING TO POUR IN.

"Governor Sayres received upward of 1000 telegrams during the day from parties in the East and West offering assistance to the flood sufferers at Galveston, and from various portions of the State reporting the collection of money and supplies.   During the day Governor Sayres estimated that the receipts in money from collections in Texas would amount to $15,000, though from reports a great deal of money has been sent direct to Galveston instead of coming through the Governor, and the amount may be much larger than that stated.

"Quite a number of Eastern newspapers are wiring the Governor offering to establish themselves as bureaus for relief funds if desired and asking what they can do to relieve the situation.   A telegram from New York informed the Governor that two relief trains of supplies had left New York for Galveston. The Cincinnati Chamber of Commerce wires that it will send any relief desired that it can give.   Chicago, Philadelphia, St. Louis and several other points did likewise."

Acting Secretary Meiklejohn of the War Department at Washington authorized the chartering of a special train from St. Louis to carry quartermaster's and commissary supplies to the relief of the destitute at Galveston.

The following telegram was received :

"Galveston, Texas, Sept. 9, 1900.—Quartermaster General, Washington.—I report terrific cyclone with an eleven foot tide.

All improvements, temporary buildings, property and stores at both Jacinto and Crockett destroyed and swept clean.

"BAXTER, Quartermaster."

A second telegram followed:

"Galveston, Texas, Sept. 11, 1900.—Referring to my telegram of yesterday, via Houston, I urgently recommend that fair compensation be made to contractors for their losses, and that they be relieved of their contracts. If fortifications are rebuilt at or near their present sites I urgently recommend that quarters for troops be purchased and built on higher ground in the city, centrally located. Wharves destroyed; all railroad bridges swept away and building operations of any nature cannot be resumed under six weeks or two months."

A VOICE FROM JOHNSTOWN.

Mayor Woodruff, of Johnstown, Pennsylvania, issued the following proclamation: "Later and more definite information of the fearful destruction of life and property at Galveston and other places in Texas recalls to our attention the awful calamity in Johnstown and vicinity eleven years ago. Whole squares of homes have been swept away, hundreds of dead are lying unburied and thousands of people destitute. This would be a fitting time to show our gratitude for what the world did for us in the hour of need. Any contributions left at the banks in this city will be acknowledged and promptly forwarded to the authorities in charge of the work of relief. Already over $200 without any call for aid has been subscribed to a relief fund."

A special despatch from Galveston tells the following story of the great calamity, showing that scarcely a building was undamaged or a family that did not lose one or more members. It is roughly estimated that the death list will approximate 6,000 and the property loss will be many millions. Scarcely a building in the city escaped injury and the loss on stocks of goods cannot be estimated. All the extreme eastern and southern part and the western portion, south of avenue Q, to the Gulf, is either washed away or demolished and the dead are thrown in every direction.

These are being rapidly gathered up and taken to temporary morgues on the strand.

Whole families are, in many instances, wiped out of existence. There is scarcely a family in the district mentioned that did not lose one or more members, while the hospitals are crowded with wounded beyond their capacity, and the county court house is being converted into a hospital for their care.

The Catholic hospital down the island, was completely demolished. All the Sisters and ninety inmates were drowned.

The waves dashed over and flooded Fort San Jacinto, demolishing the barracks, officers' quarters, and drowning fourteen privates, two buglers, and First Sergeant of Company O, First Artillery.

BUILDINGS DESTROYED BY THE FLOOD.

The Opera House, City Hall, Masonic Temple, Moody's Bank Building, Knapp's publishing house, and Ritter's saloon and restaurant, on the strand, are wrecked. From the latter seven dead bodies were removed from beneath the debris.

Parties are engaged in removing the debris of the Knapp Building. Beneath they expect to find the body of Oscar Knapp, senior member of the firm. Richard D. Swann, cashier of John D. Rogers & Co., was drowned during the height of the storm while heroically attempting to rescue two ladies from drowning. It will be days before the full extent of the frightful disaster is known or a correct list of the dead is obtainable. A meeting of citizens was held to-day and a general committee, with the Mayor as chairman, was appointed. Sub-committees on Finance, Relief, Burial of the Dead, and Hospitals were appointed, and are now actively at work to relieve the distress prevailing and give decent burials to the dead.

The terrific cyclone that produced such a distressing disaster in Galveston and all through Texas was predicted by the United States Weather Bureau to strike Galveston Friday night and created much apprehension, but the night passed without the prediction being verified. The conditions, however, were ominous, the danger signal was displayed on the flag staff of the Weather Bureau, shipping was warned, etc. The southeastern sky was sombre, the Gulf beat high on the beach with that dismal thunderous roar that presaged trouble, while the air had a stillness that betokens a storm. From out of the north, in the middle watches of the night, the wind began to come in spiteful puffs, increasing in volume as the day dawned.

By ten o'clock Saturday morning it was almost a gale; at noon it had increased in velocity and was driving the rain, whipping the pools and tearing things up in a lively manner, yet no serious apprehension was felt by residents remote from the encroachments of the Gulf. Residents near the beach were aroused to the danger that threatened their homes. Stupendous waves began to send their waters far inland and the people began a hasty exit to secure places in the city.

TWO GIGANTIC FORCES AT WORK.

Two gigantic forces were at work. The Gulf force drove the waves with irrestible force high upon the beach, and the gale from the northeast pitched the waters against and over the wharves, choking the sewers and flooding the city from that quarter. The streets rapidly began to fill with water, communication became difficult and the helpless people were caught between two powerful elements, while the winds howled and rapidly increased in velocity.

Railroad communication was cut off shortly afternoon, the track being washed out ; wire facilities completely failed at 3 o'clock, and Galveston was isolated from the world. The wind momentarily increased in velocity, while the waters rapidly rose and the night drew on with dreaded apprehension depicted in the face of every one.

Already hundreds and thousands were bravely struggling with their families against the mad waves and fierce wind for places of refuge. The public school buildings, court house, hotels, in fact any place that offered apparently a safe refuge from the elements, became crowded to their utmost. Two minutes of 6.30 P. M., just before the anemometer blew away the wind had reached the frightful velocity of 100 miles an hour. Buildings that had hitherto stood tumbled and crashed, carrying death and destruction to hundreds of people. Roofs whistled through the air, windows were driven in with a crash or shattered by flying slate, telegraph, telephone and electric light poles, with their masses of wires, were snapped off like pipe stems, and water communications were broken.

What velocity the wind attained after the anemometer blew off is purely a matter of speculation. The lowest point touched by the barometer in the press correspondents' office, which was filled by frightened men and women, was 28.04½ ; this was about 7.30 P. M. It then began to rise very slowly, and by 10 P. M. had reached 28.09, the wind gradually subsiding, and by midnight the storm had passed. The water, which had reached a depth of eight feet on the strand at 10 P. M, began to ebb and ran out very rapidly, and by 5 P. M. the crown of the street was free of water. Thus passed out one of the most frightful and destructive storms which has ever devastated the coast of Texas.

ADDITIONAL DETAILS.

The city is filled with destitute, bereft and homeless people, while in the improvised morgues are the rigid forms of hundreds. Whole families are side by side.

The city beach in the southwestern part of the city was under ten feet of water, and the barracks there are destroyed, the soldiers having a marvelous escape from drowning. Many substantial residences in the western and southwestern part of the city were destroyed, and the death list from there will be large.

A heavy mortality list is expected among the residents down the island and adjacent to the coast on the mainland, as both were deeply flooded, and the houses were to a great extent insecure. The heaviest losers by the storm will be the Galveston Wharf Company, the Southern Pacific Railway Company, and the Gulf, Colorado and Santa Fe Railway Company, and the Texas Lone Star Flouring Company.

Additional details by tug from Galveston show that west of Thirty-third street the storm swept the ground perfectly clear of the residences that once stood upon it and piled them up in a conglomerated mass five blocks back on the beach, strewing the piling with the debris and the bodies of its many victims. Many of these were lying out in the afternoon sun and were frightful to look upon. The fearful work of the storm was not confined to the district along the beach, but took in all the district in the city and the Denver resurvey, but it was near to the beach that most destruction to human life occurred.

The waves washed away the Home for the Homeless, and it is thought that the inmates, consisting of thirteen orphans and three matrons, were drowned. Out in the Denver resurvey the destruction was terrible, and victims of the storm were many. The government works were greatly damaged, the buildings on the beach were washed out into the Gulf and their occupants are thought to have perished.

COMMUNICATIONS ALL CUT.

In the north part of the west end the damage was great also, almost every building being damaged to some extent, and many completely wrecked. The cotton and lumber yards in that section of the city were completely razed, and much valuable machinery is ruined. However, the loss of life was not nearly so great in that district as it was out towards the beach.

A special to the "News" from Galveston brought to Houston by the tug "Brunswick" gave the following additional particulars of the storm :

"The big iron oil tank of the Waters-Pierce Oil Company was picked from the Fifteenth street pier and carried to Thirteenth street. The old Union Depot, in recent years used as the office of the superintendent of the wharf yards, was dashed to pieces, as were numerous small frame buildings along the wharf front. Men were sent out Sunday morning to report the condition of the bridges across Galveston Bay, but were unable to reach them.

"Telegraphic communication was also cut off on Saturday.

The linemen who went out Sunday reported that the railroad bridges were all washed away, and there was not sufficient material in Galveston to rebuild the telegraph lines. The cables under the channel are gone. The lines will have to be built to the city from the mainland. Strenuous efforts were made on Sunday to repair the damage to the Mexican cable, but on account of the sea being high it was impossible to pick up the lost end of the cable.

"Thousands of telegrams were filed at the telegraph office during the day, with the expectation that they would be sent to Houston for transmission, but the captain of the only small tug available would not venture on the trip with a new crew, his engineer and fireman having been lost, while tugs which might be hired were of too deep draught to go up the bayou.

IN THE BUSINESS DISTRICT.

"In the business district not a building escaped injury. The Grand Opera House is caved in, and the fourth story of the Hotel Grand, a part of the same building, was blown off. The third story of the City Hall was blown away. The three story building of the Ritter Cafe was demolished, and crashed into the rear of the News Building. The fourth story was torn from the Moody Building, at Twenty-second street and the strand. The Masonic Temple was partially unroofed and the tower torn away. The upper stories of the Harmony Club Building were caved in, and the frame building across the street was demolished.

"Among other buildings damaged or destroyed was the Galveston Orphans' Home, all the children being reported unhurt. The Sacred Heart Church, one of the largest churches in the city, is a total wreck. St. Mary's University, adjoining it is considerably damaged, and the athletic building was destroyed. The First Baptist Church is a wreck. The parsonage adjoining St. St. John's Methodist Church was wrecked. The Ball High School building is badly damaged."

"Over thirty persons were rescued from St. Mary's Infirmary, but quite a number perished. A mother and child, a Mexican woman and child and an elderly lady, while going to the cotton mills, were drowned. While the mill was crowded with people the tower fell in, killing and injuring several persons. Over one thousand persons sought shelter in the County Court House. A lady and child from St. Louis, names not ascertained, who were visiting the family of police officer John Bowe, were lost. Mrs. Burns, mother of motorman Burns, and daughter, also perished. motorman Parker, wife and children, were killed. Mrs. Benhill and child were drowned.

"Three undertaking establishments are all being utilized as morgues, and a fourth morgue was opened in a large building on the Strand. Some of the draymen at first refused to haul more than one body at a time, demanding the price for a full load for each trip. On Sunday evening, however, the few who made this demand agreed to bring as many bodies as their carts would hold. Owing to the streets being full of debris it is only possible to use the two-wheeled carts.

CARING FOR THE DEAD.

"Many of those who escaped tell of thrilling experiences. Mr. and Mrs. James Irwin got out on the roof of their dwelling. They were seated on the side of the comb, and when the building blew over they floated off separately on sections of the roof. Mrs. Irwin was on the raft alone all night. Mr. Irwin, who had found refuge at the Ursuline Convent, and who despaired of seeing his wife again, heard a cry for help. Hoping to rescue a human being, he pulled off through the water, and was surprised and overjoyed to find his wife still afloat on the roof.

"The city is not without a water supply, but it is in total darkness. The city street railroad has suspended business, much of its track being washed out. It will be a month before cars can be operated by electricity, but horse car service will be substituted at the earliest possible moment. The plant of the Galveston Gas Company is partially demolished, and is out of commission. Those who use gas for fuel are helpless. Fire wood was swept away, but there is plenty of drift wood to be had.

"Several members of the police force were lost, and others lost their families. The force is greatly reduced in numbers, and at present is insufficient to meet the demand upon it."

The foregoing is a horrifying account, truthful and not over-drawn. In fact, the picture is far short of the reality.

RESISTLESS POWER OF THE HURRICANE.

It is a misnomer to call the violent revolving storm which devastated the city of Galveston and the adjacent coast of Texas a cyclone. It was in reality a hurricane, and more specifically what is known to meteorologists as a West Indian hurricane. A hurricane has a much smaller centre or diameter than a cyclone, travels with far greater rapidity, and its blasts often reach a velocity of 100 miles an hour. The hurricane of the West Indies, which is really born in the heated waters of the South Atlantic, and which as a rule curves when it reaches the Yucatan Channel and follows the course of the Gulf Stream, decreases in intensity as it travels further north, broadens in diameter, and becomes the cyclone of the North Atlantic.

It is a curious feature of the Galveston hurricane that, like the great hurricane of September, 1889, which devastated Vera Cruz, it did not follow the course of the Gulf Stream, but curved westward instead of eastward, after passing the Yucatan Channel, and rushed in upon the Texan coast. Galveston was not up to this time considered as within the hurricane belt, and its awful visitation is proof that the laws of storms have exceptions to their rules.

The late Padre Vines, of Havana, the venerable and learned Jesuit priest, who made a lifelong study of the birth and course of West Indian hurricanes, was accustomed to warn by cable the many friends that he had among the captains of the vessels ply-ing to and from West Indian ports of the approach of hurricanes and their probable course.

In September, 1889, he cabled to Captain Joshua Reynolds, commanding one of the Ward steamers, and who was just leaving Vera Cruz for New York, that a hurricane was approaching from the eastward, and that he would better steam slowly to and past Progresso and let the great storm pass up and along the Gulf Stream. Captain Reynolds acted in obedience to the warning, but this particular hurricane, like the one that struck Galveston, curved to the westward instead of to the eastward, after passing the Yucatan Channel, overcame an area of high barometer that hung over the Mexican coast, and rushed into Vera Cruz, carrying death and destruction in its wake. Captain Reynolds and his ship safely weathered the hurricane and were received at Havana with great rejoicing, where it had been thought they were lost.

It was in 1859 that still another West Indian hurricane curved the wrong way and swept the waters of the Gulf over Last Island, then the great summer resort of Southern society, situated a few miles west of the mouth of the Mississippi off the coast of Barataria. Those who wish to obtain some conception of the horrors attending the Galveston hurricane should read Lafcadio Hearn's story of "Chita : The Romance of Last Island," in which that skilled word painter depicts the scenes of the awful tragedy which decimated the households of the South.

STIRRING APPEALS FOR HELP.

One of our leading journals made the following timely comments upon the Galveston calamity and the urgent necessity for quick help :

"The cry for help which comes from the stricken city of Galveston and the surrounding country is a moving appeal which should receive the readiest and most generous response. The extent of the disaster which has overtaken the city and the coast country of Texas has not been overdrawn, it seems, in the reports from the scene, and it would be impossible to exaggerate the horror of the catastrophe and the distress and suffering that follow in its wake.

"A fair city of 38,000 inhabitants was wrecked in a night. Thousands of men, women and children were drowned or killed in the wreckage of the flooded, crumbling city ; whole families suddenly blotted out ; the great mass of the survivors bereft of their habitations, goods and clothing, and by the wreck of business houses and the stoppage of industry deprived of the means of earning subsistence for a long time to come. No one need hesitate about making a contribution to alleviate the suffering of Texas on the grounds that others will give enough to supply all needs.

TERRIBLE SUFFERING AND MISERY.

"However generous or lavish may be the aid proffered, it will not be enough to repair the mischief of that storm, and however prompt the aid may be, it will not be quick enough to prevent terrible suffering and misery. Delay in providing for the impoverished and homeless means peril to more lives, deprivation and sickness, and, under the most favorable circumstances in getting aid to the district, thousands are fated to undergo the severest suffering.

"Fortunately, the Government has stepped in and, through the War Department, is lending prompt and effective aid. Tents and rations are being rushed to Galveston with all possible speed, and private liberality and relief committees are coming to the rescue. The scope of the Government's efforts will be limited to such supplies as are available in the War Department, and, in addition, vast quantities of food, clothing and medicines are needed, doctors and nurses are required, and a large sum of money is an absolute necessity to pay for these things and to form a fund for the purpose of maintaining relief until the sharp period of distress shall be tided over. Our city, in every cause that appeals to benevolence and humanity, has always been in the forefront of the generous, and, in such a case as the Texas disaster, the city's liberality should be maintained. The Citizens' Permanent Relief Committee has taken steps to render aid to the hurricane sufferers, and, through that useful and beneficent organization, every person in this vicinity will have the opportunity to join in giving aid for a purpose which must excite universal pity and sympathy."

CHAPTER IV.

The Cry of Distress in the Wrecked City—Negro Vandals Shot Down—Progress of the Relief Work —Strict Military Rule.

THE situation on the third day after the flood was vividly described by a visitor to the city as follows: It is plainly apparent that as a result of the Galveston disaster, a task confronts the public authorities such as neither Texas nor any other State has ever before had to grapple with.

Human nature at its worst has had opportunity for the display of its meanest passions, and relentless measures have been rendered necessary. Looters and vandals have ignored all moral restraints, and gunpowder has had to be used unsparingly to subdue the savagery being practiced. It is learned on unquestionable authority that the soldiers under Adjutant General Scurry have to-day (Wednesday the 12th) slain no less than seventy-five men, mostly negroes, guilty of robbing the dead.

POCKET FULL OF HUMAN FINGERS.

One of these had in his pocket twenty-three human fingers with costly rings on them. The fingers had been cut from the victims of the storm found on the beach or floating in the waters of Galveston Bay.

W. McGrath, Manager of the Dallas Electric Company, and representing large Boston interests in Texas, returned from Galveston direct. He says: "The only way to prevent an epidemic that will practically depopulate the island is to burn the bodies of the dead. The Governor of Texas should call an extra session of the Legislature and appropriate a million or half a million dollars, or whatever amount is needed. The situation must be taken intelligently in hand to save the State from a possible epidemic. Before I left Galveston about 4,000 bodies had been

61

found. Eleven hundred had been tied together in bunches and sunk into the sea. Last night some fresh water was found by forces of men who explored the ground until the principal main of the city water works was found. Tons of rubbish were removed and the main tapped. I believe the water question is solved for the present, but money, clothing, wholesome bread, ice, drugs, etc., are needed."

A bulletin from Galveston, via. Virginia Point and Houston, received here at 11 A. M., says:

"The situation grows worse every minute, water and ice needed. People in frenzy from suffering from these causes. Scores have died since last night, and a number of sufferers have gone insane."

THE STORY INCREASES IN HORROR.

A despatch from Houston summed up the situation as follows: Houston is now being rapidly filled with refugees from Galveston. Stragglers have been arriving every few hours, and this afternoon a trainload of some eight hundred reached the city thoroughly worn out and disheartened, each with a tale of woe and harrowing experiences. Contrary to the usual thing in chronicling catastrophes of the present character the story of Galveston grows worse as the time progresses and the facts become known. Each chapter is more appalling than its predecessor, and the burden of death becomes heavier as the hours roll on. The estimates of the loss of life have grown from 1,000 to 8,000, and even the latter figure is said to be too small in the opinion of many of the survivors.

ACTUAL LOSS WILL NEVER BE KNOWN.

The actual loss will never be made known. The storm overwhelmed entire families, who were swept into the Gulf with the wreckage of their homes. The bodies may gradually be thrown on the sands, but identification will be impossible. The committees are endeavoring to compile lists of both dead and living, but they will not be accurate, as many mistakes have already been made and the living reported dead. Registers have been made and posted in the city in order to facilitate this feature of the relief work.

DISPOSING OF THE DEAD.

So far the efforts of the searchers have necessarily been confined to the open places, and it will be some time before the dead swept into the fields, the alleys and the gullies are gathered and laid away for good. The city is one awful stench of decaying animal matter. Nearly every animal on the island was killed, and the thousands of human remains still scattered beneath the vast piles of debris add to the danger of the situation. Too much time was lost in consigning the dead to the sea, and the workers were compelled by the exigencies of the situation to pile the corpses where found, and cremate them as well as this could be done.

PEOPLE DELAYED FLIGHT TOO LONG.

Oswald Wilson, editor of the *Texan*, who arrived with the refugees, says that the situation cannot be painted any blacker than it really is. Fully one-third of the city has been destroyed absolutely and every building damaged. He says that one reason that the loss of life was so excessive was due to the fact that they delayed leaving their homes until too late. The water rose rapidly for several hours until the centre of the city was six feet deep and the outlying section covered to a depth of over ten feet. The people of Galveston were accustomed to high water, although they had never witnessed so great an inundation, but their fears were calmed by the fact that during this period the wind had not risen above thirty miles an hour, and every year they had seen this condition during the equinoctial periods.

REALIZED THEIR PERIL TOO LATE.

Men waded about the city laughing at the rise of the water for hours, for the sea gradually encroached during the morning, and it was only when they realized the bay was forcing its contents to meet the tide from the Gulf that they lost their confidence that the present was but another attempt of the elements to create a disturbance, and seriously endeavored to reach a point of safety.

Then it was too late, for the tide swirled in the streets and the wind had begun rapidly to increase in violence. It howled and screamed in great gusts, which increased in strength every minute, and one by one the houses along the Gulf front and in the Denver resurvey and about Fort Point began to go to pieces and pile one against the other.

The waters were filled with debris and the debris with men, women and children seeking to save their lives. Wading was impossible, save in the centre of the city, and the unfortunates were swept to and fro, dashed by the waves and bruised by the flying fragments, until death resulted in one form or another. Many were the deeds of heroism, but rescuers and all fell victims to the storm, for human efforts were unavailing.

MORE HORRORS DETAILED.

J. C. Roberts, of the firm of Behring Brothers, Houston, was sent to Galveston to learn of the family of his employers. His journey was arduous, for he was one of the first. Arriving in the city worn out, he entered a little drug store and asked for whisky. He was refused. A doctor was present and gave him a prescription for the stimulant. The druggist charged $2.50 for the whisky, and the doctor $5 for his services. He landed at Galveston at Twentieth street, and walked through dead bodies.

His description of the scenes is horrible in the extreme. The dead were everywhere. They were scattered on every hand, and nearly all in a complete state of nudity. He saw an Italian woman standing in the street holding in her hand the foot and leg of an infant severed from the little body. She was unclad, but alive and insane, and refused to leave the pile of debris which contained the remains of her little one.

Roberts witnessed one of the guards shoot five negro looters. He observed one of the men robbing a dead body. The man refused to desist and the guard shot him dead as he knelt on the sands. Four companions of the ghoul started to assault the guard, when he threw himself on his stomach, and, firing rapidly, killed them all.

LOOKING SOUTH ON AVENUE I, SHOWING CHURCH OF SACRED HEART, COMPLETELY DESTROYED

M. P. MORRISSEY

TRAFFIC MANAGER OF THE WILLIAM PARR & CO., GENERAL STEAMSHIP
AGENTS, WHO FIRST SUGGESTED AND CARRIED INTO EFFECT THE
BURIAL OF BODIES AT SEA AND THE BURNING OF OTHER BODIES
ON SHORE TO SAVE THE SURVIVORS FROM PESTILENCE

'FIRE DEPARTMENT TAKING BODIES TO A MORGUE

BODIES AMONG RUINS—CHARACTERISTIC SCENE IN GALVESTON

WRECKED RESIDENCES CORNER TWENTY-SEVENTH
STREET AND AVENUE M

REMOVING WRECKAGE IN SEARCH OF DEAD BODIES

NINETY NEGROES EXECUTED.

It is said that ninety negroes have been executed for robbery, and it is unsafe for any one to stir at night unless provided with a passport from the officer in charge. A description of the burning of the dead and the burial at sea is beyond reproduction. All sentiment is at an end. It has become a matter of self-protection and in order to avoid pestilence rapid disposal of the corpses is necessary. Several loads of lime have been sent from here, with other disinfectants. The people of Galveston have had no bread since the storm save what little has been sent from Houston. A cracker factory opened its doors Sunday and sold its entire contents in a short time. Some food was left after the storm, but this is rapidly being distributed.

Bonfires are burning all over the city. They are the funeral of a thousand festering corpses cast back upon the shore at high tide yesterday. Cremation has become a necessity to prevent an epidemic. The negroes refuse to work, and the townspeople are paralyzed with fright and suffering, or are making preparations to leave the doomed island.

The first train to carry refugees to Texas City, seven miles across the bay, was announced this morning, and since daylight a thousand men, women and children have been crowding into catboats, lifeboats, sloops, schooners and a single steamboat, the Lawrence, all bent on escaping from the city. Nearly all of them have lost some member of their families. The women wear no hats, are unkempt and ill-clad. They look as if haunted.

THE CITY OFFICIALS IN A LIVELY QUARREL.

The situation has gotten beyond the control of the authorities. The powers in control have been quarreling. Last night at 7 o'clock every citizen soldier under command of Major Fayling was called in, disarmed and mustered out of service. Chief of Police Ketchum then took charge, and the Major was relieved of his command. During an hour and a half the city was unguarded. Negro looters held high carnival.

5

As the Major's work was unusually brilliant, the citizens are furious. This morning the situation from the police standpoint is improved. A hundred of the State militia of the Houston Light Guards, Houston Artillery and Houston Cavalry have arrived. They are patrolling the west end of the city. General McKibbin, Commander of the Department of the Gulf, and Adjutant General Scurry, of Texas, are on the ground, and are advising with Mayor Jones and the Chief of Police Ketchum.

In all other respects the city is worse off than on the morning after the tragedy. A terrible stench permeates the atmosphere. It comes from the bodies of a thousand unburied dead festering in the debris, that cannot be removed for weeks on account of the paucity of laborers. Every tide brings scores back to the shore. During the early part of yesterday trenches were dug and the bodies thrown into them, but it soon became an impossibility to bury all, and the health authorities decided upon cremation as an expedient.

WORK OF THE RELIEF COMMITTEE

At a meeting of the Relief Committee held this morning reports were received from the various wards. The chairman called for armed men to assist in getting labor to bury the dead and clear the wreckage, and arrangements were made to supply this demand.

The situation in the city to-day is that there are plenty of volunteers for this service, but an insufficiency of arms. There have been two or three small riots, but the officers have managed to quell them. The committee rejected the proposition of trying to pay for work, letting the laborers secure their own rations. It was decided to go ahead impressing men into service, if necessary, issuing orders for rations only to those who worked or were unable to work.

All of the ward chairmen reported the imperative need of disinfectants. A committee was appointed to sequester all the disinfectants in the city, including the lime which escaped wetting, and to obtain more. Houston was called upon for a barge load of lime.

WORK AT THE WATER WORKS.

Work on the water works had not progressed so satisfactorily as had been hoped for. The men did not work last night. Chief Engineer Reynolds has not been at the works since yesterday morning. Alderman McMaster took charge of the work to-day. The machinery has been cleared of the debris and the pipes found to be badly damaged, and plumbers, steam fitters and boiler makers are at work on them. Mr. McMaster says he thinks it will be possible to turn water into the mains to-morrow.

All saloons were closed by the Chief of Police on Sunday. At a meeting of the General Committee with the city officials to-day, the policing of the city was discussed. Mayor Jones announced that Adjutant General Scurry would take charge of the situation with the soldiers and citizen soldiery. The city is patrolled by about 2,000 police officers, special officers, soldiers and deputy sheriffs. Deputy Chief of Police Amundsen is acting as Chief. Chief of Police Ketchum is engaged in other work outside of the police department.

STRICT POLICE RULES.

No liquor is permitted to be sold under any circumstances, unless ordered by the chairman of one of the committees or by a physician, who must state that it is to be used for medicinal purposes. All persons not having business on the streets after dark must be identified before they will be allowed to pass. Unless identification is forthcoming they are arrested. No person is allowed to work in or about any building unless he has a written permit signed by the Chief of Police or Deputy Chief. No person is permitted to carry furniture or other property through the streets unless he has a written permit from the proper authority. No gambling is permitted, and any violations of this rule are prosecuted to the fullest extent.

During the storm Saturday night the young men of the Boddiker family, with the aid of a skiff, rescued over forty people and took them to the University building, where they found shelter.

The organization of forces under the able administration of General Scurry was observable on every hand, and the chaotic condition of the city was being supplanted by a vigor of action that portended restoration in the near future. Private enterprise went to work and the people took heart.

NURSES FROM A DISTANCE.

The very presence of nurses was a sign that the calamity had attracted the attention of the world at large, and the city would not be left to succumb to the dire and terrible disaster that has overtaken it.

One of the local journals said : "Merchants are cleaning up their stores and repairing their injured buildings ; property owners are seeking everywhere to obtain men and materials with which to restore their shattered habitations. Hope has by no means departed. In a brief time the sound of the locomotive will be heard upon the island, freight will be pouring up to the ship's side, and the mechanic and artisan will find remunerative employment for years to come. Out of the destruction of the greatest wind and tide force that ever played upon the American continent, there has arisen already a feeling that what a week ago was regarded as an irretrievable disaster, will yet prove the starting point of a remodelled and reinvigorated Galveston. The whole world is behind us in generous sympathy and noble beneficence."

GOVERNOR SAYRES ON THE SITUATION.

Governor Sayres made the following statement to the Associated Press on the flood situation :

"Conditions at Galveston are fully as bad as reported. Communication, however, has been re-established between the island and the mainland, and hereafter transportation of supplies will be less difficult. The work of clearing the city is progressing fairly well, and Adjutant General Scurry, under direction of the Mayor, is patrolling the city for the purpose of preventing depredations. The most conservative estimate as to the number of dead places them at 2,000. Contributions from citizens of this State and also from other States are coming in rapidly and liberally, and it is

confidently expected that within the next ten days the work of restoration by the people of Galveston will have begun in good earnest
and with energy and success. Of course, the destruction of property has been very great—not less than $10,000,000, but it is hoped
and believed that even this great loss will be overcome through the
energy and self-reliance of the people."

During the day the contributions have fairly deluged the
Governor, upwards of $100,000 having been received. Among the
large contributors are to be noted the Standard Oil Company, with
$10,000; St. Louis Commercial Club for a like amount, and the
Huntington interests for $5,000

THE TRANSPORTATION PROBLEM.

This afternoon Governor Sayres received the following official
report from General Manager Trice, of the International and Great
Northern Railroad, who is conducting the operations of the relief
corps at Galveston :

" To Governor Sayres, Austin, Tex.—Your message of yesterday received. The cars containing the tents and rations were
turned over to the barge line this morning and forwarded to Galveston, arrangements having been made for all freight to be
handled by barges hauled by tugs from Clinton to Galveston, and
passengers by our line to Texas City, and by boats from Texas
City to Galveston. This is the best arrangement that can be made,
and it prevents delay to either the freight or the passenger service,
for, if we handled the freight with the passengers to Texas City, to
transfer from the cars to the boats would cause too much delay to
the passenger service.

" We brought in one train, consisting of about three hundred
Galveston people, to Houston to-day, and will get another train-load
to-night, mostly women and children, which will make about 600
that we will get out of Galveston to-day. The passenger and
freight service between Houston and Galveston is all free
for sufferers, and we are issuing transportation to all points
north of Houston to all sufferers not able to pay their way.

" L. TRICE,"

ADJUTANT GENERAL SCURRY'S ESTIMATE.

The following report was also received from Adjutant General Scurry:

"Governor Sayres, Austin.—Mayor of Houston ordered Houston military companies here, sixty-five men and officers came. Thirty more come to-morrow. Mayor of Galveston directed me to take command. Streets patrolled for purpose of preventing thieving. Work of clearing the city progressing fairly well.

"THOMAS SCURRY, Adjutant General."

LOSS OF LIFE AND DAMAGE AT OTHER POINTS.

Governor Sayres began receiving reports from various points along the Gulf coast, which would indicate that there has been great property damage done for several hundred miles, and that the list of Galveston fatalities and suffering will be largely augmented. Down the coast from Galveston, the town of Dickinson was laid waste and five people killed. The towns of Alvin, Alta Loma, Texas City and Brookshire, are wrecked and hundreds are destitute. Richmond is so badly demolished that it will require weeks to clear the town.

Missouri City and Stafford, just opposite, were entirely demolished, and the few remaining people at these places have no homes to cover their heads. Bay City, in Matagorda county, is reported wrecked, with much loss of life, though no official report has been made to that effect. Patton, Rollover, Bolivar Point, Quintana, Sugarland, Belleville, Wharton, Fair View, Missouri City, Sartartia, Arcola and El Campo are all reported heavy sufferers both in point of property destroyed and lives lost. Owing to the fact that the telegraph service is still badly crippled, Governor Sayres cannot ascertain the exact number of dead at the points named, but it is approximated at 500.

BOATS FOR TRANSPORTATION.

The Governor was informed that quite a number of tugs from New Orleans and other available points had either arrived or were on the way to Galveston, and the transportation problem would soon be solved so far as the getting people from the island to the mainland was concerned.

Hundreds applied to Governor Sayre for permits to go to Galveston, but he refused all, saying that there were already too many people there.

THE DEVASTATION APPALLING.

The Quartermaster's Department at Washington, received the following from Galveston :

"Quartermaster General, Washington : Referring to my telegrams of 9th and 10th, I have, subject to approval, suspended the Crockett construction contracts, and again urgently recommend that contractors be paid for labor and material in place and on the ground. All swept away and lost beyond recovery. Fortifications at Crockett, Jacinto and Travis all destroyed and cannot be rebuilt on present sites. Recommend continuance of my office here only long enough to recover Crockett office safes and morning gun, when located; also to close accounts and ship my office and recovered property where directed. I fear Galveston is destroyed beyond its ability to recover. Loss of life and property appalling.

"BAXTER, Quartermaster."

VESSEL ORDERED TO GALVESTON.

President McKinley received a telegram from Governor Sayres, of Texas, asking that a light draft vessel be sent to Galveston to assist in the communication between the island and the mainland. The message was referred to the Treasury Department, and an order was issued to the revenue cutter Winona, at Mobile, to proceed to Galveston without a moment's unnecessary delay. The Lighthouse Board also ordered the lighthouse tender Arbutus, then at New Orleans, to clear at once for Galveston.

Captain Shoemaker, Chief of the Revenue Cutter Service, is apprehensive as to the fate of the cutter Galveston, which was anchored in Galveston harbor at the beginning of the storm. It is assumed that she put to sea, but as three full days have elapsed since she was heard from there are fears for her safety.

The relief work, now under full sway at Houston, is along two lines—to succor those who cannot leave Galveston and to bring out of the city all those who can and are willing to leave.

Mayor Jones and the citizens' committee of the island city are urging that only those shall be permitted to enter Galveston whose presence is imperative, and transportation lines are straining every nerve in order that they may accord the privilege to those who are pleading to get away from the scenes of horror and desolation around them.

Hundreds of people have come to Houston from the four points of the compass, anxious to get into the stricken town, but since the exodus of islanders has begun many of these have concluded to remain here rather than run the risk of missing on the way those for whom they are in search.

ATTEMPT TO SUM UP THE LOSSES.

News has gradually been reaching here of the immense losses along the coast beyond Galveston. Damage difficult to estimate in dollars and cents has been done in a wide stretch of territory, and many human lives have been lost besides those which were wiped out in Galveston and its immediate vicinity. Based on reports believed to be accurate, the following statement is probably as near correct as can be arrived at at this time:

Place.	Lives lost.	Property loss.
Galveston	8000	$10,000,000
Houston	2	300,000
Alvin	9	100,000
Hitchcock	2	75,000
Richmond	3	75,000
Fort Bend county	19	300,000
Wharton	—	40,000
Wharton county	8	100,000
Colorado county	—	250,000
Angleton	3	75,000
Velasco	—	50,000
Other points in Brazoria county	4	30,000

Place.	Lives lost.	Property loss.
Sabine	—	40,000
Patton	—	10,000
Rollover	—	10,000
Wennie	—	10,000
Belleville	1	50,000
Hempstead	1	15,000
Brookshire	2	35,000
Waller county	3	100,000
Arcola	2	5,000
Saratatia	—	5,000
Other points	—	100,000
Dickinson	7	30,000
Texas City	5	150,000
Columbia	8	15,000
Sandy Point	8	10,000
Near Brazoria (convicts)	15	1,000
Damage to railroads outside of Galveston		200,000
Damage to telegraph and telephone wires outside of Galveston		30,000

Damage to cotton crop, estimated on average crop of counties affected, 50,000 bales at $60 per bale; total, $3,000,000. Losses to live stock cannot be estimated, but thousands of horses and cattle have been killed all over the storm district.

RELIEF PUSHED FORWARD NIGHT AND DAY.

Relief for those stricken in the awful calamity is now beginning to pour in from all over the country. Relief committees are being organized, and food, clothing and money raised to be sent here as rapidly as the special trains can carry the supplies to the people so sorely in need of them.

The Relief Committee here announces that the subscriptions in cash are in excess of $15,000, and that in addition to the provisions which have been forwarded from here the Federal Government has ordered 50,000 rations, which are now on their way from

San Antonio.   Lieutenant Ferguson, of General McKibben's staff, expects to take two car loads of food to Galveston to-day.   A telegram from New Orleans says that the exchanges there have raised $6,000 for the sufferers.

Dr. C. P. Wertenbacker, in charge of the Marine Hospital Service in New Orleans, has arrived here.   He has special instructions to look after the welfare of steamers which may be in distress in Galveston.   Dr. Wertenbacker believes that two camps may have to be established by the Government, one for those who cannot leave Galveston and one for those who may come here.   The National Government will send the necessary tents, and the local authorities are providing cots in large numbers.

AN APPEAL TO THE FREE MASONS.

Houston, Tex., Sept. 12.—An appeal has been sent out by the Masonic Grand Master to the Masonic lodges and members in Texas, urging them to remit or contribute to the assistance of the destitute.

Grand Commander W. F. Randolph, of North Carolina Knights Templar, to-day telegraphed the following to subordinate commanders of North Carolina:

"Our fraters in Texas in dire distress because of recent storm. Immediate relief imperative.   Grand Master appeals for funds. Wire or send quickly to Henry B. Stoddard, Deputy Grand Master, Galveston, Tex."

SUBSCRIPTIONS UNDER WAY.

Wilmington, Del., Sept. 12.—H. L. Evans & Co., bankers of Wilmington, to-day started a fund to help the storm sufferers at Galveston.   Bishop Monaghan, of the Roman Catholic Church, in response to a telegram from Bishop Gallagher, of Galveston, has also started a relief movement.   The money which was collected by the city during the Porto Rico famine is still in the possession of Mayor Fahey, and it is likely that it will be turned over for the relief of the people of Galveston.

Atlanta, Ga., Sept. 12.—At a special meeting of the City

Council this afternoon $2500 was appropriated for the Galveston storm sufferers. Private subscriptions have amounted to more than this amount, and to-day $4771 was sent to Galveston.

Liverpool, Sept. 12.—At a meeting convened by the Lord Mayor of Liverpool, England, it was decided to open a relief fund for the sufferers from the Galveston disaster, and £1500 was immediately subscribed, exclusive of over £500 raised by the cotton association. The Chamber of Commerce of Liverpool has passed a resolution expressing deep sympathy with the people of Galveston.

PROTECTION OF GALVESTON A COSTLY PROBLEM.

To protect the city of Galveston from the ravages of future cyclones would be almost as costly as to re-establish the city on a new site. This is the opinion of eminent engineers in Washington. To insure the maintenance of the channel it has been necessary to erect jetties, which have cost more than $6,000,000, but these jetties do not furnish any obstacle of value to the invasion of the sea when behind it is a force such as a West Indian cyclone exerts.

Because of the effect of storms upon the Gulf coast it has been customary for engineer officers stationed at Galveston to report yearly upon the appearance of atmospheric disturbances of more than usual intensity, and Captain Rich, the engineer officer, who is believed to have lost his life, stated in his report for 1899 that storms which occurred during April, May and June, 1899, "carried away nearly all that remained of construction trestle and track, and caused more or less settlement of the jetties."

The need of a safe deep water harbor on the Gulf of Mexico has long been appreciated, and in 1899 Congress passed an act directing the Secretary of War to appoint a board of three engineer officers of the army to make a careful and critical examination of the American coast of the Gulf of Mexico west of 93 degrees and 30 minutes west longitude, and to "report as to the most eligible point or points for a deep harbor, to be of ample depth, width and capacity to accommodate the largest ocean going vessels and the commercial and naval necessities of the country." The Board consisted of Lieutenant Colonels H. V. Roberts, G. L. Gillespie and Jared A. Smith. The Board reported that Galveston was the most eligible point for a deep harbor, but also called attention to the harbors at Sabine and Aransas Passes as being worthy of consideration.

STORM TRAVELED OVER THREE THOUSAND MILES.

Under date of September 13th a prominent journal commented as follows on the great storm :

" Fast disappearing into the Atlantic by way of Cape Breton Island the great West Indian hurricane is passing into history so far as the United States is concerned.

" For twelve days this storm has been under the surveillance of the Weather Bureau. During this time it has traveled more than 3,000 miles, and has described in its course a perfect parabola. When the storm began its "swing around the circle" at Galveston its intensity was greater than it has been since, although as it goes to sea to-night it is reported to be again assuming terrific proportions.

" Its course now lies directly in the path of the North Atlantic Liners, and what future destruction it may wreak remains to be seen from reports of incoming vessels. Until the West Indian hurricane made its appearance the United States had been for exactly two months without a storm, which is the longest period on record since the establishment of the Government Weather Bureau. With the disappearance of this storm, another disturbance is reported near the west Gulf coast, with an arm of barometic depression extending northward into Western Tennessee."

NOT MEN ENOUGH TO HANDLE THE DEAD.

Further details of the great disaster were as follows : The citizens of Galveston are straining every nerve to clear the ground and secure from beneath the debris the bodies of human beings and animals and to get rid of them. It is a task of great magnitude and is attended with untold difficulties. There is a shortage of horses to haul the dead and there is a shortage of willing hands to perform the gruesome work. It became apparent that it would be impossible to bury the dead, even in trenches, and arrangements were made to take them to sea.

Barges and tugs were quickly made ready for the purpose, but it was difficult to get men to do the work. The city's firemen worked hard in bringing bodies to the wharf, but, outside of them, there were few who helped. Soldiers and policemen were accordingly sent out, and every able-bodied man they found was marched to the wharf front. The men were worked in relays, and were supplied with stimulants to nerve them for their task.

At nightfall three barge loads, containing about 700 human bodies, had been sent to sea, where they were sunk with weights. Darkness compelled suspension of the work until morning. Toward night great difficulty was experienced in handling the bodies of negroes, which are badly decomposed.

No effort was made after 9 o'clock in the morning to place the bodies in morgues for identification, for it was imperative that the dead should be gotten to sea as soon as possible. Many of the bodies taken out are unidentified. They are placed on the barges as quickly as possible and lists made while the barges are being towed to sea.

A large number of dead animals were hauled to the bay and dumped in, to be carried to sea by the tides.

RELIEF TRAIN FROM HOUSTON.

A relief train from Houston, with 250 men on board, and two carloads of provisions, came down over the Galveston, Houston & Northern Railroad yesterday to a point about five miles from Virginia Point. It was impossible for them to get the provisions or any considerable number of the men to Galveston, so they turned their attention to burying the dead lying around the mainland country.

There is no fresh water famine here, as the pipes from the supply works are running at the receiving tanks. It is difficult, however, to get it to parts of the city where it is needed.

ROBBERY AND MUTILATION OF THE DEAD.

A reporter has telegraphed from La Porte the story of the robbery and mutilation of the dead in Galveston and death of the offenders.

Ghouls were holding an orgie over the dead. The majority of these men were negroes, but there were also whites who took part in the desecration. Some of them were natives and some had been allowed to go over from the mainland, under the guise of "relief" work. Not only did they rob the dead, but they mutilated bodies in order to secure their ghoulish booty. A party of ten negroes were returning from a looting expedition. They had stripped corpses of all valuables, and the pockets of some of the looters were fairly bulging out with fingers of the dead, which had been cut off because they were so swollen the rings could not be removed.

Incensed at this desecration and mutilation of the dead, the looters were shot down, and it has been determined that all found in the act of robbing dead shall be summarily shot.

During the robbing of the dead, not only were fingers cut off, but ears were stripped from the head in order to secure jewels of value. A few Government troops who survived have been assisting in patrolling the city. Private citizens have also endeavored to prevent the robbing of the dead, and on several occasions have killed the offenders. Singly and in twos and threes the offenders were thus shot down, until the total of those thus executed exceeds fully fifty.

A REFUGEE'S STATEMENT.

J. W. B. Smith, who went to Galveston from Denver, was in Saturday night's storm, and reached Houston, after having an experience which he will remember the remainder of his life.

He started from the city on Monday afternoon, and in walking from the foot of Broadway to the Santa Fe bridge, counted two hundred dead bodies hung up on wire fences, to say nothing of those floating in the water. He constructed a raft out of planks, and in company with Clegg Stewart, made for the mainland, which they reached after hours of exposure.

In every direction crossing the bay they saw the feet of corpses sticking out of the water. Upon reaching land they walked to Hitchcock, Mr. Stewart's home, and found that twenty-five persons had lost their lives there, and that, in addition, fifty bodies that had floated ashore had been buried near there.

MONEY BADLY NEEDED.

The Galveston local relief committee sent out the following:

"We are receiving numerous telegrams of condolence and offers of assistance. As the telegraph wires are burdened, we beg the Associated Press to communicate this response to all. Nearby cities are supplying and will supply sufficient food, clothing, etc., or immediate needs. Cities farther away can serve us best by ending money. Checks should be made payable to John Sealy, Chairman of the Finance Committee.

"All supplies should come to W. A. McVitie, Chairman Relief Committee. We have 25,000 people to clothe and feed, for many weeks, and to furnish with household goods. Most of these are homeless and the others require money to make their wrecked residences habitable. From this the world may understand how much money we will need. This committee will, from time to time, report our needs with more particularity. We refer to despatch of this date of Major R. G. Lowe, which the committee fully endorses.

"All communicants will please accept this answer in lieu of direct response and be assured of the heartfelt gratitude of the entire population. [Signed] "W. C. JONES, Mayor."

CARNEGIE'S PRINCELY GIFT.

The Carnegie Company, of Pittsburg, was foremost in the contributions to the relief of the sufferers at Galveston. At the meeting of the Chamber of Commerce a motion to contribute $5000 was under discussion, when a representative of the Carnegie Company entered and said that he had been authorized by Mr. Carnegie through a cablegram to give $10,000 for the distressed. The announcement was greeted with applause.

GREAT TIDAL WAVES IN THE WORLD S HISTORY.

The tidal wave along the Texan coast will rank among the most disastrous in history. History is deficient in the record of such tragedies in human life, but the records are written in physical geography, and are found in the conformation of shore lines, here and there, around all the continents. It is impossible to estimate the number of lives lost through inundations since mankind began, for purposes of commercial intercourse, the development of seaports. Doubtless the total would run into the hundreds of thousands, and might reach into millions.

Geology is quite sure that the rough Norwegian coast, pierced at intervals of every few miles with the fiords or estuaries which penetrate in many instances leagues into the land, tell the story of many cataclysms such as that which has just occurred along the northern coast of the Gulf of Mexico. Science, however, taking no note of the traditions or folklore of a people, antedates all human life on the Scandinavian peninsula in setting the time when this great rising of the sea against the land took place.

Scientists are agreed on putting the formation of the Norwegian shore lines as far back as the glacial period. But in the songs of the skalds, as late as the reign of Harold Hardrada, there are allusions to the valor of olden heroes over whom the seas had swept, but whose spirits rode upon the winds which blew the Norman galleys to other shores. In the Norway of the present day there are traditions, handed down through countless generations, from the remotest antiquity, telling how, but not when, the seas came in.

OLD AND CHARMING TRADITION.

One of the oldest and prettiest traditions in the world is that which tells of a submerged city somewhere on the Scandinavian coast, the minarets and towers of which poets can see reflected in the waters at sunset, and the bells of which musicians, with ears

VIEW OF PIER 23, SHOWING VESSEL OVERTURNED BY THE GALE

HOUSE ON CENTRE STREET BETWEEN N AND N½ AVENUES BRACED UP BY
A FLOATING CISTERN

DESTRUCTION OF GALVESTON ORPHANS' HOME

INTERIOR OF ST. PATRICK'S CHURCH WHICH WAS DEMOLISHED BY THE HURRICANE

divinely attuned to concordant sounds, can hear at vespers. With-out either the poet's eye or the musician's ear it is still possible to conclude that traditions which have survived so many centuries, and which contradict nothing of the exact truth of science as to original causes, may be as well trusted as science when it begins to speculate, which is all it does when it seeks to prove that the Scandinavian fiords were in the country before the Scandinavian himself.

STORY OF THE LOST ATLANTIS.

The world, with the lapse of centuries, has not even been able to outgrow the tradition of the lost Atlantis. Perhaps this is the oldest of all traditions of cataclysms which have blotted out cities and continents. It may be that it is because this one comes handed down to us from the illustrous hand of Plato that we yield to it a veneration which prolongs its life. Certainly it can never be more than tradition, without a return to the ages of miracles. Our lately found expertness in deep sea soundings have given us no new light on Atlantis.

And yet we cling to the old story, and are loath to turn from the spectacle of a continent in the agonies of a watery burial, or to take down from the walls of our brain cells the pictures of a submerged world in which sea moss trails over and around great temples and monuments. More than half the world believes that there is a lost Atlantis. The Egyptians believed so, long before Plato's day. It is in the mouth of an Egyptian priest, talking to Solon, that Plato puts the description of the vanished land. That description makes of Atlantis a land larger than the Texas of to-day.

BELIEVED THE SEA HAD CONCEALED A LAND.

The Greek philosopher located it off the shores of North Africa, a little to the southwest of Gibraltar. The Platonian description of the interior of the Atlantis of ancient times is surpassingly beautiful, but not more so than the rare imaginative power with which Plato writes of the country and its people, a most fabulous and engaging history.

All this, of course, is the work of pure fancy, and only im-

6

portant, beyond the fact that it is the work of Plato, as showing how deeply the conviction had taken hold upon the mind of that age that the sea had taken away a land which the ancients knew as the western shore of the Atlantic Ocean, and had left nothing but a boundless waste of waters west of Europe. Speculators have located the lost Atlantis near the Canary Islands, and these islands are, in fact, supposed to be the remnants of the lost continent. There is positively nothing tangible upon which to hang the story of the lost Atlantis.

But, like most traditions which persist in living on after the world has grown too practical to have any more use for them, it has, doubtless, a foundation in some important fact of olden time, the tragedy of which was in that sacrifice of the earth to the waters of the deep, which had become familiar even to the ancients. Byron's apostrophe to the ocean is so singularly powerful and beautiful because it expresses that awe and fear of man for the sea which is an instinct with us, and which, if it had not been instinct with us at the first, would have become so through the many and heavy afflictions visited upon the race by Neptune, god of the sea.

TIDAL WAVES ON ENGLISH COASTS.

That the coasts of England have been visited by many and disastrous tidal waves there is abundant evidence. In fact, the ocean bar, which surrounds nearly the whole of England and Scotland, is evidence enough that the entire shore line, as it exists today, is itself the result of a great submersion, or series of submersions, which ages ago overflowed the old coast, rushed in shore, made new land lines, and, hollowing out between the new line and the old, a new ocean bed, leaving what had been called the coast line to be forever after called "the bar." The bar is to be found in nearly every port of England, eloquent testimony to the tidal waves of the past. But there is comparatively little of other testimony save such as has been preserved in the records of seaport towns.

One of the greatest cataclysms ever occurring on the British coast was that on the coast of Lincolnshire in 1571. This has been commemorated in verse by Jean Ingelow in the poem entitled " High Tide Off the Coast of Lincolnshire." The Linconshire coast is almost uniformly low and marshy—so low, in fact, at some places that the shore requires the defence of an embankment to save it from the encroachments of the sea.

A sea wall had been built when the great tidal wave of 1571 came, but it appears to have been absolutely useless as a defence of the country and the people of that time.

At the present day the fens of Lincolnshire are defended from the North Sea by some of the finest engineering works in the world, and yet it is much to be doubted whether they would prove effective against such invasions as that which has just overwhelmed Galveston.

GREAT INUNDATION OF 1571.

There are ancient town records in nearly all the seacoast towns of Lincolnshire which tell of the inundation of 1571. There was then as there is now, a chime of bells in the tower of St. Botolph, Boston, and when the tide was seen to be sweeping away the barriers the Mayor of Boston himself mounted the belfry stairs and had played the old love song called "The Brides of Enderby" as an alarm to the country side.

But the tide came so unheralded, there having been no premonition of it in storm or tempest, that the meaning of the chimes was not understood. Savants have never had an explanation of the Lincolnshire tide, coming as it did so unheralded by anything threatening a cataclysm. The flood found the people unprepared and thousands fell victims to its fury.

There is nothing in literature, and nothing of course in the musty archives of the Lincolnshire towns, conveying as vivid an impression of the horror of the day and night as the Ingelow verses. They are written in the old, and what now seems to us the quaint, English of that day.

The story is told by an old woman whose daughter, out with her two children looking and calling for the cows at eventide, is overwhelmed and drowned.

A REAL TRAGEDY AT GALVESTON.

Perhaps it is a safe conclusion that the tragedy poetry as set for us on the Lincolnshire stage had found expression in real life along the Texas coasts. The old Lincolnshire woman's plaintive narrative has never seemed unreal, because it is filled with the spirit of a homely life, but just now it seems like a voice from out the past telling us of the tragedy now at our doors. The poem is a very long one, but a few selections from its narration of the wide-spread desolation of the country will picture much of the gulf coast of Texas at this time. The cry of the housewife for the cattle dies out in the evening stillness and then the old dame sees the flood:

> And lo, along the river's bed
> A mighty eygre reared his crest,
> And up the river raging sped.
> It swept with thunderous noises loud—
> Shaped like a curling, snow-white cloud,
> Or like a demon in a shroud.

> And rearing Lindus, backward pressed,
> Shook all her trembling banks amain,
> Then madly at the eygre's breast
> Flung uppe her weltering walls again,
> Then bankes came down with ruin and rout,
> Then beaten foam flew round about,
> Then all the mighty floods were out.

> So farre, so fast the eygre drave
> The heart had hardly time to beat
> Before a shallow seething wave
> Sobbed in the grasses at our feet;
> The feet had hardly time to flee
> Before it brake against the knee—
> And all the world was in the sea.

> That flow strewed wrecks about the grass,
> That ebbe swept out the flocks to sea—

A fatal ebbe and flow, alas,
To many more than mine and me.

TIDES AND EARTHQUAKES.

Many of the most fatal tidal waves of which we have any history, have been accompanied by earthquakes, adding to their horrors, but making it impossible to say whether the earthquake or the inundation has been the more fatal and destructive. The great earthquake at Lisbon in 1755 was accompanied by a tidal wave which, rolling up the Tagus river from the ocean, submerged all the lower parts of the city and destroyed thousands of lives which might possibly have escaped the earthquake shocks.

When the earthquake came to Caraccas in 1812 there was a tidal wave at La Guyra, the entrepot of Caraccas, which destroyed many lives. Five years ago a series of tidal waves, accompanied by or alternating with earthquake shocks, visited some of the most populous islands of Japan. The tidal waves reached from fifteen to twenty miles inland, being of such a height, force and volume, ten miles from the ocean, particularly when restricted to narrow valleys, as to be capable of destroying much life.

The number of human lives lost at that time has never been stated in any English newspaper, but that it ran far into the thousands there is no room to doubt. Ten thousand is more apt to be an under than an over estimate, such were the ravages of the combined seismic and cataclysmic terrors visited upon that part of the world during nearly a week of days and nights of horror, which, fortunately, come but seldom in the experience of the race.

The affliction of Texas, while much less than this, is still monumental, and will always rank among the great catastrophes of history. Perhaps there have been events more destructive of life in times or places where it was impossible that any record of them should be left. But few such are known to history. Nor is it likely that the future will often bring to any part of the world a severer affliction than that which has fallen upon our Gulf coast.

CHAPTER V.

Vivid Pictures of Suffering in Every Street and House—The Gulf City a Ghastly Mass of Ruins—The Sea Giving Up Its Dead—Supplies Pouring in from Every Quarter.

A S more definite information came from Galveston and the other coast towns of Texas that were in the path of the storm, the horrors of the situation increased. Most people were inclined to look upon the first reports, made in a hurry and in intense excitement, as grossly exaggerated, but the first reports from Texas, far from being overdrawn, greatly understated the destructive effects of the storm.

Thousands of persons lost their lives, and many thousands more lost all their homes and all their possessions. A large population was without shelter, clothing, food and medicine, in the midst of scenes of wreck and ruin. The sanitary condition of Galveston was appalling and threatened a season of pestilence.

TERRIBLE SUFFERINGS OF THE SURVIVORS.

The people were undergoing a period of the sharpest deprivation, sickness prevailed, and intense suffering was in store for them. The plight of the city and its inhabitants was such that it would be impossible to exaggerate the picture, and demanded from the prosperous and humane everywhere the promptest and most abundant outpouring of gifts.

Food, clothing, household goods, provisions of every kind, household utensils, medicines and money were needed by the stricken city and its impoverished men, women and children. There has been no case in our history which appealed more strongly for sympathy and aid.

Former State Senator Wortham, who went to Galveston as the special aid to Adjutant-General Scurry to investigate the conditions there, returned to Austin and made his report. He said:

"I am convinced that the city is practically wrecked for all time to come. Fully seventy-five per cent. of the business portion of the town is irreparably wrecked, and the same per cent. of damage is to be found in the residence district.

"Along the wharf front great ocean steamships have bodily bumped themselves on to the big piers and lie there, great masses of iron and wood that even fire cannot totally destroy.

"The great warehouses along the water front are smashed in on one side, unroofed and shattered throughout their length, the contents either piled in heaps on the wharves or on the streets. Small tugs and sailboats have jammed themselves half into buildings, where they were landed by the incoming waves and left by the receding waters. Houses are packed and jammed in great confusing masses in all of the streets.

BODIES PILED IN THE STREETS.

"Great piles of human bodies, dead animals, rotting vegetation, household furniture and fragments of the houses themselves are piled in confused heaps right in the main streets of the city. Along the Gulf front human bodies are floating around like cordwood. Intermingled with them are to be found the carcasses of horses, chickens, dogs and rotting vegetable matter.

"Along the Strand, adjacent to the Gulf front, where are located all the big wholesale warehouses and stores, the situation almost defies description. Great stores of fresh vegetation have been invaded by the incoming waters and are now turned into garbage piles of most defouling odors. The Gulf waters, while on the land, played at will with everything, smashing in doors of stores, depositing bodies of human beings and animals where they pleased and then receded, leaving the wreckage to tell its own tale of how the work had been done. As a result the great houses are tombs wherein are to be found the bodies of human beings and carcasses almost defying the efforts of relief parties.

"In the piles of débris along the street, in the water and scattered throughout the residence portion of the city, are masses of wreckage, and in these great piles are to be found more human bodies and household furniture of every description.

"The waters of the Gulf and the winds spared no one who was exposed. Whirling houses around in its grasp the wind piled their shattered frames high in confusing masses and dumped their contents on top. Men and women were thrown around like so many logs of wood.

ALL SUFFERED INJURY.

"I believe that with the very best exertions of the men it will require weeks to obtain some semblance of physical order in the city, and it is doubtful if even then all the débris will be disposed of.

"There is hardly a family on the island whose household has not lost a member or more, and in some instances entire families have been washed away or killed.

"Hundreds who escaped from the waves did so only to become the victims of a worse death, being crushed by falling buildings.

"Down in the business section of the city the foundations of great buildings have given way, carrying towering structures to their ruin. These ruins, falling across the streets, formed barricades on which gathered all the floating débris and many human bodies. Many of these bodies were stripped of their clothing.

"Some of the most conservative men on the island place the loss of human beings at not less than 7500 and possibly 10,000. The live stock on the island has been completely annihilated.

"I consider that every interest on the island has suffered. Not one has escaped. From the great dock company to the humblest individual the loss has been felt and in many instances it is irreparable. In cases where houses have been left standing the contents are more or less damaged, but in the large majority of cases the houses themselves did not escape injury."

At fifteen minutes to four o'clock in the afternoon of Thursday the 13th, for the first time since Saturday afternoon at twenty-six minutes after four o'clock, Galveston was in telegraphic communication with the outside world, although not open for business completely.

The cable left Chicago on Sunday morning and was laid across the bay, and several thousand telegraph poles on the mainland were straightened up by a force of 250 men under the supervision of superintendents of the Western Union.

Concerning the great calamity, the destruction of life and property, the view expressed by a prominent citizen was very generally approved. He said :

"The people and military officers who are dooming Galveston to eternal ruin would have consigned Lisbon to a lasting chaos after her earthquake and decried and abandoned St. Louis with vacant crumbling houses after the great cyclone. If the citizens of Chicago had listened to their despairing notes, blackened fragments of half-fallen walls and shapeless heaps of brick and stone would still be the fitting monuments to proclaim their broken spirit.

BLESSINGS IN DISGUISE.

" But all the reserves of human energy are summoned forth by the very worst disasters, and courage should be written on the heart of Galveston. It is the time to lift up the hands of her strong men, to give them a word of cheer, for they are bound to the spot and must make the best of their fate. A chorus of evil predictions simply multiplies their difficulties and is a cruelty to them, whether it is intended to be so or not.

"Let the dismal prophets reflect a moment. Though buildings have been destroyed there is not a foot of land on the island that does not represent savings. Though railroad communications have been cut off, the currents of commerce by the land and by the sea are merely waiting to resume their courses. Their is a capital in trade connections which is not necessarily wrecked along with wrecked stores, offices and houses."

C. J. Sealey, a young man of Galveston, Texas, who was in La Junta, Colorado, received a telegram from the Mayor of Galveston informing him of the death of twenty-one of his relatives, among whom were his mother, two sisters and three brothers. The young man said he did not believe he had a relative on earth.

An eye-witness of the desolation described the scene as follows :

"Galveston is beginning slowly to recover from the stunning blow of last week, and though the city appears to-night to be pitilessly desolated, the authorities and the commercial and industrial interests are setting their forces to work, and a start has at least been made toward the resumption of business on a moderate scale.

"The presence of the troops has had a beneficial effect upon the criminal classes, and the apprehension of a brief but desperate reign of anarchy no longer exists. The liquor saloons have at least temporarily gone out of business, and every strong-limbed man who has not his own humble abode to look after is being pressed into service, so that, first of all, the water service may be resumed, the gutters flushed and the streets lighted.

BODIES CONSTANTLY COMING TO LIGHT.

"The further the ruins are dug into the greater becomes the increase in the list of those who perished as their houses tumbled about their heads. On the lower beach a searching party found a score of corpses within a small area, going to show that the bulwark of débris that lies straight across the island conceals more bodies than have been accounted for.

"Volunteer gangs continue their work of hurried burial of the corpses they find on the shores of Galveston Island, at the many neighboring points where fatalities attended the storm. It will probably be many days yet, however, before all the floating bodies have found nameless graves.

"Along the beach they are constantly being washed up. Whether these are those who were swept out into the Gulf and drowned or are simply the return ashore of some of those cast into the sea to guard against terrible pestilence, there is no means of knowing. In a trip across the bay yesterday I counted seven bodies tossing in the waves, with a score of horses and cattle, the stench from which was unbearable. In various parts of the city the smell of decomposed flesh is still apparent. Wherever such instances are found the authorities are freely disinfecting. Only to-day, a babe, lashed to a mattress, was picked up under a residence in the very heart of the city and was burned.

" The city still presents the appearance of widespread wreck and ruin. Little has been done to clear the streets of the terrible tangle of wires and the masses of wreck, mortar, slate, stone and glass that bestrew them. Many of the sidewalks are impassable. Some of them are littered with débris. Others are so thickly covered with slime that walking on them is out of the question. As a general rule substantial frame buildings withstood better the blasts of the gale than those of brick. In other instances, however, small wooden structures, cisterns and whole sides of houses have been plumped down in streets or back yards squares away from where they originally stood.

LOOKING TO THE FUTURE.

" Here and there business men have already put men to work to repair the damage done, but in the main the commercial interests seem to be uncertain about following the lead of those, who, apparently, show faith in the rapid rehabilitation of the island city. The appearance of the newspapers to-day, after a suspension of several days, is having a good effect, and both the News and Tribune are urging prompt succoring of the suffering, and then equal promptness in reconstruction. It is difficult to say yet what the ultimate effect of the disaster is to be on the city. Many people have left, and some may never return. The experience of others still here was so frightful that not all will remain if they can conveniently find occupation in other cities.

" The bulk of the population, however, is only temporarily panic stricken, and there are hosts of those who helped to make Galveston great who look upon the catastrophe as involving only a temporary halt in the advancement of the city.

" What is most bothering business men at present is what attitude the railroads, and especially the Southern Pacific, are to assume with respect to reconstruction. The decision of the transportation lines will do more than anything else to restore confidence. Big ships, new arrivals, rode at anchor to-day in front of the city. They had just reached the port, and found the docks and pier damage so widespread that no accommodation could be given to them. They found sheds torn away, freight cars over-turned and planking ripped off.

"The steamships reported ashore in early reports are, save two, the Norwegian steamer Gyller and the British steamer Norma, still high and dry.

"No examination is yet possible as to the condition of those still on the sand, but the big tug H. C. Wilmott has arrived from New Orleans, and her assistance is to be given to saving those vessels which can be gotten into deep water again. Apparently, however, Galveston has no immediate need for ships. The destruction of the bridges of all the railroads entering the city makes it well nigh impossible to furnish outgoing cargoes. These bridges were each about three miles in length, and the work of reconstruction will be a stupendous undertaking.

THE CITY STILL IN DARKNESS.

" One of the most serious results of the storm has been the ripping of the electric light and street car plants. The city has been in absolute darkness for several nights, and only a few concerns who operate their own illuminating service are enabled to do business. Nearly every residence has gone back to the primitive candle. The absence of street lights drives all those who have no imperative business on the streets to their homes at nightfall, but the work of the patrol system is made more difficult thereby and the opportunity for looting greater.

" Among the worst sufferers by the disaster were the churches. Nearly every one of them felt the effect of the storm. Some of them are entire wrecks, absolutely beyond repair.

"The work of relief continues energetically. Mayor Jones and his associates are bending every nerve to open a direct line of transportation with Houston by which he may be enabled promptly to receive the great quantity of provisions which are now on the way to the city."

The War Department received the following telegram from General McKibben, who was sent to Galveston to report on conditions there :

"Arrived at Galveston at 6 P. M., having been ferried across bay in a yawl boat. It is impossible to adequately describe the condition existing. The storm began about 9 A. M. on Saturday, and continued with constantly increasing violence until after midnight. The island was inundated; the height of the tide was from eleven to thirteen feet. The wind was a cyclone. With few exceptions every building in the city is injured. Hundreds are entirely destroyed. All the fortifications except the rapid fire battery at San Jacinto are practically destroyed. At San Jacinto every building except the quarantine station has been swept away.

"Battery O, First Artillery, lost twenty-eight men. The officers and their families were all saved. Three members of the hospital corps lost. All bridges are gone, water works destroyed and all telegraph lines are down. The city is under control of Commmittee of Safety, and is perfectly quiet. Every article of equipment or property pertaining to Battery O was lost. Not a record of any kind is left. The men saved have nothing but the clothing on their persons. Nearly all are without shoes or clothing other than their shirts and trousers. Clothing necessary has been purchased, and temporary arrangements made for food and shelter. There are many thousand citizens homeless and absolutely destitute who must be clothed, sheltered and fed. Have ordered 20,000 rations and tents for 1000 from Sam Houston. Have wired Commissary-General to ship 30,000 rations by express. Lieutenant Perry will make his way back to Houston and send this telegram.

"McKIBBEN."

ALARMING RUMORS FROM GALVESTON.

The authorities at Galveston on the 13th prohibited the entry into the city of any one but men willing to work. Six hundred women and children fled from Galveston and came to Houston. The smell of the dead attained to the stifling point. Five hundred more bodies recovered from the débris were cremated in one pile. Several of the women who arrived at Houston from Galveston were fever patients. They were removed to ambulances from the train in stretchers. It was evident that the city was on the verge of an epidemic, if, indeed, it was not already in its throes. There were serious indications that the authorities were suppressing the facts.

The eagerness of the Board of Health that two miles of wreck be burned, whether it threatened to consume the other portion of the city or not, and the frantic haste of the police to get every woman and child out of the city, coupled with an order issued that no one be admitted to the island except for work, not even relatives of victims or anxious ones searching for relatives, and the seizure of the railroad running to Texas City to prevent people going to Galveston, all contributed to stamp the situation as beyond the control of the handful of inexperienced men in authority. The consensus of opinion of prominent Houston people who returned from the city was that the Federal Government owed it to the country to intervene at once. Otherwise, the danger of contagion to neighboring cities and States must continue to multiply each day.

AUTHORITIES AT ODDS.

Galveston, Texas, September 13.—(By Western Union despatch boat to Houston.)—General McKibben, commanding the Department of Texas, his aide, and Adjutant-General, Lieutenant-Colonel Roberts, arrived here last night. General Scurry, Adjutant-General of Texas, also came in from Austin. Two companies of regulars from Fort Sam Houston also arrived. Galveston is now under martial law, by whose orders has not been proclaimed, and friction has already arisen between the civil authorities and the military.

The sentinels on the street corners do not recognize the passes issued by Mayor Jones, and ignore him and his police force. If a person cannot give a good excuse for being on the street after 9 P. M., he is marched off to jail. Mayor Jones is highly indignant because his authority is usurped, and law-abiding citizens are hot because they are held up when they are on an errand of relief to some stricken friend or family. This is a matter which will be brought to the attention of General McKibben and Adjutant-General Scurry, and Mayor Jones will demand that his authority as

Chief Executive of the city be respected and recognized by the military.

Houston is the haven of the unfortunate people of Galveston. Trains have already brought in between 500 and 1,000 of the survivors, and a motley crowd they are. Men bareheaded, barefooted, hatless and coatless, with swelled feet and bruised and blackened bodies and heads, were numerous. Women of wealth and refinement, frequently hatless, shoeless, with gowns in shreds, were among the refugees. Sometimes there would be a man, wife and child or two, but such cases were rare, nearly all of those who came in having suffered the loss of one or more of their family. Never were there so many sad hearts. Men bereft of their wives and children, women who were widowed, children who were orphaned— it was enough to touch the heart of anyone. Never was there more heroism shown.

Although a week ago these people had happy homes, they are now homeless and penniless, but they bear up bravely. There is no whimpering, no complaining. They were all made to feel that Houston is now their home, that they are welcome and that everything possible for their comfort and welfare will be done. They are being housed and fed, and those in need of medical attention are placed in the hospitals, where they receive every care. Many of the refugees to reach Houston had tasted little or no food since the storm.

NO LIMIT TO HOUSTON'S HOSPITALITY.

A mass meeting of the General Relief Committee was held on the 13th to discuss the best method of handling the crowds of people who were expected to come in from Galveston within the next two or three days. It was decided to pitch the Government tents in Emancipation Park in Houston, as there is no suitable place in Galveston where they can be put up. Mayor Brashear sent a communication to Mayor Jones, of Galveston, urging that all persons be sent to Houston from that place as quickly as possible, and gave assurance that they would be amply provided for.

By "all persons" Mayor Brashear meant that not only those

who are injured or destitute should come, but it included every-body. He wished it distinctly understood that Houston was pre-pared to care for all of those who left Galveston, whether they were sick or well, rich or poor. It was his belief and the belief of those associated with him on the General Relief Committee that Galves-ton must be depopulated until sanitation can be completed, and all people have been urged to come from that city to Houston.

THRILLING EXPERIENCE OF TWO HOUSTON WOMEN.

Mrs. Bergman, wife of Manager Bergman, of the Houston Opera House, gave a thrilling account of her escape during the Galveston storm. She was summering in a cottage on Rosenberg avenue, two blocks back from the beach, at 10 o'clock on Saturday. The water was up about three feet, and she donned a bathing suit and proceeded to the Olympia to talk over the long distance phone to her husband at Houston. At the Olympia she was waist deep in water. At 2 o'clock the water about her house was so deep she became alarmed, and in a bathing suit she and her sister evacuated the high cottage they occupied.

The neighbors living in the next house, being old Galves-tonians, laughed at them. Out of that family of fifteen there were saved three, and they only because they were down town. Mrs. Bergman and her sister started for the Central Telephone office, the water being from waist to armpit deep. Both are expert swimmers, and they buffeted the winds and waves for several blocks. Finally they spied a negro with a dray. They chartered him for two dollars to take them to the Central Telephone Station. After proceeding two blocks the mule was drowned, and all were washed off the dray, the negro being lost.

Mrs. Bergman and her sister, by wading and swimming, reached the telephone station, and found refuge until the firemen commenced to bring dead bodies into the building. Then they concluded to go to Belton's livery stable, where Mr. Bergman kept his horse. This was the hardest part of the trip, although the distance was only 600 yards. It was in the heart of the city, and glass, bricks, slate and timbers flew in showers.

DESTRUCTION OF GALVESTON GARDEN VEREIN, TWENTY-SEVENTH STREET AND AVENUE O

CHINESE RESIDENCE SECTION—TENTH STREET BETWEEN WINNIE AND AVENUE H, GALVESTON

ST. MARY'S INFIRMARY, GALVESTON, AFTER THE FLOOD

At Belton's they remained until next morning. At 6 o'clock Sunday morning, the storm having abated, they started back to their home. The only vestige of it or of the houses for blocks around was a hitching-post. All was a sandy waste. In the back yard lay a dead baby. This frightened them, but before going far on the way back they saw scores of dead bodies, and men, women and children maimed and bleeding, homeless and bereft of family.

It was an awful night and day they put in, with nothing on but bathing suits, and nothing to eat. Passing a store they saw the plate glass windows all broken. The background was lined with black cloth. This they seized, and securing a pair of scissors at the stable and needles and thread, they soon had two well-fitting and well-made gowns, which they wore until they reached Houston.

TRANSPORT TO CARRY PROVISIONS.

Acting Secretary of War Mieklejohn issued orders placing the transport McPherson at the services of the Citizens' Committee of the Merchants' Association of New York for the immediate transportation of provisions donated for the relief of the storm sufferers at Galveston.

The people who had been raising contributions and supplies in New York asked President McKinley for a transport, and the War Department acted immediately on the request. It was expected that the McPherson would leave within seventy-two hours and sail direct for Galveston. It was suggested by the War Department that the relief committees of Washington, Baltimore and Philadelphia and other cities in reach of New York by rail within a few hours, place themselves at once in touch with the Chairman of the Relief Committee of New York, in order that clothing, supplies and food might be forwarded promptly to the carrying capacity of the McPherson.

Austin, Tex., September 13.—Alvin and other points along the coast are crying piteously for aid. They say that they have been overlooked in the general relief fund and that with all their property destroyed, their hopes gone, no clothing, no provisions,

7

they are fit subjects for the hand of charity along with the unfortunates from Galveston. Governor Sayers promptly wired them that they should be looked after.

Touching on the subject of needs of the flood sufferers and the funds being furnished him for the purpose, Governor Sayers stated to-day that it would take at least one million and possibly a million and one-half to render the assistance that would be beneficial to the flood sufferers. Many of them will have to be supported for possibly the next two months, and it will require an immense amount of money to do this, inasmuch as there are estimated to be 10,000 destitute at Galveston and fully twice that many along the main shore.

From points along the coast comes the report that a great amount of wreckage is being thrown up by the Gulf and hundreds of people have wandered miles down the coast, seeking among the wreckage for valuables. The household property of Galveston people is strewn from Rockport in Mantagorda Bay along 200 miles of coast front. Every conceivable household article is to be found strewn along the sands. Valuables are literally lining the coast. Trunks, valises, bureaus, chests and the like are being deposited on the shore.

People are pouring up from the coast by the train load. Many are going to relatives in the central and northern part of the State, and others are stopping in Houston. Of course, this applies to the more prosperous class of the Galvestonians, if there can be any such now.

MONEY AND SUPPLIES FOR THE SUFFERERS.

The subscriptions in New York up to Thursday, the 13th, for the relief of the Galveston sufferers were :

Merchants' Association, $52,099; Mayors' Fund, $7000; New York Mercantile Exchange Fund, $2000; New York Cotton Exchange Fund, $5300; New York Stock Exchange Fund, $11,100; New York Produce Exchange Fund, $10,500; Chamber of Commerce Fund, $25,000; miscellaneous subscriptions, $30,000. Total, $142.994.

The transport McPherson left at noon Monday, the 7th, for Galveston, carrying supplies which were contributed through the Merchants' Association.

The Citizens' Committee of the association deposited in bank $26,775, making a gross total of $40,526 so deposited. Secretary Corwine immediately afterward wired Governor Sayers authorizing him to draw $12,000 in addition to the $12,000 offered the day before. Mayor Jones, of Galveston, was also notified of the telegrams of the Governor.

The steamer El Sud, of the Morgan Line, sailed for Galveston with a large contribution of food supplies and clothing for the Relief Committee, which was contributed through the Merchants' Association.

A despatch from Clark, South Dakota, says that Governor Roosevelt has authorized Colonel William J. Young, of the Executive Department of Albany, N. Y., to issue an appeal for aid on behalf of the Galveston sufferers. J. Pierpont Morgan was named by the Governor as chairman of such committee and authorized to receive subscriptions.

CLARA BARTON GOES TO TEXAS.

Miss Clara Barton, President of the National Red Cross, and her staff, left for Galveston, accompanied by Mary Agnes Coombs, the Secretary of the Executive Committee in New York during the Spanish war.

It was the intention of the Salvation Army to equip a hospital car for Galveston. There were to be physicians and nurses on board and a large supply of hospital necessities. This car will be kept at Galveston as long as needed.

A meeting of Americans, resident and transient, in Paris was held at the Chamber of Commerce on September 13th for the purpose of devising a method for raising funds to assist the sufferers at Galveston. The United States Ambassador, General Horace Porter, was elected President; George Monroe, the banker, was made Treasurer, and Francis Kimball was appointed Secretary. Resolutions of sympathy with the people of Galveston were adopted, and a subscription list was opened, with the result that inside of fifteen minutes 50,000 francs were donated.

A committee of seven was appointed to carry out the plans of the meeting, which included canvassing the American colony in Paris. The French papers also opened subscription lists, many Frenchmen having expressed a desire to subscribe.

R. P. W. Houston, member of Parliment and head of the Houston Line of Steamers, cabled $5000 to Galveston for the relief of the sufferers.

SYMPATHY FROM FRANCE.

The following telegrams passed between the Presidents of France and the United States:

"Rambouillet, Presidence, September 12, 1900.—To His Excellency the President of the United States of America: The news of the disaster which has just devastated the State of Texas, has deeply moved me. The sentiments of traditional friendship which unite the two Republics can leave no doubt in your mind concerning the very sincere share that the President, the Government of the Republic and the whole nation take in the calamity that has proved such a cruel ordeal for so many families in the United States. It is natural that France should participate in the sadness as well as in the joy of the American people. I take it to heart to tender to your Excellency our most heartfelt condolences, and to send to the families of the victims the expression of our afflicted sympathy.   EMILE LOUBET."

"Executive Mansion, Washington, D. C. September 13, 1900. —His Excellency, Emile Loubet, President of the French Republic, Rambouillet, France: I hasten to express, in the name of the thousands who have suffered by the disaster in Texas, as well as in behalf of the whole American people, heartfelt thanks for your touching message of sympathy and condolence.

"WILLAM McKINLEY."

In response to an inquiry telegraphed to Colonel A. H. Belo, publisher of the Dallas News and of the Galveston News, the following hopeful estimate of the business future and prospects of Galveston was received:

"Although in the middle of our overwhelming disaster, the full extent of which can only be approximately estimated, the citizens of Galveston held a meeting on Sunday afternoon, as soon as they possibly could after the great storm. At this meeting the sentiment expressed was a grim and undaunted resolution to rebuild the island city. They said:

"'Galveston must rise again.'

"They fully realize the vastness of their misfortune and the magnitude of their task to repair it, yet, amid all the wreck and havoc that the elements have wrought they say, with determination, that as soon as they bury their dead and provide for the immediate necessities of their living and destitute ones, they will set about to clear away the débris, and begin anew their lives of toil and energy on their storm-stricken island.

"They are inspired with the sentiment that Galveston must rally, must survive and must fulfill a glorious destiny, as the great entry port of the Southwest. As in the case of the great Johnstown disaster, in 1889, the whole American people have responded with alacrity to their cries for help, and with such aid to assist and such sympathy to inspire them, they will surely meet the success that their patriotic efforts so richly merit. A. H. BELO."

STORY OF DEATH AND RUIN.

Reviewing the situation it may be said that again were heard the cries of those in the wilderness of devastation asking for succor, for again, as a score of times before, Galveston and surrounding coast towns are the scenes of death and desolation. Homes razed and washed away by the waters that have claimed their occupants as victims of death and horror, has more than once been the story from the shores of the Gulf.

History is now repeating itself, and the repetition has become frequent since 1860. While severe storms sweep the Atlantic coast between the mouth of the Savannah River and the Chesapeake, still the resultant damage is far less north of Savannah and the Cape Fear River.   This is because the land is higher, serving as a barrier to the encroachments of the sea, while the further south one goes, it will be found, the land is lower, increasing the liability of becoming submerged by heavy inshore winds and tidal waves.

Florida, Louisiana and Texas coast cities are but a few feet above high tide register and therefore the more subject to overflow. To compute the total loss of life and property from the storms which from time to time have devastated the coast of the Gulf of Mexico it would be found the loss of human life would extend well into the thousands, while tens of millions of dollars have been laid waste.

STORMS THAT BROUGHT DESOLATION.

There have been many such storms before whose fury has been felt by the coast people.   One of the worst storms was in September, 1860, which caused ruin and death from Rio Grande to Mobile, and when the waters had subsided the loss could be figured at $3,000,000.

Then in October of the same year, one month later, another storm swept down upon Galveston and Houston, and $5,000,000 had been wiped out.   There were other storms of less violence, as, for instance, in June, 1891, when a southeast wind blew a hurricane for four days and the city was inundated and shipping was seriously crippled.

There was another fearful visitation on September 17, 1875. A good part of the city was under water several feet deep.   Vessels were wrecked and the City Hospital was filled with water and the Ocean House, on Gulf Beach, crumbled and fell and floated away in remnants.   Thirty lives were lost.   It was the hardest storm since 1867 up to that time.   The storm raged for several days.

Indianola, one hundred and twenty miles southwest of Galveston, was almost totally destroyed.   More than one hundred and fifty of its inhabitants were found dead in the ruins of their homes. Nearly all of its three thousand houses were unroofed or badly damaged, and $7,000,000 in money has gone to waste.

A hurricane on the lower Texas coast and in Mexico on August 20, 1880, carried destruction far and wide. As many as three hundred houses in Matamoras, Mexico, were demolished, even brick buildings offering no more resistance than so many toys. Brownsville, Texas, saw its houses unroofed and the infantry barracks were demolished, and twenty-eight army horses and several mules were killed. A convent did not escape damage, and several of the occupants were injured by falling débris.

The railroads, quarantine stations and the lighthouses were seriously damaged. Thirty lives were lost and property damaged was estimated at $1,000,000. This hurricane was followed by one of equal violence on the Mexican coast, which completely wiped out the town of Altata and the port of that name. Not one house was left standing and ships in the harbor suffered greatly.

ATLANTIC COAST ALSO SWEPT.

Savannah, Ga., has not escaped the fury of the southern gale. The city suffered severely in 1881, the waters rushing into the streets and causing the death of four hundred persons by drowning. Four million dollars, it was said, was the amount of the damage to property. In 1893 Savannah was visited by another cyclone and forty persons were killed. This time the property damage was $7,000.000.

Havana, Cuba, and the West Indies were visited by a destructive hurricane in September, 1888. One thousand persons were killed and hundreds of head of cattle were killed. The loss was $7,000,000.

Sabine Pass, which is the dividing line between Texas and Louisiana, was swept by a terrific storm in October, 1886. The population of the town was about four hundred. Of these one hundred and twenty-six perished and 90 per cent. of the deaths was caused by drowning. Four houses escaped injury.

The coast of Mexico was devastated for three days in the fall of 1889 by a destructive cyclone, which first struck the coast of Campeachy. There was a drenching rain which played havoc along the peninsula for miles. The wind was so furious in the city of Carmen it uprooted trees, depositing them upon houses which they crushed. All the shipping in the harbor was wrecked. Twelve foreign barks were wrecked. Some were thrown high and dry on the beach, while others were submerged. Two steamships, many schooners and many smaller craft were wrecked. There was great loss of life.

A hurricane from the West Indies, which swept up the Atlantic coast, did great damage to Savannah, Ga., on Tuesday. September 30, 1896. Wind blew at a velocity of seventy-five miles an hour for an hour and a half. Hardly a building escaped, and thousands of houses were unroofed. The damage was $1,000,000, and twenty-two persons were killed. The roof of the United States, Pension Office was blown off. Railroad stations, churches, theatres and the Bonaventure Cemetery were ruined, monuments being overturned.

The hurricane started from the West Indies. It went from Brunswick, Ga., to Savannah ; thence it plunged through and into Pennsylvania, where the damage done was tremendous. The large railroad bridge over the Susquehanna River was wrecked.

HARDEST STORM FOR MANY YEARS.

One of the worst cyclonic storms of recent years was that on August 29, 1893, which carried havoc and destruction even into our own city, although this city escaped its utmost fury, although there came tales of shipwrecks at sea. It was a West Indian hurricane that originated in the West Indies on August 25, and reached our shores at Savannah, Ga., two days later. The storm passed through North and South Carolina, Virginia and West Virginia and into the southwestern part of Pennsylvania.

All the Atlantic coast States suffered. Port Royal, S. C., was frightfully damaged. The streets of Charleston, S. C., were literally filled with débris, parts of roofs, signs, awnings, telegraph poles and building material being jumbled together in an inextricable mass of wreckage. The streets were flooded with water. All the phosphate works were blown down or badly injured. One odd sight in the old city was a schooner lying high and dry in a street.

One of our journals commented as follows on the storm that wrought unparalleled damage :

"With the passage of the great hurricane out to sea over the Gulf of St. Lawrence the most destructive chapter in the history of storm movements in the United States was closed. Just what the total of life, property and crop losses will be is even now not ascertainable with any sure degree of accuracy, but that it will surpass all earlier estimates cannot be questioned.

TIMELY WARNINGS WERE GIVEN.

"Moving into the Gulf of Mexico, just west of Florida, on Thursday, September 6, in its week's circuit of the United States, the hurricane has at least caused a loss of 5000 lives and probably many more, and has destroyed and damaged property to the extent of $15,000,000. And yet, after its probable direction and the curve of its track were ascertained on Friday, September 7, no great cyclonic disturbance has been more carefully watched or the menace of its forward movement more decisively pointed out.

"It is to be regretted that though the Friday warnings of the Weather Bureau caused apprehensions in Galveston, few realized the extreme gravity of the situation. The bureau, however, did its full duty, and its subsequent warnings with respect to the passage of the cyclone over the lakes were fully justified. The path the hurricane took between September 6 and September 12 meteorologically was most instructive and will unquestionably prove of great value in future forecasts. And yet it followed the normal rule and kept on skirting an area of high barometer that lay over the Southern States, the lakes and the Middle States. From the moment the cyclone was first "held up" by the high pressure anti-cyclone on Thursday it kept to the left of it, and so was diverted westward with such disasterous results for Galveston.

"Though it may seem to some paradoxical to say so, the clear, bracing weather of yesterday, accompanied, as it was, by the strong winds from the south and southwest, was the hurricane's contribution to northern weather. To most people who find great difficulty

in understanding the two-fold movement in cyclonic storms—the
translation of the storm as a whole along its track and the circulation of the winds in the whirl itself—the idea that clear weather is
part of a storm movement will seem strange, and yet such is the
case.

"If you are in the right quadrant and far enough from the
vortex, or storm center, though it will control the winds in your
vicinage, cloudless and rainless weather may easily be your lot.
And this was our experience, for the cyclone at 8 A. M. was central over Quebec, whither it had traversed from Des Moines, Iowa,
over 1200 miles, in a direct line, northeast from where it was central on Tuesday morning the 11th, at 8 o'clock.

TERRIBLE VELOCITY OF WIND.

"The rate at which it made this jump, taking in the lakes in
passing, was at the speed of fifty miles an hour, while the cyclonic
winds kept blowing into the centre at a velocity of seventy miles
an hour. That these two motions have nothing in common is
shown by the fact that on Saturday, when the vertical velocities
were at their height, ninety-six miles from the northeast and 100
from the southeast at Galveston, the cyclone was moving on its
track from the Gulf to the interior of Texas at the sluggish pace
of ten and one-half miles an hour. It was this slow rate which had
prevailed ever since August 5 that accentuated all the evils of the
rotary circulation, for as the centre passed slowly over Galveston
it gave the cyclonic winds full opportunity to pile up the waters and
buffet and wreck the buildings.

"Fortunately we were over 400 miles from the vortex, and,
though we were within the sphere of its southern winds, they
merely proved an annoyance through the excessive dust and were
not disastrous. On the New England coast, as well as over the
lakes, the winds were stiffer, and we are yet to hear the full story
of the cyclone's journey from gulf to gulf. Meteorologically, it is
now a closed record, so far as the United States goes, but, unfortunately for Galveston, the horror of the visitation grows as access
to the stricken town reveals the full extent of the devastation.

CHAPTER VI.

Two Survivors Give Harrowing Details of the Awful Disaster—Hundreds Eager to Get Out of Galveston. Clearing up the Wreckage.

ALEXANDER and Stanley G. Spencer, the two sons of Stanley G. Spencer, of Philadelphia, who was killed in Galveston, reached Philadelphia Monday afternoon, the 17th. Mrs. Spencer was to come north later when their affairs in the stricken city are settled, and would bring the body of Mr. Spencer, which was embalmed and placed in a metallic coffin in a vault in Galveston.

The two boys left Galveston at 9 o'clock Friday morning. It took them until 3.30 in the afternoon to reach Houston, which is only about fifty miles distant from Galveston. "All the society ladies of Houston met the train," said Alexander, the older of the two boys. "They brought clothes and food for the people."

The boys told a remarkable story of their experiences during the flood. "Storm warnings were sent out on Friday," said Alexander, "but nobody paid much attention to them; only a little blow was expected. This did not come until Saturday afternoon. It first started with a chilly wind. Things looked rather dark and hazy and black, rapidly moving clouds sped by. Papa had finished work at the office and was getting ready to come home, when he received a telegram from the North telling him to meet Mr. Lord, with whom he was to conduct business relative to the buying of property.

Papa telephoned us that he would not be home for several hours on account of this business. That is why we were not worried about him. He and Mr. Lord met in Ritter's cafe, and it was there that he was killed. He was sitting on a desk, with his hands clasped over his head, a favorite position of his, talking to Mr. Lord and a Greek, named Marcleitis.

"Ritter's cafe was in a strongly-built brick building, which was thought to be very safe, but, unfortunately, it was at the foot

107

of a short street leading to the wharf. This gave the wind from the Gulf full sweep against it. There were several other men in the cafe, and one of them said : 'Why, did you all know there are just thirteen people in this room ?' Papa laughed, and remarked that he was not superstitious. Just then the crash came, killing five out of the thirteen. In the floor above the cafe was a large printing establishment. A beam hurled down by the weight of the presses above struck papa, killing him instantly. His body was dug out of the ruins Sunday afternoon by about a hundred friends, and his was the first funeral in Galveston."

" Were you frightened much ? "

" No, we were not very scared, because we had no idea how terrible the storm was. We were not worried about papa, thinking he was safer, even, than we were. We secured the shutters and saw that the windows were braced. After that we sat quietly on the first floor. The water never did get above the basement, as the house is situated on an eminence. After a while seven people whom we did not know came in and asked for shelter, as their homes were flooded.

THE STORM GROWS WORSE.

" When the storm kept growing steadily worse we got a rope ready, so that if the worst came we could all be tied together. One family whom I knew did this. They tied loop knots around their wrists. All were drowned together and all were buried in the same hole. All night long we could hear cries for help. To every one who came we gave shelter. Once some one knocked at the door ; when we opened it a woman fell headlong across the doorstep. She had fainted from exhaustion. We found a little girl in the basement, who had been tied to a skiff. She seemed dazed, and kept talking about a beautiful carriage she had seen.

" We did not know what she meant, but next morning we saw a neighbor's carriage perched high on top of a pile of wreckage. Even when we looked out of the window we could not tell the extent of the damage. The moon rose, giving a very clear light, by which we could see objects floating around. It did not rain. The people were drowned by the water backing up from the bay and the Gulf.

"At first the wind was to the northeast. This backed the water up from the west bay. Suddenly it turned to the southeast, causing a tidal wave. The water was from four to six feet deep. Two of the observers remained in observatory all night. The wind gauge broke when the wind was blowing from 115 to 125 miles an hour.

HOUSES IN FRIGHTFUL COLLISION.

"A house was washed against ours. In it the wreckers found eight bodies, three of these and a night sergeant of police were buried in one yard. Our house rocked dreadfully. It and the two houses on either side of it, are old houses built over. No one thought they could stand the fury of the gale ; but they were the only three left standing in that part of the city. Mr. Frank Groome and Mr. Hall had to swim home. The house in which Mr. Hall spent the night was split in two, but the side he was in was left standing. If the wind had continued for two hours longer, there would not have been one person left to tell the tale. When the storm first started my brother and I went to the beach to watch the water.

"Even then the water was backing up in the gutters and the little whitecaps were dancing on the waves. The steps of our house were washed away, but Sunday morning we found the body of a woman lodged in the brick work. Our pet donkey was drowned, but we saved the dogs and the cats as they were in the house. There were five big dogs and three little puppies. Paddy, a big dog, would sit around looking at us. He kept whining the whole time as if he knew something unusual was going on. They say black cats are lucky. Well, we had three of them. These would rub up against us in a frightened way.

"Sunday morning, Mr. Groome came out to tell us about papa. Mrs. Brown, a friend of mamma's, sent for us to come to her house. Nearly all the furniture of her house was ruined by the water. The surrender of the city of Galveston to the Union troops was written in her house and the table on which it was written is still there. We had a hard time getting to Mrs. Brown's. We walked part of the way. A colored man with a bony horse hitched to a rickety little delivery wagon—'dago carts,' we call them—hauled us the rest of the way for a dollar a piece. All through the streets we met hysterical women and dazed-looking men.

"The wife of Dr. Longino, an army surgeon, was at a friend's house, with her little baby, when the storm commenced. During the storm, from fright or something else, the baby lost its breath. Everybody thought the child was dead and tried to persuade Mrs. Longino to leave it and try to save herself but she would not do so. She caught hold of the baby's tongue and held it so it could not retard the passage of air in the windpipe.

TRYING TO SAVE THE CHILD'S LIFE.

"She blew her own breath into the baby's body. After working for a long time, during the most terrible part of the storm, the baby was revived and is still living. She kept her invalid aunt alive by pinching her cheeks. The next day she reached a place of safety in the city. She said she could hardly walk along the beach for the bodies of children. There was a Catholic orphanage about five miles down the beach, in which were a hundred children and ten nuns. All of these but three boys were killed.

"One woman who was trying to save a child was pinned down by a piano. She was just about to give herself up for lost when a big wave came and washed the piano off of her. She and the child were both rescued. We kept a little pet lamb alive, which afterwards we thought we would have to kill for food. But Mrs. Brown got a calf somewhere. It was killed and cleaned, but the ladies themselves had to cut it up. This served for food for two days. The two big cisterns in the cellar were full of salt water; there was a small one on the roof which furnished us with water for a little while. After that we had to beg it from the neighbors.

"The only clothes we have are what we have on and one change of underclothes, which we took with us when we went to Mrs. Brown's. All the rest of our clothes are mildewed.

"We did not see any of the negroes stealing, as mother kept us in the house all the time, but we could hear the shots. They commenced this dastardly work Sunday night. The ghouls are composed of negroes and foreigners. We did not get very frightened when people kept coming to us for help the night of the storm. All we could do was to thank God that He had given us a place of shelter which we could share with those less fortunate."

THREATENED WITH PESTILENCE.

A visitor to the stricken city made the following report:

"Galveston's stress and desolation grows with each recurring hour. Pestilence, famine, fire, thirst and rapine menace the stricken city. Each refugee from the storm-lashed island brings tidings which add to the tale of the city's woe.

"Of the dead that lie in piles in the desolated streets and dot the waters that girdle the city, the true number will never be known. All estimates of the total of the victims of Saturday's night's tempest must be qualified with the mark of interrogation. It is not conjecture to say that the death roll in Galveston alone will hardly fall short of 5000. Sober-sensed men, who have brought to the outer world conservative accounts of sights and scenes in the hapless city, say that there are 10,000 dead people within a half dozen miles of Galveston's centre. No one disputes that the storm victims number the half of 10,000.

"Men who have lived through the yellow fever scourge in New Orleans and other Southern cities, where the dead in the streets were more numerous than the living, hold those horrors lightly in comparison with the conditions that exist in Galveston.

"In devious ways news of the situation that confronts the living in Galveston comes to this city. There is no telegraphic communication with the island. There is no train service. Boats are plying at irregular intervals across the bay. No one in the city has time to send forth to the world more than meagre accounts of the situation in the city. The bulk of the news is gleaned from refugees who are fleeing to Houston. A few railroad men have penetrated into the desolated city and returned with fragmentary accounts of the perils that menace the living, and the gruesome work that is being carried on day and night to ward off the contagion that is threatened by the hundreds of corpses that lie corrupting under the hot sun.

"It will be days before a fairly accurate estimate of the loss of life can be made. Arrivals from Galveston to-night tell that citizens are laboring unceasingly at disposing of the dead in order that the living may not suffer.

"To graves beneath the blue waters of the Gulf the dead are being consigned as fast as they can be loaded upon barges and towed to sea. There is no other way. The city must be rid of them. No more than a tithe of the bodies can be interred. So soaked is the ground that trenches fill with water as fast as the shovel can lift the earth.

FIERCE HEAT ADDS TO THE HORROR.

"There is need of laborers in the city. The remnants of the fire department and police force, both of which organizations contributed many victims to the storm, are doing heroic work. Their efforts are supplemented by the citizens. Hordes of negroes, kin, many of them, to the unspeakable creatures who preyed upon the dead in their hunger for loot, have been commandeered and forced to lend their strength in delving in the ruins for corpses. Stern-faced men with shot guns and rifles stand over them and keep them to their toil. It is heartbreaking work but it is necessary.

"Since the storm blew itself away the weather has been semi-tropical. For four days the sun has sent down its fiercest darts. The result may be imagined. Over the city hangs the nauseating stench of decomposing flesh. Besides the humans there are thousands of carcasses of domestic animals scattered through the devastated portions of the city. Galveston is in need of everything that charity and compassion can suggest. But above all the city requires disinfectants.

THE JOHN SEELY HOSPITAL, GALVESTON,

A RESIDENCE CARRIED FROM ITS FOUNDATION BY THE RUSH OF WATERS

REMOVING DEAD BODIES TO THE BARGES FOR BURIAL AT SEA

GENERAL VIEW ALONG THE GALVESTON BEACH AFTER THE FLOOD

"Heroic measures were adopted by the citizens in charge of the work of policing and rehabilitating the city. It was determined to fire the ruins and purify the city by flame. This must be done. Hundreds of bodies will be cremated in the pyres. Fire is the best disinfectant that the city has at its command. People from the vicinity of Galveston report to-night that heavy clouds of smoke have shrouded the city all the afternoon. It is evident that the ordeal by fire has begun. This adds a fresh menace to the city's safety. The fire department is unable to cope with the flames, should they spread to the undamaged sections of the city.

"It was the weakest members of the community that suffered the greatest in the dark hours of Saturday night, when the seas leaped upon the city. Two-thirds of the corpses that are seen are those of women and children. The number of the negro dead exceed the white victims.

"A water famine has added its quota to the perils of the situation. The water works are still disabled. There are few wells in the city, and the bulk of the available water supply consists of the stores in the reservoirs. This is not sufficient to last more than a day or two. Strenuous efforts are being put forth to repair the pumps and start the water works."

ROBBERS DRIVEN FROM THEIR WORK.

Since Adjutant-General Scurry has assumed police direction of affairs, looting and plundering have ceased. No one has been shot, and order prevails throughout the city. The lawless know that they will be shot down on the spot when caught depredating, and this has had a very wholesome effect. The large force of men employed in burying and cremating the exposed dead scattered throughout the city have completed that portion of their work and are now engaged in searching for the bodies of unfortunates lying crushed and bruised beneath the immense mass of debris and wrecked buildings scattered throughout the city. Where the debris lies in detached masses it is fired and the bodies therein are consumed.

When adjacent property is endangered by fire the mass of

8

debris is removed, the bodies taken out, removed to a safe distance and around them is piled the removed debris, the whole saturated with oil and fired. Identification is impossible. The bodies being in all stages of putrefaction and giving a horrible stench, it is a most sad and gruesome task. Perhaps some of the men engaged in this work are unknowingly aiding in destroying all that is mortal of some loved one.

In gathering remains for interment a nephew of Alderman John Wagner, a youth 18 years old, was found lodged in the forks of a tall cedar tree, two miles from his wrecked home, and tightly clenched with a death grip in his right hand $200, which his father gave him, with two $20 gold pieces, to hold while the father attempted to close a blown open door, when the house went down and the whole family perished in the raging storm and flood .

THE LOSSES OUTSIDE OF GALVESTON.

While the loss of life in this city will not fall below 5000 and may be many more, every little town within a radius of seventy-five miles of Galveston was wrecked and people killed and wounded, while the damage to property will aggregate over $2,000,000. The damage to property in and around Alvin, a thriving town of 2000 people, where eleven people were killed and quite a number wounded, is estimated at $300,000, and they send out an urgent appeal for aid and relief supplies.

Fifty-four houses were wrecked in Quintana and the debris piled up in the streets. Fortunately, no lives were lost. The town of Velasco, three miles above, on the east side of the river, was completely wrecked and nine killed, three being killed in the hotel, which was badly demolished. Angleton, the county seat of Brazoria, ten miles north of Velasco, was completely destroyed and several lives lost and a number badly injured. The property loss in these three towns and country adjacent thereto will be beyond the ability of the people to repair.

Supplies for the relief of Galveston's sufferers are coming in from every quarter as rapidly as the limited means of transportation here will admit.   Its distribution here has not yet gotten on a systematic basis, and needs to be radically revised, or it will fail of its purpose and defeat the object of those who are so generously contributing.   Medical relief is much better organized.

There is not a house of any character in the city but what is foul and ill-smelling.   The water failed to materialize to day as promised, and this aggravates the situation.   With a completely crippled fire department, fire apparatus all gone, nine horses drowned, five engines useless and no water supply, should a fire break out, fanned by a stiff breeze, what's remaining of the city would be speedily wiped out.

MILITARY RULE NEEDED.

Major Lloyd P. Fayling, who was so prominent in the organization of the first relief effort, was asked what solution of the present disorganization of the policing powers he would suggest. The Major dictated the following :

"The situation demands Federal aid.   It demanded it from the very first.   An experienced United States army officer of high rank should be put in command here, preferably one who has seen years of active service.   A regiment of regular soldiers would absolutely control the situation where any number of militia might meet with difficulties.   The disaster is so great and so terrible no municipal authority in the country could be expected to handle it unaided."

The first real attempt to clear away the great mass of debris piled along the beach front for a distance of several miles was begun on the 14th.   Advertisements were printed in the papers, which appeared this morning, asking for hundreds of men and boys to do this work.   A multitude responded.   They were formed into squads and promptly put to work, with police and deputy sheriffs in charge.   It is hoped that a vigorous prosecution of this work will lead to the early recovery of bodies still in the debris.   That there are many of them there is no shadow of a doubt.   It is difficult, indeed, to imagine how half the people who did escape got free from this fearful flotsam and jetsam.

An Associated Press representative traversed the beach for some distance, and the stench at different points was absolutely sickening. Everywhere little groups of men, women and children, some of them poorly provided with raiment, were digging in the ruins of their homes for what little household property they could save. In many cases those seeking their former residences were utterly unable to find a single remnant of them, so hopeless is the confusion of timber and household furniture.

EXODUS FROM THE CITY.

The exodus from the city was heavy, and hundreds more were eager to go who were unable to secure transportation. Along the bay front there were scores of families with dejected faces, pleading to be taken from the stricken city, where, in spite of every effort to restore confidence, there is a universal feeling of depression.

Shipping men say that the damage to the wharves is by no means as serious as at first supposed. The chief damage has been in the tearing open of sheds and ripping of planking. The sheds, however, can be quickly replaced. The piling for a considerable distance along the bay front successfully withstood the pounding it got from the wind and waves, and business men find a measure of consolation in this.

More hopeful reports were received touching the water supply. C. H. McMasters, of the Chamber of Commerce, has charge of the water relief work. The company is placing men all along the mains, plugging the broken places, and thereby assisting the flow. It was serving some of its customers to-day, and hopes gradually to increase the service. The water continues to run by gravity pressure. The only difficulty the people are having is in carrying supplies to their homes or places of business. The ice supply continues bountiful, and at many corners lemonade is being served at five cents for as many glasses as you can drink at one time.

More effective measures were taken to keep undesirable people off the island. Soldiers patrolled the water front, and challenged all who could not show a proper reason for their landing, or who were unwilling to work for the privilege of coming into town.

Assurances have been received by the railroads that they will do all in their power to reopen communication, and their present plan seems to be to concentrate all forces on the work of the reconstruction of one bridge. Crews are coming down the Santa Fe Railroad from Arkansas and St. Louis with full equipments to restore the line. Local representatives of the Southern Pacific have had advices from headquarters to proceed with repair work without delay.

Telegraph communication has been partially restored, the Western Union and Postal Companies having reached the city with one wire. Large forces have been at work along the lines of both companies, and connection with Galveston has been attended with many difficulties.

BUSINESS BEING RESUMED.

A larger number of business houses than on yesterday are open, and advertising their wares at no advance in the prices. Carts with disinfectants are going through the streets. The gutters are being covered with lime. Carpenters are having all the work they can do. The storm tore hundreds of roofs off, and the people who are living in topless houses are eager to obtain coverings so as to prevent the destruction of what they have saved if a rain storm comes along. Thus far, however, the weather has been clear.

The relief committees are steadily broadening the scope of their work. They have established bureaus for the issuance of orders and rations in every ward, and though there is a multitude surrounding every bureau, applicants are rapidly being taken care of. There seems no present likelihood of inability on the part of the committee to furnish all the rations that are asked for. There is of course, a scarcity of fresh beef and of milk, but bread is being provided in abundance, as well as hams, potatoes, rice and other articles.

One of the most remarkable escapes recorded during the flood was reported to-day, when news came that a United States Battery man, on duty at the forts last week, had been picked up on Morgan's Point wounded, but alive. He had buffeted the waves for five days and lived through a terrible experience.

SURGEON GENERAL WYMAN MAKES A STATEMENT.

The following statement from Surgeon-General Wyman is dated Washington, D. C., Friday, Sept. 14:

"In response to the request concerning the situation in Galveston, I have a report from Passed Assistant Surgeon Wertenbaker, who was directed to go from his station in New Orleans to Galveston, practically confirming the press reports as to the effect of the storm and conditions existing. He says:

"'City is wrecked. Press reports not exaggerated. Deaths estimated at 5,000. Bodies being cremated as fast as found. Many bodies under debris not yet removed. Water supply limited. Very scarce now, but supplies coming in rapidly. The only means of communication is by railroad to Texas City, thence by boat, or by boat from Houston.'

"Dr. Wertenbaker is at Houston, and Surgeon Peckham and Acting Assistant Surgeon Lea Hume are giving all the aid possible in Galveston. I do not apprehend an outbreak of any epidemic of disease as a result of the storm. The law and regulations are ample to meet the emergency.

"There is danger of sickness caused by unusual exposure and deprivation of food and water, but the people of Galveston and Governor and other officials of the city and State are thoroughly alive to the necessities of the situation. Their disposal of bodies by cremation is certainly a wise measure, and I am convinced that the native energy of the people, supplemented by the tents and rations furnished by the War Department and the contributions which have been and are flowing in from all parts of the country, will obviate the outbreak of widespread disease.

"WALTER WYMAN,
"Supervising Surgeon-General Marine Hospital Service."

As already stated, the first estimates of the number lost were much too low, and all the facts show that probably 8000 is not too high an estimate.

Austin, Tex., Sept. 14.—The fund for the relief of the Galveston sufferers now aggregates nearly $1,000,000 and it will probably reach $1,500,000 by to-morrow night. Most of this amount is in the hands of Governor Sayres, who will direct the work of expending it for food, supplies and other relief measures. The Governor will not give out for publication an itemized list of the contributions for several days.

Numerous inquiries from the East have been received as to the best way to send subscriptions to the Governor for the Galveston Relief Fund. The Austin National Bank, of this city, which is the United States depository for Texas, has notified the Governor that it will make transfers of all contributions for Galveston free of charge by wire or draft. Remittances may be sent direct for transfer to Governor Sayres.

The House of Representatives has sanctioned a motion to send a cablegram to the President of the United States expressing the condolence of the Government and people of Peru over the catastrophe at Galveston.

APPEAL TO DRUGGISTS IN HOUSTON.

To all druggists: The storm stricken district is very much in need of the following drugs: Iodoform, chloride of lime, gum camphor, assafetida, crude carbolic acid, phenol sodique, gauze bandages, quinine and iodoform gauze. Contributions should be sent to the Houston Relief Committee.

A. E. KESLING,
Houston Relief Committee.

"Chicago's first offering of food and clothing for the Texas sufferers left here last night (Thursday, the 13th), over the Rock Island Road on a special train of six cars that has the right of way over all trains as far as Fort Worth, Texas. Other cars packed at Rock Island, Davenport, Muscatine, Topeka, Kansas City, St. Joseph and Wichita will be picked up on the way, and it is expected the train will consist of twenty-three cars when it reaches its destination. The train is expected to reach Fort Worth on Saturday, from where it will be taken to Houston, over the Houston and Texas route on a special train schedule."

The banking house of Munroe & Company, New York, received from its Paris branch advices to draw on that bank for $10,000 for the aid of the Galveston sufferers.

Vice-President and General Manager Trice, of the International and Great Northern Railroad, spent several hours at Bryan on the 13th. Mr. Trice has just come from Galveston, where he had been in touch with the situation since the great storm. He said the railroad losses will aggregate $5,000,000 or $6,000,000.

"We are now operating trains to Texas City, and carrying on traffic from that point to Galveston by boat," he said. "Better shipping facilities will be established at Galveston than ever as fast as men and money can place them there. Negotiations are now going on to the end that all railroads entering the city join forces and materials and establish a temporary bridge across the bay, and if the plan succeeds it is hoped that trains can be run into Galveston in thirty days. The negotiations going on also contemplate the construction of a permanent double track steel bridge, to be used by all the railroads entering the city."

PLANS FOR A NEW BRIDGE.

W. Boscheke, assistant engineer of the Southern Pacific Railroad at Galveston, has received orders by wire from New York to prepare plans at once for a double-track steel bridge across Galveston Bay, ten feet higher than the old one, and to proceed with all the force possible. Engineers are at work making a survey and running lines preparatory to the resumption of work.

J. W. Maywell, General Superindent, and J. W. Allen, General Freight agent of the Missouri, Kansas and Texas, have arrived here for the purpose of conferring with General Manager Polk, of the Gulf, Colorado and Santa Fe, and Manager Hill, of the Galveston, Houston and Henderson Railway, with the object of combining their efforts on the reconstruction of one bridge for all railways entering Galveston for the time being, and thus secure an early resumption of traffic and the partial restoration of business in Galveston. Such a plan, it is believed, will be adopted.

What Galveston needs now is money and disinfectants. Next to these two things, she needs forage. There are now, as near as can be estimated, three hundred cars of provisions on the way, and it is thought that, with what is already here, that amount will suffice for a time at least. No more doctors are needed. Galveston has begun to emerge from the Valley of the Shadow of Death into which she has been plunged for nearly a week, and to-day for the first time actual progress was made toward clearing up the city.

The bodies of those killed in the storm have for the most part been disposed of. A large number may be found when the debris is removed from some of the buildings, but at present there are none to be seen, save those occasionally cast up by the sea. As far as sight, at least, is concerned, the city is cleared of its dead.

A CONFLICT OF AUTHORITY.

A conflict of authority due to a misunderstanding precipitated a temporary disorganization of the policing of the city yesterday. It seemed that when General Scurry, Adjutant-General of the Texas Volunteer Guard, arrived in the city with about 200 militia from Houston, he conferred with the Chief of Police as to the plans for preserving law and order. An order was issued by the Chief of Police to the effect that the soldiers should arrest all persons carrying arms unless they showed a written order, signed by the Chief of Police or Mayor, giving them permission to go armed.

The result was that about fifty citizens wearing Deputy Sheriff badges were arrested by the soldiers and taken to police headquarters. The soldiers had no way of knowing by what authority the men were acting with these badges, and would listen to no excuses. After a hurried conference between General Scurry and Sheriff Thomas, it was decided that all Deputy

Sheriffs and special officers shall be permitted to carry arms and pass in and out of the guard lines. The Deputy Sheriffs and special and regular police now police the city during the day time and the militia take charge of the city at night.

At a meeting of the General Committee last night, a committee of representative citizens of Galveston was appointed to go to Austin at once to confer with Governor Sayres in regard to the situation here.

The need of sprinkling the streets with a strong bi-chloride solution and taking other sanitary precautions was discussed, and after adjournment of the General Committee the Committee on Correspondence sent the following telegram :

" Galveston, Texas, Sept. 13.—To the Associated Press : Our most urgent present needs now are disinfectants—lime, cement, gasoline stoves, gasoline, charcoal furnaces and charcoal. Nearby towns also may send bread. For the remainder of our wants money will be most available, because we can make purchases from time to time with more discretion than miscellaneous contributors would exercise. We are bringing order out of chaos, and again offer our profound gratitude for the assistance so far received."

A CAMP AT HOUSTON.

At a conference held at the office of City Health Officer Wilkinson, it was decided to accept the offer of the United States Marine Hospital Service, and establish a camp at Houston, where the destitute and sick can be sent and be properly cared for. The physicians agreed that there were many indigent sick in the city who could be removed from Galveston, and Houston was selected, because that city had very thoughtfully suggested the idea and tendered a site for the camp.

Acting upon the suggestion to establish a camp and care for the sick and needy, a message was sent to the Surgeon-General, at the head of the Marine Hospital Corps, asking for 1000 tents of four berth capacity each, also several hundred barrels of disinfecting fluid.

Congressman R. B. Hawley, who was in Washington at the

time of the storm, has arrived in the city. "Work of a vast importance is to be undertaken here," said he. "Work on different lines from that which has been our habit heretofore. There are storms elsewhere. If the people in other parts of the country built as we build, their cities would be down and out nearly every year. But they build structures to stay, and we must rebuild our city on different lines and in a different manner that will resist the gales as they do. The port is all right. The fullest depth of water remains. The jetties with slight repair, are intact, and because of these conditions the restoration will be more rapid than may be thought."

OFFICIAL REPORTS TO THE WAR DEPARTMENT.

Washington, Sept. 14.—The War Department has received several telegrams relating to the conditions at Galveston. The following is from Governor Sayres:

"Austin, Tex., Sept. 13.—Will wire you if any further aid be necessary. Please express to the Department my most grateful acknowledgment for its prompt and generous assistance.

"JOSEPH D. SAYRES,

"Governor."

General McKibbin, September 12th, reports generally upon the condition at Galveston as follows:

"General conditions are improving every hour. Repairs to water works will by to-morrow insure water supply for fire protection. Provisions of all kinds are being received in large quantities; enough are now en route and at Houston to feed all destitute for thirty days. There is no danger of suffering from lack of food or shelter. City under perfect control, under charge of Committee of Safety. Loss of life is probably greater than my conservative estate of yesterday. Property loss enormous; not an individual in the city has escaped some loss; in thousands of instances total loss.

"To-day, in company with Colonel Roberts and Captain Riche, made an inspection at Fort Crockett, and by tug of the fortifications at Forts San Jacinto and Travis, with the exception of battery for two four seven-tenths rapid fire guns batteries may be considered non-existent.   Captain Riche has forwarded by wire this evening full report of conditions to chief engineer.   I coincide in recommendation that all fortifications and ordnance property be transferred to engineer officer here for salvage.   Earnestly recommend that Battery O, First Artillery, be ordered to Fort Sam Houston for recuperation and equipment ; officers and men are entirely destitute.   At present a large number are injured and unfit for duty.   Impossible at present to furnish them with ordinary camp equipage, clothing, as all transportation facilities are being utilized to bring in food supplies.

"McKIBBIN, Commanding."

In a previous report General McKibbin praises the conduct of the regulars.   Acting upon the recommendation of General McKibbin, Adjutant General Corbin to-day ordered Battery O, First Artillery, from Galveston to Fort Sam Houston.

CAPTAIN RICHE'S REPORT.

General John M. Wilson, Chief of Engineers, received the following comprehensive report from Captain Riche as to the condition of Government property at Galveston :

"Jetties sunk nearly to mean low tide level, but not seriously breached.   Channel at least as good as before, perhaps better. Twenty-five feet certainly.   Forts as follows : Fort Crocket—Two fifteen-pounder emplacement, concrete all right, standing on piling, water underneath.   Battery for eight mortars about like preceding, mortars and carriages on hand unmounted.   Battery for two ten-inch guns about like preceding, both guns mounted and in good shape.   Shore line at Fort Crocket has moved back about 600 feet. Fort San Jacinto—Battery for eight twelve-inch mortars badly wrecked, magazines reported fallen in ; mortars reported safe.   No piling was under this battery ; some of the sand parapet left. Battery for two ten-inch guns badly wrecked.   Central portion level, both gun platforms down, guns leaning ; no piling was under this battery.

"Battery for two four seven-tenths rapid-fire guns, concrete

standing upon piling; both guns apparently all right. Battery
for two fifteen-pounder guns, concrete apparently all right, standing on piling. Fort San Jacinto battery could not be reached by
land; inspection was from a distance. Sand around these batteries seemed pretty well leveled off to about two to three feet
above mean low. Torpedo casements, nothing but concrete left
and badly wrecked. Concrete portion of cable tank left; cable in
it probably safe. Part of coal wharf still standing. Everything
else in vicinity gone. Some of the mine cases are down the beach
as far as Fort Crockett.

BATTERIES UNDERMINED.

"Fort Travis—Battery for three fifteen-pounder guns, concrete intact, standing on piling. Water underneath. Battery for
two eight-inch guns, concrete intact, except eastern emplacement,
which has cracked off; eastern gun down and twenty feet from
battery; western one all right; concrete standing on piling; water
underneath middle of battery. These batteries were inspected from
the channel. Shore line has moved back about 1,000 feet, about
on the line of the rear of these batteries. All buildings and
other structures gone. Inspection was made with General Mc-
Kibben.

"Recommendation is made that all fortifications and property
be transferred to the Engineer Department. That for the present
batteries be considered non-existent so that future work may be
chargeable as original construction. Much ordnance can be
saved if given prompt attention. Unless otherwise instructed, I
will take charge of these works at once and save all possible.
New projects for jetties and forts cannot be submitted for several
weeks until definite detailed information is had. Further
recommendations will then be submitted as soon as possible. Galveston is still a deep water port, and such a storm is not likely to
reoccur for years.   "RICHE, Engineer."

Notwithstanding the fact that the number of boats carrying
passengers between Texas City and Galveston has been largely
increased, it was impossible on Thursday, the 13th, to leave the

city after the early morning hours, and hundreds of men, women
and children, all anxious to depart, suffered great inconvenience
and hardship, and were, after all, compelled to sleep upon the
beach at Texas City, waiting for the morning.   There is but one
steamboat plying across Galveston Bay, which is able to carry
passengers in any number, and even this boat is able to make the
trip only with extreme caution, on account of the shallowness of
the bay.

Yesterday morning somebody lacked something of being
cautious in the extreme, and the "Lawrence," after jamming her
nose into the mud, remained aground all day.   Her passengers
were taken off in small boats.   This compelled all those who were
unable to come on the first trip of the "Lawrence" to trust themselves to sailboats, and by noon a dozen of them, heavily loaded,
started from Galveston to Texas City, where the fleet was scattered over Galveston Bay by a distance of anywhere between one
mile and three miles.   The wind died away utterly.

URGED TO HURRY A TRAIN.

The boats could neither go on to Texas City nor return to
Galveston.   None of them had more than a meagre supply of
water and no food, as the trip ordinarily does not require above
an hour.   Great suffering resulted.   All afternoon they were
becalmed, and, a slight breeze arising in the evening, at 9 o'clock
at night the sailing craft which had left Galveston at noon began
to dump their passengers upon the beach at Texas City.   This
place is now among the things that once were.   There are no
houses, no tents, no accommodations of any kind save a few passenger coaches standing upon the railroad track.   These were
speedily filled, and the rest of the women and children, all hungry
and the latter crying for food, were compelled to remain on the
beach.

An urgent message was sent to the railway people at Houston, saying that women and children were suffering, and asking
them to hurry a train to Texas City for the purpose of conveying
the refugees to Houston.   No reply was received, and when a

train, whose crew knew nothing of the existing conditions at Texas City, finally appeared, the announcement was made that it would not go before morning. The crowd at Texas City was more than enough to fill the train to the limit, but, notwithstanding, determined to allow the "Lawrence" to attempt once more the perils of the mud and await another consignment of refugees.

It was fully twenty hours after their start from Galveston that the people who left there yesterday noon were able to move out from Texas City, which is only eight miles away, and by the time the train had made a start for Houston, every woman in the crowd was ill through lack of food, exposure and insufficient sleep.

NO RED TAPE TO STAND IN THE WAY.

Washington, Sept. 14—General Spaulding, Acting Secretary of the Treasury, took further measures to-day for the relief of the distressed citizens of Galveston by arranging for their transportation by foreign vessels to New Orleans or other gulf ports. The law provides that American vessels only can carry passengers between American ports, but during the present conditions the Treasury Department will remit the penalties to which foreign vessels would be liable, for the relief of Galveston.

The Rev. J. F. McCarthy, of Newark, N. J., assistant pastor of St. Patrick's Cathedral, to-day received a special despatch from Galveston to the effect that all of the twenty-four Newark nuns at the Catholic Convent of the Sacred Heart at that place had been saved from the general destruction of life and property by the terrible cyclone of Saturday. Father McCarthy at once despatched a special message to the homes of the nuns' relatives with this information. They were reported lost in an account contained in in a preceding chapter of this volume.

A prominent newspaper called attention to the necessities of the situation as follows :

" As later news is received from Texas the full extent of the destruction of life and property is revealed. No such visitation of nature's force has ever before descended upon a community in this country. There is no longer any doubt that the death list will run into the thousands. It will probably never be known accurately how many perished in the track of last Sunday's storm. Many bodies have been washed out to sea, and of the hundreds of corpses that lay exposed in the streets and buried under fallen buildings only a fraction will be identified.

"For the sanitary protection of the living it has been found necessary to deny the dead an ordinary burial. A great city full of prosperous people has been suddenly left without food, water, clothing and all the daily necessaries of life. Worst of all, the survivors are absolutely without means of recuperation from the awful disaster that has overtaken them. They are totally dependent upon the outside world for assistance.

RELIEF FOR TEXAS SUFFERERS.

"In the first steps of relief for those who have been stricken our northern cities made a generous response to the call for aid. The hearts of our citizens have been profoundly stirred, and they have given out of hand without questioning or hesitancy. Everything that would contribute to the care of the suffering and the succor of the needy has been offered without stint. All alike have come forward with their donations, rich and poor, according to their means.

"From Philadelphia was dispatched a train of four cars loaded with a quarter of million pounds of supplies furnished by the people of that city for the relief of the distressed at Galveston and along the Gulf coast. With the train went eight volunteer nurses to care for the sick and injured. They will arrive on the ground none too soon, for the local resources of Texas are being greatly overtaxed.

"The supplies have been selected with judgment, so that they will not suffer in transit and in distribution, and only non-perishable goods have been chosen, for it will be weeks before the stricken district will have strength to provide for itself. But there will be time enough for future measures. It is the first aid that counts. Our people have been doubly generous, because they have not stood upon the order of their giving."

CLARA BARTON

REMAINS OF A BUILDING THAT WITHSTCOD THE FLOOD

A RUINED HOME

HON. WALTER C. JONES
MAYOR OF GALVESTON

CHAPTER VII.

Not a House in Galveston Escaped Damage—Young and Old, Rich and Poor, Hurried to a Watery Grave—Citizens with Guns Guarding the Living and the Dead.

THE all-absorbing story of the great flood is continued in the following pages, with new and thrilling incidents. Best informed residents of Galveston who have been over all portions of the city estimate that from 1200 to 1300 acres were swept clear of habitation. It can be said that not one Galveston home escaped without some damage.

Galveston's great open-air show-place was the Garten Verein. There were various structures devoted to recreation which stood on about seven acres of ground that had been brought to a degree of perfection in gardening hardly credible when the foundation of sand was remembered. Hundreds of oleander trees and flower-beds adorned the park. The Garten Verein was wiped out of existence. Among the débris have been found many bodies.

SLOWLY RECOVERING FROM THE STUNNING BLOW.

Galveston is now beginning slowly to recover from the stunning blow of last week, and though the city appears to-night to be pitilessly desolated, the authorities and the commercial and industrial interests are setting their forces to work and a start has at least been made toward the resumption of business on a moderate scale. Plans for rebuilding the city are also discussed. The presence of the troops has had a beneficial effect upon the criminal classes, and the apprehension of a brief but desperate reign of anarchy no longer exists.

The liquor saloons have at least temporarily gone out of business, and every strong-limbed man who has not his own humble abode to look after is being pressed into service, so that, first of all, the water-service may be resumed, the gutters flushed and the streets lighted.

The further the ruins are explored the greater becomes the increase in the list of those who perished as their houses fell about their heads. On the lower beach a searching party found a score of corpses within a small area, going to show that the bulwark of debris that lies straight across the island conceals many more bodies than have been accounted for.

Volunteer gangs continue their work of hurried burial of the corpses they find on the shores of Galveston Island at the many neighboring points where fatalities attended the storm. It will probably be many days yet, however, before all the floating bodies have found nameless graves.

MANGLED CORPSES WASHED ASHORE.

Along the beach they are constantly being washed up. Whether these are those who were swept out into the Gulf and drowned or are simply the return of some of those cast into the sea to guard against terrible pestilence, there is no means of knowing. In any event, the correspondent, in a trip across the bay yesterday, counted seven bodies tossing in the waves with a score of horses and cattle.

The city still presents the appearance of widespread wreck and ruin. Little has been done to clear the streets of the terrible tangle of wires and the masses of wreck, mortar, slate, stone and glass that bestrew them. Many of the sidewalks are impassable. Some of them are littered with debris. Others are so thickly covered with slime that walking on them is out of the question.

As a general rule, substantial frame buildings withstood better the blasts of the gale than those of brick. In other instances, however, small wooden structures, cisterns and whole sides of houses are lying in streets or backyards squares away from where they originally stood.

Here and there business men have already put men to work to repair the damage done, but in the main the commercial interests seem to be uncertain about following the lead of those who apparently show faith in the rapid rehabilitation of the island city. The appearance of the newspapers to-day, after a suspension of several days, is having a good effect, and both the News and Tribune are urging prompt succoring of the suffering and then equal promptness in reconstruction.

It is difficult to say yet what the ultimate effect of the disaster is to be on the city. Many people have left and some may never return. The experience of others still here was so frightful that not all will remain if they can conveniently find occupation in other cities.

WONDERFUL COURAGE AND HOPE.

The bulk of the population, however, is only temporarily panic stricken, and there are hosts of those who helped to make Galveston great who look upon the catastrophe as involving only a temporary halt in the advancement of the city.

The decision of the transportation lines will do more than anything else to restore confidence. Big ships, new arrivals, rode at anchor to-day in front of the city. They had just reached the port and found the docks and pier damage so widespread that no accommodations could be given to them.

The losses to the charitable institutions of the city were very heavy. Sealy Hospital, the gift of the late John Sealy, was one of the largest institutions of Texas. Very serious damage was sustained. Almost the first work of restoration begun on any public structure was at the Sealy Hospital.

The medical department of the University of Texas included what is known as Brackenridge Hall. This hall was the gift of George W. Brackenridge, of San Antonio. It was seriously damaged. The Old Women's Hospital is a complete ruin. St. Mary's Infirmary, on Tenth and Market Streets, was entirely destroyed. The Ursuline Convent and the Ursuline Academy were partially demolished. The convent is now a haven of refuge of 500 houseless people.

The Catholic Orphans' Asylum disappeared, leaving .but slight traces in the form of ruins. It was supposed that the inmates, some ninety-nine sisters and little children, had been swept out into the gulf when the waters receded. Within the past few days bodies of several of the victims at the asylum have been found.

It appeared that when the sisters found the waters rising all around the asylum their only thoughts were for their little charges. They tied the children in bunches and then each sister fastened to herself one of these groups of orphans, determined to save them or die with them. Two of these groups have been found under wreckage. In each case eight children had been fastened together and then tied to a sister.

Galveston's school buildings, public and private, were unsurpassed for solidity and architectural finish. An examination of the public school buildings shows that scarcely one is fit for use.

Houses of worship suffered severely, although most of them were quite substantial. St. Patrick's Cathedral, the Baptist Church, Trinity Episcopal, the Fourth Presbyterian, St. Mary's Cathedral, St. John's Methodist, the Seamen's Bethel and two other churches on Broad Street, between Twenty-first and Tremont, sustained either total destruction or such damages that they must be rebuilt. Grace Episcopal Church, in the west end, which was one of the many benefactions of the late Henry Rosenberg, escaped with slight injury.

BUSINESS HOUSES SUFFER GREAT LOSS.

One of the most notable buildings of the city was that of the Improvement Loan and Trust Company, at Post Office and Tremont street. The damage sustained was not serious. The E. S. Levy office building, on Market and Tremont streets, cost $135,000. It contained 150 offices, and was considered a marvel of the town. This building withstood the storm and the occupants escaped by staying in their offices.

The Marx and Blum Buildings, Twenty-fourth and Mechanic streets, was one of the large commercial structures. It was occupied in part by the Galveston Hat and Shoe Co. The damages to the building and the stocks are placed now at $75,000. The Clarke and Courts Building sustained a loss to building and stock of $40,000. The Galveston Cotton and Woolen Mills suffered to the amount of $75,000. The Galveston City Railroad power-house was demolished, and it is estimated that $100,000 will be required to restore the plant.

The business structures did not suffer the total destruction that occurred in so much of the residence section, but many are so badly damaged that they will have to be torn down.

LARGEST ELEVATOR BADLY DAMAGED.

Galveston had a gigantic elevator interest which had developed with the port's growing grain trade. Elevator " A " at Fourteenth street, on the Bay side, was one of the largest in the world. Its capacity was in excess of 1,500,000 bushels of wheat. All the upper works of the elevator are gone.

One of the remarkable things about the force of the storm was that it tore from their moorings several large steamships and carried them in diverse directions. For example, the Kendall Castle an English ship, was swept from Pier 33 across Pelican Island and landed on the shore at Texas City. That was a course almost due north. Possibly a dredge may be able to cut a channel which will let the Kendall Castle out of the shoal part of the Bay, where it lies high in the water.

The Norwegian Gyller, a steamer of considerable tonnage, now lies stranded between Virginia Point and Texas City. Its course varied considerably from that of the Kendall Castle. A channel would have to be cut so far to float out the Gyller that there is doubt whether it would be warranted by the amount at stake.

One of the most serious results of the storm has been the damage to the electric light and street car plants. The city has been in absolute darkness for several nights, and only a few concerns who operate their own illuminating services are enabled to do business. Nearly every residence has gone back to the primitive candle. The absence of street lights drives all who have no imperative business on the streets to their homes at nightfall, but the work of the patrol system is made more difficult thereby and the opportunity for looting greater.

The motormen deserted their cars when the fury of the wind and the rush of the water made it no longer possible to operate them. Attempts are being made now to get the cars in shape again. The great destruction of live stock has elimated the carriages and cabs as a means of transportation.

The work of relief continues energetically. Mayor Jones and his associates are bending every nerve to open a direct line of transportation with Houston by which he may be enabled promptly to receive the great quantity of provisions which are now on the way to the city. The Relief Committee is striving to systematize its work. On Tuesday an ordinance was passed authorizing rescuing and burying parties to set fire to wrecked buildings and burn them. In these funeral pyres hundreds of corpses were cremated.

CARING FOR HOMELESS REFUGEES.

Houston now is the haven of the unfortunate people of Galveston. Trains have already brought in between 500 and 1000 of the survivors, and a motley crowd they are. Men bareheaded, barefooted, hatless and coatless, with swollen feet and bruised and blackened bodies and heads were numerous. Women of wealth and refinement, frequently hatless, shoeless, with gowns in shreds, were among the refugees. Nearly all of those who came in have suffered the loss of one or more of their family. It is remarkable, however, there is no whimpering, no complaining.

The refugees are being housed and fed, and those in need of medical attention are placed in the hospitals. General-Manager Van Vleck, of the Southern Pacific, says the damage to the wharves is fully eighty per cent. The Southern Pacific, he says, expects to begin work on the bridge within two days. It is expected that trains will be run into Galveston within forty days.

John J. Moody, a member of the committee sent from Houston to take charge of the relief station at Texas City, reports as follows:

" On arriving at La Marque this morning I was informed that the largest number of bodies were along the coast of Texas City. Fifty-six were buried yesterday and to-day within less than two miles extending opposite this place and towards Virginia City. It is yet six miles further to Virginia City and the bodies are thicker where we are now than where they have been buried. A citizen inspecting in the opposite direction reports dead bodies thick for twenty miles.

"The residents of this place have lost all, not a habitable building being left, and they have been too busy disposing of the dead to look after personal affairs. Those who have anything left are giving it to others, and yet there is real suffering. I have given away nearly all the bread I brought for our own use to hungry children.

"Every ten feet along the wreck-lined coast tells of acts of vandalism. Not a trunk, valise or tool chest has escaped rifling, We buried a woman this afternoon whose fingers bore the mark of a recently removed ring."

WASHED ACROSS THE BAY FROM GALVESTON.

B. F. Cameron, a lumber dealer of Stowell, Chambers County, says that the relief party which went from Stowell to Bolivar, reported to him that there was over 1000 dead bodies on the beach at Bolivar, Yeast Bay, and in sight of the salt marshes which line the bay. The party succeeded in burying only forty of the corpses. The others are lying in the water and on land, decomposing in the heat. Many of these bodies were evidently swept across the bay from Galveston.

In view of the completeness with which Galveston has been destroyed by the storm, many believe the city will never be rebuilt. The argument is that from its very location the city is ever in danger of a similar visitation, and capital will be fearful of investment where the danger is so constant.

There are many, however, who take the opposite view and say that in no other place on the Gulf can there be found a location so advantageous, and therefore, no matter if the risk be great, capital will seek investment in Galveston, and the city will soon resume her importance as a shipping port.

This sentiment is reflected in telegrams and verbal utterances, some of which are here printed :

Dallas, Texas, Wednesday.—Much serious thought has been given to the question of the future of Galveston by the best informed men of Dallas since the calamity of last Saturday and Sunday. The outlook, to their minds, is not a bright one. The expression of judgment most frequently heard is " Galveston is doomed." Men reason that to the perils the population have ever to face from nature's elements the timidity of capital must now be added.

In the great storm of 1875 little of private or public capital ran the risk of destruction. The great wharves, elevators, compresses and railway and steamship systems had taken but slight foothold in the island city. The federal government had built jetties and general harbor improvements and coast defences, at a cost of more than $10,000,000 of public money. All these millions of public and private wealth have been put into Galveston enterprises since 1875.

CAPITAL WILL BE SHY HEREAFTER.

Capitalists will scarcely venture again in the near future to invest their money in a place where it is likely to be wiped out at a ratio of from $5,000,000 to $10,000,000 to one equinoctial storm. And when the Federal Government contemplates costly brand new coast defence fortifications, such as Fort Sam Houston, shattered by wind and waves, and ninety per cent. of the garrison killed, it will not consider the place where these ventures were made a safe one for their duplication. A harbor to be safe must be land locked.

These are the views of thinking men who have studied the situation. The question then arises, What will supersede Galveston? Some predict that Houston, fifty miles in the interior, on Buffalo Bayou, through the agency of a ship canal built at the expense of the federal government, is the coming metropolis of the Gulf.

Others say Texas City, ten miles from Galveston, will now be developed as a grand maritime successor to the unfortunate island city. Others say Clinton, on Buffalo Bayou, six miles below

Houston, because of its facilities to furnish water and rail terminals, will be the Texas seaport of the near future.

Very few expect unfortunate Galveston to rise again and
reassert herself the mistress of the Gulf. A Galveston man illustrated the problem very aptly to-night, when he said:

" Fully one-half of the population of Galveston will never go
back there to live if they be got off the island alive this time. My
opinion is that Galveston has had her rise and fall."

AUSTIN PREDICTS NO DESERTION OF THE CITY.

Austin, Texas, Wednesday.—In the first shadow of the awful
calamity which has befallen Galveston the thought of many is that
Galveston City will have to be removed to the mainland or deserted. Nevertheless, calmer opinion is that the city will not be
moved. There are too many interests concerned, too much money
invested and too many possibilities to think of moving the city.

Property losses, while great, are not beyond repair. The city
may not for many years regain the popularity it enjoyed up to last
week, but it is believed that with the passage of time and the
allaying of public fear the place will begin to revive.

Millions are invested there in harbor improvements that would
be useless were the island deserted. Millions more invested in
business weathered the storm, save as to windows and roofs, and
these can be easily repaired.

Wharfing interests representing millions will cost money to
get back into shape again, but the belief is general that it will be
done. The business interests of Texas demand a port such as
Galveston, and while the town may not regain within five or six
years the resident population it had, it is not probable that it will
be depopulated.

When the storm of 1875 swept the island it did considerable
damage, and it took several years for the public to shake off the
fear of a residence there. They did so, however, and went back,
and it is believed that they will do so again.

Prominent citizens of Galveston to a man say that no thought
of moving the city to the mainland or a more protected spot can

be entertained, as there are too many interests in Galveston that cannot be transplanted, and that have not been so badly affected by the storm as to render them useless.

Railroads are already reconstructing bridges across the bay, and trade will be moving through the port within a fortnight.

To protect the city of Galveston from the ravages of future cyclones would be almost as costly as to re-establish the city on a new site.

This is the opinion of eminent engineers in Washington. To insure the maintenance of the channel it has been necessary to erect jetties which have cost more than $6,000,000. These jetties, however, do not furnish an obstacle of any importance to the invasion of the sea when behind it is a force such as a West India cyclone exerts.

Because of the effect of storms upon the Gulf coast, it has been customary for engineer officers stationed at Galveston to report yearly upon the appearance of atmospheric disturbances of more than usual intensity, and Captain Rich, the engineer officer who is believed to have lost his life, said in his report for 1899 that storms which occurred during April, May and June, 1899, "carried away nearly all that remained of construction trestle and track and caused more or less settlement of the jetties."

GREAT NEED OF A SAFE HARBOR.

The need of a safe deep-water harbor on the Gulf of Mexico has long been appreciated, and in 1899 Congress passed an act directing the Secretary of War to appoint a Board of three engineer officers of the army to make a careful and critical examination of the American coast of the Gulf of Mexico west of 93 degrees and 30 minutes west longitude, and to "report as to the most eligible points for a deep harbor, to be of ample depth, width and capacity to accommodate the largest ocean-going vessels and the commercial and naval necessities of the country."

The Board consisted of Lieutenant-Colonels H. M. Robert, G. L. Gillespie and Jared A. Smith. It is reported that Galveston was the most eligible point for a deep harbor, but also called attention to the harbors at Sabine Pass and Aransas Pass as being worthy of consideration.

In New York the views of railroad men concerning the future of Galveston as a shipping point are far from gloomy. A. F. Walker, Chairman of the Board of Directors of the Atchison, Topeka and Santa Fe Railroad, says he expects the city to be rebuilt within three months.

"Of course," said Mr. Walker, "it is a serious blow to Galveston, and with the city covered with mud and wreckage it is easy to prophesy evil for its future, but two weeks will suffice to clear the wreckage and clean the streets, get the dead buried and make a careful estimate of the actual loss. This loss is tremendous, there can be no doubt, but it has very likely been grossly exaggerated.

"Galveston will rebuild, and quickly, because the site combines the greatest natural advantages as a Gulf port and has solid commercial backing. It is imperative that we have a port on the Gulf—the extent of shipping demands it. Galveston offers, in spite of the real handicap of her low position, the best site, and I see no reason why it should not be rapidly rebuilt."

BELIEVES CITY WILL BE REBUILT.

Vice-President Tweed, of the Southern Pacific Railroad, said this morning that he felt sure that his road would repair the damage done to its properties at Galveston, and go on with further improvements planned.

"I take it for granted," Mr. Tweed declared, "that the directors of the Southern Pacific will keep up the work they started there. I do not think that this disaster, though certainly serious, will kill Galveston as a shipping port. No definite reports have been received as to the extent of our losses there. The two piers already completed on the property of the Southern Pacific were certainly badly damaged. Any estimate of the amount of damage would be only a guess, but I should say that it would fall below $400,000. Three hundred and fifty thousand dollars had been spent on the piers, and $75,000 paid for a short line from Galveston to Houston, which was destroyed."

Concerning the suggestion that Galveston will not be rebuilt, but that another city will be established in a safer place on the Gulf, to serve as a shipping port, Mr. Henry Mallory, of the Mallory line of steamships, said:

"Texas naturally seeks an outlet through a Texan harbor, and there is none other in Texas equal to the harbor of Galveston. All railroads centre there. If the city were wiped out some man with money would begin to build there. Locally, Galveston has suffered great loss, against which there is no insurance. But that does not rob the city of its pre-eminent valve as a port."

Asked if it would be practicable to rebuild the city on an inner shore of Galveston Bay, Mr. Mallory said that it would not. "There is no better location," said he, "for the city. It is not our purpose to abandon Galveston. We have ten steamships—nine in commission and one building—and we expect to remain in the Texas service."

A CHANGE FOR THE BETTER.

A correspondent, under date of September the 14th, wrote:

"So far as the actual presence of death is concerned, nobody would know, from a glance at the streets to-day, that a terrible tragedy had been enacted here. Human corpses are out of sight. They have either been buried, taken out to sea or burned.

"But the horrors have not been obliterated by any means. The danger of pestilence still remains. While the human corpses have been disposed of, those of animals—horses, cows, dogs, etc.— have been permitted to remain above ground. There was no time and no means to remove them. Their putrifying remains lay where the waves left them—there to emit a stench that is simply unbearable.

"Lime with which to consume these carcasses is all that will save Galveston from epidemic.

"With corrupt flesh and bad water, or no water at all, Galveston is already in the grasp of typhoid and other virulent fevers. The diseases have not yet become epidemic, but if unchecked for twenty-four hours there is no doubt they will become so.

" Appreciating the situation, Adjutant-General Scurry yester-day succeeded in getting gangs of laboring men organized. The progress made is remarkable and to-day it was much greater. Large piles of refuse were gathered and burned, and the work of cleaning up proceeded in a systematic manner. Heretofore there has been no system, everybody working for the public good in his own way.

PEOPLE HURRYING TO ESCAPE.

" The exodus from the city was heavy to-day, and hundreds more were eager to go who were unable to secure transportation. Along the bay front there were scores of families with dejected faces, pleading to be taken from the stricken city, where, in spite of every effort to restore confidence, there is a universal feeling of depression.

" Shipping men say to-day that the damage to the wharves is by no means as serious as at first supposed. More hopeful reports were received to-day touching the water supply. The company is placing men all along the mains, plugging the broken places and thereby assisting the flow. It was serving some of its customers to-day, and hopes gradually to increase the service. The water continues to run by gravity pressure.

" The only difficulty the people are having is in carrying supplies to their homes or places of business. The ice supply continues bountiful, and at many corners lemonade is being served at five cents for as many glasses as you can drink at one time.

" The work of disposing of the dead continues. Several hun-dred bodies are still buried beneath the wreckage. Thirty-two sand mounds, marked with small boards, attract attention on the beach, near Twenty-sixth street, and tell the story of where seventy-five bodies have been laid to rest. In the extreme western part of the city sixty bodies were cremated with wreckage of the homes of the unfortunate victims.

" A conflict of authority, due to a misunderstanding, precipi-tated a temporary disorganization of the policing of the city yes-terday. It seems that when General Scurry, Adjutant-General of the Texas Volunteer Guard, arrived in the city with about 200 militia from Houston, he conferred with the chief of police as to the plans for preserving law and order.

"An order was issued by the chief of police to the effect that the soldiers should arrest all persons found carrying arms unless they showed a written order, signed by the chief of police or Mayor, giving them permission to go armed. The result was that about fifty citizens wearing deputy sheriff badges were arrested by the soldiers and taken to police headquarters.

FREE USE OF DEADLY WEAPONS.

"The soldiers had no way of knowing by what authority the men were acting with these badges, and would listen to no excuses. After a hurried conference between General Scurry and Sheriff Thomas it was decided that all deputy sheriffs and special officers shall be permitted to carry arms and pass in and out of the guard lines. The deputy sheriffs and special and regular police now police the city during the daytime, and the militia take charge of the city at night.

"More than 2000 dead bodies have been identified, and the estimate of Mayor Jones, that 5000 perished in Saturday's great hurricane, does not appear to be magnified. The city is being patrolled by troops and a citizens' committee, and a semblance of order is appearing.

"At a conference held at the office of City Health Officer Wilkinson it was decided to accept the offer of the United States Marine Hospital Service and establish a camp at Houston, where the destitute and sick can be sent and be properly cared for. The physicians agreed that there were many indigent sick in the city who should be removed from Galveston, and Houston was selected because that city had very thoughtfully suggested the idea and tendered a site for the camp. Acting upon the suggestion to establish a camp and care for the sick and needy, a message was sent to the Surgeon-General, at the head of the Marine Hospital Corps, asking for 1000 tents of four-berth capacity each; also several hundred barrels of disinfecting fluid.

"The health department is calling for 100 men with drays to clean the streets. The plan is to district the city and start out the drays to remove all refuse and dead animals and cart all unsanitary matter from the streets. It is anticipated that by Saturday the work will have advanced to cover the greater portion of the business district and part of the residence section.

"Prior to the hurricane Galveston was one of the richest cities in the world, per capita, and the surviving millionaries who made their money here have read with displeasure the telegrams that the city would never survive the terrible blow it suffered. They insist that the city will be rebuilt and will be another Chicago, rising superior to the calamities that palsy the ordinary people.

"The determination to rebuild the city received a strong impetus to-day, when it was learned that G. W. Boscheke, assistant engineer of the Southern Pacific Railroad, had received orders by wire from New York to prepare plans at once for a double-track steel bridge across Galveston Bay ten feet higher than the old one, and to proceed with all the force possible. Engineers are already at work making a survey and running lines preparatory to the resumption of work.

NEW SURVEY WILL BE MADE.

"A telegram from New York says that Colonel H. M. Roberts, of the Engineering Corps, United States Engineers for the southwest district, said to-day that a survey will be made of the wrecked Galveston forts and works. Captain Richie has submitted a report, in which he says the foundations which were built on piling withstood the ravages of the storm much better than the foundations without piling. In the future it is proposed to use piling exclusively.

"Congressman R. B. Hawley, who was in Washington at the time of the storm, has arrived in this city.

"'Work of vast importance is to be undertaken here,' said he; 'work on different lines from that which has been our habit heretofore.

" 'There are storms elsewhere. If the people in other parts of the country built as we build, their cities would be down and out nearly every year; but they build structures to stay, and we must rebuild our city on different lines and in a different manner, that will resist the gales as they do. The port is all right. The fullest depth of water remains. The jetties, with slight repair, are intact, and because of these conditions the restoration will be more rapid than may be thought.'

MORTALITY LIST IS ENORMOUS.

In fact, while the mortality list of the city grows larger every hour, the prospects of Galveston grow brighter. An investigation shows that industries that were supposed to be wrecked forever are only slightly damaged, and business in them may be resumed any day.

" J. C. Stewart, the grain elevator builder, after careful inspection of the grain elevators and their contents, said the damage to the grain elevators was not over two per cent. The wheat will be loaded into vessels just as rapidly as they come to the elevator to take it. Ships are needed here at once. Mr. Stewart said he would put a large force of men to work clearing up each of the wharves, and the company will be ready for business within the the next eight days. The wharves have been damaged very little outside of the wreckage of the sheds. With the wreckage cleared away, Galveston will be in good shape for business.

" At a meeting of the general committee last night the need of sprinkling the streets with a strong bichloride solution and taking other sanitary precautions was discussed, and after adjournment of the general committee, the committee on correspondence sent the following telegram :

" 'Our most urgent present needs now are disinfectants, lime, cement, gasoline stoves, gasoline, charcoal furnaces and charcoal. Nearby towns also may send bread. For the remainder of our wants, money will be most avilable, because we can make purchases from time to time with more discretion than miscellaneous contributors would exercise. We are bringing order out of chaos,

A CLEAN SWEEP OF EIGHTEEN BLOCKS BY SIX. WAS THICKLY POPULATED AND
COMPLETELY DESTROYED

TREMONT STREET, LOOKING NORTH FROM AVENUE O ½

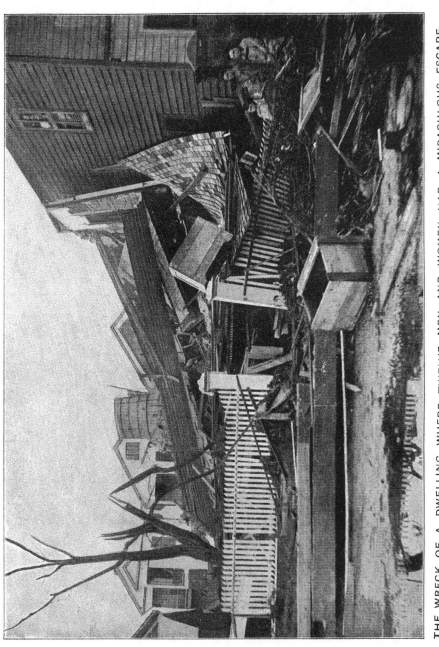

THE WRECK OF A DWELLING WHERE TWELVE MEN AND WOMEN HAD A MIRACULOUS ESCAPE

PHOTO BY COURTESY
CHICAGO AMERICAN

CREMATING DEAD BODIES TAKEN FROM GALVESTON WRECK.

and again offer our profound gratitude for the assistance so far received.'"

Surveying the situation, one of our great journals bestowed these words of praise: " Another good day's work was done yesterday in behalf of the Texas sufferers. There has been no abatement in the generous giving of supplies and money. The fearful plight of the thousands who outlived the terrors of the storm has touched every heart profoundly. In Galveston alone, where the cyclone swept inland with fiercest fury, 25,000 persons are homeless. Half the population of what a week ago was a prosperous city, in a single day was left dependent upon charity.

DANGER OF AN EPIDEMIC.

" The danger of an epidemic now threatens the survivors. Many of the people are giving way to physical exhaustion. They have been compelled to subsist upon unwholesome food, drink polluted water and breathe the foul air of their unsanitary surroundings. In spite of all that has been done for the relief of the stricken Texans, the death roll is still growing. As many as possible must be removed from the scene of destruction to more healthful conditions.

" What Philadelphia has done should go far to alleviate the immediate distress, yet this is only a drop in the great flow of charity. An additional $10,000 was sent to Governor Sayres yesterday, making $25,000 in all that has been forwarded by the Citizens' Permanent Relief Committee. And more subscriptions are daily flowing in. A number of physicians and nurses have volunteered their services and are only awaiting a reply from the Relief Committee on the ground. There will be work for them if sickness becomes prevalent, as is now feared.

" Many of our citizens who wished to make donations of food, clothing and other supplies have again had recourse to the special trains that are being sent forward. Last night a second special of four heavily-laden cars was sent to Galveston. In addition to this, many subscriptions of money have been made and will be forwarded to the authorities in Texas."

10

CHAPTER VIII.

Fears of Pestilence—Searching Parties Clearing Away the Ruins and Cremating the Dead—Distracted Crowds Waiting to Leave the City—Wonderful Escapes.

"The large force of men used in burying and cremating the exposed dead scattered throughout the city are trying to complete that portion of their work and are searching for the bodies of unfortunates lying crushed beneath the mass of debris and wrecked buildings. Where the debris lies in detached masses, it is fired, and the bodies therein consumed.

"When adjacent property will be endangered by fire, the mass of ruins is removed, the bodies are taken out and conveyed to a safe distance. Around them is piled the debris and the whole is saturated with oil and fired. It is quite impossible to identify the bodies as they are in all stages of putrefaction.

"It is a gruesome and sad task. Some of the men engaged in this work are, perhaps, unknowingly helping to destroy all that is mortal of some loved one, who, a few days before, was the light of his home. The ghastly pile may contain the body of his wife, mother, brother, or some petted child; but in nearly every instance he knows it not.

"One pathetic incident occurred. A squad of men discovered in a wrecked building five bodies, among whom one of the party recognized a brother. All were in an advanced state of decomposition. They were all removed and a funeral pyre was made. The living brother, with a wrench in his heart, assisted, and with Spartan-like firmness stood by and saw his brother's body reduced to ashes.

"The appalling loss of life by the hurricane has benumbed the people and virtually dried up the fountains of grief. Neighbor meets neighbor and, with a hearty grasp of the hand, says "I hope all is well with you." The usual reply is, "I am sorry to say I am the only one left."

146

"You hear of such incidents everywhere—on the street, in the stores, around soda-fountains where crowds collect to quench their thirst, since water is scarce and the saloons are closed for an indefinite time.

"Burial parties are organized at Virginia Point, Texas City, Port Bolivar and down the island, and the bodies there are being buried as rapidly as possible. Since something like order has come out of chaos a stop has been put to the looting and desecration of bodies at Virginia Point by the bands of ghouls that had terrorized that point, and they have been dispersed.

MONEY CLINCHED IN DEATH GRIP.

"Where the bodies are beyond identification and effects and jewelry are found, these are removed, and a memoranda taken for possible identification at some time by any one who is seeking a lost relative or friend.

"A party that was picking up bodies for burial found the corpse of a nephew of Alderman John Wagner, eighteen years old, lodged in the forks of a tall cedar tree, two miles from his wrecked home. Tightly clinched in his right hand was $200, which his father had given him, with two twenty dollar gold pieces, to hold while the father attempted to close a door, which had blown open.

"At that moment the house went down and the whole family except the father perished in the storm and flood. It would take volumes to record the many heartrending incidents of this sort and the heroism displayed during the fateful night of Saturday.

"The loss of life in this city is simply appalling. Every little town within seventy-five miles of Galveston was wrecked and torn and people were killed and wounded. The damage to property will aggregate millions of dollars. The damage to property in and around Alvin, a thriving town of two thousand people, where eleven people were killed and a number wounded, is estimated at $300,000, and they send out an urgent appeal for aid and relief supplies."

"Captain Talfor, of the United States Engineer Corps, during the hurricane was at Quintana, at the mouth of the Brazos River, where he has been supervising government works. He stated to-day that the barometer fell to 27.60, and the wind velocity was one hundred and twenty miles an hour. Fifty-four houses were wrecked in Quintana, and the debris piled up in the streets. Fortunately no lives were lost.

"The town of Velasco, three miles above, on the east side of the river, was completely wrecked. Nine persons were killed, three in the hotel, which was badly demolished. Angleton, the county seat of Brazoria, ten miles north of Velasco, was almost completely destroyed. Several lives were lost and a number of persons were badly injured.

"The property loss in these three towns and the country adjacent will be beyond the ability of the people to repair. Destitution stares them in the face, and help is urgently needed there and in all other towns within seventy-five miles of the city. The loss in proportion to population and means is just as great and as keenly felt as the loss and destruction in Galveston, and they should not be forgotten by the generous public, which is responding with such noble promptness to Galveston's cry for help.

SOLID TRAINLOADS OF SUPPLIES.

"Supplies for the relief of Galveston's sufferers are coming in from every quarter as rapidly as the limited means of transportation here will admit. Solid trainloads from the North and East are speeding towards Galveston as fast as steam will bring them, while cities, chambers of commerce and other commercial bodies in this country, England and Continental Europe are subscribing thousands of dollars for the sufferers from one of the greatest calamities of the century.

"The distribution of supplies here has not yet been put on a systematic basis. There is one general relief committee, with sub-committees in each ward. To these sub-committeemen sufferers must apply for relief, and are categorically questioned as to the extent of their distress.

"If the answers are satisfactory, an order is issued for supplies. If he is an able bodied man, although he may be houseless and may have lost members of his family, or have some injured by the storm and needing attention, he must perform labor before supplies are issued, and if he refuses he is impressed and compelled to work.

"There are many so sadly injured or prostrated by the frightful experience they have recently undergone that they are unable to apply for relief, and would suffer from thirst and exposure unless housed, fed and cared for by humane people who have been less unfortunate. No effort thus far has been made by those in charge of relief affairs to hunt out these poor creatures and care for them.

"And if they have male relatives, these are afraid to venture on the streets for fear they will be impressed and put to work, and thus taken away from those who need their constant care. The present method of relief needs to be radically revised, or it will fail of its purpose and defeat the object of those who are so generously contributing. Medical relief is much better organized.

EXODUS SERIOUSLY HAMPERED.

"The Transportation Committee is handicapped in its efforts to get out of the city the persons who are destitute by the lack of sufficient boats and rail communication. The latter want will not be supplied for many days. Present communication is by boat to Texas City, and then by the Galveston, Houston and Henderson Railway to Houston. Those who are able to pay are charged half fare; those who are not are given free transportation. Guards are stationed at Texas City to prevent the curious from invading the city, eating up the limited food supply and doing no good.

"The city in its present condition is not a healthy place for visitors. It is full of fever and other disease breeding matter, and smells like a charnel house. There is not a house of any character in the city but is foul and ill smelling. Plenty of lime-water and disinfectant is urgently needed here, or an epidemic will sweep through the city with hurricane force.

"Thousands of men are cutting passageways through the streets, clearing the sidewalks of the mass of debris, removing the sea slime from the floors of buildings and washing them out, but this does not dispose of it, and under the torrid sun it ferments and putrefies and the stench is fearful.

"The water failed to materialize as promised and this aggravates the situation. With a crippled fire department, the fire engines useless and no water supply, a fire, if it should break out, would speedily wipe out what remains of the city.

"It will be months before the business streets will be entirely cleared of rubbish and repaved, and it will be years before the damage done by the storm will be obliterated. It is impossible to conceive of the widespread destruction unless it is actually seen."

ANOTHER REPORT FROM GENERAL McKIBBEN.

Washington, D. C., Friday.—General McKibben on September 12, reported to the War Department upon the conditions in Galveston as follows:—

"General conditions are improving every hour. Repairs to water works will by to-morrow insure water supply for fire protection. Provisions of all kinds are being received in large quantities. Enough are now en route and at Houston to feed all destitute for thirty days.

"There is now no danger of suffering from lack of food or shelter. City under perfect control, under charge of Committee of Safety. Loss of life is probably greater than my conservative estimate of yesterday. Property loss enormous; not an individual in the city has escaped some loss; in thousands of cases it is total.

"To-day, in company with Colonel Robert and Captain Riche, I made an inspection at Fort Crockett, and by tug of the fortifications at Forts San Jacinto and Travis; with the exception of battery for two 4.7 rapid fire guns, batteries may be considered non-existent. Captain Riche has forwarded by wire this evening full report of conditions to Chief of Engineers.

"I coincide in recommendation that all fortifications and ordnance property be transferred to engineer officer here for salvage. Earnestly recommend that Battery O, First Artillery, be ordered to Fort Sam Houston for recuperation and equipment; officers and men are largely destitute. At present a large number are injured and unfit for duty. Impossible at present to furnish them with ordinary camp equipage, clothing, as all transportation facilities are being utilized to bring in food supplies."

CAPTAIN RICHE'S REPORT.

"CHIEF OF ENGINEERS, ARMY, Washington, D. C.:

"Jetties sunk nearly to mean low tide level, but not seriously breached. Channel at least as good as before ; perhaps better. Twenty-five feet certainly. Forts as follows : Fort Crockett—Two 15-pounder emplacements, concrete all right, standing on piling water underneath. Battery for eight mortars about like preceding. Mortars and carriages on hand unmounted.

"Battery for two 10-inch guns about like preceding, both guns mounted and in good shape. Shore line at Fort Crockett has moved back about six hundred feet. Fort San Jacinto—Battery for eight 12-inch mortars badly wrecked, magazines reported fallen in ; mortars reported safe. No piling was under this battery; some of the sand parapet left. Battery for two 10-inch guns badly wrecked. Central portion level, both gun platforms down, guns leaning. No piling was under this battery.

"Battery for two 4.7-inch rapid fire guns, concrete standing upon piling ; both guns apparently all right. Battery for two 15-pounder guns, concrete apparently all right, standing upon piling.

"Fort San Jacinto batteries could not be reached by land ; inspection was from a distance. Sand around these batteries seemed pretty well leveled off to about two to three feet above mean low. Torpedo casemate, nothing but concrete left and badly wrecked. Concrete portion of cable tank left ; cable in it probably safe. Part of coal wharf still standing.

"Everything else in vicinity gone. Some of the mine cases

are down the beach as far as Fort Crockett.   Fort Travis—Battery for three fifteen-pound guns, concrete intact, standing on piling, water underneath.   Battery for two eight-inch guns, concrete intact, except eastern emplacement, which has cracked off; eastern gun down and twenty feet from battery ; western one all right ; concrete standing on piling, water underneath middle of battery.   These batteries were inspected from the channel.

"The shore line has moved back about one thousand feet, about on the line of the rear of these batteries.   All buildings and other structures gone.   Inspection was made with General McKibben.   Recommendation was made that all fortifications and property be transferred to the Engineer Department ; that for the present batteries be considered non-existent, so that future work may be chargeable as original construction.

"Much ordnance can be saved if given prompt attention. Unless otherwise instructed, I will take charge of these works at once and save all possible.   New projects for jetties and forts cannot be submitted for several weeks, until definite detailed information is had.   Further recommendations will then be submitted as soon as possible.   Galveston is still a deep water port, and such a storm is not likely to reoccur for years."

ESTIMATES OF THE DEAD ARE TOO LOW.

Austin, Tex., Sept. 14—"I am thoroughly satisfied, after spending two days in Galveston, that the estimate of 6000 dead is too conservative. It will exceed that number.   Nobody can even estimate or will ever know within 1000 of how many lives were lost."

This was the opinion of Assistant State Health Officer I. J. Jones, who arrived at Austin directly from Galveston, where he was sent by Governor Sayres to investigate the condition of the State quarantine station.   Dr. Jones made an inspection of the sanitary condition of the city, and in his report said further :

" It was with the greatest difficulty that I reached Galveston. At the quarantine situated in the Gulf, a mile and a half from the the wharves, I found things in a state of ruin.   The quarantine warehouse and disinfecting barge, just completed, are total wrecks, as is also the quarantine wharf. A part of the quarantine residence is left standing, but so badly damaged that it is not worth repairing.

AN OFFICER'S BRAVERY.

"Quarantine Officer Mayfield showed the greatest bravery and self-sacrifice when the storm came on. He sent all of his employees and his family, except two sons, who refused to leave him, to places of safety. He remained in the quarantine house with his two devoted sons throughout the terrible night. All of one wing of the house was taken away and the floor of the remaining part was forced up and carried away by the waters. Dr. Mayfield and his two sons spent the night on a stairway leading from the upper floor to the attic.

"Despite this destruction of the station, the quarantine has never been relaxed, and all vessels are promptly boarded upon arrival at Galveston. There are now three vessels lying at quarantine. They brought cargoes to be discharged at Galveston and had cargoes consigned to them. The cargoes cannot be taken off except by lighter, and the vessels are awaiting instructions from their owners. The Mallory Line Steamer "Alamo" got in Wednesday, but was sent back to the bay, as she could not discharge her cargo.

"The sanitary condition of the city is very bad. While there has been no outbreak of sickness, every one expects that, and it is inevitable. There is no organized effort being made to improve sanitary conditions. Large quantities of lime have been ordered to the place, but I doubt if anyone will be found to unload it from the vessels and attend to its systematic distribution when it arrives.

"The stench is almost unbearable. It arises from piles of debris containing the carcasses of human beings and animals. These carcasses are being burned where such can be done with safety. But little of the wreckage can be destroyed in this manner, however, owing to the danger of starting a fire that will destroy what is left of the ill-fated city. There is no water protection and should fire break out the destruction of the city would soon be complete.

"When searching parties come across a human body it is hauled out into an open space and wreckage piled over it. The pyre is then set on fire and the body slowly consumed. The odor from these burning bodies is horrible.

"The chairman of the Central Relief Committee at Galveston asked me to make the announcement that the city wants all the skilled mechanics and contractors with their tools that can be brought to Galveston. There is some repair work now going on, but it is impossible to find men who will work at that kind of business. Those now in Galveston who are not engaged in relief work have their own private business to look after and mechanics are not to be had.

"All mechanics will be paid regular wages and will be given employment by private parties who desire to get their wrecked homes in habitable shape as rapidly as possible. There are many fine houses which have only the roof gone. These residences are finely furnished, and it is desired that the necessary repairs be made quickly.

WELL ORGANIZED.

"The relief work is fairly well organized. Nothing has been accomplished, except the distribution of food among the needy, and some attempt at clothing them. I found no one who was hungry or thirsty. About one-half of the city is totally wrecked, and many people are living in houses that are badly wrecked. The houses that are only slightly injured are full of people who are being well cared for. The destitute are being removed from the city as rapidly as possible. It will take three or four days yet before all who want to go have been removed from the island city. A remarkably large number of horses survived the storm, but there is no feed for them, and many of them will soon die of starvation.

"In the city the dead bodies are being disposed of in every manner possible. They are burying the dead found on the mainland. At one place 250 bodies were found and buried on Wednesday. There must be hundreds of dead bodies back on the prairies that have not been found. It is impossible to make a search there on account of the debris. There will be many a skeleton of vicvims of the disaster found on the prairie in the months and years to come.

"Bodies have been found as far back from the present mainland shore of the bay as seven miles. That embraces a big territory which is covered with rank grass, holes filled with water and piles of debris. It would take an army to search this territory on the mainland.

THE GULF FULL OF BODIES.

"The waters of the Gulf and bay are still full of bodies, and they are being constantly cast upon the beach. On my trip to and from the quarantine station I passed a procession of bodies going seaward. I counted fourteen of them on my trip from the station, and this procession is kept up day and night. The captain of a ship who had just reached quarantine informed me that he began to meet floating bodies fifty miles from the port.

"As an illustration of how high the water got in the Gulf, a vessel which was in port tried to get into the open sea when the storm came on. It got out some distance and had to put back. It was dark and all the landmarks had been obliterated. The course of the vessel could not be determined, and she was being furiously driven in toward the island by the wind. Before her course could be established she had actually run over the top of the north jetty. As the vessel draws twenty-five feet of water some idea can be obtained as to the height of the water in the Gulf."

They marry and are given in marriage. A wedding took place in Galveston. It occurred at the Tremont Hotel. Ernest A. Mayo, a lawyer, and a candidate for Prosecuting Attorney, was the bridegroom. Mrs. Bessie Roberts was the bride. The engagement was of long standing. Both suffered much from the storm. They decided that it was better to cast their fortunes together. Friends approved. The ceremony took place on Thursday, the 13th, five days after the flood.

Governor Sayres was advised on the fourteenth that a government vessel, which was loaded with supplies at Texas City for the Galveston sufferers, went aground shortly after leaving the wharf, and had not yet been gotten off. It was found that vessels could not cross the bay at that point, and thereafter they would be sent to some other point which had a deeper channel connection with Galveston.

The estimates of immediate losses in the aggregate vary widely. It may be said that none of them are below $20,000,000. The maximum, as given by intelligent residents, including some members of the Citizens' Committee, is $35,000,000. One of the Galveston business men sent to Austin to confer personally with Governor Sayres on the work of relief, inclined to the belief that the immediate losses might, without exaggeration, be placed at $35,000,000.

In the indirect class are the losses which must be sustained through the paralysis of business, the reduction of population, the stoppage of industries, and the general disturbance of commercial relations, and Galveston business men hesitate to form any conclusion as to what the moral losses must be.

A REFUGEE'S TALE OF HORROR.

F. B. Campbell, who was in Galveston when the floods swept upon it, was one of the first refugees to reach the North. He passed through Pittsburg, six days after the disaster, on his way to Springfield, Mass., which is his home. Mr. Campbell had his right arm fractured. William E. Frear, a Philadelphia commercial traveller, who was with Campbell in Galveston, accompanied him as far north as Cincinnati, and went home on the express. Frear's right ankle was sprained.

Campbell was a cotton broker and was overwhelmed at his boarding house while at dinner. He reached a heap of wreckage by swimming through an alley. Of the scene when he left, Campbell said :

"The last I saw of Galveston was a row of submerged buildings where a thriving city stood. A waste of water spread in all directions. In the sea were piles of wreckage and the carcasses of animals and the bodies of hundreds of human beings. The salt marshes presented an indescribable sight. Nude forms of human beings, that had been swept across the bay were scattered everywhere. No man could count them without going insane. It looked like a graveyard, where all the tenants of the tombs had been exhumed and the corpses thrown to the winds."

SOME WONDERFUL ESCAPES.

There were many wonderful incidents of the great storm. In the infirmary at Houston was a boy whose name is Rutter. He was found on Monday morning lying beside a truck on the land near the town of Hitchcock, which is twenty miles to the northward of Galveston. This boy is only 12 years old. His story is that his father, mother and two children remained in the house. There was a crash and the house went to pieces. The boy says that he caught hold of a trunk when he found himself in the water and floated off with it. He thinks the others were drowned. With the trunk the boy floated. He had no idea of where it took him, but when daylight came he was across the bay and out upon the still partially submerged mainland.

When their home went to pieces the Stubbs family, husband, wife and two children, climbed upon the roof of a house floating by. They felt tolerably secure, when, without warning, the roof parted in two places. Mr. and Mrs. Stubbs were separated and each carried a child. The parts of the raft went different ways in the darkness. One of the children fell off and disappeared, and not until some time Sunday was the family reunited. Even the child was saved, having caught a table and clung to it until it reached a place of safety.

One of the most remarkable escapes recorded during the flood was reported to-day when news came that a United States battery man on duty at the forts last week had been picked up on Morgan's Point, injured but alive. He had buffeted the waves for five days and lived through a terrible experience. Morgan's Point is thirty miles from Galveston.

Galveston, Tex., Sept. 14.--The local Board of Health

through Dr. H. A. West, its secretary, has made a demand that the work of clearing up the dwelling houses be turned over to physicians. This work has been under the direction of Adjutant General Scurry, and he has proved himself so capable that the Relief Committee declined to make any division of responsibility.

Notwithstanding the fact that the number of boats carrying passengers between Texas City and Galveston has been largely increased, it was impossible yesterday to leave the city after the early morning hours. Yesterday the "Lawrence," after jamming her nose into the mud, remained aground all day. Her passengers were taken off in small sailboats, and by noon a dozen of them heavily loaded started from Galveston to Texas City.

INTENSE SUFFERING ON THE WATER.

The wind died away utterly and the boats could neither go on to Texas City nor return to Galveston. None of them had more than a meager supply of water, which was soon exhausted; the sun beat down with a merciless severity. In a short time babies and young children became ill and in many instances their mothers were also prostrated. There was absolutely no relief to be had, as the tugs of Galveston Bay, which might have given the sloops tow, are all made for deep sea work and draw too much water to allow of their crossing the shallow channel.

Hour after hour the people on the boats, all of which were densely packed, were compelled to broil in the torturing and blinding sun. A slight breeze arising in the evening at 9 o'clock, the sailing craft which had left Galveston at noon began to dump their passengers upon the beach at Texas City. Owing to a delay in Houston trains it was fully twenty hours after their start from Galveston that the people who left there yesterday noon were able to move out from Texas City, which is only eight miles away, and by the time the train had made a start for Houston every woman in the crowd was ill through lack of food, exposure and insufficient sleep.

In the long list of the dead of Galveston the family name of

Labett appears several times.   Only a year or two ago five generations of the Labetts were living at one time in Galveston.

The family nearly suffered the destruction of the family
name in the storm.   A young man connected with one of the railroads was down town and escaped.   When the parties of searchers
were organized and proceeded to various parts of the city one of
them came across this young Labett near the ruins of his home
all alone.   He had made his way there and had found the bodies of
father and mother and other relatives.   He had carried the dead to
a drift of sand, and there without a tool, with his bare hands and
a piece of board he was trying to scrape out gravel to bury the
bodies.

GALVESTON REFUGEES AT HOUSTON.

The "Post" of Houston prints a list of 2701 names of Galveston dead, compiled from various sources, but believed to be
authentic.   There are many bodies still in the ruins of Galveston
and scattered along the beach of the mainland and in the marshes.

About 1300 people arrived here from Galveston on the 13th.
Four buildings have been set apart for the benefit of refugees, but
of the 3500 who have reached here so far not more than 800 remain
in the public charge, the remainder of them going to the homes
of relatives and friends.

MESSAGES FOR THE DEAD.

The following statement was made on Friday, the 14th ; it
was dated at Dallas :

"Galveston is no longer shut off from wire communication
with the outside world.   At 1.15 o'clock this afternoon the Postal
Telegraph and Cable Company received a bulletin from the
storm-stricken city stating that wire connection had been made
across the bay by cable, and that direct communication with the
island city was resumed with two wires working and that two
more would be ready by to-morrow.   A rush of messages followed.

"The Western Union got in direct communication with Galveston this afternoon, and soon that office was also crowded.

Probably never before has there been so much telegraphing to the dead. The headquarters of the Western Union and Postal systems located in this city report that in Dallas, Houston and Galveston are thousands of messages addressed to persons who can never call for them or receive them.

"Some of the persons addressed are known to be dead, and there is no doubt that hundreds of others are among the thousands of unknown and unidentified victims of the storm whose bodies have been dumped into the sea, consigned to unmarked graves or cremated in the great heaps that sanitary necessity marked for the torch and the incinerating pyre.

"The insurance questions are beginning to receive serious attention. Life insurance companies are going to be hit very hard. The question that particularly engages the attention of representatives is whether settlement shall be made without litigation. The general southwestern agents for eight big insurance companies were interviewed to-day, and they stated that all Dallas insurance men concur in the opinion that the insurance policies against storm losses carried by Galvestonians will not aggregate $10,000,000. They say there was absolutely no demand for such insurance at Galveston."

WHOLE FAMILY KILLED BY STORM.

Among those who were caught in the storm that devastated Galveston on Sunday night were six persons who comprised the family of Peter E. McKenna, a former resident of Philadelphia. According to news received by their relatives in that city, all perished.

When word of the Texas disaster first came it was reported that the entire family had been lost, but it later developed that a married daughter, who lives in Omaha, Neb., was not visiting her parents, as was first supposed, and therefore escaped the death that overtook her relatives.

Peter E. McKenna, the head of the family, was well known in Philadelphia during his youth. His father was one of the pioneers in the religious press. The son followed the profession

MOTHER AND CHILDREN IN PERIL FROM THE FLOOD

SHOOTING VANDALS ENGAGED IN ROBBING THE BODIES OF THE VICTIMS

PHOTO BY COURTESY
CHICAGO AMERICAN

CARING FOR THOSE INJURED BY THE STORM AT GALVESTON.

PHOTO BY COURTESY
CHICAGO AMERICAN

TRAIN BLOWN FROM TRACK SHOWN BY DOTTED LINE.

of his father, and after engaging in the publication of newspapers and religious weeklies until 1862 he sought fortune in the West.

Galveston at the time was a growing city, and as it offered the opportunities Mr. McKenna desired he settled there and devoted himself to the upbuilding of newspapers. His success was of such a nature that he made his permanent home in Galveston, and during the thirty-eight years that have passed, was recognized as one of the most foremost journalists in that city. Latterly he was connected with the Galveston "Despatch" and also conducted a publishing house for himself.

Separated as he was by thousands of miles from the city of his birth, Mr. McKenna was able to make only a few visits during the last twenty-five years, but he kept up a constant correspondence with several relatives. In these letters there was frequent mention of the fact that the city was lower than the sea and open to the attacks of any storm that might form in the Gulf of Mexico.

CLEARING THE WATER FRONT.

At a conference held at the office of the City Health Officer on Friday, the 14th, it was decided to accept the offer of the Marine Hospital Service, and establish a camp at Houston, where the destitute and invalids can be sent. The physicians agreed that there were many indigent persons in the city who should be removed. A message was sent to the Surgeon General asking that the department furnish one thousand tents, of four-berth capacity each ; also seven hundred barrels of disinfecting fluid.

Another important movement in the direction of sanitation was made by the Health Department in calling for one hundred men with drays to clean the streets. The idea is to district the city and start the drays to remove all unsanitary matter from the streets.

STRANGE BURIAL PLACES AND GRAVES.

Although the work of disposing of the dead is being pushed, several hundred bodies are still buried beneath the wreckage. Thirty-two sand mounds, marked with small boards, attract

11

attention on the beach, near Twenty-sixth street, and tell the story of where about seventy-five bodies have been buried.

One of the greatest needs of the city now is disinfectants. The local Committee on Correspondence drafted this general message to the country :

" Our most urgent present needs now are disinfectants, lime, cement, gasoline stoves, gasoline, charcoal furnaces, and charcoal. Nearby towns also may send bread. For the remainder of our wants money will be most available because we can make purchases from time to time with more discretion than miscellaneous contributors would exercise. We are bringing order out of chaos and again offer our profound gratitude for the assistance so far received."

The first real attempt to clear away the great mass of debris piled along the beach front for several miles was begun to-day. Advertisements this morning asking for hundreds of men and boys were answered by a multitude. It is hoped that a vigorous prosecution of the work will lead to the early recovery of the bodies in the debris. That there are many of them there is no shadow of doubt.

SEEKING FORMER RESIDENCES.

A correspondent walked along the beach for some distance to-day and the stench was sickening. Everywhere little groups of men, women and children, some poorly clad, were digging in the ruins of their homes for what little household property they could save. In many cases, those seeking their former residences were unable to find a single remnant of them.

The exodus from the city was heavy to-day, and hundreds more were eager to leave, but were unable to secure transportation. Along the bay front there were scores of families with dejected faces, pleading to be taken from the stricken city, where, in spite of every effort to restore confidence, there is much depression.

J. C. Stewart, a builder, after a careful inspection of the grain elevators and their contents, said the damage to the elevators was not over two per cent. Mr. Bailey said he would put a large force of men to work clearing up each of the wharves, and the company will be ready for business within eight days. The wharves have been damaged very little outside of the wreckage of the sheds. With the wreckage cleared away Galveston will be in shape for beginning business.

SOUTHERN PACIFIC WILL REBUILD.

To a journal in New York the "Galveston News" sent the following important statement:

"You ask the 'News' what is our estimate of Galveston's future and what the prospects are for building up the city. Briefly stated, the 'News' believes that inside of two years there will exist upon the island of Galveston a city three times greater than the one that has just been partially destroyed. The devastation has been great and the loss of life terrible, but there is a hopefulness at the very time this answer is being penned you that is surprising to those who witness it. That is not a practical answer to your inquiries, however.

"The principal feature is this—The Southern Pacific company has ordered a steel bridge built across the bay ten feet higher than the trestlework on the late bridges. The company has ordered also a doubling up of forces to continue and improve their wharves, and with this note of encouragement from the great enterprise upon which so much depends the whole situation is cleared up.

AN EXCELLENT PORT.

"Our wharves will be rebuilt, the sanitary condition of the city will be perfected ; streets will be laid with material superior to that destroyed, new vigor and life will enter the community with the work of construction, and the products of the twenty-one States and Territories contiguous will pour through the port of Galveston.

"We have now, through the action of this storm, with all its devastation, thirty feet of water on the bar, making this port the equal, if not the superior, of all others on the American seaboard. The island has stood the wrack of the greatest storm convulsion known in the history of any latitude, and there is no longer a question of the stability of the island's foundation. If a wind velocity of one hundred and twenty miles an hour and a water volume of fifteen feet in some places upon the island did not have the effect of washing it away, then there is no wash to it.

"Galveston island is still here, and here to stay, and it will be made in a short time the most beautiful and progressive city in the Southwest. This may be esteemed simply a hopeful view, but the conditions existing warrant acceptance of the view to the fullest extent.

"The 'News' will not deal with what is needed from a generous public to the thousands of suffering people now left with us. The dead are at rest. There are twenty thousand homeless people here, whose necessities at this time are great indeed. Assistance is needed for them in the immediate future. The great works of material and industrial energy will take care of themselves by the attraction here presented for the profitable employment of capital. We were dazed for a day or two, but there is no gloom here now as to the future. Business has already been resumed."

PLAN TO PROTECT GALVESTON.

Can the city of Galveston, almost obliterated by the recent storm, be protected from all future assaults by the Gulf?

Colonel Henry M. Robert, United States Corps of Engineers, and divisional engineer of the Atlantic and Gulf coasts, who is stationed here at present, says that Galveston can be absolutely protected from every storm by a sea wall built along the Gulf front.

Colonel Robert, during the late spring, while on a visit to Galveston, suggested a comprehensive plan for the improvement of that harbor, which was hailed by the city and State as solving the problem of the creation of a great port in Galveston Bay. This plan would also aɯord a great measure of protection to the city from inundation on its northern and southwestern sides should a strong wind from the Gulf pile up the water on the shallow floors of Galveston and West bays.

Colonel Robert's plan contemplates the construction of a great basin for harbor purposes, as well as for dry docks, to the northwest of the city. The basin would be formed by a retaining wall shutting out Galveston and West bays, and by filling in the parts of the Gulf floor between this retaining wall and the walls or shores of the basin.

The northern retaining wall would follow generally the line of the south jetty, and a deep water channel of twenty-five to thirty feet would be left between the new land and the city of Galveston, connecting the channel formed by the jetties with the inner basin. Pelican Island would be the backbone of the made land, and all of Pelican Flats would be transformed into solid land, to be used for railway and docking purposes.

THE PROJECT WAS APPROVED.

The plan also involved the extension of the jetty channel through Galveston Bay and up Buffalo Bayou as far as Houston, more than sixty miles distant, making the latter city an open seaport. Railways would have, by means of the filled-in land, ready access to the city, and, in addition, the port facilities of Galveston would be many times increased, and a continuous sea channel be constructed from the Gulf to Houston.

This project, as outlined by Colonel Robert, received the unqualified approval of the various interests concerned in the development of Galveston harbor, and steps had been taken to carry out the plan before the onslaught of the recent storm swept away water lines and much of the city itself. Colonel Robert now proposes an additional plan, simple and inexpensive, for affording the fullest and most complete measure of protection from all storms. This new plan is to construct a sea wall along the Gulf front of the city.

It is estimated that the height of the waves in the recent storm, which was the severest ever experienced on the Texas coast, was about ten to twelve feet. Colonel Robert suggests that a wall at least twelve feet above the beach, and running the entire length of the water front, or about ten miles, be built

immediately to barricade the city from the Gulf. A height of
twelve feet above the beach would give fourteen feet above the
water, and would, Colonel Robert thinks, afford ample protection.

COST OF THE SEA WALL.

As to the expense of such a structure, it is thought by engineers that a liberal estimate would be about $1,500,000 per mile.
This wall, as projected by Colonel Robert, would extend from a
point on the south jetty, where the latter crosses the Gulf front
of the city, and would follow the line of the beach, two or three
feet above the water level, until it reached the southwestern limit
of the island, in the shallow water of West Bay. At the latter
point the danger from storms is not serious.

At present the depth of water between the jetties is 26½ feet,
and it is thought that it will soon be thirty feet. The average depth
of the original channel across the twenty-five miles of Galveston
Bay is about twelve feet. It is proposed by Colonel Robert's plan
to increase this to at least twenty-five feet. An additional and
supplementary plan is to extend the improvement, so as to create
a system of coast channels that will transform Galveston into a
central port with a labyrinth of waterways.

EXTENSIVE HARBOR IMPROVEMENT.

The magnitude of the plan for the improvement of the harbor of Galveston may be imagined when it is observed that the
inner basin, or harbor, is to be about five miles long by three
broad, that it may be approached by a deep water channel accommo-
dating ocean going vessels of the deepest draught. The outlet
into West Bay will not be so deep, as the bay itself is navigable
by light draught vessels only. The new land, formed on the basis
of Pelican Island and flats will be about four miles square.

Colonel Robert said that a survey will be made at once of the
wrecked forts and other military works at Galveston. A report
received from that place says that those portions of the works
erected upon piling withstood the storm. It is proposed to use
piling entirely for similar works in the future.

CHAPTER IX.

Story of a Brave Hero—A Vast Army of Helpless Victims— Scenes that Shock the Beholders—Our Nation Rises to the Occasion.

WHEN Galveston's chapter of horrors had reached its crisis, when the people were dazed, leaderless and almost helpless, so that they went about bewildered and did little more than gather a few hundred of the bodies which were in their way, a longshoreman became the hero of the hour. It was not until Monday that the brave leaders, who are usually not discovered in a community until some great emergency arises, began to forge in front. They were not men from one rank in point of wealth or intelligence. They came from all classes.

For example, there was Hughes, the longshoreman. Bodies which lay exposed in the streets, and which had to be removed somewhere lest they be stepped on, were carried into a temporary morgue until 500 lay in rows on the floor.

A VERY GRAVE PROBLEM.

Then a problem in mortality such as no other American community ever faced was presented. Pestilence, which stalked forth by Monday, seemed about to take possession of what the storm had left. Immediate disposition of those bodies was absolutely necessary to save the living.

Then it was that Lowe and McVittie and Sealy and the others, who by common impulse had come together to deal with the problem, found Hughes. The longshoreman took up the most gruesome task ever seen, except on a battlefield. He had to have help·ers. Some volunteered; others were pressed into the service at the point of the bayonet.

Whisky by the bucketful was carried to these men, and they were drenched with it. The stimulant was kept at hand and applied continuously. Only in this way was it possible for the stoutest-hearted to work in such surroundings.

167

Under the direction of Hughes these hundreds of bodies already collected and others brought from the central part of the city—those which were quickest found—were loaded on an ocean barge and taken far off into the gulf to be cast into the sea.

There were 38,000 people in the city when the census was taken a few weeks before the flood. After a careful survey of the desolate field since the storm and flood have wrought their sad havoc, the conclusion is forced that there were in Galveston 25,000 people, or thereabouts, who had to be fed and clothed. The proportion of those who were in fair circumstances and lost all is astonishing.

Relief cannot be limited to those who formed the poorer class before the storm. An intelligent man left Galveston, taking his wife and child to relatives. He said: "A week ago I had a good home and a business which paid me between $400 and $500 a month. To-day I have nothing. My house was swept away and my business is gone. I see no way of re-establishing it in the near future." This man had a real estate and house renting agency.

STRIPPED OF ALL THEIR POSSESSIONS.

At the military headquarters one of the principal officials doing temporary service for this city said: "Before the storm I had a good home and good income. I felt rich. My house is gone and my business. The fact is I don't even own the clothes I stand before you in. I borrowed them."

Now these are not exceptional cases. They are fairly typical. They must be fed and clothed, these 25,000 people, until they can work out their temporal salvation.

And then something ought to be done to help the worthy get on their feet and make a fresh start. Some people will leave Galveston. It is plain, however, that nothing like the number expected will go. Galveston is still home to the great majority. Those who can stay and live there will do so. If the country responds to the needs in anything like the measure given to Johnstown, Chicago, Charlestown and other stricken cities and sections, Galveston as a community will not only be restored, but will enter upon a greater future than was expected before the storm.

Since Tuesday there has been no doubt of Galveston's restoration. From a central organization the relief work was divided by wards. A depot and a sub-committee were established in each ward of the city.

"They who will not work shall not eat," was the principle adopted when the organization was perfected. Few idle mouths are being fed in Galveston. There are, however, the fatherless, and there are widows, and there are sick who must have charity. But the able-bodied are working in parties under the direction of bosses. They are being paid in food and clothing. In this way the Relief Committee is within the first week meeting the needs of the survivors, and at the same time is gradually clearing the streets and burning the ruins and refuse.

PICTURES IN SHARP CONTRAST.

Of Galveston's population of 38,000 it is estimated that 8000 were killed.

The area of total destruction was about 1300 acres.

There were 5000 dwellings, hotels, churches and convents utterly destroyed,

More than 2000 bodies have been burned.

The property loss is not less than $15,000,000.

One hundred and twenty-five men, most of them negroes, were shot to death for robbing the dead. "Decimation" is the word often employed to emphasize destruction of life. Galveston was "decimated" twice over by this storm.

It took on the part of the public-spirited men a good deal of boldness to lay down the law that the support tendered by the country must be earned and to enforce it. But before two days had passed the whole community was at work cheerfully. A tour through the city, up one street and down another, showed the greatest activity. Thousands and not hundreds of men were dragging the ruins into great heaps and applying the torch. Occasionally they came on the remains of human beings and hastily added them to the blazing heaps. But it is notable that much less is said now about the dead than during the early days. The minds of the people who survived have passed from that phase of the calamity.

A soldier standing guard at a place on the beach where these fires were burning thickly was asked if the workers were still finding bodies.

"Yes," he replied, "a good many!" That was all. Three days ago the same soldier would have gone into particulars. He would have told how many had been found in this place and in that.

The commander of one of these squads came into headquarters to deliver a report to Colonel McCaleb. He had nothing to say about bodies, but wanted to tell that a trunk in fairly good condition, with valuable contents, had been taken out of one heap, and that the owner might be found through marks of identification which he had noted. So it goes; the thought is of the living rather than of the dead.

SIGNS OF RESTORATION EVERYWHERE.

The women of Galveston are working as never before. Whereever one goes carpets and clothing and mattresses and rugs are hung on fences and galleries. The scrubbing-brushes are going. A smell of carbolic acid is in the air. The housekeepers are bustling in and out. Every residence that can be called habitable is undergoing renovation most thoroughly. The sound of the hammer is heard everywhere. Amateur carpenters are patching and strengthening homes which, in the better spirit that prevails, they may now hope to save.

One of the strongest impressions that is gained of the work of restoration is from the sights in front of the stores. Merchants and clerks are overhauling stocks. Where the articles are such that it can be done they are carried out in front of the stores and spread in the sun to dry. Tons of dry goods, clothing, hats and caps, boots and shoes are spread in the streets and on the pavements, so that in places it is difficult to get past.

In these stores the watermarks on the walls and shelves varies from waist to shoulder high. Everything below these levels was saturated. The loss of stocks affected by water is very great. But the disposition of the storekeepers to make the best of it and to save something, even if badly damaged, is cheering.

Full of confidence and even optimistic are the expressions of the men who have taken the lead in this crisis. Said Colonel Lowe, of the Galveston News: "In two years this town will be rebuilt upon a scale which we would not have obtained so quickly without this devastation.

"I took it for granted that when the Southern Pacific management said to its representatives, as it has said: 'Build a bridge ten feet higher than the old one and put on a double force to do it,' our future was assured. We shall go forward and create the city. We shall have some restrictions as to rebuilding lines, especially on the beach side, where the greatest losses were sustained. The ramshackle way in which too much construction has been done heretofore will be of the past."

SAVING VAST GRAIN STORES.

If any one had predicted on Sunday or Monday that on Friday and Saturday Galveston would be doing business at the old stand, he would have been laughed to scorn. What the grain men are planning very fairly tells the story. It applies to all lines of business. The storm caught 2,500,000 bushels of wheat in cars and elevators. Superstructures of the elevators were carried away, and in other ways the immense buildings were somewhat damaged. These indefatigable people six days later are perfecting their arrangements to save that grain and export it. Robinson, the inspector, said:

"Without more rain for a few days, say six or eight, we shall begin loading that wheat on ships for export. Don't you believe anything you hear about permanent damages to Galveston as the result of the storm.

"We have got the grandest harbor here. Why, our channel instead of being filled by the storm carrying sand into it was scoured two feet deeper than it was before. We had then twenty-eight to twenty-nine feet of water. We have now thirty feet.

" None of the danger of sickness that was feared has shown itself. We are getting rid of the wreckage, and we are scattering car loads of lime and other disinfectants everywhere. I believe all danger is passed. Talk about Galveston giving up!" continued Mr. Robinson, " This great wharf property is worth $18,000,000. It sustained a loss of less than $500,000.

" The company has 1000 men at work on the repairs. It stared eternity in the face Saturday night, and was ready to go, To-day I have got more energy and ambition than I ever had. I don't know where I got it. I guess God gave it to me. Come back in sixty days, and you will not know Galveston, remembering it as you see it to-day."

TERRIBLE EXPERIENCES OF A YOUNG GIRL.

Miss Maud Hall, who was spending her school vacation in Galveston, and who passed through the storm, has written of her experience to her parents, Mr. and Mrs. Emory Hall, of Dallas. Miss Hall was in the house where she was boarding at the time the storm came. She says:

" The wind and rain rose to a furious whirlwind, and all the time the water crept higher and higher. We all crowded into the hall, and the house, a big two-story one, rocked like a cradle. About 6 o'clock the roof was gone, all the blinds torn off and all the windows blown in. Glass was flying in all directions and the water had risen to a level with the gallery. Then the men told us we would have to go to a house across the street.

" It took two men to each woman to get her across the street and down to the end of the block. Trees thicker than any in our yard were whirled down the street and the water looked like a whirlpool. I came near drowning with another girl. It was dark by this time, and the men put their arms around us and down into the water we went.

" I spent the night—such a horrible one!—wet from my shoulders to my waist and from my knees down, and barefoot. Nobody had any shoes and stockings. The house was packed with people just like us. The windows were blown out, and it rocked from top to bottom, and the water came into the first floor. About 3 o'clock in the morning the wind had changed and blew the water back into the Gulf.

"As soon as we could we waded home. Such a home! The water had risen three feet in the house, and the roof being gone the rain poured in. We had not had anything to eat since noon the day before, and we lived on whisky.

"It was awful. Dead animals every where and the streets filled with fallen telegraph poles and brick stores blown over. Hundreds of women and children and men sitting on steps crying lost ones, and nearly half of them injured! Wild-eyed, ghastly-looking men hurried by and told of whole families killed. All day wagon after wagon passed filled with dead, most of them without a thing on them, and men with stretchers with dead bodies with just a sheet thrown over them, some of them little children."

HOPING FOR THE BEST.

Says an eye-witness of the terrible scene:

"What a contrast! Last Sunday, gloom, desolation and black despair prevailed. This storm-tossed city was filled with desolation. The sorrow of the survivors for the dead was unspeakable, the destruction of property indescribable, the people were palsied, and in the gloom of devastation and death there was no silver lining to the pall that darkly overshadowed them. To-day hope and determination buoy up the people.

"They realize that the task before them is titanic yet, with the generous aid that is floating to them from all parts of the civilized world, born of a common humanity, that makes the whole world akin, aided by their own indomitable purpose, the sick and wounded will be healed, the destitute relieved and the recuperation of Galveston will be speedy and lasting. It is the spirit that turns defeat into victory, makes a people strong, glorious and prosperous. You hear no complaining, no expression of want of confidence, but of hope, zeal and determination, and this is exemplified by the vigorous enterprise visible on every hand.

"Although it is the Sabbath, work is being pushed under a

systematic plan of operation that is rapidly bringing order out of chaos. The search and burial or cremation of the unfortunate victims within the corporation limits of the city are being rapidly prosecuted by a large force in squads under military direction. Down the island and on the mainland the work of interring the dead is conducted with the same system.

"As new conditions constantly develop, the cleaning up and disinfecting the streets, stores and buildings go bravely on, and the sanitary condition of the down portion of the town has been greatly improved, and Mayor Jones stated to-day that there would be no let-up in the work until the entire city was cleaned and disinfected. Dry goods stores and clothing houses resemble great laundries, and every available space is occupied with goods hung out to dry. Fortunately the weather is clear, hot and dry for this purpose. Those merchants whose stocks were but slightly damaged have done a rushing business, and so have the restaurants, whose stocks are very limited and fresh meats difficult to obtain.

EXTORTION A RARE EXCEPTION.

"Extortion is a rare exception, although the supply of food at hotels and restaurants is limited. This will be overcome in a few days, since all the railways terminating here have united upon one bridge and are pushing the work night and day with a large force reconstructing it, while their tracks are being restored on the island and mainland by large forces, which it is confidently asserted will give this stricken city rail communication by Wednesday next.

"If this is done it will relieve the existing situation wonderfully. All supplies are now brought in by boat, and these, being principally for the sick and absolutely destitute, are being distributed with dispatch. The injured and sick, under the thorough system inaugurated by the Board of Health and local physicians, aided by volunteers from the outside, are receiving every care and attention, and are doing as well as could be under the circumstances, which are being improved daily.

"All churches in the city, either being wrecked or ruined, with but one or two exceptions. divine services were in most cases suspended.   Mass was celebrated at St. Mary's Cathedral this morning and was largely attended.   Father Kirwin preached a feeling sermon, at which he spoke of the awful calamity that had befallen the people.   After expressing sympathy for the afflicted and distressed, he advised not to lose confidence, for back of them the humanity of the world stands with relief; to hope for the future and build a more secure, a larger and better city.

"This young priest has done yeoman service in relieving and caring for the wounded, comforting the bereaved and burying the dead.   Bishop Gallagher, who has also been earnest and active in his efforts, is in receipt of a telegram from Archbishop Corrigan, of New York, stating that his diocese would see that all Roman Catholic orphans sent to his care would be provided for.   To-morrow a census of the Roman Catholic people will be begun to ascertain the number of widows and orphans caused by the storm, and the exact number of families that perished.

"The Grand Lodge Committee of Odd Fellows were here to-day and organized local relief committees to look after and care for the sick and destitute of that order, for whom an appeal has been sent to the lodges of the United States for relief."

SOUTHERN PACIFIC AT GALVESTON TO STAY.

"Galveston, September 16.—The news which was printed here this morning in the shape of a personal telegram from Vice-President Huntington, of the Southern Pacific, that that road is not to abandon Galveston, has created intense satisfaction, and has materially accelerated the movement for the speedy reconstruction of the city.

"Mr. Huntington's telegram was to Mr. A. H. Belo, of the Galveston and Dallas News, and read: 'I see it reported that we are to abandon our work at Galveston.   Nothing is further from our thoughts.   We expect to resume work there as soon as we can. You can assure the people to that effect.'

"Dr. W. H. Blount, State Health Officer, to-day printed a statement showing that no apprehensions are justified that sickness will result from the overflow just experienced.   He shows that in 1867, in the midst of the widespread epidemic of yellow fever, a severe storm occurred at Galveston in the early days of October, resulting in a deposit over a greater portion of the city of slimy mud. Not only did no sickness result, but the cyclonic disturbance cut short the yellow fever epidemic, and but few cases of fever occurred thereafter. In 1875 and 1886, when there were severe storms and no overflow, no increase in sickness occurred.

"Several thousand men are at work clearing away the débris on the beach. One hundred and fifty bodies were discovered in the wreckage and burned Friday. No attempt is now being made to identify recovered bodies. Indeed, most of them are found naked and mutilated beyond recognition. A New York relief train has arrived with a number of physicians and nurses and a large supply of provisions, which were distributed. Every effort is being made by the postal authorities to receive and distribute mail. No city delivery has yet been arranged for, and all who expect letters are requested to call at the Postoffice. No mail is being collected from the letter boxes.

"In some quarters of the city the Water Works Company is serving customers on the second stories. This is taken as indicating the rapid headway being made in putting the plant again in operation. The Street Railway Company suffered a loss of a quarter of a million, and its entire system is torn to pieces. An effort is to be made temporarily to operate cars with mules.

ENCROACHMENTS OF THE SEA.

"The residents of Galveston are plucky in the extreme in their determination to rebuild and make Galveston a greater and better city than it has ever been before, but in one direction, at least, they have suffered a loss that is beyond repair, and that lies in the extent of the territory wrested from them by the storm. The waters of the Gulf now cover about 5,300,000 square feet of ground that was formerly a part of Galveston. This loss has been suffered entirely on the south side of the city, where the finest residences were built, facing the gulf, and where land was held at a higher valuation than in any other part of the city.

HON. JOSEPH D. SAYRES
GOVERNOR OF TEXAS

SHOWING TERRIBLE DEVASTATION ON AVENUE I, BETWEEN TWELFTH AND
THIRTEENTH STREETS

CREMATING BODIES EXCAVATED FROM THE RUINS

MEDICAL DEPARTMENT UNIVERSITY OF TEXAS, GALVESTON, DESTROYED
BY THE FLOOD

" For three miles along the shore of the Gulf this choice residence property extended, but the shore line was so changed by the storm that at low tide the water is 350 feet higher along the entire three miles. In the eastern part of the city there are places where 350 feet is less than the actual amount of ground taken from the city. It is a fair estimate, however, for the entire distance. The foundation pillars of the Beach Hotel now stand in the water. Before the storm there was a beach in front of the hotel site nearly 400 feet wide. There is no possibility of any of this land being reclaimed.

A MORE HOPEFUL FEELING.

" A more hopeful feeling is observable everywhere here, and the situation is brightening rapidly. The State Health Officer, Dr. Blunt, believes that there is now no danger of an epidemic. The city Board of Health held a meeting yesterday and adopted a resolution voicing the same views. Emergency hospitals have been established in every ward for the treatment of the sick and wounded.

" The Ursulin Convent has been converted into a great general hospital for the reception and care of patients who are seriously ill, with a full corpse of physicians and trained nurses. All public and private hospitals are filled to their capacity with sufferers. Medical supplies are still much needed.

" Banks and some other branches of business have resumed. Others are actively preparing to resume. Preparations for rebuilding are already going on in the business part of the city. The railways and the wharf front are being rapidly cleaned of débris. The telegraph and telephone companies are rushing their work. The Western Union has five wires strung to their downtown office. The Postal will have some up soon, and the full telegraphic service is expected to be re-established by the close of the week. The cable connection has not yet been restored. Business on the floor of the Cotton Exchange will not be re-established for three weeks. The Exchange Building was partly unroofed by the storm.

12

"Many dead are reported as being yet unburied, especially in the extreme west part of the city. The interment and cremation of human bodies and the carcasses of animals is being vigorously prosecuted. Only about six houses remain between South Galveston and the city limits. Of probably 1000 persons living down the island, at least one-third were lost. There are 200 bodies on the beach between the Mott place and the city limits. Eighteen persons in this neighborhood got together and began burying the dead yesterday. They are out of provisions.

"Daily papers and illustrated papers have been most energetic in taking photographs of the Galveston disaster. The town is under military law, and the people are not inclined to brook photographers. Three photographers who ventured out yesterday had their instruments smashed and themselves pressed into service burying dead bodies.

"So much progress has been made here towards the rehabilitation of Galveston, and so harmoniously are the various forces working, that General McKibben, who was ordered here with his staff to assist the authorities, has decided that his presence is no longer necessary, and he has made arrangements to leave for Houston. After having largely assisted in the restoration of local confidence, the withdrawal of General McKibben is taken to mean that little is to be done here but to take care of the distressed until normal business conditions have been resumed. In this connection the information was made public through the local representatives of the Federal authorites yesterday that the War Department will undertake as soon as possible the restoration of its property at this point.

RAILROAD CAPITAL TO BE EMPLOYED.

"Dispatches quoting Eastern financiers on the future of Galveston are read with much interest. The idea, however, that the status of the city will be changed finds no local adherents. The various railroads entering here have determined to assist the citizens of Galveston to the full extent of their ability in rebuilding the city. Colonel L. J. Polk of the Santa Fé has received a very enthusiastic and encouraging message from the headquarters of the road, declaring confidence in Galveston, urging the business community to proceed at once to the work of reconstruction, and promising every help in their power. As a result of the receipt of the message, Colonel Polk said yesterday :

" The railroad interests have decided to combine their forces in order to rebuild as quickly as possible a bridge from Virginia Point to Galveston. A large number of men will go to work in the morning with this end in view. You may say to the country that in six days a bridge will have been built, and trains will be running over it. I have had a consultation with the wharf interests, and they have promised us that they will be prepared to handle ingoing and outgoing shipments by the time the bridge is finished. The bridge we will build will be of substantial but temporary character. We will subsequently replace it with a more enduring structure. There is no reason why Galveston ought not commercially to resume normal conditions in ten days."

MEDICAL COLLEGE SHATTERED.

" Colonel Prather, President of the Board of Regents of the Medical College here, and Colonel Breckinridge, a member of the Board, were among the late arrivals yesterday. They met General McKibben, and were driven to the institution. They found the building in a badly shattered condition, but on their return it was announced that the college would be immediately reconstructed by private beneficence if the State was unable to bear the cost.

" Large gangs have been at work in the business district, and splendid progress in clearing away débris has been made. The street car company has a large force of men at work cutting wires, removing obstructions, and putting their track in condition."

The News correspondent telegraphs as follows from Houston : "Inquiries as to the loss of life and property continue to pour in. The list will never be known. There have been already handled on the Galveston island, and along the bay shores of the mainland opposite the island, about 4000 corpses. The long stretch of débris along the beach and the western part of the island has not yet been heard from. The prairies of the mainland over which the waters rushed have also their tales to tell. I should say, after investigation, that a conservative estimate of the loss of life in Galveston would be 8000. The names of thousands of victims will never be known. They have simply passed out of existence. As to the property loss, it is hard to make an estimate. Colonel Lowes's estimate of $15,000,000 to $20,000,000 is conservative."

GALVESTON'S DISTRESSING APPEAL RENEWED.

Austin, Tex., September 15.—Governor Sayers last night received the following official report from Mayor Jones, of Galveston, as to conditions there:

"Hon. Joseph D. Sayers, Governor: After the fullest possible investigation here we feel justified in saying to you, and through you to the American people, that no such disaster has overtaken any community or section in the history of our country. The loss of life is appalling, and can never be accurately determined. It is estimated at 5000 to 8000 people. There is not a home in Galveston that has not been injured, while thousands have been destroyed. The property loss represents accumulations of sixty years, and more millions than can be safely stated. Under these conditions, with 10,000 people homeless and destitute, with the entire population under a stress and strain difficult to realize, we appeal directly in the hour of our great emergency to the sympathy and aid of mankind.   WALTER JONES, Mayor."

GREAT ANXIETY FOR FRIENDS.

Memphis, Tenn., September 15.—The following telegram from Mayor Jones, of Galveston, was received here to-day:

"To the Associated Press, Memphis, Tenn.: I am in receipt of thousands of telegrams offering assistance and inquiring about absent friends and relatives. All of these have been promptly answered, but restricted communication has probably served to cause delay in transmission and delivery. The telegraphic companies are doing all in their power to restore prompt communication with the outside world, and have already partially succeeded, and I am assured that within the next few days normal conditions with reference to telegraphic communication will prevail.

"The situation in Galveston has been in most instances accurately reported, and the distress of the people is great. Galveston and vicinity need at once the assistance of all people. Remittances of money should be made to John Sealy, Treasurer Relief Committee, acknowledgment of which will be made.

"WALTER C. JONES, Mayor."

DISTRESS AT ALVIN.

Houston, Texas, September 15.—The following statement and appeal came from R. W. King, of Alvin, Texas:

"I arrived in Alvin from Dallas, and was astonished and bewildered by the sight of devastation on every side. Ninety-five per cent. of the houses in this vicinity are in ruins, leaving 6,000 people absolutely destitute. Everything in the way of crops is destroyed, and unless there is speedy relief there will be exceedingly great suffering.

"The people need and must have assistance. Need money to rebuild their homes and buy stock and implements. They need food—flour, bacon, corn. They must have seeds for their gardens, so as to be able to do something for themselves very soon. Clothing is badly needed. Hundreds of women and children are without a change, and are already suffering. Some better idea may be had of the distress when it is known that box-cars are being improvised as houses and hay as bedding.

"Only fourteen houses in the town of Alvin are standing on their foundations, and they are badly damaged. While the great sympathetic heart of this grand Nation is responding so generously for the stricken city of Galveston, it should be remembered also that the smaller towns—where the same condition of total wreck exists, though miraculously with smaller loss of life—need immediate help from a liberal people."

The situation on Saturday, the 15th, is told in the following graphic description:

"Under the firm rule of the military authorities, affairs in Galveston are rapidly assuming a more cheerful aspect. The forces of law and order are crystallizing every hour, and now that the people realize that there is definite authority to which they can appeal they are going to work systematically to renovate the city and prevent any possibility of epidemic. The force engaged in burying the dead and clearing up the city has increased steadily until now twenty-five hundred men are pushing the work.

"Adjutant-General Scurry holds the town fast with a strong grip. He is compelling all men whose services can be spared from public business to join the forces at the work in the streets.

"The burial of the dead goes steadily on. All the corpses in the open, along the shores or near the wreckage, have been sunk in the gulf or burned in the streets. The labor of clearing away the débris in search of bodies began at Thirtieth street and avenue O, one of the worst wrecked parts of the town. Two hundred men were put at work, and in thirty minutes fifty corpses were found within a space thirty yards square. Whole families lay dead piled in indescribable confusion.

OLD AND YOUNG CRUSHED TOGETHER.

"Old and young crushed by the falling timbers, were one by one dragged from débris six to twenty feet deep. Aged fathers were clinging to more robust forms ; children clutching to mother's skirts, young girls with their arms around brothers, mothers clasping babes to their bosoms. These were the melancholy sights seen by those digging among the ruins. In dozens and scores the bodies were turned up by pich and shovel, rake and axe. Away to the left the wreckage stretched two miles to Seventh street ; to the right, a mile to Fortieth street down town.

"Popular sentiment insists that the west end be burned, but the military authorities have hesitated to give the order. Father Kerwin and Captain Morrissey urge that the wreckage be fired at once, and it will probably be done.

"Men are making ready to apply the torch. Fire engines are out on the beach. A road runs through the wreckage separating it from houses not wholly destroyed. When water is running freely in the mains the fire will be started. Fires are burning at intervals all along the beach over the gulf front, raising clouds of smoke, which stretches far along the coast.

"The streets are clearing rapidly; many in the centre of the town are to-day readily passable. Along the Bay and Gulf fronts, however, the wreckage still chokes the streets. Sanitary conditions are steadily improving. Physicians do not disguise the danger to the city, but do not expect an epidemic. Five of them declared to-day that if the refuse was completely burned, the streets were thoroughly disinfected and the sewers quickly put in order, there would be no pestilence.

GREAT EXODUS OF WOMEN AND CHILDREN.

"Women and children are leaving in large numbers. They include all classes and conditions. In groups and sometimes in long lines they pass down Tremont street on the way to the boat bound for Texas City. Many are going never to return, poorly and scantily clad, with handkerchiefs for hats, and all their worldly goods stuffed into pillow-cases.

"The man who has no property or relatives in Galveston is leaving for good. The future of Galveston depends upon whether or not the town can retain its shipping. If Galveston can keep her prestige as a port her revival is assured. All those who have helped to make Galveston what it was are certain that it will continue to be the great port of the Southwest. Not a man in town who has any property will desert the city. Progressive citizens have been especially cheered by the news that the English shippers will continue to patronize the port and by the generous gift of $5000 from R. P. Houston, member of the English Parliament and head of the shipping firm of R. P. Houston & Co., of Liverpool and London. This contribution came in response to the news that one of the Houston steamers, the Hilarius, was stranded on the Pelican Island.

"Business men know that if Galveston should go down its shipping would promptly be transferred to New Orleans. But it is the glory of the people of New Orleans that since the storm they have said not a word against the rebuilding of this city, but have generously and nobly responded to the appeals for Galveston's sufferers.

"In spite of any ambition of rival ports, in spite of the timidity of women and some men, the people of Galveston, patiently and soberly, with loyalty and courage, are determined to rebuild on the ruins of this once beautiful city a metropolis that shall prosper and endure. They are determined to do this, in spite of the possibility that their homes and industries may again be wrecked by storm. If you ask them why, they will tell you, " No community is immune from disasters of this kind. It merely happened that Galveston was in the path of the storm." And then they will go back to burying their dead.

"Captain Randall, of the steamship Comeno, which has arrived from New Orleans, reports that coming up the bay he saw a great many human corpses, and that the banks of Pelican Island were strewn with the dead. Pelican Island is six miles from Galveston.

BRIDGE AND TRAIN IN SIX DAYS.

" The various railroads entering the city are determined to assist to the full extent of their ability in rebuilding the city. Colonel L. J. Polk, of the Santa Fé, has received a very encouraging message from the headquarters of his road, declaring confidence in Galveston, and urging the business community to push forward the work of reconstruction. Colonel Polk said in an interview:

" The railroad interests have decided to combine their forces in order to rebuild as quickly as possible a bridge from Virginia Point to Galveston. A large number of men will go to work with this end in view. You may say to the country that in six days a bridge will have been built and trains running over it. I have had a consultation with the wharf interests, and they have promised us that they will be prepared to handle ingoing and outgoing shipments by the time the bridge is finished. The bridge we shall build will be substantial, but of temporary character. We shall subsequently replace it with a more enduring structure. There is no reason why Galveston ought not to resume normal commercial conditions in ten days.

"So much progress has been made toward the rehabilitation of the city, and so harmoniously are the various working forces ᵗworking that General McKibben, who was ordered here with his staff to assist the authorities, has decided that his presence is no longer necessary, and he has made arrangements to leave for Houston.

"The hiding place of three ghouls was discovered in a beached dredge formerly used by the Southern Pacific Railroad Company. Three satchels, filled with jewelry and money, were seized. The men, who are whites, will probably be shot.

BANKS ASK MILLION DOLLAR LOAN.

"The cashier of the Island City Bank left the city last night for Houston. He carried with him a petition from the Associated Galveston Banks̄ begging the Houston bankers to advance them $1,000,000. By an agreement made among the Galveston banks, no check for more than $25 is now honored. It is impossible for nine out of ten Galveston merchants to meet any promissory notes that are about to fall due, and if assistance is not obtained the merchants, as well as the banks, must go down.

"Every time a schooner or a catboat was filled to its safety limit with human freight, and the way was barred, women would gesticulate wildly and in choking voice implore even standing room. Nine hundred refugees left the city yesterday, and 10,000 more would have left to-day if facilities were at hand."

Excellent work in saving lives during the hurricane at Galveston was done by the officers and crew of the revenue cutter Galveston, which was stationed at that port.

The first mail through from the stricken city reached Washington on the 15th, and brought two letters from Chief Engineer W. H. Whitaker of the Galveston. Under date of September 9, he says:

"All the sheds on the wharves must have been levelled to the ground, or nearly so. I do not think there is a house that has not been more or less damaged or blown to the ground. While the wind was blowing over sixty miles an hour we sent out a boat with a rescuing party to row up one of the streets. The first trip they succeeded in saving thirteen women and children, and brought them back to the vessel in safety.

" It was useless to attempt to row the boat against the terrific wind, and, as the water was at that time not over a man's head in the streets, a rope would be sent out to the nearest telegraph pole, and by that means the boat could be hauled along from pole to pole. This was accomplished only by the most herculean efforts on the part of the men who led out the rope, but between swimming, walking and floundering along in the teeth of the gale the rope would finally be made fast.

FACING THE FIERCE BLASTS OF THE STORM.

" Then it was all that the crew of one officer and seven men could do to pull the boat against the fierce blasts of the cyclone. By working all Saturday afternoon and evening and up to one o'clock Sunday morning the brave boys succeeded in rescuing thirty-four men, women and children, whom they put in a place of safety and provided with enough provisions for their immediate needs. Finally, on account of the darkness, the increasing violence of the storm and the vast amount of wreckage in the streets, the rescuing party was reluctantly compelled to return to the vessel.

" On board the ship it was a period of intense anxiety for all hands. No one slept, and it was only by the almost superhuman efforts of the officers and crew that we rode out the hurricane in safety. With the exception of the carrying away of the port forward rigging and the smashing of all the windows and skylights, the vessel sustained no serious injury. Not a single person on board was injured in any way."

Under date of September 11 the same officer writes: " We think there have been 5000 lives lost. I cannot begin to tell the number of houses blown down or damage done. Our new distiller, which came down on the New York steamer, has been set up on deck, and we are thus enabled to relieve much suffering by supplying drinking water to the many who call on us for relief. We have also furnished as much food to the needy as we can possibly spare.

"All that can be thought of now is the disposing of the dead. Already one steamer load and four barge loads have been sent out to sea. During the height of the hurricane the tide rose seven or eight feet above the usual high water mark and three feet over the wharves.

"There are five hundred men working to repair the city water works and in the meantime we are furnishing all the water we can possibly distil to the sufferers and aiding them in such other ways as lie in our power."

With a view to the restoration of the fortifications in the harbor of Galveston, General Wilson, chief of engineers, organized a Board of engineer officers, consisting of Colonel Henry M. Robert, stationed in New York; Major Henry M. Adams, stationed in New Orleans; Captain Charles H. Riche, stationed in Galveston, and Captain Edgar Jadwin, stationed in New York, to meet in Galveston at the call of the senior officer about October 20.

RESTORATION OF PUBLIC WORKS.

The Board is instructed to make a careful examination of the jetties and fortifications of Galveston and to report to the Chief of Engineers what action is necessary for the repair and restoration of the fortifications and harbor works.

Acting Secretary of War Meiklejohn has received a telegram from Mayor Jones, of Galveston, saying: "The people of the city of Galveston desire to return to you their heartfelt thanks for your assistance in their hour of trouble and affliction."

A despatch also was received from General McKibben saying that there are plenty of doctors in Galveston, but that disinfectants are badly needed.

"Washington, September 15.—In response to the request of your journal concerning the situation in Galveston, I have a report from Passed Assistant Surgeon Wertenbaker, who was directed to go from his station in New Orleans to Galveston, practically confirming the press reports as to the effect of the storm and conditions existing. He says:

" 'City is wrecked. Press reports not exaggerated. Deaths estimated at 5000. Bodies being cremated as fast as found. Many bodies under débris not yet removed. Water supply limited. Very scarce now, but supplies coming in rapidly. The only means of communication is by railroad to Texas City, thence by boat, or by boat from Houston.'

"Dr. Wertenbaker is at Houston and Surgeon Peckham and Acting Assistant Surgeon Lea Hume are giving all the aid possible in Galveston. I do not apprehend an outbreak of any epidemic of disease as a result of the storm. The law and regulations are ample to meet the emergency.

"There is danger of sickness caused by unusual exposure and deprivation of food and water, but the people of Galveston and the Governor and other officials of the State and city appear to be thoroughly alive to the necessities of the situation. Their disposal of bodies by cremation is certainly a wise measure, and I am convinced that the native energy of the people, supplemented by the tents and rations furnished by the War Department, and the contributions which have been and are flowing in from all parts of the country, will obviate the outbreak of widespread disease.

"WALTER WYMAN,
"Supervising Surgeon General Marine Hospital Service."

WHOLE FAMILIES LOST.

Austin, Texas, Saturday.—Imagine, if you can, fifty thousand persons, many of them without clothing, all of them in immediate need of food and drink; motherless and fatherless children, men who have lost their families,—men, women and children all dazed from one of the greatest calamities of the time, and you can have some slight idea of the conditions existing at Galveston and all over the country along the Gulf contiguous to the storm centre of last Saturday and Sunday.

"The most harrowing reports have been brought to Governor Sayers by dozens of relief committees, which have been pouring in here from all the cities along the coast pleading for assistance. In response to an invitation from the Governor a special committee of Galveston citizens, headed by Major Skinner, of the Galveston Cotton Exchange, arrived for consultation with Governor Sayers.

VAST AMOUNT OF WORK TO BE DONE.

"The Relief Committee reported to the Governor that the city authorities would prefer that the city remain under the command of State Adjutant-General Scurry for the time being at least; that he not only be allowed to superintend the patrolling of the city, but that he be placed in charge of the sanitary work as well, and that he be allowed to hire 2000 laborers from other portions of the State, as the laborers in Galveston had their own homes to look after.

" Governor Sayers will not only secure the importation of 2000 outside laborers for sanitary work, but he will recognize any drafts made by Chairman Seeley, of the local Galveston Relief Committee, for such moneys as he may want from time to time, and in such quantities as are necessary, the same to be expended under the exclusive control of the chairman and the local Finance Committee of Galveston.

"In addition to the Galveston plea for assistance, several relief committees from other points were entertained by the Governor. The one from Velasco, following the Galveston committee, stated that there were 2000 destitute there. Alvin reported 8000 in the neighborhood. The Columbia District reported 2500, and several other towns reported in proportion, Fort Bend County coming with a report of some 15,000 in that county alone.

"In view of these reports Governor Sayers ordered bacon and flour to be sent to Galveston, Richmond, Fort Bend, Angleton, Velasco and Alvin in quantities ranging from 200,000 pounds of flour and 100,000 pounds of bacon for Galveston, to 5000 pounds of the former and 20,000 pounds of the latter as an emergency supply for Alvin. More supplies will follow at once."

Says one of our great newspapers:

" Galveston is showing the same splendid courage as Chicago thirty years ago, before a less dire calamity, and the country as a whole is displaying the same liberality. The Galveston News undoubtedly speaks for the city and the citizens in declaring that the city will be rebuilt and protected. Its channel, as one slight recompense, has been deepened to thirty feet. There remains its protection by sea walls. and here the General Government might well deal liberally with the stricken city. Whatever Galveston port needs to protect and prevent the city from another tidal wave ought, and we do not doubt will, be the liberal care of Congress next winter.

"Much more remains. The insurance companies rebuilt Chicago, and furnished the city with working building capital. Galveston has no such resource. Like Johnstown the city has to be rebuilt and the houses refitted. In the great flood of 1889 this was rendered possible because all the great flood of relief was managed, methodized and economically directed by the Johnstown Relief Commission, acting for the State. This prevented waste, gathered together all aid and successfully rebuilt, refurnished and re-equipped the destroyed homes.

" The Galveston disaster needs a like body. Food and shelter will before long be provided. This is but a beginning. Contributions are pouring out all over the country and organized work has not yet begun. Any sum really needed by Galveston can be raised if it is asked by an authoritative body, able to speak definitely and with precision of the losses sustained by churches, hospitals, institutions and individuals, and competent to distribute relief with efficiency and economy. If Texas and Galveston put such a body before the country in complete control the desultory giving already begun will be succeeded by organized, systematic contributions equal to the great need, great as it is."

CHAPTER X.

Details of the Overwhelming Tragedy—The Whole City
Caught in the Death-Trap—Personal Experiences
of Those Who Escaped—First Reports
More Than Confirmed.

THE centre of the West Indian hurricane, which had been predicted for several days, struck Galveston at 9 o'clock Saturday morning. At that hour the wind was in the north and the
waters of the bay were rising rapidly. The Gulf was also turbulent, and the water, forced in by the tropical storm, rolled up the
beach and gradually swept inland. About 2 o'clock P. M. the
wind was rising rapidly, constantly veering, but settling towards
the east and coming in fitful jerks and puffs, which loosened
awnings, cornices, slated roofs and sent the fragments flying in
the air.

The waters of the bay continued rising and creeping ashore,
mingled with the waters from the clouds, and filled the downtown streets and invaded stores. Despite the danger from flying
missiles, as the afternoon wore on, men ventured out in the streets
in hacks, in wagons, in boats and on foot, some anxious to get
home to their families, some bent on errands of mercy, and others
animated by no purpose save bravado.

Gaining in velocity, the wind changed to the northeast, then
to the east, and the waters rose until they covered the city. The
wind howled frightfully around the buildings, tearing off
cornices and ripping off roofs. The wooden paving blocks rose
from their places in the streets and floated off in great sections
down the streets.

At 6.30 o'clock the wind had shifted to the southeast, still
increasing in velocity. At that hour the wind gauge on the roof
of the United States Weather Bureau registered eighty-four miles
an hour then blew away. Still the wind blew harder and
harder and even the most fortunate houses lost all or a part

191

of their coverings. The storm reached its height at about 8.30 o'clock, At 9 o'clock the wind began subsiding and the waters to recede.

But the fury of the storm had not been spent until well into Sunday morning. At 1 o'clock the water had fallen until the streets were inundated no more than they would be by a big rain. Sunday morning broke clear, and the sun shone brightly on a scene of wreck and ruin, which verily beggars description.

The streets were piled with debris, in many places several feet high. Buildings were shorn of roofs, cornices, chimneys and windows. Stocks of goods were damaged by floods from below and rain from above. But it was the wind which had wrought the greatest havoc in every respect. The damage from waters of the bay was inconsequential when compared with that from wind. The eastern part of the city received the full force of the storm and suffered most, although no section escaped serious injury.

FRANTIC PEOPLE HUNTING RELATIVES.

All along the beach for about four blocks back scarcely a residence was left. The beach district was shorn of habitations. Back of that houses and timbers piled up, crushing other buildings which lay in their path. Men and women walked through the slimy mud that overspread the streets, homeless. Men and women rushed around frantic, hunting their relatives. Dead and wounded men, women and children lay around waiting the coming of the volunteer [corps organized to remove the bodies to improvised morgues and hospitals. There was no thought of property damage ; those who had escaped with their families, losing all else, felt satisfied and thanked their Maker.

Mr. A. V. Kellogg, a civil engineer in the employ of the Right of Way Department of the Houston and Texas Central Railroad in Houston, went down to Galveston Saturday morning on company business, leaving on the Galveston, Houston and Henderson train which departs from Houston at 9.45. Mr. Kellogg had an interesting tale of his experiences getting into

PHOTOGRAPH BY MORRIS, GALVESTON

INMATES OF THE HOME FOR HOMELESS CHILDREN, GALVESTON—ALL OF THESE LITTLE ONES WERE LOST IN THE FLOOD

RUINS AT TWENTY FIRST STREET AND AVENUE O ½

WRECK OF FORT CROCKET

PHOTO BY COURTESY
CHICAGO AMERICAN

AVENUE A IN "EAST END" OF GALVESTON—COLORADO AND SANTA FE RAILROAD TRACKS IN FOREGROUND

Galveston, of the storm and its effects and how he managed to get out of the city and into Houston again.

"When we crossed the bridge over Galveston Bay going to Galveston, said Mr. Kellogg, the water had reached an elevation equal to the bottom of the caps of the pile bents, or two feet below the level of the track. After crossing the bridge and reaching a point some two miles beyond we were stopped by reason of the washout of the track ahead and were compelled to wait one hour for a relief train to come out on the Galveston, Houston and Henderson track. During this period of one hour the water rose a foot and a half, running over the rails of the track.

"The relief train signaled us to back up a half mile to higher ground, where the passengers were transferred, the train crew leaving with the passengers and going on the relief train. The water had reached an elevation of eight or ten inches above the Galveston, Houston and Henderson track and was flowing in a westward direction at a terrific speed. The train crew were compelled to wade ahead of the engine and dislodge driftwood from the track. At 1.15 we arrived at the Santa Fe union depot. At that period of the day the wind was increasing and had then reached a velocity of about thirty-five miles an hour.

THE HOTEL FLOODED.

"After arriving at Galveston I immediately went to the Tremont Hotel, where I remained the balance of the day and during the night. At 5:30 the water had begun to creep into the rotunda of the hotel, and by 8 o'clock it was twenty-six inches above the floor of the hotel, or about six and one-half feet above the street level. The front windows of the hotel were blown in between the hours of 5 and 8. The roof was blown off and the skylights over the rotunda fell in and fell through, crashing on the floor below. The refugees began to come into the hotel between 5:30 and 8 o'clock until at least 800 or 1,000 persons had sought safety there. The floors were strewn with people all during the night.

"Manager George Korst and the employes of the hotel did everything in their power to help the sufferers from the effects of

13

the storm and to give them shelter. At 5 o'clock the wind was
blowing from the northeast at a velocity of about forty-five miles
an hour, and by 9 o'clock it had reached the climax, the velocity
then being fully 100 miles. The vibration of the hotel was not
unlike that of a boxcar in motion. I tried to sleep that night, but
there was so much noise and confusion from the crashing of buildings that I didn't get much rest.

STREET SIGHTS WERE APPALLING.

" I arose early Sunday morning. The sights in the streets
were simply appalling. The water on Tremont street had lowered
some eight feet from the high water mark, leaving the pavement
clear from two blocks north and six or seven blocks south of the
Tremont Hotel. The streets were full of debris, the wires were
all down and the buildings were in a very much damaged condition. Every building in the business district was damaged to
some extent but with one or two exceptions, and those, the Levy
Building, corner of Tremont and Market, and the Union Depot,
both of which remained intact and went through the storm without
a scratch.

" The refugees came pouring down into the heart of the city,
many of them had but little clothing, and scores of them were
almost naked.

They were homeless without food or drink, a great many had
lost their all and were really in destitute circumstances. Mayor
Jones issued a call for a mass meeting, which was held Sunday
morning at 9 o'clock and was attended by a large number of
prominent citizens. Steps were taken to furnish provisions and
relieve the suffering of the refugees and to bury the dead.

" Early in the morning it was learned that the water supply
had been cut off for some unknown reason. I presume that it
was caused by the English ship which was blown up against the
bridges, cutting the pipes. At all events, the city is without
water, and something should be done by the citizens of Houston
to relieve this situation. People who had depended on cisterns,
of course, had their resources swept away, and there are but few

large reservoirs of rain water to be found in the business district.

"The scene on the docks was a terrible one. The small working fleet and the larger schooners were washed over the docks and railroad tracks in frightful confusion. The Mallory docks were demolished. The elevators were torn in shreds. Three ocean liners were anchored off the docks and seemed to be in good condition. The damage to the shipping interests is simply immense, the Huntington improvement being entirely swept away.

FRIGHTFUL CONFUSION EVERYWHERE.

"I tried to get out of the town as quick as I could, and suc-ceeded in securing passage on the first sloop which sailed, which happened to be the 'Annie Jane,' Captain Thomas Willoughby, who afterward proved to be an excellent sailor. We sailed from the Twenty-second street slip at 11 o'clock, with seven souls aboard. When we got outside the harbor we found it was blowing a terrific gale and the sea running very high. Under three reefs and the peak down we set our course for North Galveston. As we passed Pelican Flats we could see the English steamer anchored off over toward where the railroad bridge should be, and came to the conclusion that she had evidently broken the water mains and cut the supply off from the city.

"Another ocean liner could be seen off the shore of Texas City, in what would seem to have been about two feet of water in normal tide. We passed within a few hundred yards of where the Half-moon light house once stood, but could see no evidence of the light house, it being completely washed away. The waters of the bay were strewn with hundreds of carcasses of dead animals. We had a very hazardous passage, going against a five mile tide running out, but managed to reach North Galveston at 1.35.

"At North Galveston we found that a tidal wave had crossed the peninsula, carrying destruction in its path. The factory building and the opera house were completely blown down and other buildings destroyed. While there were no deaths reported at North Galveston, there were many hardships endured by those who battled with the elements."

Dr. I. M. Cline, the chief of the weather bureau at Galveston, lived on the south side of Avenue Q, between Twenty-Fifth and Twenty-Sixth streets, in a strongly built frame house. It stood until houses all around it had gone down, and at last it had to give under the pressure of the wind and waves and other houses that were thrown against it, and with it about forty people went down, two-thirds of whom were drowned, among the number his wife. The first floor was elevated above the high water mark of 1875, and Dr. Cline though he was safe there.

He left his office and went to his home and family early in the afternoon. The office telephone had been in use nearly all the morning giving warning to the people who called up from exposed points along the beach to ask about the outlook. One man was posted at the telephone nearly every minute of the time, and to each inquiry the answer was sent over the wire, "The worst is not over yet."

LIVES SAVED BY FLIGHT.

Barometer readings of this tropical terror had not been taken since it left Havana and Key West, for the reason that it was travelling across the gulf and after barometer readings could have been taken nearer Galveston and reported here communication was shut off. But the weather bureau knew the worst was not over, and so perhaps thousands along the beach had warning and sought safety in the center of the island before the storm broke here in its fury. This partly accounts for so many people who lived right on the beach, whole families in instances, being saved, people who lost everything but who saved their lives. while others who lived in stronger buildings nearer in, some of whom had passed through the 1875 and other storms though of course they could weather it, and thus were lost.

When the waters rushed into Dr. Cline's home and began to rise rapidly he realized his peril, but it was then too late to escape. His brother, also of the weather bureau, Mr. Joe Cline, came to his rescue to help save the family or perish with them. Standing on his brother's front porch Mr. Cline motioned to the neighbors on the opposite side of the street to go north, meaning to get out, for no voice could be heard across the street in the teeth of that terrible northeaster.

This was the last warning that was given, and then the chief of the Weather Bureau, while with his devoted brother and their loved ones disappeared within their own homes to await their doom. It was not many hours coming. Higher and higher the water rose, and they mounted the second floor till the waves mounted higher, and buildings about them crashed and fell, adding to the number of inmates of the houses others who had been driven out and were seeking safety.

Finally, the building gave way beneath the pressure of the wreckage behind it. The Cline family was in the room and had resolved to go by threes. Dr. Cline had with him Mrs. Cline and their little 6-year-old girl, Esther. His brother, Joe, took charge of the two older girls. As the house went over Mr. Joe Cline and his charges were thrown through a window which they were near and they caught on the roof. A dresser pushed Dr. Cline and his wife against the mantle and his little one was knocked from his left arm. They were all pinioned beneath the roof.

FOUND IT WAS THE FOOT OF HIS BABY.

Dr. Cline, holding to his wife, prepared for death, but throwing his left hand above his head, felt something strike his hand He grabbed the object and it proved to be one foot of his baby that had been knocked from his grasp when the roof fell in. The water had driven her little body to the surface through an opening, which, although in an almost dying condition, he realized. By some means—he doesn't know how—he was released from the timbers that held him down, and he, too, was sent up by the rush of water to the surface. With his feet and arms he reached for his wife, who had been torn from his grasp, but he could not find her, and so she perished. Their experience in drifting on debris was that of hundreds of others. For hours they were tossed about on the raging sea. Part of the time they think they were far out in the Gulf. They know they were out of sight of lights and buildings much of the time.

Mr. William Blair, a member of the Screwmen's Association, with a party of twelve, took in what he said to be the first boat that carried news from the mainland. The trip this party made was one of the most heroic on record. Mr. Blair said :

ONE LONE HOUSE STANDING.

"We were caught in Houston in the storm, and Sunday morning as soon as the storm abated we resolved to get to our families and friends in Galveston, if such a thing was possible. A party of twelve of us left Houston on a Southern Pacific train. We got as far as Seabrook and there we found everything washed away, and dead bodies here and there. One lone house was standing. Clear Creek bridge had been washed away and the railroad track was turned over. We went back to Houston and waited there till 4.40 P. M., and took the Galveston, Houston and Henderson regular train and succeeded in getting as far as Lamarque.

"The whole country was under water, but we decided to get to Galveston any way that night. We pulled out towards Virginia Point, wading in water up to our necks, some times swimming. At one place it got so deep that we got a lot of drift together and constructed a sort of a raft and ferried over the places. I was about to forget to tell you that one of our party was a woman, a Miss Beach. She had a sick sister in Galveston at the infirmary and she had determined to get to her if possible. That brave and fearless women kept up with the men wading and swimming, and while others lagged and some dropped out along the way, she never once faltered, and I have never before seen her equal for courage and determination.

"There were six of us when we got to Virginia Point, others had turned out toward Texas City. We got as near to Virginia Point as we could, we found three railroad engines there, one of them turned over. There were some cars scattered along the track and in one caboose were some injured people. A portion of our party stopped there to do what they could for them.

"We found dead bodies all along the track, three and four in a bunch, all women and children with perhaps the single exception of one man. These bodies were strewn from the Point to Texas City and they were there by the hundreds, it seemed to me—bodies of people who had been washed and blown across the bay from Galveston. Some of the people who had made that terrible trip across the bay, driven by the force of the wind and the waves, were yet alive.

"There were all sorts of debris and wreckage piled up and washing along the mainland; furniture of every description, heavy iron, frames of pianos, fine plush-covered furniture—everything was there to be seen. The remains of cattle and horses and chickens were there in heaps and piles, drifting boxcars had been driven three miles from their original positions and turned over and blown about.

GATHERING UP THE DEAD.

"Monday, as soon as it was light enough to see, we started out looking for skiffs—something to take us to Galveston. We did not find a skiff, all had been stove in. At last we found a negro who had a boat. He had been crippled. Three of us, Miss Beach among the number, took passage on his boat, and I took charge of it. The remainder of our party stayed at Virginia Point until the arrival of a sailboat and brought a relief party to Galveston from Houston. A relief train had arrived, from Houston, bringing members of the fire department, the health officer and county officers, with provisions. They saw that there was no way for them to cross and so they remained and began the work of gathering and bringing the dead on the mainland.

"The concrete piers of the county bridge we found washed away in mainland and we saw a big steamer grounded in the West Bay. We saw a fine boat about thirty feet long that had made the trip without sailor or rudder from Galveston. In that boat I was told a drowning family took refuge.   When they were nearly over a wave struck it and threw all its occupants out except one man, and he landed in safety.   Claude G. Pond, who was with Capt. Plummer's life boat during the storm, estimates that they saved 200 people in the east end from drowning.

"They began work Saturday afternoon at 2 o'clock and kept it up as long as they could do any good in the east end from First street to St. Mary's Infirmary.   Capt. Plummer waded in water up to his chin, and in places was swimming, directing the movements of the boat, while Mr. Pond and Capt. Plummer's two sons manned the boat.

CLUNG TO THEIR PROPERTY.

"Several places they extended rescue and the people declined to go expressing the belief that their peril was not so great, and preferring to remain with their property.   Sometimes they would make the second trip to such places and sometimes the occupants would be saved and in other instances they had tarried too long. Their plan was to carry people into places where they could wade out and leave them, going back to bring others to shallow water and on the return again carrying them further in.

"In cases where parents had been carried out to wading water and deposited, they would stand there instead of pushing on, looking back for their children, and it sometimes happened that the children and parents both went down while one waited for the other, when, if the parents had pushed on after they had reached wading water, all might have been saved.

"One of the last loads carried out was about to land in front of St. Mary's Infirmary, when a piece of falling timber struck the boat and capsized it.   They had eight or nine people in the boat, and when they succeeded in righting it they could find only two or three.

"Mr. Mennis and a party of about forty people took refuge in a two-story grocery store at Forty-fifth street and Broadway. When the roof went over and the building went to pieces, Mr. Mennis and six others caught on drift.   They were driven toward the beach into the gulf, and when the wind veered to the southeast and later south, they were driven across the bay and landed on the mainland near Texas City. Of the seven who made this terrible voyage two died in the course of a day. Mr. Mennis lost his mother and two brothers.

"In the vicinity of Texas City sixty bodies supposed to be from Galveston have been buried. Nearly all were women. There was no means of identification, except possibly by jewelry, which was found on about one-half of the bodies."

Prof. Fred. W. Mally reached Houston three days after the storm, and in reply to inquiries related some thrilling experiences. He had been out at Booth, in Fort Bend County. He boarded the 7.15 P. M. Santa Fe train.

TREETOPS INTERRUPTED PROGRESS OF TRAINS.

"At Thompson," said Prof. Mally, "the train crew stopped to water and cool off a hot box, and by the time we started again the wind was blowing a gale. There is no wagon road along the windward side of the right of way from Thompson to Duke or Clear Lake. The result was that as we passed along we were kept in constant suspense of disaster by the treetops, which were being bent over so as to rasp the windows as the train passed on.

"At several places we had to stop and cut off the tops of all trees in order to get through. We finally reached Duke, which was out in the open and prairie section. Here it was impossible to proceed farther, and the train stopped to await the end of the storm. We remained here until about 3 o'clock in the morning and tried to get to Alvin. The first station out was Arcola. The dwellings in this locality were a complete wreck, and only the depot remained standing.

A TOWN IN RUINS.

"At Manvel, the next station, the ruin seemed even worse. The depot had been completely demolished and was laying across the track. Not a house standing in good condition. We came down farther within three miles of Alvin and found the track washed out. The agent from Alvin and the section boss met us and stated that Alvin was in ruins and some killed. Not being able to get through, we backed up the road, hoping to reach Eichenberg.

"The sight of seeing men, women and children wading waist deep in water over a country where we were accustomed to seeing orchards and garden patches and to hear the cries for the dear ones missing is enough to unnerve the strongest. Returning to Duke we unloaded again those we had saved at that point from the storm.

"While our train of five passenger coaches was standing on the track at this point the house in which the agent was living was literally blown to pieces. His wife and three children were with him, and soon the furious wind was tossing and rolling women and children like footballs over the earth. Men from the train faced the terrible gale and succeeded in getting all on the train in safety. This house stood within seventy-five yards of our train. About this time the depot, which was just opposite the car I was in, was unroofed and split apart in the middle.

WHOLE FAMILY SAVED BY TRAINMEN.

"Soon after a third house, 200 feet away. was blown to pieces and a man, wife and three children saved from the wreckage by those on the train. We reached the timbered section and were soon blocked by the wreckage of fallen trees across the track. Everyone who could wield an axe got one, set to work diligently to cut our way through. At the same time a large crew was working from Rosenberg down toward us. From Thompson to Duke large pecan, elm, oak and pine trees were encountered on an average every 100 feet.

"Arriving at Thompson, we found Slavin's store a perfect mass of ruin, the gin a partial wreck and many houses blown down. Here the first victim of the storm and train was placed on board. He had been knocked off the track the night before and had his leg broken. At Booth, Booth's store was badly wrecked, trees blown all over the land, several houses blown down. One negro was killed in a falling house. At Crabb everything was blown down, and we reached Rosenberg at noon.

"We had many dire expectations all night, worked hard all morning and had nothing to eat since supper the night before. I reached Houston over the Macaroni in time to reach my nurseries and people at Hulen. I found only one house standing here intact, my large barn and packing shed are damaged but not wrecked. My large office building was blown from its foundation and considerably twisted, but left it so my manager can live in it with his family until something else can pe provided for. None of my employees were hurt, and, in fact. no deaths or injuries at Hulen."

TERRIBLE TALES OF VANDALISM.

Passengers who arrived at Dallas told terrible tales of the work of the vandals in that city. According to them, men inflamed with liquor were roaming among the wreckage over the city rifling the hundreds of bodies of even the clothing and leaving them to fester in the semi-tropical sun. Much of this horrible depredating, it is claimed, is being done by negroes, who will not work and cannot be made to leave town. This was before the saloons were closed.

Among those who arrived from Galveston was J. N. Griswold, division freight agent of the Gulf, Colorado and Sante Fe Railway. His story is as follows :

"There were many acts of vandalism. Fingers and ears that bore diamonds were lopped off with knives. Upon our arrival at Texas city I saw an old man who was drunk. Sticking out of a pocket in his pants was a bank deposit book full of bank notes.

"I asked him where he got it. He said he fouud it on the bank.

"'How much have you got?' I asked him. "Oh, about twenty-seven dollars,' was his reply. He must have had several times that amount at least.

"The darkies are doing most of the pilfering. Sunday morning before daylight they were breaking into warehouses and looting stores and saloons particularly. The town was full of drunken negroes Sunday morning at daylight.

"And the worst of it is that nearly all the soldiers were lost. Of the detachment stationed at Galveston I don't believe there are more than thirty left. At present the crying need of Galveston is water and ice—and soldiers. The fresh water on the island was ruined by the brine from the sea. The ice is needed to prevent the decomposition of the corpses. The soldiers are needed to keep down vandalism. And along this latter line I want to say that the militia must come quickly. The negroes should be sent to the cotton fields of north Texas. Those who will work can be kept there, but the others should be sent away just as soon as possible, for they merely eat up the supplies and are a constant menace. They should either be killed or made to get out, for one or the other is the grim necessity of the situation.

FLOATING BODIES IN THE BAY.

"As to the loss of life in Galveston, I can't figure it. We counted ninety-three floating bodies on our way from the wharf to Texas City. The prairies across the bay this side of Galveston are covered with piles of cotton and wreckage of all descriptions—dead bodies and the like.

"I got to Galveston at 10 o'clock Saturday morning. My wife and I took a car and started to the beach. The water was rather high and we thought we would have a jolly good time splashing around. When we got within five blocks of the beach the motorman stopped his car and said that he could go no further. We came back downtown and got on another car. This time we could get within but seven blocks of the beach. This shows you how fast the water was rising.

"We got back to the Santa Fe ticket office about 11.30 o'clock. I made up my mind that I wanted to go over to the general offices, but the water was in all the streets and I waited awhile, hoping it would get lower. But at noon it was between knee and hip deep in front of the Santa Fe ticket office. At 2 o'clock my wife and I waded into the Washington Hotel.

"From that time on the wind grew stronger. At 5 o'clock the water was six feet deep in the lower floor of the Washington Hotel. Why, it covered the telephone box in the office. The wind blew not less than ninety-five miles an hour from then until 9.30 o'clock.

"The first rise came from the bay, and the bay rise lasted until about 8 P. M. Then the tide from the Gulf met the rise from the bay and forced it back. That's when we had our highest water. And I want to say to you right now that but for those two forces meeting there wouldn't be a stick left on Galveston Island to-day.

"About 9 o'clock the water commenced to fall rapidly, and at 10 o'clock the wind had subsided fully 50 per cent. The damage had all been done. At daylight we got out and went down to the beach. From the beach back for four or five blocks it was just as clean as this floor. Up and down the island there was wreckage as high as this ceiling. This had something to d with breaking the force of the water. And that wreckage was full of dead bodies. The only way to get rid of it is to burn it with the bodies in it, for they can never be taken out.

MAKING A HURRIED ESCAPE.

"Monday at noon we left the wharf on the sailboat 'Lake Austin' in company with five others. We paid $100 for passage to Texas City. The names of those in the party were, J. A. Kemp, of Wichita Falls; Henry Sayles, of Abilene; A. W. Boyd, of Houston; W. A. Frazer, of Dallas, and myself and my wife. Mrs. Griswold was the first woman to leave the island after the disaster. We landed at Texas City at 2.30, caught the Texas Terminal Railway to a junction with the Galveston, Houston and Henderson. From there we walked for a mile to where they were repairing the track, and caught a freight train into Houston, arriving about 10.30 at night.

"The buildings in Galveston that are not totally wrecked are damaged in such a manner that I believe it will cost as much to repair them a; it would to build new ones outright. There is not a church left standing. The general offices of the Santa Fe are badly wrecked. On the floor next to the top some of the inside door casings are forced out of the frames, and the entire building will have to be replastered before it will be safe to occupy. The train sheds are gone.

"On the Mallory wharves is a conglomerated pile of boxcars and boats and cotton wreckage of every description. The Mallory liner 'Comal' arrived there just after the storm, and, thank goodness, the crew has sense enough to stay on board the boat. Dead bodies are in all the wreckage under the wharf just like dead rats. The Santa Fe officials and the heads of the different departments in the general offices, so far as reported, are all safe. The families of a good many of the clerks have been lost entirely, and in other instances partially so.

"The Blum family came to the Washington Hotel at daylight Sunday morning with nothing on them but shreds. They had lost everything. When they left home they had thousands of dollars worth of diamonds on their persons. These were all lost in their battle with the elements. Their bodies were a mass of bruises.

"There is scarcely a stock of goods in Galveston that isn't a total loss. But the Sealy residence, standing even as it does, where it seems as if the slightest breeze would strike it, hasn't a scratch on it.

ENTIRE FAMILIES LOST.

"The brother of John Paul Jones, the general agent of our road, lost his entire family. Will Labatt, assistant ticket agent of the Santa Fe, lost his entire family, with the exception of his wife, who is visiting in the North. He turned up Sunday morning at 6 o'clock more dead than alive and covered with bruises and cuts.

"John Paul Jones, the general agent of the Santa Fe, succeeded in saving his family. His wife was very sick, but he saved her by swimming accross the street with his child on his head and his wife between himself and another person.

"Mr. Crane, chief rate clerk to the general freight agent of the road, spent the entire night with his wife on the roof of his residence. His wife had been confined about six weeks ago, and in addition had an abscess on her leg, which bent it nearly double. They were saved. He was a mass of bruises. His heel was crushed.

"I don't see how any man who passed Saturday night in Galveston can stay there and make it his home."

W. A. Fraser, of Dallas, general deputy of the Woodmen of the World of Texas, arrived in Dallas from Galveston where he had been for several days. He stated that complete as are the reports published in "The News," the half has not been told of the terrible calamity that has visited the coast country. "On the approach of the storm," he said, "I tried to leave on the International and Great Northern Railroad at 1.30 o'clock, but found that the bridges had been washed away and the water had risen to such an extent that it was impossible for me to get away from the depot, where I took shelter with about 150 other persons who had sought the same place of refuge.

THE CRIES OF THE DYING.

"The depot was badly damaged, but no lives were lost there, although bodies were floating in every direction and the cries from the dying could be heard almost constantly. When daybreak came Sunday morning the sights presented were something terrible. It was hardly possible to walk along the streets without tumbling over dead bodies, and the only thing, in my estimation, that saved the city from being completely wiped out was the fact that the wind blew from the bay during the first part of the night —blowing the water up through town, in some places as high as fifteen feet—and the wreckage from destroyed houses was piled up along the Gulf front to a height of forty or fifty feet. When the wind changed and blew from the Gulf this wreckage acted as a breakwater and kept the waves from washing everything into the bay.

" As soon as daylight appeared the work of rescue commenced, but it was soon found that after several vacant stores and all the undertaking establishments had been crowded with the dead, that it would be impossible to handle them in this way. Barges were employed and into them the wagons unloaded the bodies, which were taken to the bay and there deposited. It can be safely said that there is not a single house in the entire town that has not been badly damaged in some way and there are whole families who will never be heard from again.

"Looting and vandalism are rife upon the island. The few soldiers they have are exhausted and unable to properly guard the city, and in my estimation the State troops should be sent there at once. Cases of where the fingers of women had been cut off so as to deprive them of their rings and their ears cut to get the ear-rings are common. It is a hard matter to get a negro to assist in any way in burying the dead, as they all seem to be very much interested in accumulating all the wealth they can possibly get from the dead and from the wreckage.

WHITE MEN AND NEGROES PLUNDER TOGETHER.

"They are not alone in this, but I am sorry to say that white men are side by side with them in their damnable work. Women could be seen on the first morning after the flood with baskets over their arms taking everything they could possibly pick up, without regard to whom it belonged to or what its value might be. What the city needs most, in my estimation, is pure water, food and able-bodied men who are willing to work, so the bodies can be removed from the wreckage and carried from the island and the carcasses of animals be burned or disposed of as quickly as possi-ble. Whatever is to be done should be done at the earliest pos-ble moment, as provisions are scarce and it is next to impossible to get fresh water. The sewerage system is also choked, and this combined with the stenches from decaying animal matter makes it almost impossible for people to exist for many days.

"Immediately on my arrival here a meeting of the Woodmen was called and $200 in cash subscribed and turned over to me, and about $300 more pledged to be placed in my hands on demand. All camps throughout the State are requested to immediately call

EXTERIOR VIEW OF ST. PATRICK'S CHURCH, WHICH WAS DEMOLISHED

WRECKAGE AT CENTRE STREET, LOOKING NORTH FROM AVENUE 6½

RUINS OF PUBLIC SCHOOL, TWENTY-FIFTH STREET AND AVENUE P

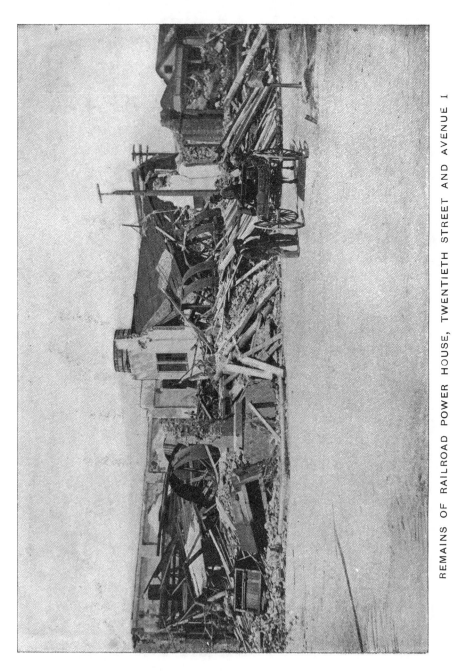

REMAINS OF RAILROAD POWER HOUSE, TWENTIETH STREET AND AVENUE I

meetings and forward such subscriptions as they may see proper to me at Dallas. This will be used for the benefit of Woodmen and their families, many of whom are in absolute want and distress, and we hope to raise at least $30,000, which is less than $1 each from our members."

From Houston came the following heartrending news of the Galveston horror two days after it occurred :

"The dreadful fatality of Galveston is looking worse, in the face of facts brought out to-day. Three men, who reached here this morning, tell of so and so many dead bodies being found in a single house or yard or on one block, that the conclusion is almost irresistible that a greater number than 1000 has been lost. They tell that twenty or forty or a hundred were lost by the collapse of a single large house, they having gathered there for safety, but they are unable to say anything about the hundreds of small houses that were swept away, some vacant, of course, but many occupied, but without a mark, a sign or a memory to recall the lost.

NAMES OF DEAD WILL NEVER BE KNOWN.

"The outline of the terrible disaster is now known over the United States, and even farther. The details are wanting; no list of names approaching completeness can be had for weeks, and it is almost sure that a complete list will never be found. As time wears along the names of different persons will be recalled by those who were neighbors, and they will be set down on the death roll that will be made up ; but where neighbors do not know neighbors, the names will never be called, and the identity of the lost will pass with eternity—without recall or remembrance.

"This city and her people are devoting themselves assiduously to relieving the unfortunates. Her business men are losing not a moment. They thoroughly realize that seconds are valuable. Last night large wagons jostled along the streets with boxes of prepared food to load them on boats and cars. The Mayor has sent out calls to the large cities of this and other

14

States for immediate help, and everybody here feels that the response will be generous and speedy. These people know the justness of their demand, and hence their confidence in getting the answer.

"W. O. Ansley, a well known cotton man of this city, received a letter this morning, brought by private messenger, from A. W. Simpson, a cotton man at Galveston, saying:

"'It's awful. Not a complete house in the city. Help urgently needed. Thousands are homeless. Food is being distributed to the destitute, but lots more will be needed.'"

MISSING ONES SWELL DEATH LIST.

A newspaper writer who got through from Galveston, made the following statement: "The condition at Galveston is heart-rending in the extreme for the injured, and it grows worse momentarily. The list of the dead will not be fully known for weeks ; the list of the missing will swell rapidly as soon as the people have begun to report their losses to the authorities, and gradually this list of missing will change into the list of dead as the bodies are recovered from the ruins in the city or are picked up on the beach of the mainland, where many of them now lie, it is believed. A meeting was held Sunday morning at the Tremont Hotel, and at this meeting measures were considered for the relief of the stricken.

"The conclusion was quickly reached that the citizens are not equal to the task, notwithstanding their willingness, and an appeal for aid was made to the President and the Governor. The messages have already gone to them, and will probably be made public all over the country by this afternoon. But no tardy aid will suffice. It is present necessity that must be met."

H. Van Eaton, who travels for a Dallas firm, arrived from Galveston, where he spent the perilous hours during the storm. He reached that city Saturday morning and was unable to cross to the mainland until Sunday afternoon.

"Just after it started to rain," he said last night, "several of us thought we would walk down to the beach, but on seeing our danger decided to return to the hotel, which we succeeded in doing by wading in water waist deep.   Inside of a few minutes the women and children began to come to the hotel for refuge. All were panic stricken.   I saw two women, one with a child, trying to get to the hotel.   They were drowned within three hundred yards of us.

"After the worst was over in Galveston we went over to Virginia Point, which cost us $15 each.   When we got over there we found a caboose and an engine chained together with some twenty-five people in it.   While we were in the caboose three bodies, two men and a child, drifted against the car and we tied them to one end to keep them from floating away.   We saw fourteen bodies there, all having floated across the channel and all more or less disfigured from coming in contact with so much wreckage. Most of them were women and children.

"We walked six miles from Virginia Point, swimming at intervals, in order to catch the relief train, which could not come in further from washouts.   We met people coming and going.   A party of twelve persons, including one woman, had built a raft and were intending to cross to Galveston.   We saw three launches six miles inland, north of Virginia Point on the bald prairie. Only one of them seemed to have anyone in it.   We reached Houston at 3.30 this morning.   There are only two houses in anything like perfect condition between Houston and Galveston. From Houston up to Hearne things were badly torn up.   The whole east end of Galveston and the entire west end are completely gone."

CHAPTER XI.

Galveston Calamity One of the Greatest Known to History—Many Thousands Maimed and Wounded— Few Heeded the Threatening Hurricane—The Doomed City Turned to Chaos.

GALVESTON has been the scene of one of the greatest catastrophies in the world's history. The story of the great storm of Saturday, Sept. 8, 1900, will never be told. Words are too weak to express the horror, the awfulness of the storm itself, to even faintly picture the scene of devastation, wreck and ruin, misery, suffering and grief. Even those who were miraculously saved after terrible experiences, who were spared to learn that their families and property had been swept away, and spared to witness scenes as horrible as the eye of man ever looked upon—even these can not tell the story.

There are stories of wonderful rescues and escapes, each of which at another time would be a marvel to the rest of the world, but in a time like this when a storm so intense in its fury, so prolonged in its work of destruction, so wide in its scope, and so infinitely terrible in its consequences has swept an entire city and neighboring towns for miles on either side, the mind can not comprehend all of the horror, can not learn or know all of the dreadful particulars.

One stands speechless and powerless to relate even that which he has felt and knows. Gifted writers have told of storms at sea wrecking of vessels where hundreds were at stake and lost. That task pales to insignificance when compared with the task of telling of a storm which threatened the lives of perhaps sixty thousand people, sent to their death perhaps six thousand people, and left others wounded, homeless, and destitute, and still others to cope with grave responsibility, to relieve the stricken, to grapple with and prevent the anarchist's reign, to clear the water-sodden land

212

of putrefying bodies and dead carcasses, to perform tasks that try men's souls and sicken their hearts.

The storm at sea is terrible, but there are no such dreadful consequences as those which have followed the storm on the sea coast and it is men who passed through the terrors of the storm, who faced death for hours, men ruined in property and bereft of families, who took up the herculean and well-nigh impossible task of bringing order out of chaos, of caring for the living and disposing of the dead before they made life impossible here.

The storm came not without warning, but the danger which threatened was not realized, not even when the storm was upon the city. Friday night the sea was angry. Saturday morning it had grown in fury, and the wrecking of the beach resorts began. The waters of the Gulf hurried inland. The wind came at terrific rate from the north. Still men went to their business and about their work while hundreds went to the beach to witness the grand spectacle which the raging sea presented.

WATERS CREPT HIGHER AND HIGHER.

As the hours rolled on the wind gained in velocity and the waters crept higher and higher. The wind changed from the north to the northeast and the water came in from the bay, filling the streets and running like a millrace. Still the great danger was not realized. Men attempted to reach home in carriages, wagons, boats, or any way possible. Others went out in the storm for a lark. As the time wore on the water increased in depth and the wind tore more madly over the island.

Men who had delayed starting for home, hoping for an abatement of the storm, concluded that the storm had grown worse and went out in that howling, raging, furious storm, wading through water almost to their necks, dodging flying missiles swept by a wind blowing 100 miles an hour.

Still the wind increased in velocity, when, after it seemed impossible that it should be more swift, it changed from west to southeast, veering constantly, calming for a second and then coming with awful terrific jerks, so terrible in their power that no building could withstand them and none wholly escaped injury.

Others were picked up at sea. And all during the terrible storm acts of the greatest heroism were performed. Hundreds and hundreds of brave men, as brave as the world ever knew, buffeted with the waves and rescued hundreds of their fellow men. Hundreds of them went to their death, the death that they knew they must inevitably meet in their efforts. Hundreds of them perished after saving others. Men were exemplifying that supreme degree of love of which the Master spoke, "Greater love hath no man than this, that he give his life for his friend." Many of them who lost their lives in this storm in efforts to save their families, many to save friends, many more to help people of whom they had never heard. They simply knew that human beings were in danger and they counted their own lives

TREMENDOUS FURY OF THE GALE.

The maximum velocity of the wind will never be known. The gauge at the Weather Bureau registered 100 miles an hour and blew away at 5.10 o'clock, but the storm at that hour was as nothing when compared with what followed, and the maximum velocity must have been as great as 120 miles an hour. The most intense and anxious time was between 8.30 and 9 o'clock, with raging seas rolling around them, with a wind so terrific that none could hope to escape its fury, with roofs beginning to roll away and buildings crashing all around them, men, women and children were huddled in buildings, caught like rats, expecting to be crushed to death or drowned in the sea, yet cut off from escape.

Buildings were torn down, burying their hundreds, and were swept inland, piling up great heaps of wreckage. Hundreds of people were thrown into the water in the height of the storm, some to meet instant death, others to struggle for a time in vain, and thousands of others to escape death in most miraculous and marvelous ways.

Hundreds of the dead were washed across the island and the bay many miles inland. Hundreds of bodies were buried in the wreckage. Many who escaped were in the water for hours, clinging to driftwood, and landed bruised and battered and torn on the mainland.

All attempts at burying the dead has been utterly abandoned, and bodies are now being disposed of in the swiftest manner possible. Scores of them were burned the 12th, and hundreds were taken out to sea and thrown overboard. The safety of the living is now the paramount question, and nothing that will tend to prevent the outbreak of an awful pestilence is being neglected.

This morning it was found that large numbers of the bodies which had previously been thrown in the bay were washed back upon the shore and the situation was rendered worse than before they were first laden in the barges and thrown into the water.

TOO MANY ON THE COMMITTEE.

Relief committees from the interior of the State have commenced to arrive, and, as usual, they are much too large in numbers, and to a certain extent are in the way of the people of Galveston, and an impediment to the prompt relief which they themselves are so desirous of offering. Several of the relief expeditions have had committees large enough to consume 10 per cent. of the provisions which they brought. The relief sent here from Beaumont, Tex., arrived this morning and was distributed as fast as possible. It consisted of two carloads of ice and provisions, and came by way of Port Arthur.

The great trouble now seems to be that those people who are in the greatest need are, through no fault of those in charge of the distribution, the last to receive aid. Many of them are so badly maimed and wounded that they are unable to apply to the relief committee, and the committees are so overwhelmed by direct applications that they have been unable to send out messengers.

The wounded everywhere are still needing the attention of physicians, and despite every effort it is feared that a number will die because of the sheer physical impossibility to afford them the aid necessary to save their lives. Every man in Galveston who is able to walk and work is engaged in the work of relief with all the energy of which he is capable.   But, despite their utmost endeavors, they cannot keep up with the increase in the miserable conditions which surround them.   Water can be obtained by able-bodied men, but with great difficulty.

Dr. Wallace Shaw, of Houston, who is busily engaged in the relief work, said that there were 200 people at St. Mary's Infirmary without fresh water.   They had been making coffee of salt water and using that as their only beverage.   Very little stealing was reported and there were no killings.   The number of men shot down for robbing the dead proved a salutary lesson, and it is not expected that there will be any more occurrences of this sort.   The soldiers of the regular army and of the national guard are guarding the property, and it is impossible for thieves to escape detection.

SOLDIERS HAVE MIRACULOUS ESCAPE.

The loss of life among the soldiers of the regular army stationed in the barracks on the beach proves to have been largely overestimated.   The original report was that but fifteen out of the total number in the barracks on the beach had been saved.   Last night and to-day they turned up singly and in squads, and at present there are but twenty-seven missing, whereas the first estimate of casualties in this direction alone was nearly two hundred.   It it probable that some of the twenty-seven will answer roll call later in the week.

One soldier reached the city this afternoon who had been blown around in the Gulf of Mexico and had floated nearly fifty miles going and coming, on a door.   Another one who showed up to-day declared that he owed his life to a cow.   It swam with him nearly three miles.   The cow then sunk and the soldier swam the balance of the way to the mainland himself.

Efforts were made this afternoon to pick up the dead bodies that have floated in with the tide, after having been once cast into the sea.   This is awful work, and few men are found with sufficiently strong nerves to last it more than thirty minutes at a time. All of the bodies are badly decomposed, swollen to enormous proportions and of so dark a hue that it is possible to tell only by the hair, when any hair is visible, whether the corpses are those of white people or negroes.

Gen. McKibben U. S. A., and Adjt. Gen. Scurry arrived last night and have assumed entire charge of the city, with the result that conditions have very much improved as far as order and method in the distribution of supplies and the direction of the work is concerned. Gen. McKibben represents the government in a general way, but has not assumed direct charge of the city, which is under the command of Adjutant Gen. Scurry.

Several of the very young soldiers have been a trifle over-zealous in the matter of guarding the property, carrying their energy to a point which made it somewhat uncomfortable for the people whose property and person they came to guard. Gen. Scurry repressed them promptly and several of them have been disarmed. The service of the militia, on the whole, however, has so far been of a most excellent character.

SIGHT-SEERS BARRED OUT.

Every effort is being made to induce people to leave Galveston, and it is extremely difficult for anyone, no matter what his business, unless he is in direct charge of a relief train, to gain admittance to the place. Hundreds of people left Houston to-day for Galveston, but could get no further than Texas City, which is on the north side of Galveston Bay, and there they were compelled to remain until the train brought them back to Houston. No persuasion, no sum of money, would induce the guard to pass them into the stricken city.

Orders had been issued that no sightseers were to be allowed, and the order was obeyed with the utmost rigidity. It will be at least a week before there is full and free communication with Galveston, but matters are now steadily progressing toward a solution of the problems that confront the relief committee. Every effort is being made to induce people to leave, and one train, which arrived in Houston at 5 o'clock this evening, carried 350 women and children ; another at 10 o'clock carried twice as many

more, and it is expected that fully 2,000 of the women and chil-
cren will be out of the place by to-morrow night. Mayor Jones
estimates that there are at least 10,000 of these helpless ones
who should be taken from Galveston at the earliest possible
moment. They are all apparently anxious to get away and will
be handled as rapidly as possible.

Another trainload of provisions and clothing, making the
third within the last twenty-four hours, came here from Houston
to-night.

The steamer Charlotte Allen arrived at noon to-day from
Houston with 1000 loaves of bread and other provisions. The
amount of food which has been sent so far has been large, but
there are still in the neighborhood of 30,000 people to be cared
for on the island.

BOYS RESCUE FORTY PEOPLE.

During the storm Saturday night, the Boddinker boys, with
the aid of a hunting skiff, rescued over forty people and took
them to the University building, where they found shelter from
the wind and waves. The little skiff was pushed by hand, the
boys not being able to use oars or sticks in propelling it, and is
to be set aside in the University as a relic of the flood.

Many stories of heroism are coming out. People tell of getting out of their houses just before the roof fell in on them.
They tell of seeing people struck by flying timbers and crushed
to death before their eyes. One man was cut off from his family
just as he had them rescued, and saw them sink beneath the
water, just on the other side of the barrier. He turned in and
helped to rescue others who were about gone. One woman carried her five month's old baby in her arms from her house only
to have a beam strike the child on the head, killing it instantly.
She suffered a broken leg and bruised body.

The lightship, which was moored between the jetties at the
point where the harbor bar was located before it was removed, was
carried to Half Moon Shoal and grounded. There was nobody
aboard except Mate Emil C. Lundwall, the cook and two men.

She broke her moorings and with a 1500 pound anchor and 600 fathoms of 2-inch cable chain, drifted to the point where she grounded, a distance of about four miles.

The damage to the lightship was slight, consisting principally of broken windows. The mate showed himself to be a skillful seaman and managed to save the vessel by his skill as such.

Along the whole East Sealy avenue the oak trees have been partly dragged up by the roots and brittle chinaberry trees are practically all gone. All the tender plants have been washed out or broken down by debris or blown away literally. Not a tree is standing in its natural attitude. Not a building in the East end escaped injury. One or two, like that of Capt. Charles Clark, suffered but the loss of a few slat shingles while others were torn from their foundations.

TWISTED INTO ALL SORTS OF SHAPES.

They were carried around and twisted into such shapes that they can not be occupied again although they can be entered and the sodden furniture and bedclothing removed. This applies to buildings that are still standing. As stated, there is a vast territory of blocks in width on which there is not a vestige of a house standing, these having been blown down and carried away with the other debris.

Dr. J. T. Fry, who has been an observer of the weather for years, has a theory that the storm which visited Galveston originated in the vicinity of Port Eads, and was not the hurricane which was reported on the Florida coast. On Thursday a storm was reported moving in a northeasterly direction from Key West. It moved up the Atlantic coast. The Mallory steamer "Comal" ran into it and reported a great number of wrecks as was reported in the "News" at the time. The supposition that this was the same storm that reached Galveston by doubling back on its tracks is a mistake.

The first knowledge of the Galveston storm was the report of a wind velocity of forty-eight miles an hour at Port Eads on Sat-

urday morning. The "News" also reported high winds at Pass
Christian. The Port Eads storm was a distinct storm from that
of Florida and was confined to the Gulf. The proof of this is that
the steamer "Comal" came in from Florida in beautiful weather
and apparently followed in the wake of the storm.

Eighteen people were caught in the Grothger grocery store,
Sixteenth and N streets, and it is presumed all were lost, as many
have been reported dead who were known to have been in the
building which was swept away entirely. The firemen buried
twenty-six people south of Avenue O, between Thirty-Third and
and Forty-Second streets, on Tuesday. The graves were marked
with pieces of the garments worn by the persons.

Will Love, a printer of the "Houston Post," who formerly lived
in Galveston, swam the bay Monday to reach his family, whom he
found to be alive in Galveston. He swam from pier to pier on the
railroad bridges and at each he rested.

AWFUL NIGHT IN THE LIGHTHOUSE.

In the Bolivar lighthouse, which stands 130 feet high on
Bolivar Point, across the bay from Galveston, some one hundred
and twenty-five people sought refuge from the storm on Saturday
evening. Many of the unfortunates had deserted their homes,
which were swept by the hurricane, and other residents of Galveston, who had come to the bay shore in their frantic endeavors
to reach Galveston and their families. Among the latter was
County Road and Bridge Superintendent Kelso. Mr. Kelso
stated to a "News" reporter, when he reached Galveston on
Monday afternoon, after having been carried across the bay in a
small skiff by Mr. T. C. Moore, that the hundred and more
refugees spent an awful night in the lighthouse Saturday night
during the life of the hurricane.

The supply of fresh water was soon exhausted and an effort
was made to secure drinking water by catching rain water in
buckets suspended from the top of the lighthouse. The experi-
ment was a success in a way, but it demonstrated a remarkable
incident to show the force of the wind. The bucket was soon

filled with water, but it was salty and could not be used. Several attempts finally resulted in a fresh water supply to quench the thirst of the feverishly excited refugees.

The salt water was shot skyward over 130 feet and mingled with the rain water that fell in the buckets. From the top of the light tower several of the more venturesome storm-sufferers viewed the destructive work of the wind on Galveston Island. Twelve dead bodies were recovered near the lighthouse.

Mr. A. Mutti, a storekeeper, lost his life after a display of heroism that won for him the honors of a martyr. When the storm struck the city he hitched up a one-horse cart and started out to rescue his neighbors. Cartload after cartload he carried in safety to fire company house No. 5. On three occasions his cartload of human beings, some half dead, others crazed with fright, was carried for blocks by the raging currents, but he landed all the unfortunates in the fire house, even to his last load, when he met his death. As he attempted to pass into the building on his last trip the firehouse succumbed to the wind and collapsed. Some of the wreckage struck poor Mutti and he was mortally injured. He lingered for several hours.

GENEROUS OFFER OF HELP.

Prof. Buckner, of the Buckner Orphans' Home of Dallas, arrived in the city and made his way at once to the gentlemen in charge of the relief work. He offered to throw the doors of his establishment wide open for the orphans of Galveston, who have been deprived of their shelter at the various asylums, and announced that he was ready to care for about 100 to 150 of the children. His offer was taken under consideration for advisement at a meeting to be held of the managers of the homes.

The official records of the United States Weather Bureau have been made up and forwarded to Washington. The reports give some very valuable additional information about the storm. Unfortunately the recording instruments were destroyed or crippled beyond operation about 5:10 p. m. on Saturday, as previously reported, and before the storm had reached the center of severity.

The wind gauge recorded a two-minute blow at the rate of 100 miles an hour and was then demolished by the hurricane, which continued to increase in violence.   While the exact velocity of the wind was not recorded after the destruction of the instruments, the Weather Bureau representatives estimate the maximum velocity at between 110 and 120 miles an hour.   It did not maintain this terrific rate for any length of time, probably a half minute or minute gusts, but sufficient to wreck anything that met the full force of the storm.

A journal of the local office of the Weather Bureau contains the report of an apparent tidal wave of four feet which swept in from the Gulf some time between the hours of 7 and 8 P. M., and the time the wind veered to the southeast and attained its highest velocity of between 110 and 120 miles an hour.   It should be remembered that there was a tide of about five feet and a terrible swell in the Gulf during the storm, and that the tidal wave of four feet rode this wall of water and increased the force and speed of the sea that washed over the city.

VIVID DESCRIPTION OF THE CALAMITY.

Hon. Jeff McLemore, of Austin, a well known journalist and ex-member of the Legislature, returned from Galveston and gave the following vivid description of the horrors :

" We were five hours making the trip from the mainland, and it was not until 7 o'clock Monday evening that we reached the wharf.   When within two miles of the city we discovered a number of human bodies floating in the bay, and as the boat passed each it caused a shudder of horror among the living.   Soon after the sun went down the moon came up in a cloudless sky.   The bay was as a large mirror, and the scene seemed so peaceful and serene that for a moment it was hard to realize that we were soon to gaze upon the saddest, darkest picture in the book of time.   A gentle breeze wafted our boat lightly over the smooth waters, and as we entered the harbor and neared the wharves, formerly the scene of busiest life, a silence deep and awful prevailed.   No one on board spoke a word and the silence was only broken by the sound of a rifle sending some robber of the dead into endless eternity.

"After landing we made our way over huge heaps of wreckage that were piled almost mountain high and emerged into an open space only to be hailed by armed sentries who were guarding the town against ghouls, vandals and looters. After explaining who we were the sentries permitted us to pass, and directed us to the Tremont Hotel, the chief place of rendezvous for the stricken people.

GHOSTLY SCENES OF NIGHT.

"As we made our way to the hotel, a thing we did with difficulty, because of the wreckage that covered the streets, we saw only desolation and ruin on every hand. The pale of the moon added weirdness to the chaos and look where we might there was nothing to gladden the searching eye. We passed several small groups of men who spoke in whispers and those we addressed looked at us strangely and wondered what we came for.

"At last the hotel was reached and here most of us found friends and acquaintances who inquired after those we left behind. The city being under martial law, most of our party, after doing all in their power to relieve the anxiety of anxious men and women, disposed themselves about the hotel until morning, it being unsafe to roam about the city at night for fear of being mistaken for vandals and ghouls that have infested the city ever since the storm. To some of us it seemed that morning would never come, but it did come come at last, and it came bright and fair.

"I then started out to view the stricken city by daylight and such a scene as I witnessed is beyond the power of words to tell. The wildest flight of imagination can never paint the picture that lay before my view, and if none can imagine it, then there is no way to give one even a faint conception of it in words. The horror of it is beyond the pale of exaggeration, and the worst that may be said cannot even approach it. Acres and acres of houses were scattered in ruins over the earth and beneath the broken and shivered timbers were the decaying bodies of human beings, who suffered tortures worse than death.

"Along the pebbled beach, once the most beautiful in the world, and a scene of wonted gayety, now all is desolation and awe. Human bodies, swollen and unrecognizable, were mingled with those of dead animals and reptiles, and the whole formed a scene so gruesome and so misshapen that the thought of it even sends a sickening thrill coursing through one's veins.

"To add to the horror of the situation, human hyenas moved stealthily among the dead, robbing those who were powerless to resist, but these ghouls in human guise are meeting with just retribution, for armed sentinels are now on guard and have orders to shoot them down as they would mad dogs.

"If the situation along the East Side was more horrible than that along the West, it was only because more people dwelt there and there were more houses to be destroyed. Along either beach gaunt destruction held full sway, and each wave seemed more cruel than that which it succeeded. Nor were the waves alone in their cruelty, for the winds reveled in maddened fury and seemed to vie with them in spreading ruin and desolation.

HUNDREDS OF PEOPLE CARRIED OUT TO SEA.

"The loss of life at Galveston will never be known. The storm came first from the northwest and hundreds, perhaps thousands, were carried far out to sea never more to return. At 10 o'clock at night the wind suddenly veered to the southeast and hundreds more were swept into the bay and caught by the current and also carried out to the sea before daylight Sunday morning. That is the opinion of old seamen with whom I conversed, and if they do not know the actions of the ocean, then no one does.

"Monday evening and Tuesday morning I myself saw more than a hundred bodies floating out to sea and these were scarcely one per cent of those who perished. Responsible men with whom I talked and who had been from one end of the island to the other, estimated the loss at from 5,000 to 10,000, and all thought it would come nearer the last named figures than the first. Day by day as the debris is cleared away bodies will be found and many are buried beneath the ruins that will never be removed.

TAKING BODIES ON THE RAILROAD BARGE FOR BURIAL AT SEA

BURNING WRECKAGE TO CREMATE DEAD BODIES

SEARCHING FOR THE DEAD ON SOUTH TREMONT STREET

WRECK OF THE CHURCH OF THE SACRED HEART, THE LARGEST IN GALVESTON

"Every portion of the island was submerged and it seems a miracle that the entire city was not swept away. At least two-fifths of the houses on the island have been razed to the ground. Of the remaining three-fifths, at least half are damaged beyond repair, while the others are all damaged to greater or less extent. No house escaped without some damage and to have some idea of the cyclonic nature of the storm it will be only necessary to state that steel shutters on large business buildings were twisted around as one would twist a small piece of copper wire.

"Large splinters were whirled about in the air like darts, and many found lodgment in human bodies, no doubt producing instant death. Oh, the horror and terror of that dismal night! The wind howling, the sea roaring and lashing, houses falling and crashing, men, women and children screaming; the shrieks of dying animals; imagine it, if you can, and you may form a faint idea of the situation at Galveston last Saturday night.

HUMAN VULTURES PILFERING AND LOOTING.

"Tuesday morning I passed a partially wrecked home, in the door of which stood a young face and snow-white hair.

"'Saturday morning,' said the man who accompanied me, 'that woman's hair was dark brown; Sunday morning it had turned to snow.' I did not doubt him, for he told me of the woman's experience and how she had been saved as if by a miracle.

"But the woeful part of the terrible disaster has not yet been told. Hundreds of human vultures, almost before the storm had abated, began the work of pilfering and looting. Dead bodies were robbed and in some instances fingers were cut off to secure the rings that were on them. Most of these vultures were negroes, and they kept up their horrible work all day Sunday and Sunday night. Monday morning martial law was declared, and those placed on guard had strict orders to shoot all pilferers and looters. Many met their just fate, and by Tuesday morning the looting had almost ceased.

"Sunday the negroes refused to help bury the dead for either love or money. But when martial law was declared they were

15

forced at the point of the bayonet and made to do their share of the gruesome work. Up to Monday noon many of the dead were identified, but after that identification was impossible because of the swollen and decomposed condition of the bodies.

"Monday afternoon several hundred were loaded on barges and carried far out into the Gulf, where they were thrown over to become the food of sharks and fishes. Sunday and Monday morning many were buried down the island in the shallow sand, but by Tuesday morning these, as well as other bodies gathered along the beach, were piled on wood and burned.

"There is still great danger to Galveston from sickness and pestilence. The streets are filled with sediment from the Gulf and bay, and this is beginning to smell almost as bad as the dead bodies. Because of the immense heaps of wreckage it will be impossible to flood the streets for weeks to come, even if there were plenty of water."

BURYING THE VICTIMS IN TRENCHES.

Four days after the disaster the following account was an accurate picture of the condition of Galveston : This evening the committees in charge of clearing up the city, caring for the destitute and arranging for transportation feel much encouraged. Something like order has been been brought out of chaos. There is organized effort and the day's work has been big. It was impossible to handle the dead bodies of human beings or the carcasses of animals to get them to sea, because of putrefaction. Hundreds were buried in trenches and many were cremated. It was necessary to handle fire with great caution, as there is no water supply as yet.

The city is not suffering much for drinking water, but water is needed in the mains, that fire may be controlled. The water has been flowing steadily from the Alta Loma supply pipe into the tank. Unfortunately there was no connection from the rig tank to the mains, except through the pumps, and it is impossible to get the water through by that route. Alderman McMaster, who has been directing the work to-day, is getting out the connection from the pumps to the mains and is making a connection from rig tank to mains.

Some of the large pipe needed was not available, but carpenters are making a wooden section which will stand the slight pressures. It is expected that water will be turned into the mains from the rig tank before morning. This will give a supply in yard hydrants and fill plugs from which the steamers can work. The men at work on the pumps and pipes are well along with their work, but the boilermakers are not so far along. Mr. McMaster thinks the pumps can be started by to-morrow, and that they will give the usual pressure in the mains.

VISITORS DO NOBLE WORK.

In addition to the arrangements made for handling people from here to Texas City and thence via the Galveston, Houston and Henderson Railroad to Houston, the prospect is that the Southern Pacific will be ready for passengers within the next few days. Mr. W. S. Keenan, general passenger agent of the Santa Fe, said this evening that he expected that their track would be completed to both ends of the bridges by to-morrow evening. The company has chartered three boats and will take passengers by train from Galveston to the bridge and there transfer by boat to the mainland.

A large number of people reached here to-day from Houston and other points. Some of them came to lend helping hands, and are doing noble work ; others came to look for relatives. But there are many who come out of sheer curiosity and who do nothing but eat provisions and drink the water. They are taking up room in the boats returning to mainland which women and children ought to have. People who are not coming to help, or on other urgent missions, ought to remain away ; sightseers are not wanted, and those who have no higher purpose in coming will do Galveston the greatest service within their power by staying way.

The police and soldiers have orders not to permit the landing of strangers, and the order is being carried out as far as possible. The committee on transportation purposes to see that women and children get a chance to leave here first, and able-bodied men will not be permitted to leave during the first few days. If sightseers come anyway they will find it difficult to get in and still more difficult to get out of the city.

Mayor Jones received a telegram to-day from President McKinley, expressing his sorrow that Texas had been vis·ted by such a dreadful calamity, and advising that he had instructed the Secretary of War to render all the assistance possible.

The Mayor also received a telegram from the Kansas City Chamber of Commerce, saying that body stood ready to help, and asking what it could do.

The steamer " George Hudson " arrived from Beaumont this afternoon with a carload of ice, 5000 barrels of water, and pro-visions. Mr. John F. Keith, who came with the tug, said he would take 100 passengers with him in the morning, and he would bring the tug on another trip with lime and provisions. Fortunately, Galveston has not been entirely without ice. The Red Snapper Company had a large supply on hand, and it has been letting people have it at wholesale prices. This supply will last a day or two, and ice will then be gladly received. Three of the schooners of the Red Snapper Company reached here from Campechy banks to-day, filled with fish.

DEAD ANIMALS CARRIED ACROSS THE BAY.

The fish were given away by the thousands to all who came for them. Animals are being dumped into the bay, which go out with the tide and coming ashore by the hundreds at Bolivar pen-insula. Parties started to bury them, but the few people on the peninsula found it impossible. They came to the city to implore the authorities to send men there to bury these animals and to quit throwing them into the bay. The dumping into the bay had already been stopped, as there was little wind and the carcasses were cremated.

Between Fifteenth street and Avenue C, running on a line parallel with the island, a great mass of wreckage is piled as high as a man's head at any point and from that to the height of three-story houses. This line extends as far along as there were houses to wreck and consists of all kinds of buildings. A half of the section mentioned was traversed by a "News" man this morning. Names of fully 400 people were found who lived in that section. The debris is so high above these bodies that it may be days before all will be removed.

There were a great many injured by the storm, and these are being cared for at the hospitals, both of which are located at the east end of the St. Mary's University building at Fourteenth and Sealy avenue. This is a building quite well suited to the purpose, but of course it is lacking in conveniences. A large number of people with broken bones and badly torn limbs are confined there, and nearly every one of them has lost either whole families or some member. Drs. Starley and Ruhl are in charge and have been working night and day tending to those rescued from the wrecks of their homes.

SCHOOL BUILDING CARRIED A BLOCK AWAY.

The tower of the Rosenberg school fell in and killed about eleven people during the height of the storm. It was a place of refuge for all the people driven from their homes by the high water and terrific winds.

The parochial school situated on the corner of Eleventh and Sealy avenue, was taken from its foundations and carried by wind and water a full block to Twelfth street and Sealy avenue, landing on the north side of the street, whereas it was located on the south side previously. This stands amidst a great pile of driftwood, and having been carried to that location undoubtedly formed a barrier for the collection of great piles of drift that were brought in from gulfward. It shoved some smaller buildings out of their former locations, but did not wreck many of them.

The drift is something terrible. It includes every kind of house used by men, and represents all the city south of the line described to the beach in which it is reported that large numbers of dead bodies, which floated to sea yesterday, have been washed during the day. The houses are sometimes to be found quite intact, but turned bottom up like an upturned dry goods box. Others are but so much kindling wood.

The greatest wreck is possibly the Sacred Heart Catholic Church, at Fourteenth and Broadway. The front wall is nearly all standing, with the steeples on either side, and the curved wall that surrounds the chancel seemed in pretty good shape, but the two side walls are gone beyond repair. The east side is standing about half way up, and the west side was thrown to the ground. Sand covers the campus in that neighborhood.

The University building suffered a good deal from the blow, but it was the haven of rest for all the people in that neighborhood, as it is now the hospital for the injured and the place of succor for the women and children.

GREAT WRECK OF ST. MARY'S INFIRMARY.

The next greatest wreck is the St. Mary's Infirmary on Market and Eighth streets. Practically everything there is gone but the new part, which was completed about two years ago. This is badly damaged, but is being used. It does not cover more than a quarter of the floor space of the entire building when intact. This is used to support injured and is the place of refuge. Sealy Hospital, between Ninth and Tenth streets, escaped serious injury, beyond damage to the roof.

The colored school, on the corner of Broadway and Tenth streets, is a mass of wreckage, piled up with the debris along the mountain chain previously described. This was a large two-story frame building of eight rooms, and stood high in the air. A little Episcopal mission, located on the corner of Fifteenth and Avenue L, was carried northwest along Fifteenth street and broke up a block away. The gentleman who was in charge of the mission, Henry Hirsinger, was lost.

This great line of wreckage forms the division point between a mass of houses unroofed and partly damaged and a great prairie, which up to Saturday was the location of the homes of thousands of Galveston's people. This was generally known as the colored section of the city, but the colored people as a rule lived close to the beach. As a consequence they got scared early in the day and moved into town.

The result is that the death list is not as great proportionately among the colored people as it is among the whites, although a great many of them are missing. Prominent among the colored people missing are S. C. Cuney, a nephew of Wright Cuney, formerly collector of customs at this port. The rector of the colored Episcopal church, Rev. Thomas Cain, and his wife are lost.

The poles of the East Broadway street railway line are standing erect to Fourteenth street, beyond which there is but one pole. The wires are all down, as a matter of course, and the track is filled with wreckage. The line of wreckage crosses Broadway, between Thirteenth and Fourteenth streets, and in it at that point are several bodies which cannot be reached on account of the high pile of lumber.

HOUSES PLACED BACK TO BACK.

The great bulk of this debris is unbroken and sides and roofs of houses still intact, and the vast amount of loose boards can be used for rebuilding, so that there will be lessened cost in that direction. In some places whole houses have been moved from their foundations and carried around back of others, thus forming a barrier which caught the floating debris and prevented the whole north side of town being swept from Gulf to bay and carried into the bay.

The roof of the elevator is gone and the wheat there is exposed, but if fresh water can be obtained soon it is expected the wheat can be saved by drying. The sheds on the wharves are practically all gone, but the wharves are supposed to be in such shape that they can be repaired at a nominal expense and can be resumed.

The following letter was received at Fort Worth from C. H. Fewell, who is night yardmaster of the Santa Fe Railway Company, at Galveston :

" The only means of sending mail or anything is by water

to Houston.   All bridges and wires are gone, and it will be weeks
before they can possibly get a train out of here.   The city is a
complete wreck.   Very few buildings are standing that have not
in some way been wrecked by the storm.   The loss of life will
never be known ; it will run into thousands.   You can't imagine
what a terrible shape this place is in.   We are thankful to be
alive, but cannot help but feel sad when we think of the many
friends we have lost, and the hundreds that are left without homes
and without a mouthful of anything to eat.   Relief must come
soon or many will starve to death.

"Our rooming house stood the storm well, with the exception of a corner blown off and part of the roof.   I got up about 4
o'clock Saturday.   It was then raining and blowing hard.   I left
the house and started for the Tremont hotel and came near not
making it.   We stayed there all night.   For four hours I thought
every minute that the building would certainly go with the many
that were going to pieces around it.   We would have been as well
off had we stayed at home, but was afraid our house would not
stand the storm.

HORRIBLE BEYOND DESCRIPTION.

"Wagons have been passing all day piled full of dead bodies.
Many of them will never be identified, and they are now taking
them right to the Gulf for burial.   This seems terrible, but it
must be done, as it is impossible to bury them on the island.
Hundreds of bodies are floating in the bay and outskirts of what
was once the city.   I cannot describe how horrible it is.   I have
been over most of the city since Sunday morning and know
exactly how everything is situated.   From the beach for at least
four blocks in there is not a sign of anything left to show for
what was once fine residences.

"Not one thing is left to show that there ever was anything
at the beach.   Everything is piled up ; all rubbish for about four
blocks from the beach beyond which it looks as clear as the prairie.
The east and west end of the town is entirely gone.   At the east
end not a thing remains standing to Twelfth street.   Dead bodies

can be seen every place except in the business part of the city, to-day, two days after the storm. They are bringing them in by the wagon loads every hour. Nearly every one you meet has lost some friend and is looking for them. I visited three places where they have been taking the bodies to-day with a friend looking for relatives, and I know there could not have been less than 200 bodies in each place, lying cold in death. The general offices are a complete wreck ; the wharves, elevators and everything connected with the railroads are more or less racked and many of them a total loss. Not a splinter is left of our yard office. You might say hundreds of cars are turned over and can be found nearly a block from where they were left before the storm."

CHAPTER XII.

Thrilling Narratives by Eye-witnesses—Path of the Storm's
Fury Through Galveston—Massive Heaps of Rubbish—
Huge Buildings Swept into the Gulf.

AT GALVESTON on that fatal Saturday night there were deaths far more horrible than any of which even a Sien-kiewicz could conceive. Mothers and babes, fathers and husbands, were hurled headlong into the world beyond without a chance to make peace with their Maker, with a farewell kiss or a last fond embrace. Upon every hand the dead were piled up like drift-wood cast up by the sea, even as they were at Waterloo and Gettysburg and behind Kitchener in the Soudan. The bodies of men that the day before were perfect specimens of physical develop-ment were swollen and discolored by the fierce rays of the autumn sun, and were food for flies and maggots which buzzed or crawled hither and thither unceasingly. In the bay the sharks were over-fed, and on the prairies the buzzards could no longer be tempted.

If those who live far from the awful scene of woe, believe that this is over-drawn, let them ask the pale-faced nerve-racked refugees, from that terrible place, and they will be told that it is impossible for either pen or brush to give the picture as it is. The photo-grapher, with all his art, stands baffled. The artist, with all his talent, is incompetent. The newspaper man, accustomed to the dark side of life, shudders and turns from description to the work of reciting details, horrible enough in themselves, but far more pleasant.

There arrived in Dallas a score or more of men who told of decomposed bodies, and maggots and flies and starvation and dis-tress until their hearers rushed away in horror. Some of these heart-breaking tales are given herewith.

Ed. A. Gebhard of The Dallas News came in from Texas City. He said:

"Among the many stories of the Galveston disaster I have

seen none that fully describe the sight that presented itself around Texas City and Virginia Point on Monday. They all seem to lose the impressiveness that the narrator gave them when the centre of an excited group who were eager to know if friends or relatives were among the dead. Every word is heard or read ravenously all over the country, and when one has seen the ghastly faces of friends and acquaintances strewn ruthlessly among the grass and rubbish around Texas City and along that part of the bay shore he will not wonder that the world stands aghast.

"The corpses that had been thrown up by the cruel waters on the mainland were for the time being neglected for the field that contained thousands instead of hundreds. The remains of the old man of many winters, with the determined looking face, who gazed with intentness into the now cloudless skies, was kept silent company by a little miss whose smile would melt the heart of the most cruel man alive. Further on were the forms of women and children, most of which were entirely nude, the wind having been that severe that even the shoes were torn from their feet.

THROWN TOGETHER IN UTTER CONFUSION.

"I have seen tracks of many cyclones, but never have I seen the path of one that held the misery, the suffering and the general destruction that were occasioned by this hurricane, assisted by the sea.

"Furniture, household articles, pianos (complete and in part) and the carcasses of every kind of domestic animal were to be found in chaos. Even from the mainland could be seen the dire effects of the storm on the seaport of Texas—jagged walls, broken smokestacks, tin roofs suspended from their proper places or lying curled up at my feet in the bay, a distance of several miles from where they belonged. While it is natural for a person drowning to cling to whatever comes in their reach with that intensity that they cannot be disengaged, after death, without much trouble, this very thing lent much grewsomeness to the scene. Mothers with their children in their arms could not be separated from them, even by death.

The piling of the destroyed railroad bridges had an occasional figure clinging to them. On nearer approach the head was seen to be thrown back as if to keep above water, and the features were distorted with horror as if in their last moments they realized the fatality of the attempt. The sea, not content with drowning the living and washing them away, desecrated the tombs of Galveston and several caskets were seen floating on the bosom of the quiet bay that morning and two or three were found on shore as if resentful at having their rightful rest disturbed.

"Many people from a distance moved only by a morbid curiosity, which I consider little short of criminal, crowded to Houston in order that they might go to the devastated city and view the misery and devastation, not willing to alleviate suffering or help to bury the dead. As for me, I trust I will never look on a sight as appalling, as heartrending, as desolate, while life lasts."

A ST. LOUIS MAN STORMBOUND.

George MacLaine, of St. Louis, arrived at Dallas from Galveston, where he spent the time from Friday until Tuesday. "I was intending to leave on the 1.50 train Saturday afternoon," he said, "but I could not get away on account of the storm, the water having risen to such an extent that it could not cross the bridge.

"My experience was pretty much the same as a large number of others have given. During the storm I was in a building located at the corner of Twenty-fifth and Market streets, two or three blocks above the Santa Fé depot. We were in the parlor of the hotel on the second floor, with about eight feet of water in the lower story. The parlor was crowded with guests and refugees, men and women, and from the windows I witnessed a great many affecting and pathetic sights, particularly in the way of appeals to the men in the hotel to assist in rescuing women with children in the neighborhood who had become separated from their husbands.

"One case I particularly noticed—that of a woman and five young children, whose house fell on top of them, but, fortunately, in such a way as to protect them from the force of the waves and wind. Several attempts were made by various parties to rescue this family, but the rescue parties always returned with the statement that on account of the débris and the swift current they were unable to get near enough to the house to render any assistance. The first attempt was made about 6 o'clock in the evening.

"They were eventually given up for lost, when, to the surprise of everyone, cries for help were heard from the ruins about 5 o'clock in the morning. Appeals were again made to some of the white men in the house to go to their relief, but, I am very sorry to say, they were in vain until finally two colored men who worked in the kitchen and one of the whites volunteered their services and succeeded in bringing the party to the hotel. They had practically nothing on them when they came, but they were taken in hand and the best done with them in the way of giving them clothing and food that was possible. There were so many cases of this kind that, as I say, it is simply a repetition of the experience of others.

DRUNKEN REVELRY IN THE STREETS.

"On Sunday morning, immediately after the storm and as soon as daylight appeared, the scene on the streets was one I shall never forget. There were drunken women, almost nude, with their male companions, also under the influence of liquor, parading the streets and laughing and singing as if returning from a prolonged spree. There were some of the best citizens of Galveston hurrying to and fro, asking this one and that one if they had heard anything of their sisters, wives or some other member of their families.

"There were others who had been present when their families had perished, weeping and wailing over their losses, young children crying for their parents who had perished, parents crying for the loss of their children, and others walking aimlessly about or standing around as if they were stunned. Everyone appeared so thoroughly unnerved that there was a total lack of organized effort to search for the missing or to collect food.

"Almost immediately after the waters receded sufficiently to permit people to wade or walk in safety men and women could be seen with their long poles and baskets, whose principal aim and object seemed to be to profit by the misfortunes of the poor people who had lost their lives or their homes. On Sunday afternoon I took a walk out Tremont avenue to inquire as to the safety of some of my friends who lived on that street, and after making a few visits proceeded to the beach to witness the destruction that had taken place in that neighborhood.

"Of course it has been told by several how everything had been swept off the face of the land in that direction, but I could not help noticing the large number of colored people with their baskets and shawls searching through the ruins of what had been the finest homes in Galveston for bric-a-brac, silver and other articles of value. I stood for some time, amazed that they could have the audacity to do what they were doing, but as nobody seemed to interfere with them or question their right, I passed on as every one else did, simply feeling astounded that people could be so inhuman at such a time. I saw one colored woman who had filled her basket and was returning to the city when she met one of the unfortunate owners of the property, who, by the merest chance, noticed sticking out of the woman's basket some article that she was able to identify as her property.

CURSED FOR INTERFERENCE.

"She called upon the darkey to give up the article, but she declined to do so, taking the position that in such times it was anybody's property. Fortunately for the rightful owner a gentleman friend happened to come along during the controversy, and, hearing the nature of it, forcibly took the basket from the woman, who was even then bold enough to stand cursing the man for his interference. I did not see any parties mutilating or robbing the dead, but I met several others in Galveston who had.

"I left on Tuesday morning, being fortunate enough to get passage on a schooner that carried me to Texas City. From there I caught a train to Houston. All day Monday in Galveston it seemed to be one continual procession of bodies, which were being carried in wagons, drays, fire ladders, and every other imaginable conveyance. Some of the bodies were minus heads, arms or feet, which, added to the advanced stage of decomposition, not only made the scene particularly horrible to witness, but extremely nauseating on account of the smell from the bodies. Particularly toward the close of Monday the bodies were found so rapidly that any effort to carry them to any special point for burial had about ceased and they were covered up in the sand, laid down on the wharf or left where they were found. Even after I was fortunate enough to get a schooner to carry me to Texas City it seemed that there were almost as many floating in the bay and being carried off or lying around on the mainland as I had seen in Galveston itself.

"It was a horrible experience which I passed through, which I hope will never occur again in my lifetime, and I feel that I cannot too strongly call attention to the urgent needs, both in food and clothing, not only of the poor classes, but of the best people in Galveston, who up to the time of this terrible calamity had not known what want was, and who even now seem ill at ease in knowing how to make their wants known."

STORM OF INDESCRIBABLE FURY.

Rudolph Daniels, Assistant General Passenger Agent of the Missouri, Kansas and Texas Railway, was in Galveston during the storm, and returned to Dallas on the 12th. Mr. Daniels said: "I can only give you my experience and what I saw. The storm was indescribable in its fury, and it was hard to realize the extent of the devastation and destruction even when on the scene. It does not seem real or possible.

"I was in a restaurant near the Tremont Hotel when the storm broke. It began blowing a gale about 2 o'clock in the afternoon, but the wind did not reach an alarming height until about 4 o'clock. Myself and friends saw that it was going to be a storm of more than ordinary fury and started for the Tremont. The street was three feet deep in water and we got a carriage. We had to draw our feet up on the seats to keep out of the water.

"At 5 o'clock the wind was blowing a hurricane, and the water came over the sidewalk in front of the Tremont.

"The water in the street was full of telegraph poles, beer kegs, boxes and débris of all sorts. The wind was carrying all sorts of missiles. On a great many roofs in Galveston oyster shells were used instead of gravel. The wind tore them off and hurled them through the air with great force, injuring people and breaking windows. The air was full of flying glass and every imaginable thing that could be blown away. Mixed with the roaring of the hurricane was a bedlam of strange noises, the crash of breaking glass, rumble of falling walls and rattle of tin roofs making an infernal sound.

"The people for blocks around endeavored to make their way to the Tremont. Rescuers stood on the sidewalk to assist those who were trying to cross the street, which was over waist-deep in water. The water was lashed to foam by the wind and the air was thick with spume and spray. When a person, man, woman or child, would get in reach, those on the sidewalk would seize them and drag them into the hotel.

"Soon there were about 1000 people in the hotel. Women with hardly clothing enough to cover them, and that wet, were crowded along the halls and stairways. They were moaning and babies were crying. Outside in the storm all seemed a sort of haze. No definite shapes could be seen across the street.

WINDOWS BROKEN AND ROOMS FLOODED.

"The wind reached its strongest about 6 o'clock. Then the water was in the rotunda of the hotel. Part of the skylight had blown off and the rain was pouring in. Many of the windows were broken by flying pieces of débris and the rooms were flooded. My room was among those flooded. Joe Morrow had a room that was dry, and he and Harry Archer and myself crowded into it. Morrow got four inches of candle somewhere, and we had half a dozen dry matches. We burned the candle from time to time during the night to cheer us up. All of us were scared and did not know what minute everything would go. After midnight the storm began to go down, and at 5 o'clock in the morning the water had gone out of the hotel and part of Tremont street was above it.

"We set out to find W. H. McClure, who had had an awful

AVENUE L AND TWENTY-FIRST STREET, SHOWING THE URSULINE CONVENT THE REFUGE OF HUNDREDS OF PEOPLE

RUINS OF THE GAS WORKS AT THIRTY-THIRD AND MARKET STREETS

BURYING BODIES WHERE THEY WERE FOUND

AVENUE L AND FIFTEENTH STREET—SHOWING DESTRUCTION DONE BY THE HURRICANE

experience. He came to the hotel and offered a hackman any price to go to his house after his family, but could not induce him to go. Failing in that, he started back home to his wife. That was 7 o'clock, and he did not manage to reach home, one-half mile away, until 2.30 in the morning. We found them all safe. We saw several bodies on Tremont street on the way there.

"The organization of relief work began at once. It was soon seen that there was no time for the identification of bodies, and the work of taking them to sea for burial began. Along the Gulf front for three blocks back there is not a house standing, and I could see only one or two on the Denver resurvey.

"There was a meeting of all the railroad men in Galveston at 9 o'clock Tuesday morning, at which it was arranged that freight would be handled through Houston and the Clinton tap to Clinton and by barge to Galveston. The Galveston, Houston and Henderson to handle passengers to Texas City and then to Galveston by the steamer Lawrence."

W. H. McGrath, general manager of the Dallas Electric Company, returned from Galveston yesterday. He said:

HOUSEHOLD FURNITURE STREWN FOR MILES.

"No words can express the scenes of death and desolation. Nothing can be said that will convey the full meaning. I went over to Galveston in a schooner and came away as soon as possible. What they need there is not people, but ice, water and supplies. All along the shore of the bay for twelve miles inland are strewn pianos, sofas, chairs, tables paving blocks and all sorts of broken lumber and debris from Galveston.

"General Scurry detailed my party to bury the dead on a stretch of beach about two-and-one-half miles long. In that space we found fourteen bodies, all women and children but two. The hot sun beating down and the action of the water had caused decomposition to set in at once. They were horribly bloated, and the eyes and tongues protruding and the bosoms of the women bursting open.

"None of the corpses had any clothing upon them. One man
16

had a leather belt about his waist and the shreds of his trousers. The women were nude except that corsets and shoes still remained on some of them. All the lighter portions of the clothing had been beaten off by the water. There was no time for indentification. We simply pulled them up on the beach and buried them where they lay.

"It is frightful to think of. The bay is still full of floating bodies. Forty-three were counted from the schooner I was on as we went down. Gangs of men are at work all the time under martial law burying as fast as they are cast up.

"The city of Galveston is a wreck. Not a building in the town escaped injury. The people there who went through the storm seemed dazed and in a sort of stupor. All they know is that they want to get away from the spot, and when they get on the mainland they go wild with joy. They are utterly bewildered and demoralized.

ARRESTED FOR ROBBING THE DEAD.

"General McKibben had just arrived when I was there and martial law reigned. I was told that seventy ghouls had been arrested for robbing bodies and that they would be court-martialed and shot. The tramp steamer Kendal Castle is lying high and dry 200 feet from the water's edge. She is standing on an even keel, just as though she was at sea. General Scurry wanted a boat to go across to Galveston and informed the captain he was under martial law and his boats would be required. The boats were sent and General Scurry went across the bay in the captain's gig.

"The stench along the wharves in Galveston is something terrible, but the people are making every effort to dispose of everything that is putrifying.

"The railroad and telegraphic companies are making tremendous efforts to get into Galveston. The Postal Telegraph Company has two wires strung down the Galveston, Houston and Henderson to the junction of the Texas Terminal. Below that not a pole was left. The Western Union is making rapid progress and will lay a cable across the bay."

George Hall, a traveling man who lives at 133 Thomas avenue, this city, returned from Galveston yesterday morning, having passed through the terrible scenes enacted there during and after the storm. To a News representative he said last night:

"I arrived at Galveston Friday afternoon, and my wife and little girl were to come down Saturday. At noon Saturday I noticed that the storm, which had been blowing all the morning, was getting worse. At that time I went to the tower of the Tremont Hotel and saw the waves rolling in toward the land. I took just one look over the city and came down. The wind increased in violence from that on and the rain fell in sheets, and I sent a telegram to my wife and advised her to stop in Houston. I think that was the last telegram that was sent from the island, as a few moments afterwards the girl told me the wires had snapped. The storm was accompanied by no thunder or lightning.

CHILDREN CRYING AND WOMEN PRAYING.

"About 4 o'clock the people who were able to get conveyances began to come in from the residence districts. The hotel did not serve any supper. From 6 to 10 o'clock was the worst of the storm, and during that time there was about 1200 people in the house. We were just as nearly like rats in a wire cage as anything could be. At 10 o'clock the water was four feet deep in the office, and it was certain death to go out doors. We were in pitch darkness all the time, although some one had secured one candle and set it up in the dining-room. Children were crying and women praying and throwing their arms around the mens' knees and asking them to save them. It was certainly as horrible a night as any one ever put on earth. I have been on the road thirty years, have been in all parts of the world, have had many hairbreadth escapes, but they did not amount to a snap of the fingers besides this.

"We had one particularly hard gust that lasted about five minutes, and on looking at my watch I saw that was a little after 10 o'clock. At 12 o'clock it had died down considerably, and the water fell two feet in about twenty minutes.

"In the early morning we ventured out, although it rained

most of the forenoon. In the afternoon I took a walk down to the beach which is ordinarily ten minutes' walk, but it took me an hour and one-half on this occasion. Once I slipped and twisted my ankle slightly. My foot came down on something soft, and I found that it was the breast of an old man with long whiskers.

"As I returned to the hotel I counted thirty-five bodies, five in one bunch. I saw a negro go out of a house with a load of bed-clothes and other stuff and a soldier stopped him. The man claimed that he had been sent there by the owners of the property. I personally saw no looting.

"I stayed there over Sunday night, and on Monday morning seven of us bunched together and paid a man $100 to take us over the bay. On the way over we counted more than ninety bodies passing close to us, and on Sunday forenoon I believe there were about as many bodies in the bay as there were fish. I am certain in my own mind that I saw over 1000 bodies.

STRONG MAN FAINTS.

" Early Sunday morning Jack Frost, of this city, walked into the Tremont Hotel, nearly naked and broken and bruised from head to foot. He fainted and was carried to a room and a doctor sent for. The doctors said that the bones of his right hand were broken, one clavicle broken and his left shoulder dislocated, besides being horribly bruised and mangled. Several inquiries from the doctors elicited the information that it was a close question of life and death when I left. He was caught at Murdock's pavilion when the storm came up, and could not get away. No one knows just where he landed."

M. F. Smith, of the Chicago, Milwaukee and St. Paul Railroad was in Galveston during the hurricane and got home to Dallas yesterday. He said that nothing he could say would convey an adequate idea of the storm. "I was in the Tremont Hotel Saturday when the hurricane began," he continued. " The water came up into the rotunda and the wind blew with fearful force. Eight hundred or a thousand people took refuge in the hotel. It was a scene of pathos to see the women and children with hardly any clothing, not knowing where relatives or children were scattered about the corridors in deepest distress. It was remarkable that so few of them gave any outward sign or cry. Sunday morning the water was gone out of the rotunda and it was ankle deep in mud. I went out Tremont street to Avenue N½, where I came to water. People were coming in toward the higher ground sick, wounded and homeless. One hundred men were sworn in by the Mayor Sunday morning as a guard and relief work began at once. I came out Monday morning on the Charlotte M. Allen. From her I saw a barge loaded with corpses going to sea for burial and another at the dock was being loaded. A passenger on the Allen counted fifty floating bodies in the bay on the way up to Virginia Point. We had to walk to Texas City Junction and I saw Galveston paving blocks on the prairie north of Texas City."

CAST UP BY THE HEAVY WAVES.

Officers Williams and Curly Smith stated that the body of a woman that had been buried at sea on the east end was washed ashore on the beach near the foot of Tremont street. Attached to the body was a large rock weighing about 200 pounds. The body was carried to a place back from the water's edge and placed in a grave.

While working with a gang of men clearing the wreckage of a large number of houses on Avenue O and Centre street to-day Mr. John Vincent found a live prairie dog locked in a drawer of a bureau. It was impossible to identify the house or the name of its former occupants, as several houses were piled together in a mass of brick and timber. The bureau was pulled out of the wreckage a few feet from the ground, where it had been buried beneath about ten feet of débris. The little animal seemed not to be worse for his experience of four days locked up in a drawer beneath a mountain of wreckage. It was taken home and fed by Mr. Vincent, who will hold the pet for its owner if the owner survived the storm.

Some idea of the extent of the destructive path of the hurricane can be got from a view of the beach front east of Tremont street. Standing on the high ridge of débris that marks the line of devastation extending from the extreme west end to Tremont street an unobstructed view of the awful wreckage is presented.

Drawing a line on the map of the city from the centre of Tremont street and Avenue P straight to Broadway and Thirteenth street where stands the partly demolished Sacred Heart Church, all the territory south and east of this line is leveled to the ground. The ridge of wreckage of the several hundred buildings that graced this section before the storm marks this line as accurately as if staked out by a surveying instrument. Every building within the large area was razed by the wind or force of the raging waters, or both.

This territory embraces sixty-seven blocks and was a thickly populated district. Not a house withstood the storm and those that might have held together if dependent upon their own construction and foundations were buried beneath the stream of buildings and wreckage that swept like a wild sea from the east to the west, demolishing hundreds of homes and carrying the unfortunate inmates to their death either by drowning or from blows of the flying timbers and wreckage that filled the air.

WIND A HUNDRED MILES AN HOUR.

The strongest wind blew later in the evening, when it shifted to the southeast and attained a velocity of from 110 to 120 miles an hour. The exact velocity was not recorded, owing to the destruction of the wind gauge of the United States Weather Bureau after it had registered a 100-miles-an-hour blow for two minutes. This terrific southeast wind blew the sea of débris inland and piled it up in a hill ranging from ten to twenty feet high and marking the line of the storm's path along the southeastern edge of the island.

In one place near Tremont street and Avenue P four roofs and remnants of four houses are jammed within a space of about twenty-five feet square. Beneath this long ridge many hundred men, women and children were buried, and cattle, horses and dogs and other animals were piled together in one confused mass. While every house in the city or suburbs suffered more or less from the hurricane and encroachment of the Gulf waters, the above section suffered the most in being swept as clean as a desert. Another area extending east to Thirteenth street and south of Broadway to the Gulf suffered greatly, and few of the buildings withstood the storm, none without being damaged to a more or less extent. From Tremont street and Avenue P½ the wind came northward for about two blocks and then cut across westward to the extreme limits of the city; in fact, swept clear on down the island for many miles. The path of the levelled ground west from Avenue P cleared the several blocks, extending south to the beach and west to Twenty-seventh street. It cut diagonally southwest on a straight line within three blocks of the beach and down west on the beach many miles beyond the city limits. This does not mean that the path of the storm was confined to this stretch of territory—not by any means. There were many blocks in the centre of the city almost totally demolished by the fury of the wind and sea, but the above long line of about four miles of the city proper and many miles of country land were swept clean of buildings and all other obstructions.

NO VESTAGE LEFT OF BUILDINGS.

A few of the piles that once supported the street-railway trestle extending from Centre street to Tremont street on the beach are all that remains to mark the curved line of right-of-way. Not a vestage of the three large bath-houses of Keef's Pagoda and Murdock is to be seen.

The Midway, with its many old shacks and frame houses, concert halls and other resorts, was swept to the sea, and the Gulf now plays twenty feet north of where the Midway marked the beach line. The Olympia-by-the Sea likewise fell an early prey to the storm, and the surf which formerly kissed the elevated floor of the Olympia now sweeps across the electric railway track about fifteen feet north of the big circular building. On Tremont street and Avenue P½ two buildings stand, or rather two structures mark where two frame buildings battled with the raging elements. The two houses were occupied by Mr. Joseph Magilavaca and family and Mr. C. Nicolini and family. Both houses were stripped of every piece of furniture, wall-paper, window-frames and doors on the first floor and second floor remained intact. The houses were blown from their elevated foundations and dropped down on the ground and the sea washed the interior of the first floors almost up to the ceilings. The families took refuge in a house across the street, which gave way and was leveled almost to the ground, but all the inmates escaped with their lives. These two dwellings stand like charmed structures in the centre of the hurricane's track.

The Rosenburg School-house suffered severely on the east side of the building. The roof of this wing fell in and carried the second floor and nearly all of the south wall with it. It was reported that a number of people sought refuge in this building and that all of them escaped without serious injury.

TO HASTEN ONE BRIDGE.

The indications this morning are that there will be reasonably free intercourse with the outside world within ten days at the most, although those in charge of transportation lines are rapidly finding that the storm did more damage than they had at first calculated upon. At another conference the question of utilizing one of the railroad bridges across the bay and repairing that for the use of all lines prior to the repairing of the other bridges or the building of a steel bridge was practically settled. Colonel L. J. Polk, general manager of the Gulf, Colorado and Santa Fe, said that it was reasonably certain that this would be done, all the roads concentrating all their efforts to the completion of one bridge. In regard to his own line he said :

"I do not know when the wrecking gangs will get to Virginia Point. The statement I made to you yesterday that I expected we would have a train to the point to-day was based on information from the other side, but it appears that they did not know the amount of work there was before them. Practically they have to build a new track from Lamarque to the Point.

"We shall probably not reach the bay on the island side

VIEW OF CENTRAL PARK, SHOWING DAMAGED HIGH SCHOOL IN THE CENTER, TRINITY CHURCH IN THE REAR AND TREMONT HOTEL AT THE RIGHT

THE CITY HALL, GALVESTON—SHOWING DAMAGE DONE BY THE STORM

MEMBERS OF THE GALVESTON CENTRAL RELIEF COMMITTEE

JUDGE NOAH ALLEN	WILLIAM A. McVITIE	RABBI HENRY COHEN
	CHAIRMAN	
J. H. KAMPNER		CLARENCE OUSLEY
REV. J. M. K. KIRWIN	BERTRAND ADONE	WILLIAM V. McCONN
OF ST. MARY'S CATHEDRAL		

THE BALL HIGH SCHOOL, GALVESTON—AFTER THE FLOOD

before Saturday, as the same conditions prevail, and we did not realize the immense damage the storm had done.

"We have practically decided to unite in the repairing of one bridge for the use of all lines for the present. Our chief engineer, Mr. Felt, and Mr. Boschke, of the Southern Pacific, went to the mainland this morning to establish communication with the parties at interest who are on that side. J. M. Barr, third vice-president of the Santa Fe system, and James Dun, chief engineer of the system, both of Chicago, are on the mainland. They came down here to assist in any way they could in the re-establishment of the business."

DAMAGE TO THE WHARVES.

The wharf company did not suffer badly so far as the actual wharves are concerned, and it comes from General Manager Bailey that they will be ready to handle the business within seven or eight days. Of course a good deal of wharf flooring is torn up. The most serious damage was to the sheds, some of which are complete wrecks. Business can be done without sheds, and as long as the wharves themselves are in shape business can be done. With the rail lines established and running again, freight can move over the wharves. As a matter of fact coal was being discharged at the coal elevator at pier 34 yesterday. The West End wharves are all right, and some of these sheds are standing. Of course there is an immense amount of repair work to be done, but this need not interfere with the movement of freight.

Secretary S. O. Young, of the Galveston Cotton Exchange and Board of Trade, said this morning that it would be three or four weeks before quotations could be actually received here, owing to the condition of the exchange building and the lack of wires over which to do business. The exchange building is pretty badly wrecked, the slate shingles having been carried away on one side early in the afternoon, which let in great floods of water and ruined the ceilings and walls.

Dr. Young suffered several severe bruises as a result of the storm and some of his employes are gone. His janitors are employed in the public work of relieving the general situation. A good many cotton men who had interests in the market left a day or so ago for Houston and New Orleans, where they could look out for their interests.

The Masons started early Monday to furnish relief to their brethren. They established headquarters in the Masonic Temple, which was partly wrecked, and have furnished food and the necessaries of life. All Masons in distress are asked to go to them. They bought provisions to the amount of $500 and have been distributing what they had. A meeting this morning was held at the temple to organize a central relief committee for more systematic work, now that the first distress has been relieved.

LOSSES REPORTED EVERYWHERE.

The Gulf, Colorado and Santa Fe Company notified Chairman Sealy of the relief committee that there was $5000 there for its use. The Santa Fe has suffered great loss itself and is a flood sufferer of great proportions in dollars and cents. Thomas Taylor, a cotton man, on Monday bought $500 worth of men's clothing, which he immediately distributed to the needy. The other men of means are coming forward with donations for permanent relief.

The Galveston Brewing Company suffered comparatively slight property loss, although it will amount into the thousands. Their utility was not impaired in the least, however, and they are making ice as fast as they can, and selling it at the regular Galveston rate 30c. per 100 pounds. During the storm the brewery building was the haven of between 300 and 500 people. The men employed at the establishment were instrumental in saving between seventy-five and 100 people during the storm by going out in it and swimming and wading as best they could, dragging the people into safety in the brewery.

Captain Owens stated this morning that in the jumble of confusion mention of the practical destruction of the towns of Arcadia and Alta Loma had been omitted. At Arcadia there are about 150 people living. Arthur Boddeker lost his life during the storm and two or three were hurt. At Alta Loma two children of Mr.

Steele were killed. There are six houses standing. All the groceries at both places were damaged by water and these people are in great need of provisions, medicines and food for stock.

One old man was found this morning who stated that he had one hundred kinfolks in Galveston and he is the only survivor.

Galveston was a place where there were large families by intermarriage, many of which had been established when the city was but a village, fifty or more years ago. These had lived here and increased until a family of 100 was not improbable in the least. The case of this old man is probably an extreme one in the line of annihilation, but others have lost almost as heavily.

STEAMERS TORN FROM THEIR MOORINGS.

General Agent Denison was unable to give any definite information about the movements of steamers out of Galveston. There are now three here. The Alamo is aground on the north side of the channel, having been torn from her moorings at the wharf during the storm and swept to her present position.

Mr. Denison expressed the opinion that it might be possible that dredging would be necessary to relieve the steamer. The Comal arrived in port Monday and berthed at pier 26, but was unable to discharge much cargo. She moved down into the roads Wednesday afternoon, driven there because of the stench at the wharves and the impossibility of doing any business. The Sabine arrived this morning and also anchored in the roads to await an opportunity to discharge. The wharf is in bad shape for the handling of cargo, being wet and muddy and torn up in a good many places.

There was talk of urging Governor Sayers to call a special session of the Legislature to take action to relieve the situation at Galveston. This was done by Governor Culberson in 1897 in the case of El Paso, and is said to be sanctioned by the State Constitution. Representative Dudly G. Wooten, of Dallas, said:

"In regard to the necessity for a specially called session of the Legislature, it is difficult to speak intelligently unless we know all the conditions. So far as the immediate physical wants of the flood-stricken district are concerned, the liberal contributions of private charity will readily meet the emergency, as has been demonstrated by the generous manner in which the people everywhere, both in Texas and outside, have responded to the appeals for help. Food, money and all the necessaries to alleviate the present distresses of Galveston and the adjacent coast are already in sight and being rapidly utilized.

"But I think the most serious problem is the one of sanitation. It must be borne in mind that the results of this flood are such as to create a condition that will inevitably produce a pestilence unless it is dealt with promptly, intelligently and firmly. Not only Galveston Island, but all the towns on the mainland and all the coast for many miles have been subjected to an overflow that has left the country in a deplorable unsanitary condition. This is the season of the year when yellow fever, cholera and other epidemic diseases have usually originated and done their worst ravages. If a plague were to add its horrors to the fearful havoc of the winds and waves, then indeed would the coast be ruined, and the spread of the disease would speedily involve the whole State and the South generally, resulting in a paralysis of commerce and a state of terror and helplessness, the cost of which cannot be even approximated or imagined.

CALL FOR MILITARY GUARDS.

"The strictest police and sanitary discipline and vigilance will be required to prevent something of this kind, and that is where the possible necessity of a legislative appropriation may become imperative. There is practically no fund at the command of the State authorities for those purposes. If the volunteer militia is to be used to police the stricken districts, there is only a nominal sum at the disposal of the Governor and Adjutant-General. That fund would not last a week.

"Besides, it is likely that a horde of vandals and vagabonds will congregate at the seat of the calamity to prey on the provisions and supplies that a generous public has contributed to the relief of the real sufferers.

" To establish and enforce proper sanitary regulations, remove the débris and sources of infection and maintain an effective police protection will require rigorous and intelligent organization under State control and adequately supported by public funds. It is not to be expected that the local authorities will be equal to these demands, for they are completely demoralized by the terrible calamity that has so recently swept over their country. They are exhausted, unnerved and broken in body, mind and spirit by the strain through which they have passed, and are in no condition to meet these after perils. This, in my judgment, is the phase of the problem that is most serious and may require legislative aid.

HOW TO MEET THE EMERGENCY.

" The cost of a special session, if the necessity exists, is not to be considered, for it is insignificant compared with the inestimable cost of the failure of the State to do its duty in the premises. Besides, the expense of a called session and of an adequate appropriation would be distributed over the entire taxpaying population of the State and would be inappreciable on each taxpayer. It is an emergency in which the responsibility for a mistake makes it a very troublesome question for the Governor.

" If there is the danger that I speak of, and I think no doubt can be entertained as to that, delay may be fatal to any action to be hereafter taken, for if the plague should once take root and begin its work, no amount of outlay and vigilance can ever compensate the loss caused by a hesitating or dilatory policy. On the other hand, the contributions made and to be made and the agencies already at the command of the authorities may be adequate for the necessities. I do not personally know just what the conditions and resources may be, but if anything is to be done it must be done speedily, and the responsibility for errors is not a light one. I do not doubt that the Governor is in touch with the situation and will do his duty."

General H. B. Stoddard, deputy grand master of the grand encampment of Knights Templars of the United States, one of the most exalted positions in America, returned to Houston from a visit to Galveston and made his headquarters there. He went down to size up the situation for the grand order of which he is the head. He was there two days, all of which time he used to get accurately at the facts. He moved about through the city to see for himself, and also talked to the prominent business men in order to reach a nearly accurate conclusion. He met prominent officials of his own and other orders, together with distinguished physicians.

"I agree with statements that it is a terrible disaster, but I think some of the estimates have been made too high," said he. "I want you to bear in mind if my investigation would indicate it, I would put the loss of life at any figure, no matter how great."

MACHINERY A COMPLETE LOSS.

Major R. B. Baer, receiver of the Galveston City Street Railway, who is in this city now, says that to-day he telegraphed the Guarantee Trust Company, the owners of the property, that it would take $200,000 to $250,000 to repair the damage to the street railway. The powerhouse and machinery are a complete loss and seven miles of track is gone, as well as all of the trestle work.

"After the storm and until I left Galveston yesterday I walked an average of ten miles a day," said Major Baer, "and I know there is hardly a building in the city that is not damaged, while the stocks of merchandise are damaged from 25 to 90 per cent. The Galveston, Houston and Northern and the Santa Fe both expect their roads to be open to Virginia Point by Saturday, and then some light draught steamboats will be put on to ply between Virginia Point and Galveston. Both of these roads will commence work on their bridges across the bay as soon as material can be gotten on the ground. The Santa Fe has now a force of 400 men working toward Virginia Point and a large force on the island repairing their track. The Southern Pacific is putting to work all the men they can get."

One of the Texas journals made editorial comment as follows : "Duty is still all that all can do. Many of the survivors of the storm are ill, others bruised, wounded, broken, hungry and breadless, others hapless orphans, too young to realize their sad condition.

There has never been in this country any other disaster to be compared with this. Where others have had to battle against wind or water, here the man and the woman and the child have found a dual foe—both wind and wave. Considering all the conditions and forces and dangers and dreadful results, it may be asserted without any word to modify the statement that this is the most grievous calamity of modern times.

TOO AWFUL FOR WORDS.

"It is a stunning blow to every Texan whose heart is in the right place. It is a calamity so dread that no one can afford to stop to consider himself or his own wounds. The duty which one owes to others comes first. Many are too far away from the scene of desolation and death to do anything; but they are not too far away to give something, and thus to help along the heartrending work which is now going on in Galveston and in other places along the coast. The work of uncovering bodies, of burying the dead, of supplying the needs of those who require assistance, is going on, and a beginning has been made in cleaning and clearing the city to prevent a general spread of sickness, which is sure to come unless this work is thoroughly done. This task will require a week more, possibly many weeks more.

"The removal of huge masses of bricks, stones, timber and decaying stock in large houses which have gone down is necessarily a slow business, yet this difficult task must be performed before even the work of burying the dead can be completed. From the ruins of some houses of this kind scores of bodies are yet to be taken. Unless ample help is procurable this task is almost a hopeless undertaking. It is in order to repeat that it is a duty which must be performed without delay. So far Texans have responded nobly. The same may be said of people the country over. The main purpose is to keep before all the fact that the service of sympathy and mercy must be continued for a little while if the victims of the storm are to be saved and succored.

"As an exchange says, the elements seem to have been wreaking vengeance on Texas this year. In April the Colorado and

Brazos Valleys were swept by floods, entailing great loss in life and property. Austin suffered severely. This flood followed a more disastrous one of last year, which laid waste some of the best farms in the State, destroyed crops too late for replanting, drowned thousands of cattle, horses, mules and hogs, and many people. With all these recent disasters Texas is in a more prosperous condition than the State has ever been in before, taking the whole country over.

"While certain of the river valleys have been swept by flood, the rich uplands, particularly those of north Texas, the orchard and garden lands of east Texas and of the coast country and the small grain and pasture lands of the west have brought forth abundant crops, and, speaking generally, the people are in a good way. The high prices for wheat, corn, cotton and other products of the field or ranch have told a hopeful story, and a wise change from the old-time one-crop habit has done much to help along. In spite of the disasters of this and of last year, barring the victims of the floods alluded to, the people of this State are in good condition and quite ready to do all in their power to help along their less fortunate fellow citizens.

TEXAS HAS IMMENSE TERRITORY.

"Texas is a vast State, and this fact might make it appear that more storms or other direful visitations fell to the lot of this people than residents of other parts of the country find it necessary to endure. The fact is that many States have been visited by floods this season, and in some places floods are feared year after year. So it is of other destructive visitations. They must be expected now and then anywhere from Maine to California, or, for that matter, at any place the world around. There is only one thing to do about it.

"People must prepare in advance for such troubles as far as possible and must stand ready to take the consequences and make the best of them. So it is now. So it will continue to be, here and elsewhere.

CHAPTER XIII.

Refugees Continue the Terrible Story—Rigid Military Patrol —The City in Darkness at Night—Hungry and Ragged Throngs.

PERSONS who arrived in Dallas from Galveston not only confirmed all that had been said before or written about the disaster there, but gave more details of the horror. Each interview was more distressing than the one preceding it, and it seemed that even an approximate idea of the truth was yet to be given. Some accounts told of the deadly flood. Others told of the work of vandals and their speedy death at the hands of Uncle Sam's fighters, and of hunger and sickness, woe and misery.

Newt M. Smith, of Dallas, who was sent to Galveston by the local insurance men to assist in the relief of the needy brethren in that city, was one of those to return with important information.

" When we arrived in Houston we were informed that no one would be permitted on the train without a pass from Mayor Brashear, of Houston," he said. " We hunted the Mayor up and were told that 2000 passes had already been issued and that the train would carry only 800 people. We finally succeeded in getting on board without passes, some of the men climbing through the windows. Nearly all the dwellings and business houses of the small stations on the International and Great Northern between Houston and Galveston are either blown down or seriously damaged.

"At certain places along the railroad every telegraph pole was down for a distance of one-half or three-quarters of a mile, poles and wires being across the track. Some twelve or fifteen miles this side of the bay at one place I counted the carcasses of fourteen large cattle and horses that had drowned. Just before reaching Texas City Junction it was necessary for the passengers to abandon the train for the purpose of repairing and rebuilding a bridge across trestle which had washed away. Volunteers were called for to go into the mud and water, and more men volunteered than could get around the bridge timbers to replace them.

"It required three or four hours in which to repair the track at this point, during which some 250 passengers left the train, taking with them their valises, jugs of water and provisions, and walked a distance of six miles through the mud and water to Texas City. About two and a half miles west of Texas City, and about two miles from the bay, out on the bald prairie, is a large dredge-boat. For fifteen miles back from the bay can be seen millions of feet of débris of every description, including tops of houses, sashes, doors, pianos and pieces of household furniture of every kind. There were something over twenty-six bales of cotton that I counted out on the prairie inside of that distance, all compressed cotton which had evidently come from the wharf at Galveston.

BURYING THE DEAD.

"After arriving at Texas City we had to wait two or three hours for a boat, and during the time a number of the party walked down the beach and discovered and buried the bodies of eight men, women and children. A memorandum was taken describing as well as possible the people buried, and a headboard put up with a number corresponding to the one in the book. We left Texas City at 3.30 Tuesday evening, arriving at Galveston at 9.30.

"While on the way over we discovered the bodies of several people and quite a number of horses and cows, and as we got off the boat, just under the wharf was a pile of twenty or twenty-five drowned people. Just after leaving the wharf we saw the remains of seven people which were being prepared for cremation. The town is under martial law, and on my way up to the city I was hailed by guards three different times, but after explaining I was permitted to proceed.

"I do not think the conditions at Galveston have been overdrawn by the newspaper reports. In fact, it is more deplorable than any words or picture could portray to the mind. Before we arrived several parties had been shot for robbing the dead and looting houses. Some of our party walked down the beach and found a couple of white men who were breaking open and robbing the trunks which had floated ashore, taking the garments from them and drying them on the grass. These trunks contained all kinds of family wearing apparel.

"We found that all the insurance men of Galveston and their immediate families were safe excepting two married sisters of Mr. Harris, who were drowned with their eight children. They were drowned in their own yards and the bodies afterward recovered and buried there. The loss to the insurance companies from a financial standpoint will be very heavy on account of the cancellation of policies under which there is now no liability, the houses having been destroyed. Again, a great many people who are indebted to the insurance agents cannot pay for the reason that they have lost everything.

CITY WILL RECOVER FROM THE BLOW.

"If the Government and the railroads will repair and rebuild their property in Galveston the city may recover from the blow, but unless this is done there will be very slim chances for the city to attain the position as a commercial point it has heretofore held. The losses of life and accident insurance companies will be something enormous.

"What the people of Galveston need most, in my opinion, is lime and workingmen, especially carpenters and tinners. The citizens are fully aware of the sympathy they are receiving and the liberal manner in which the people of the country have come to their relief from a financial standpoint, but the immediate need is a sufficient number of hands to clean up the city and remove the débris. Among the important buildings destroyed were the cotton mills, baggage factory and the electric light and power houses, the large elevators and the Texas flouring mills, with several million bushels of wheat."

W. E. Parry, of Dallas, was one of those who weathered the hurricane in the union depot at Galveston. He said that he was particularly fortunate, and did not even get wet. In telling the story of his experience he said: " I left Houston Saturday morning and knew nothing of the storm until we reached Virginia Point. The wind was blowing a gale and the water in the bay was high and a considerable sea running. We got over on Galveston Island at 10.30 and found the track washed out. A switch engine and a coach was sent to us and everybody, including the train crew, was transferred. The water was rising all this time and the wind was increasing in violence. The water got over the track and put out the fire in the engine, but the steam lasted long enough to get into the depot. While going in the train crew had to go ahead and push floating poles and ties and wreckage off the track.

" We got to the depot at 2.10 in the afternoon. The wind was still growing stronger and the air was full of sheets of water. The streets were waist-deep and the water was running like a millrace. We could see people wading around trying to collect their families and effects, and the bus was still running between the depot and the Tremont. I knew the depot was a new, strong building, and I decided to stay there.

GREAT GUSTS OF WIND.

" Every gust of wind seemed fiercer and more wicked than any. It was blowing in a straight line from the northeast in great, vicious gusts, as if it would tear down everything. Soon the water came into the ground floor of the depot, and we had to go to the second floor. The wind kept increasing in velocity and began to blow the windows in, tearing out frames and all and throwing them across the rooms. Men went to work and put additional braces across the large panes of glass and wedged them tight with newspapers.

" I saw a boy driving an express wagon, trying to reach the depot. A gust struck him, and over went the wagon, horse and all, the boy landing on the sidewalk. He was a nervy youngster and came back, and I could see the knife in his hand as he cut the horse loose in the water. He mounted and rode back to town.

" Night came on, and still the storm grew worse and worse. No man can describe the pandemonium of sound. The wind would yell and shriek until it resembled the cry of an enraged animal. All sorts of missles were flying through the air and clattering against the walls. Cornices, section of tin and thousands of slates from the roofs were flying every way. The instinct to escape was strong among all in that depot, and it was suggested that we join hands and try to make our way up town. I told those who wanted to go that they would be killed with flying slate, and it was decided to stay.

"It is hard for men to sit still and do nothing when in mortal fear of their lives, and I saw men sit, clench their hands and set their teeth, and sweat breaking out all over them. It was an awful strain on the nerves. We reasoned that we were in as good a place as we could get, though no one expected to live through it.

OLD GENTLEMAN WITH BAROMETER.

"There was an old gentleman in the depot who seemed to be a scientist. He had a barometer with him, and every few minutes he would examine it by the solitary lantern that lit the room, and tell us it was still falling and the worst was yet to come. It was a direful thing to say, and some of the crowd did not like it, but the instrument seemed to be reliable. About 9 o'clock the old man examined it and announced that it stood at 27.90. I give the figures for the benefit of any one who wants to know the reading at the heighth of the storm. He announced to the crowd that we were gone and that nothing could exist in such a storm.

"At that time the hurricane was awful. Once in a while I could hear a muffled detonation, a sort of rumbling boom. I knew that it was a house falling, and it did not add to my comfort. There was no lightning or thunder, and at times the moon gave some light. The clouds did not appear to be up any distance, but to drag the ground.

"About 10 o'clock the old man looked at his instrument and gave a whoop of joy: 'The worst has passed,' he shouted. 'We are all safe. The storm will soon be over.' Few took in the full meaning of his words for the wind was still a hurricane. Within almost as many minutes it had risen ten points and we felt safe.

"I went over the island the next day and words can not describe what I saw. Everything was wrecked along the gulf front for three to four blocks back, the ground was clear and the houses which had stood there were piled in a windrow which in many places must have been fifty feet high

"What is needed is able-bodied, honest men to clean up this wreck and remove bodies and bury them. They want no idlers or surplus people to feed and protect. Disinfectants to purify the streets from the slime and silt left by the water are necessary.

"I saw 600 bodies in an undertaker's house. I saw them loaded on floats, piled up like cotton, black and white alike, with arms and limbs sticking out in every direction. I must have seen nearly a thousand bodies along the wharves and coming across the bay. It was frightful."

ON THE BOAT ALL NIGHT.

T. L. Monagan, of Dallas, who went down with the Dallas relief committee, returned and said: "We got there by wagon and boat about 10 o'clock Tuesday night and remained on the boat during the night. We went over to the hotel in the morning and found relief work well organized. They need men to clean the débris out of the streets and to get the city cleaned up. They are disposing of the dead as fast as possible, and the safety of the living precludes any delay for identification. Many are being buried at sea and some cremated.

"We went over the city and along the gulf front saw the immense windrow of wrecked houses. Not a street from Tenth to Twenty-Third was so we could get through. The ground fronting the beach is clear of houses the whole length of the city. The Denver Resurvey was washed away. In my opinion the salt meadow to the southwest of Virginia Point on the mainland must be covered with dead and wreckage. It is an awful thing and it will be thirty days before they can get in shape down there at the present rate."

F. McCrillis arrived from Galveston. He was in the storm and saw the frightful destruction. He said: "The relief committees are doing noble work on the island. The people of Galveston are rising to the occasion and I never saw braver, stronger-hearted or more intelligent men. It is wonderful the way they face the fearful disaster. They have made no mistakes.

"Some negroes were killed for looting, but since that time it has stopped. The work of cleaning up is being pushed as rapidly as possible. Every Galvestonian is confident that the city will rise from the disaster and sustain its commercial and industrial position."

HON. MORRIS SHEPPARD'S ACCOUNT.

Hon. Morris Sheppard, son of Congressman John L. Sheppard, returned to Texarkana from Galveston, sound and well, though a little broken up from the shock. When seen he said concerning his experience in the Galveston storm:

"I had gone there to address the Woodmen Saturday night, but the weather got so bad I concluded to leave. I went to the Union Depot about 5 o'clock to catch a train that was to leave for Houston a little later. When the storm broke we all ran up stairs. There were about 100 men and three ladies, and all remained in one room for thirteen hours. While the storm was at its height and the waters were wildest a number of men in one corner of the room struck up the familiar hymn, 'Jesus Lover of My Soul,' and sang with great effect, especially the lines 'While the nearer waters roll, while the tempest still is high,' etc.

"We all expected death momentarily, yet nearly all seemed resigned; several actually slept. The wind ripped up the iron roof of the depot building as though it were paper. A wooden plank was driven through the iron hull of the Whitehall, a large English merchantman, whose captain said that in his experience of twenty-five years he had never before known such a fearful hurricane. One lady clung to her pet pug dog through it all, and landed him safely at Houston Monday morning. When daylight finally came, an old, gray-bearded man was seen near the building wading in water to his armpits. We hailed him and requested him to get us a boat. He turned upon us and cursed us with a perfect flood of oaths, then turning around walked deliberately out into the bay and was swept away."

APPEAL TO COLORED PEOPLE.

Professor H. C. Bell, of Denton, Grand Master of the Colored Odd Fellows, issued the following self-explanatory circular:

"To the Lodges and Members of the Grand United Order of Odd Fellows in Texas: Dear Brethren—The greatest calamity that has ever visited any city in America visited Galveston on the 8th instant, leaving in its wake thousands of dead and helpless people of our race, together with the white race. It is our duty to help, as far as we are able, to relieve the suffering condition of the citizens of Galveston. It goes without saying that the white citizens of Texas have always contributed freely to ameliorate and alleviate suffering humanity; it is, therefore, our bounden duty, and, indeed, this is a most fitting opportunity for us, as members of the greatest negro organization in the world, to show to our white fellow-citizens of Texas the charitable spirit that has always characterized Odd Fellows. Besides this, many members of our fraternity are victims of the direful storm of the 8th instant at Galveston. They appeal for our assistance. Therefore, I, H. C. Bell, do issue this appeal to the lodges and members for relief for our brethren in Galveston."

The well-known writer and correspondent, Joel Chandler Harris, writing from Galveston, says:

"As was naturally to be expected, the facts already brought to light show that the devastation wrought at Galveston and other coast towns in Texas by the unhappy conjunction of wind and sea outrun and overmatch the wildest conjectures of those who were calm enough immediately after the event to give out such estimates as tallied with what their own eyes had seen.

"The tremendous loss of life which has been verified by all accounts gives this harrowing catastrophe a first place among events of the kind. Indeed, among modern disasters it has an awful pre-eminence, and this fact lends wings to a suggestion which I should like to emphasize.

"It is this: If the horror of the calamity is to be measured by the loss of life, the same measure should be applied to the pressing necessities of those who have been stripped of everything save life. However much we may deplore the loss of life, the dead are done for. They are beyond and above the crying demands and necessities which press upon those who are left alive.

"In the nature of things, the condition of thousands of those who have been spared is far more pitiable than that of the dead. Their resources have been swept away by wind and tide, and they are desolate in the midst of desolation. The catastrophe was so vast in extent and so furious in its sweep that it will be many a long day before the survivors are able to recover from its effects.

NEVER WEARY OF GIVING.

"Outside aid is absolutely necessary in order to prevent suffering even greater than that which accompanied the outburst of the elements. The large-hearted public is never weary of giving in cases where the necessity of giving is absolute. With the American public sympathy and pity provoke unbounded generosity.

"All geographical lines, all differences are completely broken down by any emergency which stirs the tender heart of the people. But it frequently happens that this native generosity is not as prompt to act as necessity demands, especially in cases where the least delay adds to the suffering of those who have been left helpless. No tongue can tell, and no pen can describe the awful results of a storm such as that which has visited the Texas coast.

"The sea island of the South Atlantic coast had a similar visitation several years ago, and the present writer was commissioned to visit the scene and depict the results. He arrived upon the ground more than a fortnight after the hurricane had passed through the islands, and though Miss Clara Barton and her assistants of the Red Cross Society had been able to get in touch with the sufferers more promptly than usual, there were many still on the point of starvation. No doubt many perished within sight and hearing of the succor which the public and the Red Cross Society were so anxious to give.

" Fortunately, the islands are but sparsely populated, as compared with the region which has recently been devasted, and in consequence, there was far less suffering than is to-day to be found in the track of the hurricane which has just wiped out whole communities and caused such an extraordinary loss of life. If the fact to be emphasized and insisted on is that it was necessary for generosity to act promptly after the sea island catastrophe, there is a far greater necessity for promptness in the present emergency, owing to the larger number of people involved.

REFUSED TO BELIEVE THE TIDINGS.

" The difficulty in the case of the sea island hurricane was that a large number of conservative people—the very class which may be depended on to respond most liberally to appeals in behalf of the unfortunate—refused to believe the stories sent out by the press agents and newspaper correspondents who made haste to visit the scene of disaster, placing them in the category of newspaper sensations.

" The fact remains, however, that the naked details of the sea island hurricane never were put in possession of the public. Curious incidents and queer results were dwelt upon and described, but a detailed account of the effects of that storm has never been printed. Those who have never visited the scene of one of these elemental disturbances can have no idea of the extent of the havoc and ruin wrought by them. The results must be seen and felt before they can be understood and appreciated.

" They are of such a character as to elude and evade all efforts at description. All the newspapers can do is to give a bald account of incidents.

" But to-day we are face to face with a few of the horrors of a calamity that outdoes any similar visitation with which the nation is familiar. The situation in the afflicted territory is piteous in the extreme. And may the nation's blessing rest on all who give succor to those stricken by this awful hurricane curse of the sunny southland."

" It would be difficult to exaggerate the awful scene that meets the visitors everywhere," said Clara Barton, after arriving in Galveston. "The situation could not be exaggerated. Probably the loss of life will exceed any estimate that has been made.

"In those parts of the city where destruction was the greatest there must still be hundreds of bodies under the debris. At the end of the island first struck by the storm, and which was swept clean of every vestige of the splendid residences that covered it, the ruin is inclosed by a towering wall of debris, under which many bodies are buried. The removal of this has scarcely even begun.

PEOPLE DAZED INTO CALM.

"The story that will be told when this mountain of ruins is removed may multiply the horrors of the fearful situation. As usual in great calamities the people are dazed and speak of their losses with an unnatural calmness that would astonish those who do not understand it.

"I do believe there is danger of an epidemic. But the nervous strain upon the people, as they come to realize their condition may be nearly as fatal. They talk of friends that are gone with tearless eyes, making no allusion to the loss of property.

"A professional gentleman who called upon me this afternoon, a gentleman of splendid human sympathies and refinement, wore a soiled black flannel shirt, without a coat, and in apologizing for his appearance said in the most casual, light-hearted way: 'Excuse my appearance: I have just come in from burying the dead.'

"But these people will break down under this strain, and the Red Cross is glad of the force of strong, competent workers which it has brought to its relief.

"Portions of the business part of the city escaped the greatest severity of the storm and are left partially intact. Thus it is possible to purchase here nearly all the supplies that may be wanting. Still, the Galveston merchants should be given the benefit of home demands.

"Mayor Jones has offered to the Red Cross as headquarters

the best building at his disposal. Relief is coming as rapidly as the crippled transportation facilities will admit. No one need fear, after seeing the brave and manly way in which these people are helping themselves, that too much outside aid will be given."

Reported dead several times, their obituaries printed in Galveston and Houston, Peter Boss, wife and son, formerly of Chicago, were found, after having passed through a most thrilling experience.

TRIED TO ESCAPE WITH HER MONEY.

Mrs. Boss' story of her experience in the disaster was a thrilling one. With her husband and son she was seated at supper in her home on Twelfth street when the storm broke. She seized a handkerchief containing $2000 from a bureau, and, placing it in her bosom, went with her husband and the son to the second story.

There they remained until the water reached them and they leaped into the darkness and the storm. They lit on a wooden cistern upon which they rode the entire night, clinging with one hand to the top of the cistern. Several times Mrs. Boss lost her hold and fell back into the water, only to be drawn up again by her son. Timbers crashed against their queer boat, people on all sides of them were crushed to death or drawn into the whirling waters, but with grim perseverance the Boss family held on and rode the night out.

Mrs. Boss was pushed off the cistern several times by her excited husband, but young Boss' presence of mind always saved her. With her feet crushed and bleeding, her clothing torn from her body and nearly exhausted, the woman was finally taken from her perilous position several hours after the hurricane started.

Her companions were without clothing and were delirious. They were the only persons saved from the entire block in which they lived. They were taken to emergency hospitals, where they all tossed in delirium until Sunday. Mrs. Boss lost her money, and the family, wealthy a week before, was penniless. They had to appeal to the city authorities for aid, and got but little.

A Chicago journal established a Relief Bureau at Galveston, and sent thither a special commissioner who, under date of September 15, gave the following account:

"I spent part of last night with the Chicago American Relief Bureau. I had no business there. The nurses and doctors had done all there was to do. They have worked like great big-spirited Trojans. The babies were all abed and asleep. The women were fed and the homeless and destitute men who had wandered in for shelter had been tucked away in the gallery and made as comfortable as possible.

A HEROIC LAD.

"The gas was out in the great theatre, and a few candles shed a flickering light. A lad told this story: He lost every one on earth he loved and who loved him in the flood. He swam two miles and over with his little brother on his back, and then saw his brother killed by a piece of falling timber after they had reached dry land and what he supposed was safety.

"He is sixteen years old, this boy of mine; tall and strong in every way, and when he had dug a shallow grave in the sand for his little brother he went up and down the prairies and buried those he found. Alone in the declining sun, without food or water, impelled by some vague instinct to do something for some one, this boy did this, and yesterday they found him fainting in a field and brought him to us. We put him to bed, made him take a bowl of soup and gave him a bath.

"He seemed perfectly amazed at the idea that any one should want to do anything for him. We only got his story out of him by persistent and earnest questioning. He said there was none to tell. Last night he was talking in his sleep.

"'That's all right, Charley,' he said over and over again. 'Brother won't let you get hurt. Don't you be scared, Charley, and I will save you!' and he threw his arms out and about as if he was swimming.

"Hour after hour he swam and hour after hour he comforted his little brother, and when I laid my hand on his forehead and he

woke and remembered where he was, he smiled up into my face as
a tired child would smile into the face of one he loved, and went to
sleep and began to swim through the black and troubled waters
with Charley on his strong young shoulders again.

"He is utterly alone in the world now. The doctors are a
little afraid of brain fever for him, but I believe we can stave it off,
and if we can we are going to keep him in the relief corps and
give him work and something to do and live for as long as we are
here. His name is on the list of patients published with this article. If anyone who sees it remembers and wants to befriend this
boy telegraph to the American Relief Bureau at Houston and we
will attend to it.

HUNGRY AND HALF CLAD.

"There was a new party of them which came in last night
late from Galveston. About fifty came in after 10 o'clock, hungry,
half clad and worn to the very edge of human endurance. They
stood timidly at the door and one of them begged for shelter as if
she thought she would be refused. Most of our cots with mattresses in them were taken, but that did not make any difference.
Dr. Bloch, of Chicago, and Dr. O'Brien, of New York, got their
heads together and in less than half an hour every one of those
fifty people had some sort of a bed to sleep on and in three-quarters
of an hour they were all fed.

"We engaged two cooks, a man and a woman, yesterday, but
neither of them came. That did not make the slightest particle
of difference. Whoever was hungry was fed at the relief station,
and whoever was naked was clothed and whoever was sick was
attended. Nobody knew or cared how long they had been working or whether they themselves had time to get a morsel of food.
Everybody did everything. I saw Dr. O'Brien down on his knees
taking off a pair of soaked shoes for a woman who was so tired she
could not lift her hand to her head.

"The fear of pestilence has become so widespread that the authorities are taking measures to prevent a wholesale exodus of able-
bodied men, whose services are urgently needed at the present time.

The dread of plague has seized upon the negro population so strongly that in some instances they refuse to work in cleaning up the city.

"The tidal wave caused a heavier loss of life along the coast west of Galveston than was at first supposed. Scores of corpses are being found lying along the beach. Some of the bodies may be those who were buried at sea from Galveston and floated into shore again, but the position of many shows that they were natives of the little coast towns suburban to Galveston. When more order is made at Galveston attention will be turned to those places and the bodies of the dead there will be buried or burned.

"The work of disposing of the bodies is being expedited as rapidly as possible, but the crying need is disinfectants. Hundreds of barrels of lime are being asked for in order to prevent contagion. Health officers say that the worst is to be feared from the small pools of stagnant water which fill cellars of the wrecked houses and the clogged drainage system.

CLOTHING AND PROVISIONS.

"The Chicago corps of surgeons and nurses, under Dr. L. D. Johnson, buried thirty-two bodies between the hours of 1 A. M. and 8 A. M. to-day in Alvin, Hitchcock and Seabrook, and gave provisions, clothing and medicine to 300. Its members also attended to twenty-six persons suffering from broken bones, cuts and other wounds requiring surgical work, and nursed more than fifty.

"This is considered the greatest piece of relief work done since the storm. The bodies buried had been lying in the fields a week, and were decomposed and spreading disease germs. An extra car of provisions is being shipped to that district.

"Insanity is developing among the sufferers at a terrible rate. It is estimated by the medical authorities that there are 500 deranged men and women who should be in asylums, and the number is increasing. These poor creatures form the most pitiable side of Galveston's horror. They stand in groups and cry hysterically. They are harmless, for their troubles have left them without strength to do harm.

"Mentally unbalanced by the suddenness and horror of their losses, men and women meet on the streets and compare their losses and then laugh the laugh of insanity as a newcomer joins the group and tells possibly of a loss greater than that of the others. Their laughter is something to chill the blood in the veins of the strongest men. They are maddened with sorrow, and do not realize their losses as they will when reason returns, if it ever returns.

"Some of them are absolute raving maniacs. One man, Charles Thompson, a gardener, as soon as he was out of personal danger that awful night, commenced rescuing women and children, and saved seventy people. He then lost his mind. Two policemen were detailed to capture him, but he heard them approaching and leaped from the third-story window of an adjoining building and escaped.

THE YOUNGEST NURSE.

"The Chicago Relief Corps has the youngest, and, considering her years, most efficient nurse among the hundreds engaged in relief work. She is Rosalea Glenn, eleven years old, a refugee from Morgan Point. Together with her mother, Mrs. Minnie F. Glenn, and two smaller children, she was received at the hospital last night.

"To-day Rosalea asked to be assigned to part of one of the wards. She astonished trained nurses by her cleverness, and her services proved as valuable as those of any one on the force. She is now the hospital pet. Her father is Albert W. Glenn, a boatman. The home of the Glenns was washed away, but the family were saved by a flight of seven miles into the country.

"Some of the advertisements in the Galveston News are very striking. Garbadee, Iban & Co. make this announcement: 'Our help has generously volunteered to work to-day to assist the necessities of the flood sufferers. Our store will open from 9 A. M. until 5 P. M. Orders from the Relief Committee will be filled.'

CHAPTER XIV.

Dead Babes Floating in the Waters—Sharp Crack of Soldiers' Rifles—Tears Mingle With the Flood— Doctors and Nurses for the Sick and Dying.

ONE of the most harrowing experiences during the scene of destruction and death at Galveston was that of a young lady belonging to Elgin, Illinois. Stamped upon her mind until she shuddered and cried aloud, that she might forget all its horrors and terrible memories, Miss Pixley stood in the Dearborn Street Station and told of the Galveston flood. Surrounded by her relatives and friends who had given her up as dead, Miss Pixley, who was the first arrival from the storm swept district, told her story between outbursts of bitter tears.

"Oh, those eyes," she cried, "that I might put them from my mind. I can see those little children, mere babies, go floating by my place of refuge, dead, dead! God alone knows the suffering I went through. Thousands, yes, thousands, of poor souls were carried over the brink of death in the twinkling of an eye, and I saw it all."

MISS PIXLEY'S GRAPHIC STORY.

This is her story, as she told it: "I had been in Galveston for about six weeks, visiting Miss Lulu George, who lives on Thirty-fifth street. It was not until after the noon hour of Saturday that we were frightened. Buildings had gone down as mere egg shells before that death-dealing wind.

"About 1.30 o'clock I told Miss George that we must make our way to another building about half a block away. The water had risen over five feet in two hours, and as I hurried to the front door the wind tore down my hair and I was blinded for a time.

"I turned my eyes to the west and for three long miles there was not a building standing, everything had been swept away.

How we ever reached the two-story building a hundred yards away I do not know.   We waded through the water and every few minutes we were carried off our feet and dashed against the floating debris.

ALMOST DROWNED IN CELLAR.

"The building we were trying to reach was a store and the foundation kept out the water. We hurried to the cellar and stayed there for several hours.   At last the wind-swept waves found an opening and broke through the foundation and we had a mad run to escape the rushing, swirling waters.

"We reached the first floor and I shrank into a corner, expecting every second to be carried out to my death.   How it happened I can never tell, but this and one other building were the only ones left for blocks around. As it was, several people were killed in the building we occupied and the other house that was left standing.

"After a time I felt faint from hunger and, while too weak from fright to seek food, I told Miss George that I would go into another room.   I staggered along the floor until I reached a window, and fell, half fainting, through it. As I leaned there I witnessed sights that I pray God will never make another see.

BLOOD-CHILLING SCENES.

"Whirling by me, bodies, more than I could dare count, were crushed and mangled between a jumble of timbers and debris. Men, women and children went by, sinking, floating, dashing on I know not where.   I wanted to close my eyes, but I could not.   I cried aloud and made an attempt to go to my friends, but I was exhausted, and all I could do was to watch the terrible scenes.

"Babies, oh, such pretty little ones, too, were carried on and on, gowned in dainty clothing, their eyes open, staring in mute terror above.   Thank Providence they were dead.   I was partly blinded by tears, but I could still see through the mist.   Little arms seemed to stretch toward me asking assistance and there I lay, half prostrated, too weak to lend assistance.

"How it all ended I know not.   I must have fainted for I awakened with 'We are saved, Alice,' ringing in my ears.

FLEES FROM HORRIBLE SIGHTS.

" When I found we could get out of the city I declared I would go at all cost. I thought of home and my parents and I wanted to telegraph, just like thousands of others, that I was safe.

" It was days before we could get away, however, and then it was in a most terrible confusion. Eighty-eight persons crowded on a small boat and started for Houston.

" The day we left the militia was out in all its force. I could hear the sharp reports of a rifle and the wail of some soul as he paid the penalty for his thieving operations.

" Later I saw the soldiers with their glistening rifles leveled at scores of men and saw them topple forward dead. Oh, they had to shoot those terrible beasts, for they were robbing the dead. They groveled in blood, it seemed.

" I saw with my own eyes the fingers of women cut off by regular demons in the search for jewels. The soldiers came and killed them and it was well.

HUMAN BODIES IN FIRE HEAP.

" As we made our way toward the boat that was to take us from the City of Death I saw great clouds of smoke rising in the air. Upon the top of flaming boards thousands of bodies were being reduced to ashes.

" It was best, for the odor that arose from the dead bodies was awful. Still it made one's heart ache with a sorrow never to be equaled as one witnessed little children tossed into the midst of the hissing flames. Do you wonder I cry?

" Before me, no matter which way I turned, I could see dead iodies, their cold eyes gazing at me with staring intentness. I closed my eyes and stumbled forward, hoping I might escape for a moment the sight of dead bodies, but no; the moment I would open them again, right at my feet I would find the form of some poor creature.

" Coming to Chicago on the train I read the papers. They are mistaken, away wrong. They only say 5,000 dead. It will be more than 10,000. I know I am right; every one in Galveston talks of 12,000, 15,000 and 18,000 dead, but it will be 10,000 at the very least.

"I believe the worst sight I witnessed was the 2,800 bodies being carried out to sea and buried in the gulf. Huge barges were tied to the wharfs and loaded with the unknown dead. As fast as one barge was filled it made its way out from the shore, and weighting the bodies, men cast them into the water."

I. Thompson, a young man who was very active in saving life during the night of the storm, became insane because of the awful scenes he witnessed. Thompson's friends first noticed his condition when he told that one of the persons he rescued had deposited $10,000 in one of the banks to his credit, and that he was going to live in luxury the rest of his life.

TRAGIC INCIDENTS.

Thompson retired to his room, on the third floor of the Washington Hotel, seemingly sane. Soon afterwards he began to moan, and soon became violent, rushing from one side of his room to the other and declaring his determination to commit suicide. Employes of the hotel did all they could to pacify the man, and during the night he became more rational and lay down. The person engaged to watch him was compelled to leave the room for a short time early in the morning, and when he returned he found that Thompson had wrenched the shutters off his window and leaped out upon an awning and thence to the street.

Thompson was seen to run toward the bay, and in all probability he threw himself overboard and was drowned, as he was not seen or heard of afterward.

Another case is that of a young woman who was caught in the rain, and, with two other women and about fifty men and boys, found refuge in an office. It was with the utmost difficulty she could restrain herself during the fearful storm, and she frequently became hysterical and cried out for her mother, sisters and her brother and his family. As the storm gradually subsided the young woman became more calm, and when morning broke she started for her home quite reassured. She found a wild waste of waters sweeping over the site of her home. Her dear ones were missing.

Among the first victims carried into the temporary morgue were the young woman's mother, brother and two children. These were quickly followed by her brother's wife and her two sisters. The shock overthrew the girl's reason, and she became a nervous wreck, without a relative in the world.

Hundreds of such tragic incidents as these marked the week, and the number of men and women who lost their reason was very large.

HARROWING TALES TOLD BY SURVIVORS.

Many strange incidents of the hurricane were gathered from the tales of the survivors. They told of pitiable deaths, of fearful destructions of property and of strange incidents of the great force of the storm. The following are just a few of the many that were told by refugees in this city:

One of the most remarkable escapes recorded during the flood was that of a United States batteryman on duty at the forts, who had been picked up on Morgan's Point, wounded but alive. He had buffeted the waves for five days and lived through a terrible experience. Morgan's Point is thirty miles from Galveston.

Another man who passed though a similar experience was found floating on the roof of a house on the open sea, over one hundred miles distant from Galveston. He was half famished, but quickly recovered upon being taken aboard.

Dr. H. C. Buckner, of the Buckner Orphan's Home at Dallas, brought with him from Galveston thirty-six little children who were made homeless, fatherless and motherless by the storm. Many of the children were suffering from cuts and bruises, and all were destitute of clothing except the tattered and torn garments which they had on their backs. They were taken to the Children's Hospital in Haskell avenue, in Dallas, to have their wounds treated and to recuperate before being sent to the home proper, six miles east of the city. The children are from all walks of life, and were taken in charge by Dr. Buckner while in Galveston as the ones most in need of immediate attention.

Reports show that three-fourths of the Velasco people lost their homes and four persons were drowned. Eight bodies were washed ashore at Surfside, supposed to be from Galveston. At Quintana 75 per cent. of the buildings are destroyed. No lives were lost there, though a number were injured. Velasco has hardly a house that will bear inspection. People are suffering for the necessities of life and many who are sick need medicines.

At Seabrooke, Texas, thirty-three out of thirty-four houses floated away and twenty-one people were drowned. At Hitchcock a large pile-driver of the Southern Pacific works at Galveston, and also a large barge partly laden with coal, are lying in the pear orchards several miles from the coast. Box cars, railway iron, drawbridges, houses, schooners and all conceivable things are lying over the prairie, some fifteen miles from their former location.

A TRAGIC WEDDING CEREMONY.

At the Tremont Hotel in Galveston a wedding occurred Thursday night, which was not attended with music and flowers and a gathering of merrymaking friends and relatives. Mrs. Brice Roberts had expected some day to marry Earnest Mayo. The storm which desolated so many homes deprived her of almost everything on earth—father, mother, sister and brother. She was left destitute. Her sweetheart, too, was a sufferer. He lost much of his possessions in Dickinson, but he stepped bravely forward and took his sweetheart to his home.

A pathetic story of the Galveston flood is that of Mrs. Mary Quayle, of Liverpool, England, who is now on her journey home. She had only been two days in the city with her husband when the storm came. She goes home, her husband dead, and herself a nervous wreck. Mr. and Mrs. Quayle had taken apartments in Lucas terrace, Galveston. During the storm Mr. Quayle went to a window, when a sudden burst of wind tore out the panes and sucked him, as it were, out of the house. Mrs. Quayle, in the rear of the room, was thrown against a wall and stunned. No trace of her husband's body has been found.

It will be a long time before many of the survivors of the Galveston catastrophe can appreciate the nature of the calamity which has befallen them. One woman laughingly told another that she had saved her baby, but that her two boys and her husband had been drowned. She was evidently insane.

An eye-witness, writing on September 16th, said: "Galveston is striving manfully to rise from its ashes. A reign of terror has been averted, Hope crowns the day. More than a thousand men are clearing the streets of debris. They are working night and day. Their efforts so far have been expended in picking up carcasses and gathering bodies into piles and burning them. Separate pyres are built for human bodies and animals, and the work progresses rapidly. The task is heartrendering, and many able bodied men have succumbed to the ordeal.

GIGANTIC DISINFECTION.

"Hundreds of women and children who are trying to get away from the city to the mainland find the task difficult. The slowness of the distracted ones is not due to tardiness or hesitation on their part. On the contrary, it is a scramble to get away, and the shattered wharves are lined with persons awaiting their turn. Transportation facilities are very meagre. There are few boats to be had. The Lawrence, a 200-ton propeller, is the only steamer carrying persons across to Texas City.

"One of the most hopeful features of the situation is the arrival of hundreds of barrels of disinfectants, such as carbolic acid and chloride of lime. Two thousand barrels of these could be advantageously used. The Board of Health shows signs of vigor and of an appreciation of the danger that confronts the city and contiguous territory. Every effort is being made to deodorize the ruins and to quickly dispose of the dead as soon as they are reached.

"The work of cleaning and disinfecting the streets is carried on with vigor, and the results are quite noticeable, especially in the central part of the city. Gutters in Tremont street were opened and the slush and debris from them carted to the city dump. This allowed the water to drain off. Centre street and the Strand were also worked on with excellent results, the gutters being

opened and disinfectants generally distributed. Several other streets
in the central part of the city were put in a sanitary condition.

"The depot for sanitary supplies established by the Board of
Health issued yesterday fifty-four sacks and eighty-four barrels of
lime, twenty-five sacks of charcoal, twenty boxes of powdered disinfectants, ten cans of oil and three barrels of carbolic acid.   All
of this was distributed over the city for disinfection.

"Out in the suburbs large forces were at work cleaning the
streets and opening the gutters.   The result of their work is very
noticeable to one who went out in the evening after having gone over
the same ground the day before.   The work of clearing the streets
of broken telephone and telegraph poles and wires, as well as poles
and wires of other kinds, has been begun in earnest.   The great
broken poles with their loads of wires are lowered to the ground
and the wires removed as rapidly as possible.

THE SHERIFF'S WORK.

"Sheriff Thomas reports that he and his posses buried and
cremated thirty-eight bodies in Hurd's lane, twenty-one bodies at
Sydnor's Bayou, and thirteen bodies in Eagle Grove.   Sheriff
Thomas says there are still one hundred bodies to be buried just
outside the city limits, and he has no idea of how many more down
the island.

"Fully $1,500,000 worth of vessel property is tied up on
the lowlands.   There was more than this until the British
steamer Mora was floated on Wednesday.   There are seven ocean
going steamers grounded in different parts of the bay, and the prospect of some of them ever getting from their positions is quite
remote.

"The steamer Roma is probably in the tightest place.   She
broke from her moorings at pier No. 15 during the storm and went
westward to the county bridge, tearing her way through the other
bridges until she went aground on or near Deer Island.   It is
feared her days of usefulness are over, for it would take as much
as she is worth to dredge a channel from her position to water deep
enough to float her.

"Another possible total loss is the steamer Kendal Castle, which is in shallow water near Texas City, having gone there during the storm from pier No. 31. She lies partly broadside on. Like the Roma, she is far from deep water, and until the Texas City channel is completed it does not seem probable that she can get out.

"The quarantine barge, belonging to the State, is probably gone beyond redemption. She dragged her anchor from the mooring place to Pelican Island, where she went aground and fell over on her side with the receding waters. Her machinery is propably badly wrecked, and she is in such a position that it would be difficult to right her, although the effort may be made.

"Small craft in the bay suffered as much in proportion to value as the big vessels, if not more, for practically every one was swamped. Some of them struck the piers and had holes stove in their bottoms. Owners have been repairing them, and for that reason few, if any, will be entirely lost."

GALVESTON IN DANGER FROM FIRE.

"A danger which Galveston faces is fire. Not a drop of rain has fallen since the hurricane, and the hot winds and blistering suns have made the wrecked houses and buildings so much tinder, piled mountain high in every direction. In nearly all parts of the city the fire hydrants are buried fifty feet, in some places a hundred feet deep under the wreckage, and as yet the water supply at best is only of the most meagre kind.

"Galveston's fire department is small and badly crippled and would be powerless to stay the flames should they ever start. There is no relief nearer than Houston, and that is hours away. In view of all the existing conditions it is no wonder that the cry is, 'Get the women and children to the mainland, anywhere off the island,' nor is it a wonder that with one small boat carrying only 300 passengers, and making only two trips a day, people fairly fight to be taken aboard.

"All yesterday fears were entertained by the authorities that even this service would be cut off and Galveston left without any means of getting to the mainland, owing to the trouble with the owner of the boat.

"The sanitary conditions do not improve. Dr. Trueheart, chairman of the committee in charge of caring for the sick and injured, is going on with dispatch. More physicians are needed, and he requests that about thirty outside physicians come to Galveston and work for at least a month, and, if needed, longer. The city's electric light service is completely destroyed, and the city electrician says it may be sixty days before the business portion can be lighted.

"A glorious and modern Galveston to be rebuilt in place of the old one, is the cry raised by the citizens, but it would seem a task beyond human power to ever remove the wreckage of the old city.

"The total number of people fed in the ten wards Saturday, the 15th, was 16,144. Sunday the number increased slightly. No accurate statemen: of the amount of supplies can be obtained as they are being put in the general stock as soon as received."

"SEEMS LIKE AN AWFUL DREAM."

Destitute save for a few personal effects carried in a small valise, and with nerves shattered by a week of horror, Mr. and Mrs. C. A. Prutsman, with their two daughters, twelve and six years old, reached Chicago from the flood-swept district of Texas. They came direct from Galveston, via. Houston and St. Louis.

During all of one afternoon the little family sat at the Rock Island station waiting for a train to take them to Putnam, Ill., where Mrs. Prutsman has relatives. When it was learned that they were from Galveston, they were besieged with questions concerning the details of the terrible storm. Crowds of waiting passengers flocked about them, and they told the gruesome story over and over.

"Yes, we were fortunate," said Mrs. Prutsman, as she leaned wearily back in a rocking chair, and tenderly contemplated the two children at her side. "It seems to me just like an awful dream, and when I think of the hundreds and hundreds of children who were killed right before our very eyes, I feel as though I always ought to be satisfied no matter what comes."

Mr. Prutsman said: "The reports from Galveston are not half as appalling as the situation really is. We left the fated city Wednesday afternoon, going by boat to Texas City, and by rail to Houston. The condition of Galveston at that time, while showing an improvement, was awful, and never shall I forget the terrible scenes that met our eyes as the boat on which we left steamed out of the harbor. There were bodies on all sides of us. In some places they were piled six and seven deep, and the stench horrible.

"I resided with my family fourteen blocks away from the beach, yet my house was swept away at 5 P.M. Saturday, and with it went everything we had in the world. Fifteen minutes before I took my wife and children to the courthouse and we were saved, along with about 1,000 others who sought refuge there. When we went through the streets the water was up to our arms and we carried the children on our heads.

WOMAN SHOT TO END HER SUFFERING.

"I assisted for several days in the work of rescue. In one pile of debris we found a woman who seemed to have escaped the flood, but who was injured and pinned down so she could not escape. A guard came along, and, after failing to rescue her, deliberately shot her to end her misery.

"The streets present a gruesome appearance. Every available wagon and vehicle in the city is being used to transport the dead, and it is no uncommon thing to see a load of bodies ten deep. The stench in the city is nauseating. Since the flood the only water that could be used for drinking purposes was in cisterns, and it has become tainted with the slime and filth that covers the city until it is little better than no water at all.

"Since the city was placed under martial law conditions have been much better and there is little lawlessness. The soldiers have shown no quarter and have orders to shoot on sight. This has had a wonderful effect on the disreputable characters who have flocked into the city.

SAW FOUR MEN SHOT IN ONE DAY.

" Everybody who remains in Galveston is made to work, and the punishment for a refusal is about the same as that meted out to ghouls. I saw four colored men shot in one day. There were confined in the hold of a steamer in the harbor, six colored men who were found by the soldiers with a flour sack almost filled with fingers and ears on which were jewels. These men probably have been publicly executed before this time.

" In the work of rescue we found whole families tied together with ropes, and in several instances mothers had their babes clasped in their arms.

" Scores of unfortunates straggle into Houston every day and their condition is pitiable. Several have lost their reason. The citizens of Houston are doing all in their power to meet the demands of the sufferers, and every available building in the city has been converted into a hospital. When we arrived in Houston we scarcely had clothes enough to cover us, and the citizens fitted us out and started us north. The fear of fever or some awful plague drove us from Galveston.

" Already speculators are flocking into the city, and there is some activity among them over tax-title real estate. In several instances whole families were wiped out of existence, and the opportunities in this line seem to be great."

General Chambers McKibbin, U. S. A., and Adjutant General Scurry were both emphatic regarding the necessity for prompt work in clearing the streets and surroundings of Galveston.

" I am personally in favor of burning as much rubbish as possible," said General McKibben, " and of burning it as quickly as the power of man will permit. I am not an alarmist by any means, and I do not predict a pestilence, but I think things are coming to that point where a pestilence may be possible unless prompt measures are taken, and there is nothing so effective as fire. Burn everything and burn it at once."

" I haven't a dollar to pay the men who are working in the streets all day long," said Adjutant General Scurry. " I am unable to say to a single one of the men ' You'll be paid for your work.' I have not the money to make good the promise. I hope and believe that the country will understand the situation. We must have this city cleaned up at any cost and with the greatest speed possible. If it is not done with all haste, and at the same time done well, there may be a pestilence, and if it once breaks out here it will not be Galveston alone that will suffer.

"Such things spread, and it is not only for the sake of this city, but for others outside that I urge that above all things we want money. The nation has been most kind in its response to the appeals of Galveston, but from what I hear, food and disinfectants sufficient for temporary purposes at least, are here or on the way. The country does not understand. It cannot understand, unless it could visit Galveston, the awful situation prevailing here."

NO DANGER OF PESTILENCE.

Dr. A. B. Chamberlain said that Galveston would now escape epidemic in any form. He had been through two of these Gulf coast visitations, though upon a smaller scale. "We may have some mild cases of fever as the result of the shock and the exposure," he said, "but I am confident there will be nothing serious."

This seems to be quite generally the opinion of the doctors who are not advising any wholesale exodus. They put great faith in the free use of disinfectants and in the bracing salt air which blows continuously over the island.

"A barrel of lime is worth more to us now than a ton of food," was the expression of Dr. J. O. Dyer. "Let us appeal," he continued, "for 10,000 barrels of lime and 500 barrels of tar. Each block will require at the least ten barrels scattered on its respective lots and streets, burn the tar in offensive localities."

Ladies of Galveston are engaged in a work which is perhaps without precedent in relief effort. They are making many little bags, into which they place two or three lumps of camphor. The bags have strings by which they can be fastened at the head, so that they will rest on the lip just under the nose. They are to be worn by the men engaged in the search and cremation of bodies.

It is proposed to all people whose houses are still standing that whenever they locate a corpse or carcasses in their vicinity the position be indicated by a flag of some kind.

Some of the notices and paragraphs in these first issues of the Galveston papers are as interesting as stories of the storm. For example:—

"The First Church of Christ, Scientists, cordially extends the use of their church to any denomination whose church was so damaged by the recent storm as to render it unfit for services."

DOCTORS CARING FOR THE SUFFERERS.

In the advertising columns merchants seem to vie with each other in announcing, "Positively no advance in prices." Here is an editorial leader which could hardly be found outside of a hurricane issue:—

"It is important that all who are injured enough to necessitate a stitching of their wounds should have their dressings changed every twenty-four hours. Some of the wounded have neglected to do this, with a result that the doctors have more work to do than is necessary. Every doctor in town is doing work free of cost to all who apply."

There have been accounts of negroes caught in the act of robbing the dead and shot. Galveston citizens are prompt to say that there have been exceptional cases. They gave the mass of colored people credit for doing their part.

On September 14th a writer described as follows events in the stricken city: "The evacuation of Galveston has begun. Do what they will, the newspapers and authorities cannot convince thousands who have made up their minds that this island is doomed to remain a moment after their first chance of escape.

"Schooners by the dozen are leaving for Texas and their crews have to stand guard to keep the people from overcrowding and sinking the craft. People are leaving with no destination, but with a strong determination to get many miles from this panorama of wrecked business houses, blockaded streets, hospitals filled with wounded and dying victims of the awful disaster.

" Galveston may again become the prosperous port it was five days ago, but its principal population will be of people who have not seen the awful work of wind and water. Men who have large business interests here may remain, but their families will be on the mainland, and every sign of approaching storm will drive thousands away. A workingman who paid $3,900 for a cottage and lot offered to sell for $500 yesterday, throwing in all the house contained. The house is very little damaged, but he lost a wife and baby whom he had taken to what he thought was a place of safety. It is impossible to write anything that would convey a faint idea of the wreckage and ruin.

FIRES ALL OVER THE CITY.

"The number of dead under debris in the central parts of the city will never be known, as burning is going on all over the city. The east end, beginning at Fifteenth street and Avenue L, running on a line parallel with the island, has a great mass of wreckage piled as high as a man's head and from that to the top of houses three stories high.

" This line extends as far along as there were any houses to wreck, and consists of all manner of buildings. It is a desolate scene from Eighth street east, when one compares it with the life that was present there but a short time ago. Two buildings of all the colony at the Point are left standing. These are the houses of the quarantine officer and the lighthouse. The quarantine warehouse is gone. All the barrack buildings and the dirt mounds that surrounded them are gone, and in place of all is a watery waste, with the exception of a few little islands that appear above the water.

" The water has cut into the lands from the jetties, covering all the ground practically from Seventh street east. For a block or more in the neighborhood of the hospitals there is a prairie waste, and then begins the mass of debris. One man had several houses out there and now he can find his fine porcelain tubs in the debris, while all about him are the things that composed his home and the houses he owned.

"Lucas Terrace, a large three-story brick building, divided into flats of three and four rooms each is almost a total wreck. Out of thirty-seven persons reported to have been in the building when the storm started its work of destruction, the Terrace had fifteen killed. Business concerns of the larger order in the East end suffered with the corner groceries and the smaller merchants.

WELL-KNOWN BUILDINGS DAMAGED.

"Boysen's mill is considerably damaged, the smokestack, some of the windows and part of the roof being gone. Across the street the bonemeal mill stands, with scarcely any north wall whatever. The Neptune Ice Company, Eighteenth street and Avenue A, is almost a total wreck.. A part of the building is gone into a mass of debris while other parts remain standing. The oil mill at Eighteenth street and Strand, suffered little apparent damage except to the windows. A big blacksmith shop in Eighteenth street, between Strand and Mechanic, suffered the loss of the upper story entirely. These are but a few specimens of what has happened all over the city."

W. S. Abernethy, with the Chicago relief forces, wrote on the 15th: "Yesterday was a day of anguish, as all the days of this week have been.

"There was no cessation of tear-stained faces appearing here and there to tell of the lost. And it is a wonder if the end of this sad divulgence will ever come. A motherless boy or a fatherless girl, newly childless mother or father, or whatever it may be, they still come to tell of their woe ; and the stolid men who glide over the water or who search the shore still bring in the swollen and unrecognizable victims of the storm. It will end some day, and agonizing hearts may rest from the painful throbbings of this hour.

"It is likely that Dr. Grant will increase his force to fifty deputy marshals at once. He cancelled his political appointments in Ohio to render this service to Galveston. Speaking of the disaster he said:

"It is the tragedy of the century, and is impossible of description. I have never seen anything like it before, and I hope I never shall again. As sorrowful as it is, however, I do not believe the people of Galveston will give way to despair. There is still a great future for this city, and those who survive must wisely realize the present and build to the future.

"Such destruction is impossible of repetition, and all Texas will regret if Galveston halts and refuses to improve the possibilities within her grasp. The horrible past—and thank God it is past—with its innumerable heartaches, is too awful to discuss."

MAYOR SETS ALL AT WORK.

"Mayor Walter C. Jones has issued a proclamation revoking all passes heretofore issued, and placing Brigadier General Thomas Scurry in command of all forces. General Scurry has appointed Hunt McCaleb his adjutant, and only passes signed by him will be recognized. All able men without the passes will be put at work clearing the wreckage and burning and burying the dead.

"At a meeting of the relief committee yesterday it was decided not to pay for labor, but time checks will be issued and paid later. Only those sick and those working will receive assistance from the relief committee."

HUGE TANK MOVED SIX BLOCKS.

To those acquainted with the wharf front a peculiar thing is presented near the foot of Twenty-first street. The big steel tank of the Waters-Pierce Oil Company, in which was stored during the season cotton seed oil, at the foot of Fifteenth street, was blown to Twenty-first street, a distance of six blocks. It landed on its bottom and rests now in an upright position. It is a large tank and heavy, but the elements got the better of it.

This morning the streets are pretty well crowded with business vehicles; a great many large concerns are doing business, and there is a general appearance of activity which will in a great measure relieve the feeling of unrest and stem the tide of people trying to get away from Galveston.

The prospect for rail communication is improving, but no day can be set when trains can be run to the island. Large forces are

19

at work on both ends of one of the four bridges across the bay, but as the bridge is two and one-half miles long and the piling in bad shape, it is impossible to say when the work will be completed. It may be in three or four days, or may be longer, although railroad officials hope for the best—that is, the lowest estimates of time.

FEAR TO LOOK ON THE SEA.

"It matters not how great the number of the dead, there are enough to shock the sympathies of the world, and they are gone forever. But we fear here to look upon the sea, lest some heartless wave shall bring to view the cold, stark form of another whom somebody lived with and loved.

"The victims are still growing into larger thousands, and the bereft are still coming in to tell of losses. It is a continued story of anguish and death such as Texas has never known before and prays it shall never know again.

EVERY WAVE HAS ITS TRAGEDY.

"It is said that every wave of the sea has its tragedy, and it seems to be true here. In Galveston it has ceased to be an anxiety for the dead, but concern for the living. The supreme disaster, with its overwhelming tale of death and destruction, has now abated to lively anxiety for the salvation of the living.

"Men are at work clearing the streets of piles of timbers and refuse. Men are beginning to realize that the living must be cared for. It is now the supreme duty. There is much work to be done and it is being done. Women and children are being hurried out of the city just as rapidly as the limited facilities of transportation will permit. The authorities and commissioners are rational, and idleness is no longer permitted.

"There is an element with an abundance of vital energy who intend to save the town, and the town is being saved. Burying the dead, feeding the destitute, cleaning the city and repairing wrecks of all character are under fair headway, and will be pushed as rapidly as men can be found to do the work.

"The great utilities of the city are being repaired to a state of usefulness.   Men are in demand and workers are coming to engage in the duty of restoration.   Life is beginning to supersede death, and there is apparent everywhere a desire to save the city and rebuild it.

" Before another week has passed, the listlessness of mourning people will have been changed into a lively interest in life, and as this comes so, Galveston will begin to realize just what the world expects of her.   General Scurry now has charge of the town, and it is really under martial law.

" Of course there is some friction.   Martial friction, like the martial law, is a matter only temporary   It would be difficult to challenge the necessity of this measure.   There are many defense-less women and children in the city, living in houses without locks and keys, and they must be protected against prowlers of all kinds. How long such protection will be necessary cannot be known now, but General Scurry can be depended upon to discharge the important obligations which he has assumed.

" There are political factions here who resent the idea of martial law, but this fact does not, for a moment, abate the necessity for it.   United States Marshal John Grant has arrived with twelve deputy marshals.   He tendered his services to General Scurry and they were accepted.

WALKING OVER CORPSES.

" One hundred people at present are at Virginia Point, some waiting for transportation over to Galveston, some for day to break so as to permit of the burial of corpses, of which there are many scattered up and down the beach and all over the prairie for a radius of ten miles.   Others are waiting for a first chance to get as far away as possible from this terrible scene.   Men who will work are very scarce.   Those willing have a desire to boss, which does not facilitate matters in the least.   An organized force of considerable proportion should be sent here at once.

" An eight-mile walk from where the passengers were put off the train last night to this place, over the corpses of human beings and animals, piles of lumber, household articles of every description and furniture was an experience so horrible that a small proportion of those who started are here this morning.

"A caboose and engine are standing just above this place. In it are four train men all crippled and sick, only one of them being able to get about. With them are a father and son, the remainder of a party of eight who tried to cross the bay Saturday. A half mile farther down, or a hundred yards from the bay, is another engine and caboose, in it a family of six, four of them small children, are congregated. They lived at this place and had a hard fight for their lives. They are caring for a switchman, who will live only a few hours. They are in a destitute condition.

REFUGEES CRAZED BY THEIR SUFFERINGS.

"Refugees from Galveston tell awful tales of suffering and death, and in every case that came to my notice are in such mental state that there can be no reliable facts obtained from them. The only newspaper man who has got into Galveston came out last night deathly sick, and would not stop when hailed.

"Thieves have been robbing the bodies as they came ashore. One man was caught last night and will be taken to Galveston to-day. When searched, a baby's finger was found with a ring on it. He afterwards gave the hiding place of articles and money and much jewelry was found. A cry of "lynch him" met with little favor; enough death is here.

"Frantic refugees from Galveston gave vent to all sorts of invectives against the world in general and Houston (fifty miles north) in particular, for what they believe to be dilatoriness in relief work. It does not seem that more could have been done in one day. Almost nothing has been done.

"Some in their frenzy blaspheme their God for not preventing such a catastrophe. Two relief boats are to leave shortly but only enough men to man them will be allowed to accompany them. There is no shelter here except the two cars mentioned. Box cars were strewn along the west side of the railroad grade for two miles from this point."

CHAPTER XV.

Family in a Tree-Top All Night—Rescue of the Perishing— Railroad Trains Hurrying Forward with Relief— Pathetic Scenes in the Desolate City.

AFTER suffering untold privations for over a week on Bolivar peninsula, an isolated neck of land extending into Galveston bay a few miles from the east end of Galveston island, the Rev. L. P. Davis, wife and five young children reached Houston, famished, penniless and nearly naked, but overcome with amazement and joy at their miraculous delivery from what seemed to them certain death.

Wind and water wrecked their home, annihilated their neighbors and destroyed every particle of food for miles around, yet they passed through the terrible days and nights raising their voices above the shriek of the wind in singing hymns and in prayer. And through it all not one member of the family was injured to the extent of even a scratch.

When the hurricane struck the Rev. Mr. Davis' home at Patton Beach the water rose so fast that it was pouring into the windows before the members of the family realized their danger. Rushing out Mr. Davis hitched his team and placing his wife and children into a wagon started for a place of safety. Before they had left his yard another family of refugees drove up to ask assistance, only to be upset by the waves before his very eyes. With difficulty the party was saved from drowning, and when safe in the Davis wagon were half floated, half drawn by the team to a grove.

With clotheslines Mr. Davis lashed his 12 and 14 year old boys in a tree. One younger child he secured with the chain of his wagon, and lifting his wife into another tree he climbed beside her.

While the hurricane raged above and a sea of water dashed wildly below, Mrs. Davis clung to her 6-month-old babe with one arm, while with the other she held fast to her precarious haven of refuge. The minister held a baby of 18 months in the same manner, and while the little one cried for food he prayed. In other trees the family he had rescued from drowning found a precarious footing.

When the night had passed and the water receded, wreckage, dead animals and the corpses of parishioners surrounded the devoted party. There was nothing to eat, and, nearly dead with exhaustion, the preacher and his little flock set out on foot to seek assistance. They were too weak to continue far, and sank down on the plain, while Mr. Davis pushed on alone. Five miles away a farmhouse was found, partially intact, and securing a team, Davis returned for his half-dead party.

SUBSISTED ON RAW MEAT.

For two days they remained at the home of the hospitable farmer, and then set out afoot to find a hamlet or make their way over the desert-like peninsula to Bolivar Point. In the heat of the burning sun they plodded on along the water front, subsisting upon a steer which they killed and devoured raw, until finally they came upon an abandoned and overturned sailboat high on the beach.

With a united effort they succeeded in launching the boat, and with improvised distress signals displayed, managed to sail to Galveston. There, because of red tape, they were unable to secure clothing, although they were given a little food and transportation to Houston. Clad in an old pair of trousers, a tattered shirt and torn shoes, with his family in even worse plight, the circuit rider of the Patton Beach, Johnston's Bethel, Bolivar Point and High Island Methodist Churches rode into Houston, dirty, weak and half-starved. Here the family were sent to a hospital and cared for.

Bolivar reported that up to date 220 bodies had been found and buried, and many were still lying on the sands. Assistance was needed at once. It is a fact generally commented upon, and merely emphasized by the clergyman's experience, that while succor is being rushed to Galveston, other sufferers are neglected. The relief trains en route from Houston to Galveston traverse a storm-swept section, where famishing and nearly naked survivors sit on the wrecks of their homes and hungrily watch tons of provisions whirling past them, while there is little prospect of aid reaching them.

Winifred Black, a lady journalist, furnishes the following, vivid account of her experiences in reaching Galveston : "I begged, cajoled and cried my way through the line of soldiers with drawn swords, who guard the wharf at Texas City, and sailed across the bay on a little boat, which is making irregular trips to meet the relief trains from Houston.

"The engineer who brought our train down from Houston spent the night before groping around in the wrecks on the beach looking for his wife and three children. He found them, dug a rude grave in the sand, and set up a little board marked with his name.

ALL HAD LOST LOVED ONES.

"The man in front of me on the car had floated all Monday night with his wife and mother on a part of the roof of his little home. He told me that he kissed his wife good-bye at midnight and told her that he could not hold on any longer ; but he did hold on, dazed and half-conscious, until the day broke and showed him that he was alone on his piece of drift-wood. He did not even know when the woman that he loved had died.

"Every man on the train—there were no women there—had lost some one that he loved in the terrible disaster, and was going across the bay to try and find some trace of his family—all except the four men in my party. They were from outside cities—St. Louis, New Orleans and Kansas City. They had lost a large amount of property and were coming down to see if anything could be saved from the wreck.

"They had been sworn in as deputy sheriffs in order to get into Galveston. The city is under martial law, and no human being who can't account for himself to the complete satistaction of the officers in charge can hope to get through. We sat on the deck of

the little steamer.   The four men from outside cities and I listened
to the little boat's wheel plowing its way through the calm waters
of the bay.   The stars shone down like a benediction, but along
the line of the shore there arose a great leaping column of blood-
red flame.

"What a terrible fire," I said.   "Some of the large buildings
must be burning."

A man passing on the deck behind my chair heard me.   He
stopped, put his hand on the bulwark and turned down and looked
into my face, his face like that of a dead man ; but he laughed.

"Buildings !" he said.   "Don't you know what is burning
over there ?   It is my wife and children—such little children !
Why, the tallest was not as high as this"—he laid his hand on the
bulwark—"and the little one was just learning to talk. She called
my name the other day, and now they are burning over there—
they and the mother who bore them.   She was such a little,
tender, delicate thing, always so easily frightened, and now she's
out there all alone with the two babies and they're burning !"

The man laughed again and began again to walk up and
down the deck.

HAD TO BURN BODIES OF THOUSANDS.

"That's right," said the Marshal of the State of Texas,
taking off his broad hat and letting the starlight shine on his
strong face.   "That's right. We had to do it. We've burned
over 1,000 people to-day, and to-morrow we shall burn as many
more.   Yesterday we stopped burying the bodies at sea ; we had
to give the men on the barges whisky to give them courage to do
the work.   They carried out hundreds of the dead at one time,
men and women, negroes and white people, all piled up as high
as the barge could stand it, and the men did not go far enough out
to sea, and the bodies have begun drifting back again."

"Look !" said the man who was walking the deck, touching
my shoulder with his shaking hand.   "Look there !"

" Before I had time to think I had to look, and saw floating in
the water the body of an old woman, whose hair was shining in

the starlight. A little farther on we saw a group of strange drift-wood. We looked closer and found it to be a mass of wooden slabs, with names and dates cut upon them, and floating on top of them were marble stones, two of them.

DEAD WASHED FROM THEIR GRAVES.

"The graveyard, which has held the sleeping citizens of Galveston for many, many years, was giving up its dead. We pulled up at a little wharf in the hush of the starlight; there were no lights anywhere in the city except a few scattered lamps shining from a few desolate, half-destroyed houses. We picked our way up the street. The ground was slimy with the debris of the sea.

"We climbed over wreckage and picked our way through heaps of rubbish. The terrible, sickening odor almost overcame us, and it was all that I could do to shut my teeth and get through the streets somehow. The soldiers were camping on the wharf front, lying stretched out on the wet sand, the hideous, hideous sand, stained and streaked in the starlight with dark and cruel blotches. They challenged us, but the marshal took us through under his protection. At every street corner there was a guard, and every guard wore a six-shooter strapped around his waist.

"We got to the hotel after some terrible nightmare fashion, plodding through dim streets like a line of forlorn ghosts in a half-forgotten dream. General McKibben, commander in charge of the Texas Division, was in the hotel parlor reading dispatches. He was horrified to see me.

"How in the world did you get here?" he said. "I would not let any woman belonging to me come into this place of horror for all the money in America.

OLD SOLDIER SHUDDERED AT THE SIGHTS.

"I am an old soldier, madame. I have seen many battle-fields, but let me tell you that since I rode across the bay the other night and helped the man at the boat steer to keep away from the floating bodies of dead women and little children I have not slept one single instant. Five thousand would never cover the number of people who died here in that terrible storm.

"In the short time I have been here I have met and talked with women who saw every one they loved on earth swept away from them out in the storm. As I look out of my window I can see the blood-red flame leaping with fantastic gesture against the sky. There is no wire into Galveston, and I will have to send this message out by the first boat.

"For the present the two things needed are money and disinfectants. More nurses and doctors are needed. Galveston wants help—quick, ready, willing help. Don't waste a minute to send it. If it does not come soon this whole region will be a prey to a plague such as has never been known in America. Quick-lime and disinfectants, and money and clothes—all these things Galveston must have, and have at once, or the people of this country will have a terrible crime on their conscience.

MAKING A FIGHT FOR LIFE.

"The people of Galveston are making a brave and gallant fight for life. The citizens have organized under efficient and willing management. Gangs of men are at work everywhere removing the wreckage. The city is districted according to wards, and in every ward there is a relief station. They give out food at the relief stations. Such food as they have will not last long.

"I sat in one relief station for an hour this morning and saw several people who had come asking for medicine and disinfectants and a few rags of clothing to cover their pitiful nakedness, turned away. The man in charge of the bureau took the last nickel in the world out of his pocket and gave it to make up a sum for a woman with a new-born baby in her arms to buy a little garment to cover its shivering flesh.

"The people of the State of Texas have risen to the occasion nobly. They have done everything that human beings, staggering and dazed under such a blow, could possibly do, but they are only human. This is no ordinary catastrophe. One who has not been here to see with his own eyes the awful havoc wrought by the storm cannot realize the tenth part of the misery these people are suffering.

"I asked a prominent member of the Citizens' Committee this morning where I should go to see the worst work which the storm had done. He smiled at me a little, pitifully. His house, every dollar he had in the world, and his children were swept away from him last Saturday night.

"Go?" said he. "Why, anywhere within two blocks of the very heart of the city you will see misery enough in half an hour to keep you awake for a week of sleepless nights."

"I went toward the heart of the city. I do not know what the names of the streets were or where I was going. I simply picked my way through masses of slime and rubbish, which scar the beautiful wide streets of the once beautiful city. They won't bear looking at, those piles of rubbish. There are things there that gripe the heart to see—a baby's shoe, for instance, a little red shoe, with a jaunty tasseled lace—a bit of a woman's dress and letters. Oh, yes, I saw these things myself, and the letters were wet and grimed with the marks of the cruel sea, but there were a few lines legible in it.

"Oh, my dear," it read, "the time seems so long. When can we expect you back?" Whose hand had written, or who had received, no one will ever know.

THE STENCH IS OVERPOWERING.

"The stench from these piles of rubbish is almost over-powering. Down in the very heart of the city most of the dead bodies have been removed, but it will not do to walk far out. To-day I came upon a group of people in a by-street, a man and two women, colored. The man was big and muscular, one of the women was old and one was young. They were dipping in a heap of rubbish, and when they heard my footsteps the man turned an evil, glowering face upon me and the young woman hid something in the folds of her dress. Human ghouls, these, prowling in search of prey.

"A moment later there was noise and excitement in the little

narrow street, and I looked back and saw the negro running, with
a crowd at his heels. The crowd caught him and would have
killed him but a policeman came up. They tied his hands and
took him through the streets with a whooping rabble at his heels.
It goes hard with a man in Galveston caught looting the dead in
these days.

"A young man well known in the city shot and killed a negro
who was cutting the ears from a living woman's head to get her
earrings out. The negro lay in the streets like a dead dog, and
not even the members of his own race would give him the tribute of
a kindly look.

DESOLATION ON EVERY SIDE.

"The abomination of desolation reigns on every side. The big
houses are dismantled, their roofs gone, windows broken, and the
high water mark showing inconceivably high on the paint. The
little houses are gone—either completely gone as if they were
made of cards and a giant hand which was tired of playing with
them had swept them all off the board and put them away, or they
are lying in heaps of kindling wood covering no one knows what
horrors beneath.

"The main streets of the city are pitiful. Here and there a
shop of some sort is left standing. South Fifth street looks like
an old man's jaw, with one or two teeth portruding. The merchant's are taking their little stores of goods that have been left
them and are spreading them out in the bright sunshine, trying
to make some husbanding of their small capital. The water
rushed through the stores, as it did through the houses, in an
irresistible avalanche that carried all before it. The wonder is
not that so little of Galveston remains standing, but that there is
any of it at all.

"Every street corner has its story, in its history of misery and
human agony bravely endured. The eye-witnesses of a hundred
deaths have talked to me and told me their heart rendering stories,
and not one of them has told of a cowardly death.

"The women met their fate as did the men, bravely, and for

the most part with astonishing calmness.   A woman told me that
she and her husband went into the kitchen and climbed upon the
kitchen table to get away from the waves, and that she knelt
there and prayed.

"As she prayed, the storm came in and carried the whole
house away, and her husband with it, and yesterday she went out
to the place where her husband had been, and there was nothing
there but a little hole in the ground.

" Her husband's body was found twisted in the branches of a
tree, half a mile from the place where she last saw him.   She
recognized him by a locket he had around his neck—the locket
she gave him before they were married.   It had her picture and
a lock of the baby's hair in it.   The woman told me all this
without a tear or trace of emotion.   No one cries here.

"They will stand and tell the most hideous stories, stories
that would turn the blood in the veins of a human machine cold
with horror, without the quiver of an eye lid.   A man sat in the
telegraph office and told me how he had lost two Jersey cows and
some chickens.

"THEY WERE ALL DROWNED."

" He went into minute particulars, told how his house was built
and what it cost, and how it was strengthened and made firm
against the weather.   He told me how the storm had come and
swept it all away, and how he had climbed over a mass of wab-
bling roofs and found a friend lying in the curve of a big roof, in
the stoutest part of the tide, and how they two had grasped each
other and what they said.

"He told me just how much his cows cost, and why he was so
fond of them, and how hard he had tried to save them, but I said:
"You have saved yourself and your family ; you ought not to
complain."

" The man stared at me with blank, unseeing eyes.   " Why, I
did not save my family."   He said.   "They were all drowned.   I
thought you knew that ; I don't talk very much about it."

"The hideous horror of the whole thing has benumbed every

one who saw it. No one tells the same story of the way the storm
rose, or how it went. No two men tell the story of rescue quite
alike. I have just heard of a little boy who was picked up floating on a plank. His mother and father and brothers and sisters
were all lost in the storm. He tells a dozen different stories of
his rescue on the night of the storm.

"But the city is gradually getting back to a normal understanding of the situation, just as one comes out of a long fainting
fit, and says : 'Where am I ?'"

"The Mayor is doing everything in his power to straighten
matters out. Martial law is strictly enforced. The Chief of
Police is busy, very busy. I caught him in the hotel rotunda
this morning. There were five or six men around him, all trying
to get permits. He would not listen to one of them.

TOO BUSY TO TALK.

"He transfixed me with a stony stare when I asked him for
some information. He did not have time to bother with me. He
was too busy feeding the hungry and comforting the destitute
and taking care of thieves to care whether the outside world knew
anything about him or his opinions or not.

"The little parks are full of homeless people. The prairies
around Galveston are dotted with little camp fires, where the
homeless and destitute are trying to gather their scattered families together, and find out who among them are dead and who are
living.

"There are thousands and thousands of families in Galveston
to-day without food or a place to lay their heads.

"But oh, in pity's name, in America's name, do not delay help
one single instant ! Send help quickly, or it will be too late.

"One week has passed since the awful calamity which laid
low beautiful Galveston and the story has not yet been half told.
The people against whom the appalling catastrophe was visited
are just beginning to awake from the horrible nightmare which
had its inception in the roaring torrents of the Gulf of Mexico.

"With the awakening comes memory—remembrance of awful

scenes following the storm which up to now have been untold. Accounts of personal experiences are just becoming available, and the narration of the different stories is like a long, hideous dream.

"Quartered in the Chicago hospital in the Auditorium Theatre are persons whose minds were a blank all the week until the ministering of the "Chicago American's" nurses and physicians restored, at least partly, the shattered nerves and senses. During this morning's early hours these unfortunates related their awful experiences.

"The story of Thomas Klee was possibly the most pitiful. Klee lived near Eleventh and N streets. When the storm burst he was alone in his house with his two infant children. He seized one under each arm and rushed from the frail structure in time to cheat death among the falling timbers of his home.

LODGED HIS CHILD IN A TREE.

"Once in the open, with his babies under his arms, he was swept into the bay among hundreds of others. He held to his precious burden and by skillful manœuvring managed to get close to a tree which was sweeping along with the tide. He saw a haven in the branches of the tree and raised his two-year-old daughter to place her in the branches. As he did so the little one was torn from his arm and carried away to her death.

"The awful blow stunned, but did not render senseless. Klee retained his hold on the other child, aged four years, and was whirled along among the dying and dead victims of the storm's fury, hoping to effect a landing somewhere. An hour in the water brought the desired end. He was thrown ashore, with wreckage and corpses, and, stumbling to a footing, lifted his son to a level with his face. The boy was dead.

"Klee remembered nothing until last night, when he was put ashore in Texas City. He had a slight recollection of helping to bury dead, clear away debris and obey the command of soldiers. His brain, however, did not execute its functions until early to-day in the hospital.

"George Boyer's experience was a sad one. He was thrown into the rushing waters, and while being carried with frightful velocity down the bay saw the dead face of his wife in the branches of a tree. The woman had been wedged firmly between two branches.

"Margaret Lees' life was saved at the expense of her brother's. The woman was in her Twelfth street home when the hurricane struck. Her brother seized her and guided her to St. Mary's University, a short distance away. He returned to search for his son, and was killed by a falling house.

Galveston, Tex., Sept. 15.—The sound of the hammer is beginning to be heard throughout the city. Every man not engaged in looking for and cremating the dead is repairing the damage wrought by Saturday's great tidal wave.

The spirit that has been displayed by the citizens remaining here is remarkable. They seem determined to begin immediately the work of rebuilding the stricken city, and to that end are endeavoring to secure building material as speedily as possible. Business houses are being restored and restaurant keepers are conducting business on the sidewalks.

MIRACULOUS ESCAPE FROM DEATH.

Some of the escapes of people of Galveston from the storm were nothing less than miraculous. Charles Rutter, aged twelve, was in his father's house when the waves and wind swept it away. The boy seized a floating trunk and was found at Hitchcock, twenty miles north.

The Stubbs family, consisting of father, mother and two children, was in its home when it collapsed. They found refuge on a floating roof. This parted, and father and one child were swept in one direction, while the mother and the other child drifted in another. One of the children was washed off, but last Sunday evening all four were re-united.

Mrs. P. Watkins is a raving maniac as the result of her experiences. With her two children and her mother she was drifting on a roof, when her mother and one child were swept away. Mrs. Watkins mistakes attendants in the hospital for her lost relatives, and clutches wildly for them.

Harry Steele, a cotton man, and .his wife sought safety in three successive houses which were demolished. They eventually climbed on a floating door and were saved. W. R. Jones, with fifteen other men, finding the building they were in about to fall, made their way to the water tower, and, clasping hands, encircled the standpipe, to keep from being washed or blown away.

Mrs. Chapman Bailey, wife of the southern manager of the Galveston Wharf Company, and Miss Blanche Kennedy floated in the waters, ten to twenty feet deep, all night and day by catching wreckage. Finally they got into a wooden bath-tub and were driven into the Gulf over night. The incoming tide drove them back to Galveston, and they were rescued the next day. They were fearfully bruised. All their relatives were drowned.

A Texas journal commented as follows upon the great disaster :

" Galveston thanks the nation. Her citizens, still staggering under the blows dealt by the hurricane, have been aroused to confidence again and inspired for the work of restoring their home city, by the magnificent expression of sympathy and kindliness which their fellow countrymen have made by means of their great relief fund.

NEW LIFE IN THE CITY.

" For two days after the hurricane the people of Galveston heard practically nothing from the outside world. Then meager news came. To-day for the first time the story of the response of the American people to the stricken city's involuntary appeal for relief has been brought in.

" The hundreds of thousands of dollars in cash given for the use of the city, the many relief trains, laden with supplies of food, so much needed, and of medical and surgical appliances, still more needed, the oncoming bands of doctors and nurses and guards, mean new life to this city.

" Despair is gone. To-day the spirit of the citizens may well

20

be expressed in the fine words which one of them quoted to-day. They are taken from the doorway of a church in Tyrol, where the half-obliterated letters represent the wisdom of centuries, and the thoughts of Galveston men of to-day.

> " Look not mournfully into the past.
> It comes not back again.   Wisely
> Improve the present.   It is thine.
> Go forth to meet the shadowy future
> Without fear and with a manly heart.

"The contributions and gifts of the people of the United States are the subject of conversation wherever men meet on the streets.   That a city, which had met with disaster only five days ago, could now be the recipient of a fund which is already approximating half a million dollars, seems well-nigh incredible.

"Galveston has been better treated than was Chicago after its great fire, or than were the sufferers in western Pennsylvania after the Johnstown flood.   The spirit is the same, but has grown great with good times and swift with good hearts.

SWIFT TRAINS LOADED WITH SUPPLIES.

"The bulletins which come through Governor Sayres at Dallas, who is earning the gratitude of Galveston people by his good work for them, tell of swift trains coming from the Atlantic and the Pacific laden with supplies.   They tell of gifts of many thousands of dollars from great corporations and rich men of the country, and as well of gifts from the poorer classes in cities and villages in all parts of the Union.   How Governor Roosevelt stopped on his speaking tour long enough to wire an appeal to the citizens of his State for relief funds, how other governors have issued appeals, and how Americans even as far away as Paris have spontaneously met and contributed large sums, have all been heard here.

"It is a wonderful thing," said Mayor Jones, "and one which speaks for the high character of our American citizens, that so much should be done for this city so quickly.   I have just heard from Governor Sayres that all sorts of people are contributing. His message said that many of the churches of the land would take special contributions for our benefit.

"I cannot say how grateful I and all the people of Galveston are for this splendid treatment. We will show our thankfulness by going ahead with our own work, and making a new Galveston on the spot where the old one was so nearly annihilated."

The mayor's confidence in the future of Galveston is shared by the greater part of the business men. Two days ago all were downcast, pessimistic and despondent. Many even talked of abandoning Galveston entirely and helping to build a new city on some other location. Already the mournful past has begun to be cast behind. The conditions of the present are being studied, and the very best that is possible will be made out of the future.

"GALVESTON SHALL RISE AGAIN."

Two daily papers have already resumed their issues, and their appearance helped to restore confidence. Both of them had stirring editorials, and that of one had for its keynote, " Galveston Shall Rise Again." There was not a half hearted word in the editorial. It urged that people bury their dead, succor their living, and then start resolutely to work to mend the broken things and to build the city anew.

Galveston will not be abandoned for a location on higher ground somewhere else. It has too fine a climate, it is too well known as a summer resort, and it has too great advantages in its bathing beaches to make abandonment a possible thing, even should business seek to move away.

But business will not go away. If the railroads replace their bridges, terminals and wharves, that means that they have confidence in the future of the city, and adds to the confidence of the citizens. It is perfectly clear already that the railroads entering Galveston are quickly going to do their share in the work of reconstruction.

The Southern Pacific railroad has had men investigating its wharves and tracks, and it has announced through General Manager Van Vleck that, although the damage to its property in this city is fully 80 per cent, it will proceed to restore it as rapidly as possible.   Mr. Van Vleck says that men and mortar are already being carried to Virginia Point for work on the bridge, and that inside of forty days he expects to be running trains into Galveston again.   He will not work in connection with any other road, nor build a joint bridge to the city, but he says his company will permit other roads to use the bridge when it is ready.

The scenes on the streets when provisions are being distributed are pathetic in the extreme.   Many families, among whose members hunger was possibly never felt before, are being supplied with provisions.   Wizened-faced, bare-footed children were to be seen on the street eagerly appropriating spoiled and cast-off stocks of food.

SYSTEMATIC RELIEF.

The committee is trying to systematize the work, so as to relieve the worst cases first.   Mayor Jones said :

"We have made such arrangements as will make it possible for us to feed the needy until we can get in full supplies.   We are relieving every case presented to us.   I think within a day or two our transportation facilities will be sufficient temporarily to meet our needs.   Galveston has helped other cities in their distress, despite her size, and we are consoled by the generous response of the country to our appeal."

The committee has instructed the local drug stores to provide the poor and needy with medicine at the expense of the relief fund.

Every strong-limbed man who has not his own home and property to look after is being pressed into the service of the city. First of all, it is necessary to get the waterworks in good condition, so that water may be turned into the mains, the gutters flushed, and the sewers made usable.   The lack of water since the flood has contributed much to the discomfort and the danger to health.

Volunteer gangs continue their work of hurried burial of the corpses they find on the shores of Galveston Island at the neighboring points where fatalities attended the storm.   It will probably be many days, however, before all the floating bodies have found nameless graves. Along the beach they are constantly being washed up. Whether these are those who were swept out into the Gulf and drowned or are simply the return ashore of some of those cast into the sea to guard against terrible pestilence, there is no means of knowing.

In various parts of the city the smell of decomposed flesh is still apparent. Wherever such instances are found the authorities are freely disinfecting. Only to-day a babe lashed to a mattress was picked up under a residence in the very heart of the city and burned.

The following editorial, signed by the publishers, A. H. Belo & Co., appeared September 13th in the "Galveston News":

HOMES MUST BE REPAIRED.

"At the first meeting of Galveston's citizens, Sunday afternoon, after the great hurricane, for the purpose of bringing order out of chaos, the only sentiment expressed was that Galveston had received an awful blow. The loss of life and property is appalling—so great that it required several days to form anything like a correct estimate. With sad and aching hearts, but with resolute faces, the sentiment of the meeting was that out of the awful chaos of wrecked homes and wretched business Galveston must rise again.

"The sentiment was not that of burying the dead and giving up the ship, but rather bury the dead, succor the needy, appeal for aid from a charitable world, and then start resolutely to work to mend the broken chains. In many cases the work of upbuilding must begin over. In other cases the destruction is only partial. Still, the sentiment was, Galveston will, Galveston must, survive and fulfill her glorious destiny. Galveston shall rise again.

"Galveston having been isolated since the storm of last Saturday night, the stricken citizens of the town have not been informed as to the thrill of horror which went over the world when the news of the catastrophe was spread. The Associated Press brings the cheering news that in every town and city in the United States, commercial, religious and charitable bodies have organized into relief committees. At present thousands of dollars and hundreds of cars of supplies are en route and will reach the sufferers of Galveston just as soon as it is possible to boat them across the bay. If the desolation here has been awful, the sympathy and humanity of a great nation has been ample, and very soon the local committees will be enabled to assist the destitute thousands.

"What the 'News' desires most to say to the surviving victims of last Saturday's catastrophe, is that in the knowledge of a world-wide sympathy which is encompassing us, we must not give way to despair. If we have lost all else, we still have life and the future, and it is toward the future that we must devote the energies of our lives. We can never forget what we have suffered; we can not forget the thousands of our friends and loved ones who found in the angry billows that destroyed them, a final resting place. But tears and grief must not make us forget our present duties.

TIME FOR DAUNTLESS COURAGE.

"The blight and ruin which have desolated Galveston are not beyond repair. We must not for a moment think Galveston is to be abandoned because of one disaster, however horrible that disaster has been. We have our homes here, even if those homes are in ruins, and if we loved Galveston before, how much stronger must that affection be and how much more sacred it must be when we think of our loved ones, whose dust consecrates not only the land but the very waves which lash its shores.

"It is time for courage of the highest order. It is time when men and women show the stuff that is in them, and we can make no loftier acknowledgment of the material sympathy which the world is extending to us than to answer back that after we shall have buried our dead, relieved the sufferings of the sick and destitute, we will bravely undertake the vast work of restoration and recuperation which lies before us, in a manner which shall convince the world that we have spirit to overcome misfortune and rebuild our homes. In this way we shall prove ourselves worthy of the boundless tenderness which is being showered upon us in the hour of desolation and sorrow.''

Refugees from Galveston, Alvin, Angellon and other places are fast scattering throughout the State. Over fifty have arrived at Austin and have found temporary homes with friends and relatives. Many have gone to places in other States. A local Relief Committee has been organized in Austin to look after the wants of the destitute people as fast as they arrive. They are clothed and fed at the expense of the local people,

Similar committees are being formed in all the principal cities and towns of the State. It is expected that this action will assist the Relief Committees of Houston and Galveston greatly and will also reduce the amount of money required to be expended out of the general fund that is accumulating for the benefit of the sufferers.

Word reached here from Houston that evidences had been found there of imposition on the part of chronic tramps who are pouring into the city from all directions and claiming to be just from Galveston and to have lost everything in the storm. Many of these frauds have been exposed and driven out of the city. A plan is being arranged whereby all parties seeking help must be identified as having come from Galveston or other storm-swept towns.

SERMONS ON GALVESTON.

The Galveston catastrophe furnished the theme for Rev. Dr. Russell H. Conwell's sermon on Sunday, September 16th, in the Temple of Grace Baptist Church, Philadelphia. He attributed the disaster to the working of God's immutable laws, and declared that the calamity in its end was for the good of all things. At the conclusion of his sermon he made an appeal for the aid of the sufferers. There was a generous response. Many pledged themselsves for specific sums.

Dr. Conwell took his text from Genesis xiii, 36. He said in part : " It was Jacob who said 'all things are against me,' but Paul said, ' All things work together for good to them that love God.' Paul's position was true. Jacob's was untrue. Yet Jacob had philosophy in his expression ; but his philosophy was so much inferior that Paul's inclosed it, left it out of sight. There is no sorrow or affliction or pain or death but it worketh out in God's hands a greater good.

"The disaster at Galveston fills me with terror. It was a lovely city ; its people kind-hearted and enterprising. The destruction of that city so suddenly was God's doing, and consequently it must be for good. It was His doing and what He does is right. The hurricane was the necessasy outcome of all the working laws of God. He sent it and it must be for good. We can not understand that ; we sit back in our heart's darkness and say, 'God is wrong ; He is not governing the universe.'

BLESSINGS IN DISGUISE.

"The people who now live in Galveston will be better all their lives. This experience has deepened their natures, enriched their sympathies, enlarged the boundaries of their feelings, and the people of that city will be blessed by that awful experience. They are going to be better inspired, more loving toward others, more affectionate toward each other, and they are going to be different men even without their riches, for riches do not make good men. The people of Galveston have been taught that there is something more than dollars in this world. The rich will now feel what it is to be poor. It does man good to feel the depths of life. Many of the survivors will thank God they have to begin life over again.

"This great calamity is good also in that it arouses the sympathies of the whole country. When it arouses the sympathies of many tens of thousands it must be a gigantic force to work out an ultimate good. Just think when they begin to build the city again ! How many will be benefited ? They will order lumber from the North, where the suffering people are waiting for the order. They will order millions of dollars worth of goods from Philadelphia, and there are poor people here waiting for that work. When you consider how that disaster locally is going to bless so many people outwardly, then the measure of its good may be far greater than the measure of its evil."

Rev. Dr. Colfelt, pastor of Oxford Presbyterian Church, touching on the Galveston disaster in his sermon on " Repentance," said :—

" The changes are so quick and excessive in our mortal life that none of us know what to-morrow will bring forth. Not one of us knows whether our money will be a blessing or a curse, separating us from our good work. Christ declares that disasters are not to be interpreted as judgments, but they are simply personal. The object in every instance of disaster and calamities is to bring us fast to repentance."

The ministers in nearly all of the churches referred to the Galveston calamity in their sermons. At the close special collections were taken.

MAKES THE WHOLE WORLD KIN.

Galveston's great calamity was the central thought in many sermons preached in Chicago, and in a majority of the churches a collection was taken for the benefit of the sufferers. Some of the expressions were as follows :

The Rev. William A. Burch (South Park Avenue Methodist Church)—"Such catastrophes reveal the worst and the best. There was mutilation of the sacred dead. But so on every battlefield a glittering diamond on the finger or in the ear excites the passions of men. But look at the better side. A cry for help went up and the nation was moved. Responses started with tens of thousands of dollars, and will run into hundreds of thousands. Human sympathy has mightily grown."

The Rev. Charles Reynolds (North Congregational Church, Fifty-ninth and La Salle streets)—" We have heard the news of the terrible calamity, also heard of the depravity of the human ghouls who pounced upon the dead for robbery, and how they were shot down like dogs. The whole has been like a terrible nightmare. Then we must look for a bright side. We rejoice at the noble gifts made by the people of the United States, especially Chicago. The lesson of the terrible catastrophe is that we at all times must be prepared to meet our God. We are facing death, which may come at any moment, like it did upon those poor souls in Galveston."

The Rev. Samuel Fallows (St. Paul's Reformed Episcopal Church, Adams street and Winchester avenue)—" From breaking hearts we must say, 'Father in heaven, all is well, though faith and form are sundered in the night of fear.' The lesson of self-help which this calamity teaches will not be lost. God intended man to conquer nature, to bind its forces, to ride triumphantly on its seemingly resistless energies. Galveston must not be blotted out. It must rise to newness of life. Like our own Chicago, it must be rebuilt on a higher level. It must rear its structures so that the angriest waves shall not dash them to pieces. Another lesson of American pluck and energy will thus be learned by mankind. "

MISFORTUNES MAKE US ONE.

The Rev. Frank DeWitt Talmage (Jefferson Park Presbyterian Church)—"We know not why this misfortune happened. Only eternity can solve for us the mystery, but we can learn two or three lessons that may be of help to us. God has made of one blood all nations. The misfortunes of mankind make us one, and when we hear the call we can hear Christ say, 'Inasmuch as ye have done it unto one of the least of these, ye have done it unto Me.'"

The Rev. J. Kittredge Wheeler (Fourth Baptist Church, Ashland Boulevard and Monroe street)—" The Galveston horror brings more prominently into notice the universal brotherhood of· mankind, and shows that when suffering humanity calls, the response is liberal and widespread. Such a disaster puts aside all superficial distinction, and man comes to regard man as a fellow being without prejudice as to color or social position. "

The Rev. W. H. Carwardine (Adams Street Methodist Church)—"It was builded upon the sand, and its destruction is a warning to those builders who forget the foundation in the beauties of the upper structure. The highest light that comes to the victims of the most appalling disaster of the century is the unfolding of the world's friendship. "

The admirable courage and determination with which the survivors faced the terrible situation are well expressed in the following editorial of a leading journal :

"While the catastrophe at Galveston is calling forth proofs of sympathy and a spirit of practical helpfulness on every hand, the people of Galveston themselves are giving the world an equally notable proof of courage and sturdy resolution. The situation as it has developed from day to day has afforded a striking evidence of their ability to pull themselves together and prepare to face the future. The conditions which they had to confront on the days immediately following the catastrophe, when they were cut off even from communication of the outer world and were alone in their knowledge of the extent of the calamity, must have been appalling beyond conception.

NO WEAK FIBRE IN GALVESTON PEOPLE.

"Stunned by a disaster in which individual griefs were lost in a common horror and the presence of death on all sides made the finding of the dead an incident of commonplace, they could scarcely have been expected to act with energy, organization or promptitude. The blow sustained by the city must have seemed irreparable.

"Irreparable it would have been if the Galveston men and women had been of weaker fiber. It stands to their credit that as soon as the clear comprehension of their misfortune came to them they faced it resolutely, and pushing aside individual griefs, set themselves to protect those who were still living. They recognized the futility of lamentation, and the necessity of foregoing the rites and formalities which men hold to be sacred obligations to the dead. Now that the worst part of their terrible task is over, the reports indicate that they are setting themselves in the same spirit to the work of rebuilding Galveston and making of it such a city as it had never before been expected to be.

"There is no more talk about abandoning the site or allowing the city to pass into a stage of decadence. The town is to be rebuilt, from its ruins, and it is not merely to be rebuilt but to be improved. Judging from the feeling manifested among the people of the city, they will come in the future to celebrate 'flood day' in much the same spirit that Chicago commemorates the anniverary of its great fire.

"The outside world has a double duty to discharge in helping the people who are showing this resolution and pluck in a time of severest trial. It would have been a duty to have given them aid in any event. But the way in which they are meeting their calamity indicates a courage and a strength of character to which the world can well afford to pay tribute. No effort should be spared to help those who are so bravely trying to help themselves.

"'The Daily News' is glad to say that in discussing Galveston's future it is discussing what is to be a fact—a fact, moreover, inspiring in its lesson of invincible Anglo-Saxon will and courage that rises equal to all occasions and throws down the challenge to despair.

HOPE FOR THE RUINED CITY.

"Outside of Galveston, when the news came of the awful destruction by hurricane and ocean combined, there were not a few who asked, as did 'The Daily News,' 'Will Galveston be rebuilt?' and paused for a reply. The answer has come promptly and with a ring of determination and hope that makes Americans proud of the Galvestonians—Yes, Galveston will be rebuilt. 'It will rise greater and better than ever.'

"And it is now known that this resolution, taken on Sunday afternoon, almost before the great storm had begun to subside, has been caught up not only by Galvestonians themselves but by all the great business interests centering there, and is re-echoed from all parts of the United States. Chairman Walker of the board of directors of the Atchison, Topeka & Sante Fe Railroad says the city will be rebuilt and doing business at the old stand in three months. The officials of this road further say that in six days the bridge from Virginia Point will have been built and trains running over it.

"A like spirit is being manifested by other steamship companies, whose trade doubled Galveston's export business between

1892 and 1899, making it rank fourth as an export port in the United States, only New York, Boston, and Baltimore surpassing it.

"Leading business and representative men of Galveston, also, instead of sitting down in despair, have been busy at work burying or otherwise disposing of their dead, clearing away the debris and getting the city in shape again as rapidly as possible.

"In the face of such a gallant spirit and purpose, difficulties and discouragements which at first were appalling will disappear. In its heroic work its strength and hope will be all the greater for the friendly aid and encouragement and the munificent generosity of America and Europe which will help Galveston to get upon its feet again."

CHAPTER XVI.

Startling Havoc Made by the Angry Storm—Vessels Far Out on the Prairie—Urgent Call for Millions of Dollars— Tangled Wires and Mountains of Wreckage.

COLONEL "BILL" STERRETT, a well-known publisher of Austin, went to Galveston after the storm and the sights he saw during his stay there are thus described by him :

"How to commence the story bothers. Whether to start out with the absolute truth and wind the sheet about the whole thing with the simple expression ' unspeakable ' or to go on and hint the details inexpressibly sad, intimate the horrors, is the question.

"It would be better for the heart if a veil could fall from heaven and conceal what it has done. It would be better if a fog, thick, like a wall, should come up between the sea and the land that the latter might never see the crime of the former. For if calm humanity shrieked against the awfulness of the one element, it has done it now.

"The broad pampa between Houston and Galveston had been flooded. The towns which in the last ten years had grown were scared and torn by this fiend. Its anger was shown in pastures as well as in towns, and yet none knew the fury of it. There were reports of destruction further on, and the truth of them impressed each man in the cars as the cars counted off its rattleteteck in toll-off the miles.

" Against a barbed wire fence the bloated carcasses of cattle had floated, their swollen limbs stiff toward the sky, and yet others browsed around in the meadow now which was a roaring sea but four days ago. The sight was the first he saw of death, and every man in the car, as to avoid the fear that arose in the mind of each, began to express wonder how this could be, that is, that some of these poor brutes were dead and others living. There were vessels of all tonnage, kinds and degrees on the prairie.

"Out there was a tramp steamship, the other way was the

dredge boat; there were yachts, schooners and launches, but near us was the hobby horse of a child. And so help me, I would rather have seen all the vessels of the earth stranded high and dry than to have seen this child's toy, standing right out on that prairie, masterless. Because one represented—well, why, say God, man's heart is so weak. But surely he will forgive it when it is soft for those who are weak.

"Débris of all kinds covered the prairie. It was from Galveston, because it could be from no other place. Every ant hill was covered with the remnants of homes in the city, six miles away. There were lace curtains, furniture of all kinds, but mostly of the cheap kind. There were toys, ladies' toilet articles, bed clothes, and, in fact, everything that goes to make up a home. This point was Texas City, six miles away from Galveston, across the bay. The town had suffered badly.

GENTLE AS A COUNTRY POND.

"Human lives were lost there, and the agony of it was great, but above all was the idea, 'What of across the bay?' It was six miles dead across, and a schooner was in waiting to take us over. But before it landed there was a chance of observation of the bay, in which the waters now gently lisped. For the bay was as gentle as a country pond. It lisped and kissed the few blades of grass that grew down where the rise and fall of the ridge was natural. It did not moan like the sea. It merely gurgled. But every little wave threw up and agitated the dead. Bloated horses and cows which provident housekeepers in the city across the water had owned and petted were there. Chickens, rats, dogs, cats and everything, it seemed, that breathed, was there, dead and swollen and making the air nauseous.

"But by their sides were people. The worn-out people of the district, having saved their own lives and buried their dead, were quick to respond to natural instincts and do right by their kind. I saw them take swollen women and swollen men and swollen children and with quick shift place them in two-foot graves. It was terrible, but what could they do?

"There were no burial services. The men who did work were simply doing what they could to relieve the air of them. They were not gentle, but how could they be gentle, when the bodies lay there with their black faces, with their terribly swollen tongues and the odor of decomposition threatening those who lived?

"In the debris from Galveston was everything. I was struck with the idea that this must have impressed the people that the world had come to an end. For twenty-five miles on the land into the interior this disorderly element raged. It destroyed and it mangled, and when it ceased really the sea had given up its dead and the secrets of life were revealed, for walking among the debris I found a trunk. It had been broken open by the waves.

"Letters were blurred by the waves. I picked up one, and it began, 'My darling little wife,' and I closed it and threw it among its fellows on the drift. She was dead. She had kept this letter. Their sacred relations were exposed by this terror to those who would read them. There were dozens of men who picked up those letters. No one read them, for man is not so bad after all.

WRINGING THEIR HANDS IN AGONY.

"Two women—I talked to them—had left two children each in Galveston in the destroyed district, and they sat through that whole five hours' trip wringing their hands and trying to curb the volcano of lamentation which lies in the mother's heart when those of her flesh are imperiled or dead.

"We passed corpses. We passed the corpses of men and women and children. The moon was out, floating real brilliantly, and the boat cut past, barely missing a woman with her face turned toward God and the sky. I fervently prayed I might never the the like again. And when we reached the wharf, torn and skinned so that we had to creep to land, I saw beneath me, white and naked seven bodies.

"My very soul turned cold at the grewsome sight. Horrible! The contemplation of it yet makes me sick, though I have seen things since then that make me and would make the world sick, if I were able to describe them, unto death."

Of the pitiful tales, that of Thomas Klee, of Galveston, is one of the most pitiful. His wife was away from home when the house was destroyed, and has not since been heard from. Klee with his infant boy and girl in his arms was carried for an hour in the whirling water. Once he tried to fasten the four year old girl in the branches of a tree, but she was torn from his arms while he was trying to make her fast. When he finally gained a firm foothold he found his boy dead in his arms. Since that time he has hardly been a conscious being and he is still in the hospital at Houston, where he was taken Friday.

The body of a nephew of Alderman John Wagner, a youth eighteen years old, was found lodged in the forks of a tall cedar tree on Galveston Island, two miles from his wrecked home, and tightly clinched with a death grip in his right hand was $200 which his father gave him to hold while the father attempted to close a door, when the house went down and the whole family perished in the storm and flood.

CLASPED HANDS AND ESCAPED.

Encircling a water stand pipe with clasped hands, W. R. Jones and fifteen other men prevented themselves from being carried away by the water, and so saved their lives at Galveston.

In a wooden bathtub Mrs. Chapman Bailey and Miss Blanche Kennedy were carried out into the gulf, where they spent Saturday night. Not till the next morning did the tide bring them back to where the rescuing parties could reach them. Neither of them has a relative in Galveston left alive.

Captain John Delaney, chief customs inspector of the port of Galveston, is one of the courageous men of the town. He lost his entire family, wife, son and daughters, but his sixty years were not bowed by his fate. The day following the disaster he was at his post, attired in a suit of overalls, the only clothing he had saved from the wreck of his home, and he has inspected all the vessels that have arrived since then.

Along the Galveston wharf front the storm was particularly violent. The big steel tank of the Waters-Pierce Oil Company,

21

in which was stored during the season cotton seed oil, at the foot of Fifteenth street, was blown to Twenty-first street, a distance of six blocks. It landed on its bottom and rests now in an upright position. It is a large tank and heavy, but the elements got the better of it.

RESCUED TWO BABES FROM DEATH.

Ray Ayers, an eight year old boy, unwittingly rescued his sister's two babies during the flood. He was floating on a raft in Galveston when he passed a box with the two children in it. He siezed them, but the weight was too heavy for his raft, and so he placed them on two bales of hay on top of a floating shed. When he found his sister he learned that her children were lost, and when a searching party discovered them, they were still sleeping, unconscious of their danger.

James Battersole, of Galveston, was one of the men who were carried far out to sea during the storm, whirled back again in the rush of waters, and lived to tell of it. The roof of his house, on which he had sought refuge, served as his raft, and the spot on which he landed was very close to the location his house had formerly occupied.

Margaret Lee's life was saved at the expense of her brother's. The woman was in he Twelfth street home, in Galveston, when the hurricane struck. Her brother seized her and guided her to St. Mary's University, a short distance away. He returned to search for his son, and was killed by a falling house.

While George Boyer, of Galveston, was being carried with frightful velocity down the bay he saw the dead face of his wife in the branches of a tree. The woman had been wedged firmly between two branches.

Mrs. P. Watkins is a raving maniac as the result of her experience. With her two children and her mother she was drifting on a roof, when her mother and one child were swept away. Mrs. Watkins mistakes attendants in the hospital for her lost relatives, aud clutches wildly for them.

Harry Steele, a cotton man, and his wife sought safety in

three successive houses, which were demolished. They eventually climbed on a floating door and were saved.

Though separated by the storm and washed in different directions all the members of the Stubbs family, of Galveston, were rescued. Father, mother and two children were on a floating roof that broke in pieces. The father, with one child, went one way. The mother went another, and the remaining children went in still a third direction. Sunday evening all four were reunited.

L. F. Menage, of Austin, who returned from Galveston Friday night, reached the Tremont Hotel, Galveston, the Friday evening before the terrible storm began. He says it has been the most terrible week in his experience, the most awful two days a man could imagine were the Sunday and Monday succeeding the hurricane.

"ALL GONE!—ALL GONE!"

"One man would ask another how his family had come out," said Mr. Menage last night, "and the answer would be indifferent and hard—almost offish: 'Oh, all gone.' 'All gone' was the phrase on all sides.

"The night before the disaster, when I reached the hotel, it was blowing rather hard, and the clerk said we were in for a storm, and I asked him if his roof was firmly fixed, and he said, 'Well, it won't be quite as bad as that,' but by the next night at the same time there was three feet of water in the rotunda and the skylight had fallen in and the servants' annex been blown to pieces, and the place was crowded with refugees who arrived from all points of the city in boats. Saturday night there was little sleep, yet no one realized the extent of the disaster.

"On Sunday morning one could walk on the higher streets, so quickly had the water gone down. I took a walk along the beach, and the place was one great litter of overturned houses, debris of all kinds and corpses. I met one woman who burst into tears at sight of a small rocker, her property, mixed in among the wreckage. She had lost all her family in the flood. People were for the most part bereft of their senses from the horror, and a single funeral would have seemed more terrible—more solemn—than a pile of cremated bodies.

"The tales of looting are only too true, and as I passed north-ward in a sailboat on Tuesday I heard the shots ring out which told that some ghoul was paying the penalty. Galveston will rise again on the old site, and without as much difficulty as is at present anticipated. Most of the people will, however, try and live on the mainland.

Miss Sarah E. Pilkington, a well-known young woman of Chester, Penna., was one of those who escaped the terrible storm which broke over Galveston. Miss Pilkington left Houston just a few hours before the dreadful storm broke, but she was suffi-ciently near its origin to hear the rush and roar of the wind. "I distinctly remember," said she, "the approach of the hurricane. It sounded like two express trains, each rumbling in opposite directions. Suddenly there was a loud report similar to the noise of a big collision, and the tornado was separated, one portion going in the direction of Galveston, the other wending its way toward Houston. I was staying at Milliken."

For some time after the hurricane Miss Pilkington could not be communicated with, and it was thought for a week that she had perished in the tornado.

NO TIME TO DIG GRAVES.

Galveston, Texas, Tuesday.—The work of digging bodies from the mass of wreckage still continues. More than 400 bodies were taken out of the débris which lines the beach front to-day. With all that has been done to recover bodies buried beneath or pinned in the immense rift, the work has hardly started. There is no time to dig graves, and the bodies, beaten and bruised beyond identification, are hastily consigned to the flames.

Volunteers for this work are coming in fast. Men who have heretofore avoided the dead under ordinary conditions are now working with vigorous will and energy in putting them away. Under one pile of wreckage this afternoon twenty bodies were taken out and cremated. In another pile a man pulled out the bodies of two children, and for a moment gazed upon them and then mechanically cast them into the fire. They were his own children. He watched them until they were consumed and then he resumed his work, assisting in removing other bodies.

A large force of men are still engaged in removing the dead from Hurd's lane, about four miles west of the city. At this point the water ran to a height of fourteen feet, and left in trees and fences the bodies of men, women and children, which are now being collected and cremated.

On the mainland the search for and cremation of bodies is being vigorously prosecuted. Reports received from Bolivar Peninsula, where between 300 and 400 bodies were lying along the beach and inland, show that the dead are being buried as rapidly as possible. The man bringing the report says the force is inadequate and should be immediately increased.

DISINFECTING THE CITY.

The manner of disposing of the wreckage and its mass of bodies in this city has not as yet been definitely decided upon. Every energy is now employed in getting rid of the dead, opening streets, cleaning alleys and gutters and disinfecting the city. When this is done the removal of the immense mass of debris will commence. Everything is in readiness to turn on the current for the electric lights in the business district, but because of the danger from hanging wires on the circuit, the lighting has been indefinitely postponed. Three telephone wires are now working between Galveston and Houston.

Chairman Davidson, of the Relief Committee, says the greatest sufferers from the storm are those persons of limited means who owned homes near the beach. There are hundreds of these, who owned lots, and by giving liens upon them, had homes constructed by loan companies.

A. Holzman, representing Frederick G. Holzman, of Cincinnati, purchaser of the sewerage bonds of the city of Galveston to the amount of $300,000, arrived to-day and consulted with the city officials as to whether it was proposed to accept a sewerage system in accordance with plans adopted prior to the storm. He received assurances that the storm would in no way affect the construction of the sewerage system, and as soon as possible work would commence.

W. B. Groseclose, assistant general freight agent of the Missouri, Kansas and Texas Railroad, reached Galveston this evening. He says the road will commence to receive grain for shipment to Galveston on September 22. A large force of men is engaged repairing one of the railroad bridges across Galveston Bay.

A force of Deputy United States Marshals under Marshal Grant is guarding the entrance to Galveston, at Texas City, and keeping away all persons who can show no good cause for coming here. Crowds are daily leaving the city, a majority being women and children. The city is still under martial law, and will remain so indefinitely. Idlers and sightseers who elude the guards on the mainland are upon their arrival here pressed into the street service.

SOME ACCOUNT OF CLARA BARTON.

Galveston, Tex., September 18.—Clara Barton, President of the Red Cross Society, who came here to distribute relief supplies, was stricken down at her work to-day while ministering to the victims of the Galveston storm. She succumbed, like a soldier, at her post. To-night she lies seriously ill at the Tremont Hotel.

She was stricken at a conference in her rooms at the Tremont, with her staff of nine gathered about her. She had just finished an outline of her work, assigning each member of her staff to the particular part of the work that one was to do. Suddenly she ceased speaking. Turning to Mrs. Ellen Spencer Mussey, Vice-President of the Red Cross, who sat at her side, she whispered:

" Begin talking. I am going to faint. Don't let them see."

Miss Barton leaned back in her chair and Mrs. Mussey arose, and, standing before her, began speaking. Without a sign to the others Mrs. Mussey finished what she had to say and then dismissed the conference.

Galveston people arose with heavy hearts this morning. Thousands of them were driven from their beds. Shortly after sunrise there came a downpour of rain, the first since the storm. If there was a house in town that had been sufficiently repaired to shed the rain it was a rare exception. Cremation of the dead and clearing the streets have taxed the energies. There has not been time to give attention to roofs. Such repairs as have been made to buildings have been in the form of straightening and strengthening them so that they might not fall down. Many, while still standing, are leaning like the tower of Pisa or are partly off the foundations.

FACES OVERSPREAD WITH SADNESS.

From this it will be understood that when the rain poured down it entered the houses still called habitable and drenched the contents again. The faces of the people showed the influence of the rain. They were overspread with sadness. The hopefulness which had been lighting up the features was gone. But it was only an hour of depression. Then the shower, for that was all it proved to be, passed. The sun come out.

All Galveston went to work with renewed energy. Three or four horse cars made their appearance and, drawn by mules, were operated over several streets. At the wharves there was activity. The loading of wheat for export was commenced. Cremation and cleaning went on. The finding and burning of over 100 bodies in the day shows that the end of this duty is not yet in sight.

In the southern and southwestern part of the city the great windrow of wreckage still stands, concealing from sight but not from smell what is underneath. Word was sent along the inner side of the windrow to occupants of houses near that they must move back a block. The impression is that this means the authorities have decided they will apply the torch to the great heaps whenever a favorable wind from the north will make burning safe for the rest of the city. This action has been strongly advocated.

The tents have come and with board floors and fences separating them now make a white city on the beach front where the houses were swept away. They will be much safer and more healthy than many of the shattered buildings which are still occu-

pied by the poorer classes.   There have been till now some people
finding shelter in the wooden cisterns which the wind blew off
their foundations and left lying about the streets and parks.
Others are in houses without roofs and windows and still others in
buildings the walls of which are far from perpendicular.

The following detailed account of the experience of the Rev.
Judson S. Palmer and his family, formerly of Sharon, Penna., in the
disaster at Galveston, was received at the former place in a letter.
Mrs. Palmer and her son were drowned.

ROOF BLOWN AWAY.

About four o'clock Dr. Cline, who was in charge of the Weather
Bureau at Galveston, the letter stated, passed, and Rev. Palmer
asked him what they had better do.   He advised them to stay
in the house, as he thought it was perfectly safe.   The storm
increased and the water flowed into the yard.   Mr. Palmer went
downstairs and found the wind had blown down the front door
and several windows.

About dark sections of the roof were blown off and all the persons in the house went into Mr. Palmer's room.   There a prayer
meeting was held, all joining in prayer and singing.   Little Lee's
prayer was: "Dear Jesus, do make the water recede and give us a
nice day to play to-morrow."

After that all who could went into the bathroom.   The water
arose until it came up to the necks of Mr. Palmer and his wife.
They then stepped upon the edge of the bathtub, Mr. Palmer holding Lee, with his little arms clasping the father about the neck.
Mrs. Palmer held to the shower-bath fixtures overhead and passed
her other arm around her husband's neck.   Suddenly there was a
grinding noise.   The house upset.   There was a rush of water
and all were engulfed in the flood.

Mr. Palmer and his family became separated and he never saw
them again.   He went to the bottom as he was sure he was drowning.   Suddenly he was caught by a swift current and arose to the
surface.   He crawled upon what he believed to be a bundle of shutters and drifted until his raft struck a shed and it sank.   After

several hours he succeeded in getting on one of the outbuildings of the Catholic convent, where he remained until the water receded. Mrs. Palmer's body and that of her son were not recovered.

On September 20th a correspondent furnished the following facts : " Normal conditions are being restored swiftly in Galveston. The work of clearing the streets of debris continues unabated and all relief work is now thoroughly systematized. Several human bodies were found to-day. No attempt was made to identify them, and they were immediately cremated.

NECESSARY BUREAUS.

" A census bureau was placed in operation to-day. A mortuary bureau has also been opened where relatives or friends are to make oath of the known death of persons lost in the storm. Hanna & Leonard's new elevator began business to-night. The British steamer Endeavor went under the spouts and is taking on a full cargo of wheat.

" At a meeting of the general relief committee to-day no one was found who would undertake the job of removing the city's debris on contract, as all state it would be impossible to make a definite estimate. The nearest estimate expert wreckers will make is that it will take 2000 men ninety days to clear away the debris and get all of the bodies out, and that this will cost $500,000. The board adopted a resolution stating that it was its opinion that the best way to solve the problem of clearing the debris was to let a contract to some one to do this work.

" Dr. George H. Lee, inspector of hospitals and dispensaries, made a favorable report on the sanitary condition of the city. The losses to the life insurance companies are estimated at $500,000. Most of those who carried old line life policies escaped. The fraternal orders will lose heavily."

Governor Sayers, speaking of the situation at Galveston said :

" I look for the rebuilding of Galveston to be well under way by the latter p   of this week. The work of cleaning the city of unhealthful refuse and burying the dead will have been completed by that time.

"The loss of life occasioned by the storm in Galveston and elsewhere on the southern coast cannot be less than 12,000 lives, while the loss of property will probably aggregate $20,000,000.

"If the laboring people of Galveston will only get to work in earnest, prosperity will soon again smile on the city. The money and food contributions coming from a generous people have been a great help to the people of Galveston, as it has relieved them of the necessity of spending their money to support the needy, and it can now be applied to the improvements of their own property and putting again on foot their business enterprises.

"The work of clearing the streets of débris is progressing rapidly under the perfect organization instituted by military rule under Adjutant-General Scurry. Over two thousand men are engaged on the work. Ninety-eight bodies are reported as having been found in the wreckage and removed to-day. Bodies found are buried or cremated and no systematic record has been kept. The storm wrecked almost every vault in the six cemeteries of the city, and many of the dead were washed to sea in metal cases. So far only one casket has been found. It had been carried three miles from the vault.

WORK PUSHED WITH VIGOR.

"The work under the direction of the health department is pushed with vigor and rapidity. Over a carload of disinfectants was taken from the wharves to-day and sent to the heath department supply depot, and almost as much was taken from that place and distributed over the city. Much was done in the way of removing debris and disposing of animal carcasses. The sick and wounded are receiving the best of treatment. Besides the other hospitals and medical relief station already in service, the marine hospital and refuge camp was opened this afternoon and will accommodate a large number of patients. The outlook from a health standpoint is very encouraging.

"Three pile drivers are at work closing up the breach in the Galveston Bay bridge made by the steamship Roma. The rebuilding of the bridge is progressing rapidly. A message from General

Superintendent Nixon, of the Santa Fé Railroad, to General Manager Polk this evening, said trains will be able to cross on Thursday. Orders have been issued to allow freight to proceed to Galveston. The tracks on Galveston Island will be completed to the bridge to-morrow noon. Engines are again running into the Union Depot, and are bringing freight to the ships in port.

"The water works system is being gradually restored and the mains are now supplying the various hospitals. Miss Clara Barton, of Red Cross Society, has opened a depot for supplies. She has sent orders for medicine and surgical dressings, food for the sick and clothing and shoes.

WANTS A BREAKWATER.

"Congressman Hawley advocates the building of a break-water, beginning at the south jetty and extending westward, parallelling the shore of Galveston Island for a distance of about seven miles. With a base of twenty-five feet and crown of eight feet, capped with heavy granite blocks, he believes this would break the force of a tidal wave and adequately protect Galveston.

"The people are still leaving the city in considerable numbers, but the relief work locally has now been gotten down to such a fine point that it is likely there will be a marked diminution of the exodus during the next two or three days. Fears of an epidemic have been allayed by the distribution of medicines and disinfect-ants, and a feature which would undoubtedly have had the effect of causing many to seek succor elsewhere has been eliminated from the situation.

"Supplies and money are now pouring in from all over the country, and at least seven figures are needed to express the amount of cash so far received. This is being used judiciously, and the good effects of the presence of such a relief fund in the city are already apparent. An order of the military government directed against idle negro women went into operation to-day. It has been decided by the Central Relief Committee to establish a camp in which these women will be held and kept off the streets and out of the way of those who are burying the dead."

To put Galveston on her feet will require $5,000,000. Such is the opinion of Congressman Hawley, one of the representative business men. This does not mean that the sum mentioned will come anywhere near restoring the city to the condition before the storm. Far from it.

Mr. Hawley was simply asked: "What measure of relief will burn your dead, clean and purify your streets and public places, feed and clothe the living and place your people where they can be self-sustaining and in a way to regain what has been lost?"

His reply was: "It will take $5,000,000 to relieve Galveston from the distress of the storm. At least that sum will be needed to dispose of the dead, to remove the ruins and to do what is right for the living.

SOME MEANS TO HELP PEOPLE.

"I think that we should not only feed and clothe, but that we ought to have some means to help people who have lost everything to make a start toward the restoration of their homes. To do this will require every dollar of $5,000,000."

There are now on the scene more nurses and physicians than are required. The injured are rapidly recovering from their wounds, which are largely superficial. Many men and women are suffering from severe nervous shock, and find it impossible to sleep. Food is coming in by the boatload and carload faster than it can be handled, in such generous quantities that no further doubts are entertained about supplies. Relief headquarters in each of the twelve wards deal out supplies to applicants in their respective wards.

Estimates of the numbers dependent upon the relief committees vary. Mayor Jones makes it about 8000, while other authorities put the number as high as 15,000. In the business centre the streets have been cleaned and opened. All buildings still show marks of wind and water, but goods are displayed and business is being transacted. The city is gradually assuming its bustling ante-flood appearance. Stenches no longer assail the nostrils, except where much debris still remains untouched.

Cremation of the dead is being pushed, but it will be many days before the working parties get out the last of the bodies. The whole twenty-two miles of the island was submerged. The horrors of the western portion beyond the city limits are just being learned. At San Luis 181 bodies were burned to-day. Between twenty and thirty bodies were counted among the piles of th' railroad bridge between the island and Virginia Point. In Kinkead's addition about 100 were lost, eighteen in one house. There were also losses at Nottingham, one of the Galveston island villages, where nothing but wreckage remains.

One hundred bodies were buried in Galveston on Sunday. The further the men work in the Denver reservoir section the more numerous do they find the dead. Fires are burning every 300 feet on the beach and along many of the streets. Mayor Walter C. Jones to-day, in response to a request, made a statement of conditions and needs of Galveston people, basing his conclusions on the most current information which has come to him. Mayor Jones' statement is as follows:

"WE ARE BROKE."

" It is almost impossible to speak definitely as yet of the needs of our people. We are broke, the majority of us. Galveston must have suffered, in my estimation, based upon all of the reports I have to the extent of $20,000,000. We now need money more than anything. From the advices I have received I believe that the shipments of disinfectant and food supplies now on the way will be sufficient to meet the immediate wants. By the time these are used we shall have regained our tranquility."

This is the ninth day after the storm and still the grewsome works goes on of recovering the dead from the gigantic mass of debris that lines the southside of what remains of the city. Among the scores of bodies recovered and cremated yesterday was a mother with a suckling babe tightly clasped to her breast.

The body of Major W. T. Levy United States Immigrant Inspector of this district, was among the number. He had made a struggle to save his wife and three children but all were lost.

The bodies of the wife and children have not been recovered, or if so they are still among the uninterred dead.

The task of recovering the bodies that are beneath or jammed into this immense rick of debris, extending from the eastern to the western limits of the city, a distance of over three miles, is a herculean one, and the most expenditious way of removing the whole from a sanitary point of view, is by fire. This, however, in the crippled condition of the fire department and water works, would endanger the remaing portion of the city. As it now stands this immense mass of debris, strewn with dead bodies, the carcasses of decaying animals, etc., is a sore menance to the health of the city and is the most difficult problem the Board of Health has to deal with.

OPENING UP THE STREETS.

The work of opening up the streets and disinfecting them is being vigorously prosecuted. The debris and garbage is being removed, 250 vessels of every description carrying it out to a safe place, where it is burned. In a few days all streets will be opened for the passage of vehicles. It was decided at a meeting of the Central Executive Commiltee that all the laborers employed in burying the dead, cleaning the buildings and moving the debris from the streets and sidewalks shall receive $1.50 per day and rations. Heretofore they have been working for nothing, and if they refused were impressed by the military.

The work of relief of the sick and injured is well in hand and under the direction of skilled physicians and nurses it is improved daily. Eleven hundred tents were received by the Board of Health. All except 300, retained for hospital purposes, will be distributed by the chairmen of various ward sub-committees to shelter the homeless in their respective wards.

Houston, Tex., September 17.—The day after the report of the storm at Galveston had been published to the world the Houston representative of a Northern journal received this " rush " telegram : " Get photographs of Galveston storm scenes, no matter what the expense ; rush them through."

At that time no one had gone from the outside to Galveston, not even newspaper men. Galveston was practically cut off from the outside world. The scores of people hurrying to Houston with the desire of getting to Galveston by the railroad and boats plying between there and that city could not make the trip.

The representative endeavored to charter a tug to send a photographer and some newspaper men through, but the captain refused to go.

CAPTAIN WOULD NOT RISK THE TRIP.

" I will sell you my boat," he said, "but neither myself nor my men will risk the trip."

By putting several thousand men at work all day Monday and Monday night one railroad line was put in condition for a train to go from Houston to Texas City, six miles from Galveston, the island being across the bay.

This, the first train out of Houston, was to leave early Tuesday morning. The news of its intended departure spread to all parts of the country. Hundreds of grief-stricken, bewildered people, nearly crazed with anxiety for relatives in the storm-swept country, stayed up all night, with the hope of getting into Galveston. The railroad men let all that they could possibly stow away in the coaches get on board, telling them in advance, however, that no one would be able to get from Texas City to Galveston.

Arriving there with the train was the special photographer of the newspaper with his camera. When this crowd of men and women reached Texas City they found no means of riding further.

The only possible way to make the perilous trip was to walk to Virginia Point, two miles away, and this was across the marsh filled with débris and bodies from the Galveston wreck. The photographer and the ten other men attempted the task. They were nearly exhausted when the two miles were finished. They had taken off their shoes and walked up to their waists in water. Their feet were bruised. The photographer carefully kept his camera from coming in contact with the water, however, and got several graphic views when he reached the place.

The ten men found a skiff that was thrown up the bay by the rush of water on that fateful Saturday night. They dragged it for many weary yards, finally getting it into the water, and managed to row to Huntington Wharf, Galveston, a distance of two miles. Worn out as they were, they walked to the city, the man with the camera being the first photographer in from the outside.

His troubles were not over, though. There were hundreds of terrible scenes to photograph; at every turn there was a graphic picture; but the people of Galveston, crazed with grief as they were, seemed to think it a desecration that he was there, and that views of their wrecked town and their dead should be thus recorded by the camera. They muttered and they threatened.

The photographer moved from one place to another.. He hid himself and only took a snapshot when he knew he was safe from the scrutiny of the men and women who thought his work was a mockery of their grief. To show the real mind of the people it will only be necessary to state that many newspaper men who have visited all parts of the world as special correspondents, who have had ingress to courts and Parliament, who have traveled everywhere there has been news to find, found it impossible to get into Galveston.

GETTING OUT OF GALVESTON.

Getting out of Galveston, however, is comparatively easy. It was Wednesday morning when the photographer finally reached Houston, exhausted and nervous to a degree that made working a torture. He managed to develop his pictures, and that evening that man rushed forward the first photographs of actual storm scenes to leave the city.

One hundred and thirty bodies of storm victims were recovered and cremated to-day (September 17), nine days after the hurricane, and still there are hundreds more to be found. They lie for the most part under the twisted heaps of debris that line the city for miles along its southern side.

The problem of clearing away the wreckage in this part of the city, where it is thickest, is still a very troublesome one despite all the work that has been done. The quickest and best way would doubtless be by fire, but the very mention of fire has a terror for Galvestonians now. The city is practically without protection from fire, and if the flames once get a good start, a holocaust might be the result, which would be only second in horror to the hurricane.

The problem is all the more serious because the danger of an epidemic caused by the many dead bodies of men and animals is still great. Sickness of a malarial type is already prevalent. The debris and garbage is being removed with the aid of 250 wagons to places where it can safely be burned, but that is a very slow process. Men are still being impressed for the work under the oversight of the soldiers, but hereafter all the laborers will be paid $1.50 a day out of the relief funds.

ABOUT 17,000 PEOPLE RECEIVING RELIEF.

Health Officer Wilkinson stated that 40 per cent. of the debris of every description had been removed from the streets; that 95 per cent. of the dead bodies had been disposed of, and that 95 per cent. of the carcasses of animals had been removed from the city.

Among the bodies found was that of Major W. T. Levy, United States emigrant inspector for Galveston. His wife and three children perished, but their bodies have not been recovered. In one place the body of a mother was found with a babe of a few months tightly clasped to her breast.

About 17,000 people are now receiving relief each day, and the supplies are sufficient for their immediate wants. This morning the first supplies brought by the Chicago relief train arrived here by way of Clinton. The train reached Houston at midnight Saturday, having made a run of 270 miles from Fort Worth at an average speed of thirty-seven miles an hour. Owing to a change in its schedule the people who had been watching for its arrival failed to see it, and it was rushed over the Southern Pacific Road to Clinton, where barges were waiting for the supplies.

The Chicago train was the largest that has yet been sent to Galveston, and many expressions of gratitude to Chicago are heard

22

here.   Mayor Jones, for instance, said to-day : " Chicago people are the best kind of friends to have when one is in trouble.   We cannot express our thanks to them.   We will show by our future what their help has meant to us.   Like Chicago we will rise above all disaster and rebuild our city better than it has ever been before."

Eleven hundred tents were received to-day by the Board of Health.   All except 300, which were retained for the marine hospital on the beach, have been distributed to the homeless in the different wards.

Miss Clara Barton is giving her time and attention to assisting in the work of relief and ascertaining what supplies are necessary to meet the exigencies of the situation.

NUMEROUS CASES OF INSANITY.

The city takes on more of the appearance of a business place each day.   To-day horse cars are running downtown, while there is both water and electric service in limited portions of the city. Telephone communication has been opened with Houston, and both of the telegraph companies have greatly improved their service. All the railroad companies announce they will have trains into the city inside of three days, although at first only trains with construction material may risk the trip across the repaired bridge. The Santa Fé Road expects its first train on Thursday.

A systematic effort was begun this morning to obtain the names of the dead, so that the information can be used for legal purposes and for life insurance settlements.   Sworn statements from witnesses of death are being recorded, and communication with people with information who have left the city is being opened.

There are numerous cases of insanity in Galveston as a result of the terrible bereavements sustained by the survivors.   Judge John J. Reagan, a prominent lawyer, is at the Mas   c relief station in a pitable condition.   Judge Reagan lost every relative he had in Galveston.   He sits hour by hour in pathetic silence.   Then he bursts out laughing, and his laughter is followed by tears.

There are now about 200 soldiers in Galveston doing police

duty, and more have been called for.   The Dallas Rough Riders, the Houston Light Guards, the Galveston Sharpshooters, Battery D, of Houston and Cavalry Troop A, Houston, are the commands.

The affiliated labor organization of this city, over 500 of its members having lost everything, has issued an address appealing to every labor organization throughout the country for assistance. It has appointed T. W. Dee and James F. Grimes as agents to visit all large cities in behalf of aid for their stricken members. Dee and Grimes have also received credentials from Mayor Jones, and they left to-night on their mission.

Not a day goes by but new stories of almost miraculous escapes and of prolonged suffering are told here.   The conditions of the hurricane were such that it was luck alone that permitted men to escape death.

ESCAPE OF REV. L. P. DAVIS AND FAMILY.

The escape of Rev. L. P. Davis, his wife and his five young children on Boliver Peninsula and their seven days of suffering before they reached here is of a kind rarely to be equaled in the annals of disasters.   This has already been detailed in these pages.   Mr. Davis started to drive his family away from his home at Patton Beach when the water began to rise high.   He saw a neighbor's family washed out of their wagon and rescued them.

The party made their way to a grove, where the adults tied the children and themselves in the branches of trees.   They spent a fearful night.   On Sunday, when the waters went down, they made their way past many corpses till they found a farmhouse not entirely destroyed.   There they got a little food and then set out on foot, living on the raw flesh of a steer till they found an over-turned sailboat and managed to reach Galveston.   From here they went to Houston, where they will be cared for.

CHAPTER XVII.

Governor Sayres Revises His Estimate of Those Lost and Makes it 12,000—A Multitude of the Destitute— Abundant Supplies and Vast Work of Distribution.

GOVERNOR SAYRES issued a statement September 19th, in which he said in part: "The loss of life occasioned by the storm in Galveston and elsewhere on the southern coast cannot be less than 12,000 lives, while the loss of property will probably aggregate $20,000,000. Notwithstanding this severe affliction, I have every confidence that the stricken districts will rapidly revive, and that Galveston will, from her present desolation and sorrow, arise with renewed strength and vigor."

Speaking further of the situation at Galveston, the Governor said: "I look for the rebuilding of Galveston to be well under way by the latter part of this week. The work of cleaning the city of unhealthful refuse and burying the dead will have been completed by that time, and all the available labor in the city can be applied to the rebuilding.

"If the laboring people of Galveston will only get to work in earnest, prosperity will soon again smile on the city. Arrangements have been made to pay all the laborers working under the direction of the military authorities $1.50 and rations for every day they have worked or will work. An account has been kept of all work done, and no laborer will lose one day's pay.

"The money and food contributions coming from a generous people have been a great help to the people of Galveston, as it has relieved them of the necessity of spending their money to support the needy, and it can now be applied to the improvement of their own property and putting again on foot their business enterprises.

"Five dollars a day is being offered to the mechanics who will come to Galveston, and with the assurance from reputable physicians that there is no extraordinary danger of sickness, outside laborers will flock to Galveston, and before many days a new city will rise on the storm-swept island.

"The telegraph and telephone companies and railroads have been exceedingly generous since the great calamity. They have not only given money, but everything has been transported to that city free of charge, while those desiring to get away from the harrowing scenes of Galveston have been transported free. The people of Texas will long remember with grateful hearts the kindness of these companies. It is now an assured fact that trains will be running into Galveston this week, and, with uninterrupted communication with the outside world, Galveston should soon assume her normal condition."

DISTRIBUTING $40,000 A DAY.

Twenty thousand people are being fed and cared for daily in Galveston with the supplies which are pouring in from all parts of the country. This will be cut at least one-half in ten days, is the statement of W. A. McVitie, chairman of the central relief committee.

The estimated cost of the aid which is now being extended is $40,000 a day. The great bulk of the aid is going to the 4,000 men who are at work cleaning up the wreckage, digging for bodies and cleaning the streets. Through them it goes to their families. No able-bodied laboring man is allowed to escape the work, whether he needs aid or not, though most of them do. The business men who are in position to resume are allowed to attend to their stores, and their clerical forces are not interfered with.

The debris-hunting and street-cleaning work will be put upon a cash basis, the wages being $1.50. Time has been kept from the beginning, though the records are not complete, and it is the expectation, if the money which comes in from outside is adequate, that the men will be paid for the full time they have worked. This will apply to those who had to be made to work at the point of the bayonet, as well as those who volunteered their services. This will not be given in cash, but in the form of orders for tools for mechanics, lumber for those who have homes they wish to repair, etc.

Heretofore practically every able-bodied man has been made to work, and unless he worked he got no supplies. The first few days' wages consisted entirely of rations, which were given according to the number and needs of the laborer's family, regardless of the amount of work he accomplished. Since other supplies have begun coming in they have been added.

The work of distribution is being conducted systematically and with an apparent minimum of imposition and fraud. There is a central committee, of which W. A. McVitie, a prominent business man, is chairman. Then there is a committee for each one of the twelve wards. As fast as goods or provisions arrive from the mainland they are placed in the central warehouse, from there the different ward chairmen requisition them, and they are taken to supply depots in the different wards. All day long there is a motley crowd around every one of these depots, negroes predominating at least two to one. Every applicant passes in review before the ward chairman.

ONLY THE DESTITUTE HELPED.

" Ah want a dress foh ma sistah, " says a big negress.

"You're 'Manda Jones, and you haven't any sister living here," replied the chairman.

"Foh de Lord, ah has ; ah ain't 'Mandy Jones at all ; we done live on Avenue N before de storm, and we los' everything."

"Go out with this woman and find out if she has a sister who needs a dress," says the chairman to a committeeman. In this way check is kept on all the applicants for aid.

At the 5th ward distributing station clothing was being given away this evening. A negro woman, who had been refused a supply, went outside and by way of revenge pointed out different ones of her friends and neighbors whom she alleged were similarly unentitled.

"Dat woman done los' nothin' at all, " she shrieked. "Ah did not los' nuthin' mahself and doan wan' nuthin."

"What's the trouble?" asked a bystander. An old negress who was lined up waiting her turn, replied: "Oh, she's mad 'cause de white folks won't give her nuthin." So far no woman has been required to work, but a strong feeling is developing to compel negro women to work cleaning up the houses. There are plenty of people who are willing to hire them, but as long as free food and clothing can be secured it is hard to get colored women to go in and clean up the partially ruined homes.

"Our supply of foodstuffs is adequate," said Chairman McVitie, "but just now we are a little short of clothing. This, however, may not be true to-morrow. We have no idea of the contents of the cars on the road to us. Frequently we don't know anything is coming until the cars reach Texas City. With the money which has been coming in we have been augmenting our supplies by purchasing of local merchants in lines where there was a shortage.

SAYS MONEY IS MOST NEEDED.

"What do we need worst? Money. If we have money we can order just what we need and probably get better value than the people who are buying it. Many people have made the mistake of sending money to Houston and Dallas and asking committees there to buy for us. They do not know just what we need, and if we had the money we could do better for ourselves. Money should be sent to us."

One of the most remarkable things attending the Galveston disaster is the fortitude of the people. Their loss in relatives, friends and property has been so overwhelming that it seems too much to be expressed with outward grief.

Two men who had not seen each other since the disaster met in the street. "How many did you lose?" they asked by common impulse.

"I lost all my property, but my wife and I came through all right."

"I was not so fortunate. My wife and my little boy were both drowned."

There was an expression of sympathy from the other, but nothing approaching a tear from either.

"They are making good progress cleaning up," remarked the one whose losses were heaviest, with a pleasant smile. The other one makes light answer and they pass on.

The people of Galveston have seen so much death that they are temporarily hardened to it. The announcement of the loss of another friend means little to a man who has seen the dead bodies of neighbors and townspeople hauled to the wharf by the drayload.

No services have been attempted for the dead. Neither has there been memorial services. The Rev. J. M. K. Kerwin, priest in charge of St. Mary's Catholic Cathedral, said : "It was impossible. Priest and layman had to join in the work of cleaning the city of dead bodies. I don't expect there will be memorial services for a month."

STOOD THE STORM WELL.

Father Kerwin's church is among the few which are comparatively little damaged. He sets the value of Catholic property destroyed in the city at $300,000. Included in this loss is the Ursula convent and academy, which was badly damaged. It covered four blocks between Twenty-fifth and Twenty-seventh streets and Avenues N and O. It was the finest in the South.

The city is rapidly improving in its sanitary conditions. The smell from the ooze and mud with which most of the streets are filled is stronger than that which comes from the debris heaps containing undiscovered bodies. When these heaps are being burned and the wind carries the smoke over the city, the odor is very similar to that which afflicts Chicago at night when refuse is being burned at the stockyards, and no worse. Soon even the odor of the slime will be gone. Every dumpcart in the city is at work.

Every Galveston business man talks confidently of the future of the city, though many of the clerks announce their intention of going away as soon as they can accumulate money enough.

"I'm not afraid of another storm," said a clerk in one of the principal stores. "But I'm sick and tired of the whole business."

The Southwestern Telephone and Telegraph Company, which is a branch of the Erie system, will rebuild its telephone system here. "This will take us three months, and in the meantime we will give no service save long-distance," said D. McReynolds, superintendent of construction. "We will install a central emergency system the same as that in Chicago and put all wires under ground. We will employ five hundred men if necessary to do the work in ninety days. The company's losses in Texas are $300,000 —$200,000 here, $60,000 at Houston and the rest at other points."

Residents here are greatly pleased at this announcement, as it shows the confidence of a foreign company in the future of Galveston.

ONLY ONE WHO ESCAPED.

Cooped up in a house that collapsed after being carried along by a deluge of water, John Elford, brother of A. B. Elford, Chicago, his wife and little grandson, met death in the flood during the Galveston storm. Milton, son of John Elford, was in the building with the family at the time, and is the only one of the many occupants, including fifteen women, that is known to have escaped.

A. B. Elford was dumbfounded when he received the first information of the disaster, for he had no idea of his brother being in Texas. John Elford was a retired farmer and merchant of Langdon, N. D. He recently had taken his family on a trip to old and New Mexico. Mr. Elford yesterday received the following letter from Langdon, N. D. :

"We have just received a letter from Milton. Father, mother, Dwight and Milton went to Galveston from Mineral Springs, Texas, where they had previously been stopping. They were so delighted with Galveston on reaching there that they sold their return tickets and decided to remain about two months. They were at first in a house near the beach, but moved farther away and to a larger and stronger house when the water began to rise.

"All at once the water came down the street, bringing houses and debris. They started to build a raft, but before it could be got together the house started to float. It had gone but a short distance when it went to pieces. Milton was struck with something and knocked out into the water. He came up, caught a timber and climbed to a roof, and thus managed to make his escape.

"He saw no one escape from the building as it collapsed. We do not believe the bodies have yet been recovered. We have wired for more definite news regarding the bodies, but have heard nothing more.   EDGAR ELFORD."

William Guest, a Pullman car porter, returned to Chicago from the storm-stricken district. He said:

"I left Harrisburg night before last, and things then in the neighborhood were in a dreadful state. Galveston is about twenty miles distant, and the refugees were pouring in the direction of Houston in great numbers. Many well-to-do colored people have lost all they had. The Rev. W. H. Cain, a colored Episcopal minister and his entire family were killed, and it was reported to me that Mrs. Cuney, the widow of Wright Cuney, was also lost, as well as a number of colored teachers employed in the public schools. At Houston relief committees have been organized."

The Rev. Mr. Cain was well known in Chicago, having preached several times from the pulpit of the St. Thomas Episcopal church in Dearborn near 30th street.

The Quinn chapel congregation decided at a meeting that the church at 24th street and Wabash avenue should be opened in order that contributions of clothing and food for the sufferers might be received.

KAISER MOURNS FOR GALVESTON.

Washington, D. C., Sept 17.—President McKinley has received the following message of sympathy from Emperor William of Germany:

"Stettin, Sept. 13, 1900.—President of the United States of America, Washington: I wish to convey to your excellency the expression of my deep-felt sympathy with the misfortune that has befallen the town and harbor of Galveston and many other ports of the coast, and I mourn with you and the people of the United States over the terrible loss of life and property caused by the hurricane, but the magnitude of the disaster is equaled by the indomitable spirit of the citizens of the new world, who, in their long and continued struggle with the adverse forces of nature have proved themselves to be victorious.

"I sincerely hope that Galveston will rise again to new prosperity.   WILLIAM, I. R."

PRESIDENT THANKS THE KAISER.

The President's reply was as follows :

"Executive Mansion, Sept. 14, 1900.—His Imperial and Royal Majesty, William II., Stettin, Germany : Your majesty's message of condolence and sympathy is very grateful to the American government and people, and in their name as well as on behalf of the many thousands who have suffered bereavement and irreparable loss in the Galveston disaster, I thank you most earnestly.   " WILLIAM McKINLEY."

W. B. McGown, a member of the Dallas Rough Riders, to-day arrived at Dallas from Galveston on sick leave. He denies the reports that have been current in Dallas and other Texas cities of trouble with soldiery at Galveston or of any misconduct on the part of the militia. Mr. McGown says more and fresh troops are needed at Galveston. One-half of the Houston Light Guard have had to be relieved and placed on sick leave. A number have died from malarial fever contracted at Galveston.

The Houston Cavalry, the Navasota Infantry, the Trezevant Rifles, of Dallas, and the Rough Riders were the only troops on duty last night, and a considerable part of these companies were unfit for duty. Two infantry companies from Fort Worth, Claburn, and the Dallas Artillery were expected to-day.

There were twenty-five fires kept burning to consume dead bodies in the debris in a stretch of three miles. McGown says information was received at the Dallas headquarters of the Gulf, Colorado and Santa Fe Railroad that construction trains with materials had already crossed the bay from the mainland to Galveston Island. Local Santa Fe officials say supplies and building materials will be rushed to the island rapidly from now on. Galveston now has railroad, telegraph and telephone connection with the outside world.

A special correspondent writing from Galveston on September 19th, said:

"The most serious problem which now confronts those in authority here is the disposition of the dead and the removal of wreckage. This matter is being attended to by a large force scattered through the city, but the number is inadequate to meet the requirements.

EXHAUSTION THINS OUT THE WORKERS.

" At a meeting of the Auxiliary Health Board to-day a committee was appointed to suggest to Adjutant General Scurry, in charge of city forces, and the General Relief Committee, the advisability of having the work done by contract and importing men to do it. Reports from various wards where men have been engaged in this work show a decrease in numerical strength, due to exhaustion and other causes. In some instances men who are skilled mechanics and have assisted in the disposition of the dead have obtained employment at their regular trades.

"It was announced this evening that a contract will be let for the removal of bodies and the huge mass of debris, which, in some parts of the city, reaches a height of fifteen feet. To do this, about three thousand men will be brought here from the interior. They will come with their own cooks and rations and camp on the beach, and will be paid $2 a day. It is estimated that it will require from twenty to thirty days to remove the wreckage.

" Under one pile of debris to-day thirty bodies were found and cremated. Bodies are still being washed ashore at Texas City, Bolivar Point, Pelican Island and other coast points near Galveston. There is no time to dig graves, and the bodies are hastily consigned to the flames.

" The city is still under martial law, and guards are patrolling the streets day and night.   An example was made of a man arrested for selling liquor.   The offender was marched to general headquarters, and, after a severe reprimand, was put to work on the street gang, removing and disposing of bodies.   He will serve without pay for an indefinite period.

"All hospital relief stations and all points in the city are thoroughly disinfected.   Dr. Peckham, of the United States Marine Corps, has established a camp for the injured and ill at Tremont and Beach avenues.   Directly opposite is a camp for refugees.   Camps will be established on the beach at the foot of Fifteenth street.

"Reports from Sealy Hospital, St. Mary's Infirmary and other temporary hospitals are that sanitary rules are strictly followed, and the buildings are in fairly good shape.   A great many patients from Sealy and St. Mary's have been sent to Houston.

SERIOUS CASES OF INJURY.

"In the vicinity of the hospitals there is a mass of debris containing many bodies, and the Health Board has sent an urgent appeal to headquarters to have this debris cleared.

"Emergency hospitals report wounds dressed on an average of 150 to 200 a day.   Many report serious cases.

"A census has been taken of St. Mary's Catholic parish, embracing the territory from Sixteenth to Twenty-seventh street. It shows a loss of 267 from this parish alone.   A census of the city is now being taken, which will embrace a list of the survivors, the dead and the amount of personal and property losses.

"Death from a broken heart was the doctor's verdict when Miss Clara Olson died at an early hour this morning.   When the storm was at its height the little house Miss Olson occupied with her aged mother collapsed.   Mother and daughter found refuge on a floating housetop for several hours.   A floating timber driven with terrible force crushed Mrs. Olson's skull.   The girl drifted to the Ursuline convent, where she was cared for by the Sisters. She grieved constantly for her mother, and at last died of a broken heart."

Houston, Tex., Sept. 20.—Official reports of conditions of interior towns have begun to come in from agents sent out by Governor Sayres. Following are summaries of reports so far received showing the conditions of half a dozen towns on the Santa Fe. There are probably fifty small towns, which are in just as bad shape and from which reports have not been received, but which are being supplied with provisions, clothing, and drugs from Houston by the committees :

Pearland—Fifty families depending on Relief Committee ; some supplies received but assistance in other ways than provisions needed. Families at Erin and Superior are to be supplied through Pearland.

Algoa—Twenty-five families to be supplied ; enough provisions for the present.

DESTRUCTION IN OUTLYING DISTRICTS.

Alvin—In the town of Alvin and vicinity there are probably six houses on blocks out of a total of 1,000. The population of Alvin now to be fed is about 1,500 ; Manvel, 250 ; Liverpool and Amsterdam, 250 ; Chocolate and Austin Bayous, Chigger neighborhood, Dickinson Bayou, east and outside, or the surrounding country, 2,500, making a total of 5,000 persons under the supervision of the Alvin committee. The committee admits having a sufficient amount of clothing. They have received a cash subscription of about $2,000 and have spent $400. Have received two cars of flour from Dallas, one car of meal from Dallas, one car of mixed goods from Tyler. Along the bay shore, from Virginia Point to Liverpool, for a space of six or eight miles from the bay front, there are many thousands of dead cattle that should be immediately cremated or properly looked after.

Arcadia—In the town there are 300 destitute, and those in the immediate vicinity will make the aggregate 500. Provisions already supplied sufficient for immediate needs only.

Hitchcock—In this town and immediate vicinity are more than 500 destitute. Of about 300 houses, only about ten are standing. A wave of salt water, from four to ten feet in depth, covered this section ; thirty-eight lives were lost, and, for the time being, it is feared that the soil has been seriously damaged by the effect of salt water. Supplies of provisions were sent yesterday. There are probably 10,000 dead cattle within a space of a few miles south and surrounding the town, and every house should be supplied for at least ten days with disinfectants. Fever is now settling in there, and Dr. J. T. Scott, of Houston, went there yesterday. An idea of the velocity of the wind and wave of salt water that swept over this immediate section may be imagined when it is known that the Texas City dredge boat is now lying high and dry in a garden at this place, a distance of eight miles or more from its moorings.

HOUSES AND OTHER PROPERTY GONE.

Alta Loma—This committee reports about seventy-five families, or 300 persons, to be cared for. Have received 530 rations. People have no money and their property destroyed. In the neighborhood of 100 houses existed ; forty destroyed and about twenty untenantable. There are about four houses now on blocks. Two lives were lost. The population is mainly of northern people. A shipment was made them of provisions and medicines, but other things are needed at once.

Col. B. H. Belo, publisher of the "Galveston News," said that Galveston would be rebuilt at once.

"The storm and flood taught us several lessons," said Col. Belo, in an interview. "The loss of life would have been comparatively light if the buildings had been of a more solid character. The Ursuline convent, for instance, was surrounded by a brick wall, and there was no loss of life there, although it stood right in the path of the flood and storm. There were no lives lost in the 'News' office, and we would not have been badly flooded had it not been for a building falling and battering in a part of our wall.

"I believe that all buildings will be of a more solid and enduring character than formerly. I think, too, that the streets along the water front will be built higher than they were. The

city must be rebuilt.   It is the only outlet worthy the name on
the Gulf west of New Orleans.   The government spent $6,000,000
to make a thirty-foot harbor there, and the shipping is so extensive that rebuilding the wrecked portions of the city is imperative."

A tale of self sacrifice comes from the western part of the city.
A young man by the name of Wash Masterson heard the cries of
some people outside.   They were calling for a rope.   He had no
rope, but improvised one from bed sheets, and started out to find
the people who were calling.   The wind and water soon tore his
rope to shreds and he had to return to the house, where he made
another and stronger rope.

THE CRIES OF THE PEOPLE.

The cries of the people still filled his ears.   He went out a
second time and after being gone for what seemed an hour or more
to those who were waiting he returned with the people.   They had
clung to the branches of a salt cedar tree.   Mr. Masterson was not
satisfied with that, but went out for other people immediately,
the water having begun to fall about that time, and worked all
night.

A little black dog stood barking over a sand hill in the west
end beyond Woollam's lake.   Those who endeavored to stop his
barking by driving him away did not succeed for he returned as
soon as they ceased their attempts.   It was suggested that he was
guarding a body, but others scouted the idea.

Finally they dug beneath the spot where the dog stood, and
there they found the remains of a young girl whom they identified by the rings she wore as Miss Lena Everhart, a popular little
lady, well known both in Galveston and Dallas.   This whole
family, with the exception of one son, Elmer Everhart, and a
daughter, Mrs. Robert Brown, who lives near Dickinson and was
there at the time, was lost.   The father ran a dairy just southwest of Woollam's lake.

At Twelfth and Sealy avenue there lived a colored man and
his wife.   There was a grocery on the corner and those who

weathered the storm report that he stood near the beer keg in the bar room of the grocery drinking steadily until he was swept away, his idea evidently being to destroy consciousness before the storm did it for him. His body was picked out of a pile of debris between Twelfth and Thirteenth on Sealy avenue.

The Catholic Orphans' Home on the beach at the west end of the city went some time after 5:30 o'clock Saturday evening. Mr. Harry Gray, who lived in Kinkead subdivision, just beyond the city limits, was compelled to leave his house at that hour and says the home was standing then. Now not a vestige of it remains. Eight nuns and all but one of ninety-five children were lost. This child, a little tot, was found on the north side of the island in a tree. "I'se been 'seep," he lisped. "My head was in de water."

MR. GRAY'S STORY.

Mr. Gray's story is interesting. His house fell and he fought his way out with a wife who was just out of a sick bed. He managed to get to the next house with her. This was the home of Ed. Hunter. That house went between 6.30 and 7, and the Hunter family was lost. Mr. Gray caught a transom, put the arm of his wife through it, and soon found that the transom belonged to the side of the house, about 20x20 feet in size. It was nothing but the side of the house made of ordinary siding and studding. He swung onto this and even now does not understand how it stood up under them.

All the time he kept telling his wife to hold onto him, and this she did. Along in the night the raft struck a tree and was swept from under them. Gray caught a limb with his wife still clinging to him. By this time he was almost completely exhausted but he managed by a hundred successive efforts to get his wife into the tree.

A little later a colored man was seen coming through the water. Gray called to him to take to the lower limbs and not come higher, for he was afraid the tree with three people on it would be made top-heavy. When daylight came he took his wife in his arms and told the negro to go ahead for a house they saw

23

in the distance, for had there been any holes he wanted to be advised of it before he went into them with his wife, for it was all he could do to push through the water in his exhausted condition.

After working until 10 o'clock he reached the high land in the Denver resurvey and eventually got to town. Not until yesterday had he sufficiently recovered from his exhaustion to come onto the streets. He is cut and bruised in a dozen places. He says the water in Kinkead addition was ten feet deep.

Robert Park and a party of men came in from Hitchcock Sunday, arriving that evening. They started in a skiff, and finally reached a prairie, over which they carried the boat. Finally they reached water again, and along about noon went alongside the British steamer " Roma," which was dragged from her moorings in the roads between the jetties, about seven miles up the channel and landed in the draw of the county bridge. They report the steamer in good condition. They got water and food there and came on across.

A GRUESOME SIGHT.

Mr. Park says twenty people arrived at Hitchcock on rafts from Galveston before he left. These had been carried by the storm from Galveston to Hitchcock, a distance of about eighteen miles. They also saw a pile driven from the Huntington wharves high on the prairie far beyond Viginia Point.

A gruesome sight passed along the street Monday afternoon. Workmen in digging bodies from the debris found one of a handsome man with dark hair and mustache and dressed in a light suit of clothes. He was on his knees, his eyes were uplifted, and his clasped hands were extended as in prayer. It was evident that the man had been praying when he was struck and instantly killed. As a rule, the attitudes of those who were found were with hands extended up as if endeavoring to save themselves.

The destruction of the Catholic Orphans' Home and the loss of seventy-five lives with it was told by one of three boys who came through a terrible experience by dint of good Providence and nothing else. It is a fact that three boys came into the city nom there who had passed through a terrible experience. With these three and one reported on the bay shore but four out of a total of seventy-eight people lived to tell the tale.

According to the story all the children were gathered with the Sisters and the two workmen in the chapel on the ground floor in the west wing of the building. The storm was raging terribly outside and they all engaged in prayer. The east wing finally went down and they were driven from the chapel to the floor above, the water coming in and threatening to drown them. Some clambered out on the roof of the part remaining, but not all. Finally along about 8 o'clock—they are not positive as to the time by an hour—the remainder of the building went and the roof went into the water.

DESTRUCTION OF CATHOLIC ORPHANS' HOME.

What became of the others nobody can say. Campbell only knows that he got out from the building somehow and caught a piece of drift, either a part of the roof or something of the sort. The Murney boy broke through a transom and got out. He drifted for some time and finally caught a tree to which he clung and soon found that the two other boys had caught the same tree. Prior to that they had been separated, but a strange fate attracted them to the same place.

This tree, it developed later, had caught in the masts of the wreck of the schooner "John S. Ames," which lies almost south of the home. There they remained all night. At one time Campbell was about to give up and cried that he was drowning. The Murney boy caught him and lashed him to the mast with a piece of rope that he found there. In that way was his life saved.

When morning came they found that they were alone in the open Gulf on a tree. The tree soon broke adrift from the mast, and, strange as it may seem, brought them in shore. They finally landed and started west, not knowing which direction to take. They finally brought up at a house something like two miles from the place where the home had been but so recently located. There they found their location, but were unable to get anything to eat because the woman in the house had nothing herself.

So they came on toward the city, but it was a long, hard pull through wet sand, and hungry and faint for the want of fresh water and food. They brought up at a house that had gone through the storm, was partly demolished and at the back of which was another house supporting it. There they remained during Sunday night, and were afraid every minute that the force of the little blow that came up during the night would demolish the place of refuge. But it stood, and in the morning they started on, reaching the home of young Murney during the day. There they got food and dry clothes. The other two boys were taken to the infirmary, where they are being cared for.

NEW FEATURES OF THE CALAMITY.

Another account is as follows and contains new pictures of the scene :

The elements, which had been cutting up didoes and blowing every which way during the preceding twenty-four hours, got down to it in earnest fashion Saturday morning, when a strong wind, accompanied by rain, which first came in great splashing drops which one could almost dodge, but afterwards became a hard, driving rain, began to get in its work.

Along the bay front the waves rose higher and higher and tossed about the small craft anchored in the slips like cockle shells. Striking the bulkheading of the wharves with mighty force the waves broke into clouds of spray, which leaped over the wharves and drenched the men whom duty or curiosity caused to be in that neighborhood.

Although the wind was in the north, a heavy sea was running and the breakers rolled up the beach with angry roars. The little bath houses on wheels scattered along the beach were picked up by the great waves and dashed against the row of little, flimsy structures along the Midway and piled up against them in uneven stacks. Early in the forenoon the Midway presented a picture almost of desolation, filled as it was with debris from the small platforms, stairways and landings along the beach front, which had been carried away and washed up by the sea. At times the waves would recede, leaving the beach almost·bare of water, and then, as if gathering force anew they would sweep in, rolling several feet high, passing over the shelving beach, lapping over tracks of the street railway and gushing the water into avenue R.

Early in the forenoon the waves were leaping at times over the trestle work of the street railway along the beach front, making it impossible to operate the cars around the belt, as the water would have burned out the motors. The cars were therefore operated between town and the Gulf on the double tracks of either side of the belt line. A little later in the forenoon the waves undermined the track at Twenty-fourth street and avenue R. They washed under the little Midway houses on the south side of avenue R, which were built on piling, and in places carried away the sidewalks in front of the buildings, which were not thus supported.

THE ANGER OF THE SEA.

The platform which supported the photograph gallery at the Pagoda bath house was washed away. This was not a part of the original structure, and was not as strongly built as the remainder of the bath house. The bath house proper and its pier, extending out to sea, were not at that time (Saturday noon) disturbed by the waves, although the high rollers at times dashed so near the flooring of this and the other bath houses that it looked like a rise of a few inches would punch up the flooring.

The scene at the beach was grand. The sea in its anger was a sight beautiful, though awe-inspiring, to behold. Notwithstanding the wind and the driving rain, thousands of people went to the beach to behold the maddened sea, and the street cars were kept quite busy. Down town, during the early morning, when the rain was not so heavy, there seemed no apparent necessity for getting into rainy day garb to make this trip to the beach, and many people went out in their best bibs and tuckers, to their sorrow. Well dressed men and women disembarked from the cars at the beach and picked their way amid swirling pools of

water and the spent waves to get into midway and to pass along
to places where a good view of the sea might be obtained.

For a few minutes they succeeded in keeping feet and bodies
reasonably dry, but using umbrellas counted for naught, and
were soon turned wrong side out or ripped into ribbons, and their
owners getting partially wet, abandoned themselves to the inevitable and went around seeing the sights, caring not for the
weather, nor worrying about their good duds. Some people, with
abundant foresight, appeared on the scene in bathing suits, and,
of course, they were right in it from the jump.

At Twenty-fifth street the big waves rolled up the shelving
beach, crossed the street railway tracks, leaving the water
impounded behind the embankment. These waters backed up in
the ditches and the low places of the street as far as avenue N,
and the supply being ever replenished, both from the sea and
from the clouds, there was no opportunity for this water to
run off.

IMPOSSIBLE TO NAVIGATE.

The shell man and others of the Midway folk moved their
stocks out during the morning to be on the safe side, but others,
who have long been acquainted with the sea and who were less
timorous, stayed by their places and kept their goods and chattels
there.

At that hour the water was on a level with the wharf at pier
23, and was rapidly rising. Later it was almost impossible to
navigate along the wharf front on account of the deep water and
the high wind. Of course, it was wholly out of the question for
any vessels to move for any purpose, and equally impossible for
steamers to make an entry into the harbor. The pilot boat would
not have been able to get alongside, and if any vessel approached
the harbor she would have to put to sea for fear of grounding if
she came too close. Several vessels are due.

No attempt at doing any business was made after noon, for it
was equally out of the question to load steamers as it was to move
them. If damage was done it was the result of pounding. Some
cement stored on the pier head was damaged by the water washing

up under it in the morning, and as it was not practicable to move it, it is a total loss.

While working with a gang of men clearing the wreckage of a large number of houses on avenue O and Center street, Mr. John Vance found a live prairie dog locked in the drawer of a bureau. It is impossible to identify the house or the name of its former occupant, as several houses were piled together in a mass of brick and timber. The bureau was pulled out of the wreckage a few feet from the ground, where it had been buried beneath about ten feet of debris. The little animal seemed none the worse from its experience of four days locked up in a drawer beneath a mountain of wreckage. It was taken home and fed by Mr. Vance, who will hold the pet for its owner if the owner survived the storm.

CHAPTER XVIII.

An Island of Desolation—Crumbling Walls—Faces White With Agony—Tales of Dismay and Death—Curious Sights.

ONE of the most graphic and thrilling accounts of the overwhelming calamity is contained in the following pages. It is from the brilliant pen of a visitor to the city and eye-witness of the awful ruin :

The story of Galveston's tragedy can never be written as it is. Since the cataclysm of Saturday night, a force of faithful men have been struggling to convey to humanity from time to time some of the particulars of the tragedy. They have told much, but it was impossible for them to tell all, and the world, at best, can never know all, for the thousands of tragedies written by the storm must forever remain mysteries until eternity shall reveal all. Perhaps it were best that it should be so, for the horror and anguish of those fatal and fateful hours were mercifully lost in the screaming tempest and buried forever beneath the raging billows. Only God knows, and for the rest let it remain forever in the boundlessness of His omniscience. But in the realm of finity, the weak and staggered senses of mankind may gather fragments of the disaster, and may strive with inevitable incompleteness to convey the merest impression of the saddest story which ever engaged the efforts of a reporter.

Galveston ! The mournful dirges of the breakers which lash the beach can not in the remaining centuries of the world give expression to the sorrow and woe which throbs here to-day ; and if the sobbing waves and sighing winds, God's great funeral choir, fail, how can the weak pen and appalled imaginations of men perform the task ? The human heart can merely feel what language will never be able to express. And in the case of Galveston, the heart must break before it can begin to feel.

I struggled all day Tuesday to reach this isle of desolation.

With Gen. McKibben, Gen. Scurry, Gen. Stoddard and several who had relatives here about whom they were anxious, I spent five hours on the bay in a row boat, kindly loaned by the captain of the "Kendel Castle," a British steamship hopelessly stranded at Texas City, but finally we landed on the island just as the stars were coming out.

The very atmosphere smelt of death, and we walked through the quiet streets to the Tremont Hotel. Long before we landed we had seen the naked forms of men, women and children floating in the bay and were depressed until the entire party was heartsick.

Men were grouped about the streets talking in quiet tones. Sad and hopeless women could be seen in dismantled houses, destitute children were about the streets, and all about them was nothing but wreck and ruin. Night had drawn a gray pall over the city and for awhile the autumn moon covered her face with dark clouds to hide the place with shadows. The town was under martial law, every saloon was closed, and passers-by were required to give an account of themselves before being allowed to proceed. The fact, however, that the streets were almost impassable on account of the debris kept us reminded that we were in the midst of unprecedented desolation.

REVEALED A SCENE.

Wednesday the sun drew aside the curtains of darkness and revealed a scene that is impossible of description. I spent hours driving or riding about the city, and witnessed the saddest spectacles ever seen by human eyes. What were once Galveston's splendid business thoroughfares were wrecked and crumbled. The Strand, known to every business man of the State, was lined on both sides with crumbling walls and wrenched buildings, and the street was a mass of debris, such as metal roofs rolled up like a scroll, splintered timbers, iron pillars, broken stone and bricks ; the same was true of Mechanic, and Market, and Tremont, and Twenty-first and Twenty-second, and every other street of the great business heart of Galveston.

The stores were ruined and deserted, and the blight of destruction was visible as far as the eye could reach. As horrible as all this was, it was as nothing to the hopeless faces of the miserable men, women and children in the streets.

I will not undertake to describe them, but as long as I live I will never forgot them. Many I knew personally, and these gave greeting, but God, it was nothing but a handshake and tears. It seems that everybody I had ever known here had lost somebody. The tears in their eyes, the quiver of their voices, the trembling of lips! The brand of agony was upon their faces and despair was written across their hearts. I would plunge a dagger through my heart before I would endure this experience again.

The readers of this must pardon the personal nature of this narrative. It is impossible to write without becoming a part of the story this time. I met Elma Everhart, formerly a Dallas boy. I had known him from childhood, and all his people. Indeed, I had once been an inmate of their home in Oakcliff. I hardly knew him when he stopped me, he had grown so much. He said: "Katy and her baby are at Dickinson. That town was destroyed, but they are alive. I am going there and leave Galveston forever."

A TERRIBLE FATE.

I knew he had woe in his heart, and I queried.

"I am the only one left," he answered. "Papa, mamma, Lena and Guy—they are all gone."

I remember the last time I saw this family before they left Dallas. I remember Lena, one of the most beautiful children I ever saw. I recall her beautiful eyes and long, dark curls, and I remember when she kissed me good-bye and joyously told me she was coming to Galveston to live! And this was her fate.

With all my old fondness for the ocean, recalling how I have lain upon the sand hour after hour, looking at its distant sails and listening to its mysterious voices, recalling happy moments too sacred for expression, when I think of that sweet child as one of its victims, I shall hate the sea forever.

And yet, what can this grief of mine amount to in the presence of the agony of the thousands who loved the 5000 souls who took leave of life amid the wild surging waters and pitiless tempest of last Saturday night?

After surveying the dismantled business section of the city, a cabman made his tortuous way through the residence sections. It was a slow journey, for the streets were jammed with houses, furniture, cooking utensils, bedding, clothing, carpets, window frames, and everything imaginable, to say nothing of the numerous carcasses of the poor horses, cows and other domestic animals.

HOUSES COMPLETELY CAPSIZED.

Some of the houses were completely capsized, some were flat upon the ground with not one timber remaining upon another, others were unroofed, some were twisted into the most fantastic shapes, and there were still others with walls intact, but which had been stripped of everything in the way of furniture. It is not an uncommon thing for the wind at high velocity to perform miraculous things, but this blast, which came at the rate of 120 miles an hour, repeated all the tricks the wind has ever enacted, and gave countless new manifestations of its mysterious power. It were idle to undertake to tell the curious things to be seen in the desolate residence streets; how the trees were uprooted and driven through houses; how telegraph poles were driven under car tracks; how pianos were transferred from one house to another.

More ominous than all this were the vast piles of debris, from which emanated odors which told of dead victims beneath, men, women and children, whose silent lips will never reveal the agony from which death alone released them.

More sorrowful still the tear-stained faces of the women, half-clad, who looked listlessly from the windows, haunted by memories from which they can never escape—the loss of babies torn from their breasts and hurled into a maelstrom of destruction, to be seen no more forever.

What were those dismantled homes to the dismantled hearts within? How can it be described? Will the world ever know the real dimensions of the disaster which crushed Galveston and left her broken and disconsolate like a wounded bird fluttering on the white sands of the ocean?

And the beach? That once beautiful beach, with its long stretches of white sand—what has become of that? Misshapen, distorted, blotched and drabbled and crimsoned, it spread away to the horizons of the east and west, its ugly scars rendered more hideous by the glinting rays of the sun. Part of it had disappeared under the purling waters. Far out here and there could be seen the piling, where once rested the places of amusement.

The waves were lashing the lawns which once stretched before palatial homes. And the pools along the shore were stinking with the remains of ill-fated dogs, cats, chickens, birds, horses, cows and fish. Shoreward, as far as the eye could reach, were massive piles of houses and timbers, all shattered and torn.

A cloud of smoke was noticed, and driving to the scene, we found a large number of men feeding the flames with the timbers of the wrecked homes which once gave such a charm to Galveston beach.

BURNING 1000 HUMAN BODIES.

And why the fire? The men were burning 1000 human bodies cast up by the sea, and the fuel was the timber of the homes which the poor victims once occupied! And yet this awful spectacle was but a fragment of the murderous work of the greatest storm which has swept the ocean's shore for a century!

There were dozens of piles of sand in every direction along that mutilated shore. And men were noticed in the distance shoveling these uncanny mounds.

We saw what they were doing. The bodies brought in by the tide were being buried deep in the sand. Driving beyond the grave diggers we saw prostrate on the sand the stark and swollen forms of women and children and floating farther out in the tide were other bodies soon to be brought in to be buried. The waves were only the hearses bringing in the dead to be buried in the sand along the shore. It is the contemplation of such scenes as these that staggers consciousness and stings the human soul.

They told me with sad humor that what I had seen was as nothing to what I could have seen had I been here Sunday and Monday mornings. I am glad, then, that I did not come sooner, and I am sorry that I ever came at all. What I have seen has been sufficient to make me miserable to the longest day of my life, and what I have heard that I could not see and could not have seen had I been in the storm, will haunt me by day and night as long as my senses remain.

I am telling an incident repeated to me by one of the most prominent and distinguished citizens of Galveston. On Monday seven hundred bodies had been gathered in one house near the bay shore. Recognition of a single one was impossible. The bodies were swollen and decomposition was setting in rapidly. Indeed, the odor of death was on the air for blocks. What disposition should be made of this horrifying mass of human flesh was an imminent problem.

IMPOSSIBLE TO DISPOSE OF THE DEAD.

While the matter was under discussion, the committee was informed that there was no time to waste in deliberation, that some of the bodies were already bursting. It was impossible to bury them, and they could not be incinerated in that portion of the city without endangering more life and more property, as there was no water to extinguish a fire once started. It was decided to load the bodies on a barge, tow it out to sea and sink them with weights. That was the only thing to be done.

Men were called to perform this awful duty, but they quailed at the task. And who could blame them? They were told that quick action was necessary, or a pestilence might come and sweep off the balance of the living. Still they were immovable. It was no time for dallying.

A company of men with rifles at fixed bayonets were brought to the scene, and a force of men were compelled, at the point of the bayonet, to perform this sad, sad duty. One by one the dead were removed to the barge, everybody as naked as it had come into the world—men, women and children, black and white, all classes of society and station and condition, were represented in that putrid mass. The unwilling men who were performing this awful task were compelled to bind cloths about their nostrils while they were at work, and occasionally citizens passed whiskey among them to nerve them to their duty.

Who can conceive of the horror of this ?

After awhile the seven hundred dead were piled upon the barge and a tug pulled them slowly out to sea. Eighteen miles out, where the sea was rolling high, amid the soughing white caps, with God's benediction breathed in the moaning winds, all that was mortal of these seven hundred was consigned to the mystic caves of the deep.

And yet, this was but another incident of the sad tragedy of which we write.

STORIES OF SORROW.

George H. Walker, of San Antonio, known well in theatrical circles, was a member of the party which struggled all day Tuesday to get to Galveston, and he landed late at night. It was an anxious day for him, for this was the city of his birth and before the storm he had six brothers and five sisters living here, in addition to his son, an aunt and his mother-in-law.

He found his son safe and many other members of his family. They told him how the boy, Earl, a lad of 15, had at the height of the tempest placed his grandmother, Mrs. C. S. Johnson, on the roof of the house after it was floating in the current, and had made a second trip to bring his aunt to the roof. When the lad returned the grandmother was gone, finding in the raging current her final peace. The boy and his aunt, another Mrs. Johnson, clung to the roof throughout and successfully weathered the gale.

George Walker found later on, however, that his brother Joe, and his stepbrother, Nick Donley, had been swept away to feed the fury of the storm.

I met W. R. Knight, of Dallas, who arrived yesterday at noon. He told me that he had found his mother, two unmarried sisters and married a sister, Mrs. E. Webster, safe. But he, too, had his sorrow. A sister, Mrs. Ida Toothaker, and her daughter Etta, were lost, and his brother-in-law, E. Webster, Sr., and five children, Charley, George, Kenneth, Julia and Sarah, had joined the other two loved ones on the bosom of the unresting sea.

How many stories of sorrow like this that remain to be told cannot now be numbered. The anxious people who have been straggling into Galveston from a distance have usually found some dear relative or many of them missing and numbered among the thousands who became in a few brief hours the victims of the remorseless furies.

It is with reluctance that I relate one case that came under my own observation. It was so horrible that perhaps it ought not to be told at all, but only such instances can convey a faint idea of the horror of the Galveston disaster. While rowing near the Huntington wharves the naked upturned body of an unfortunate woman was observed floating in the water, with a half-born infant plainly in view.

MASSACRE OF THE LIVING.

Mr. L. H. Lewis, of Dallas, arrived yesterday looking for his son, George Cabell Lewis, who was found alive and well. Mr. Lewis said : "I helped to bury sixteen at Texas City last (Tuesday) night—all Galveston victims. They buried fifty-eight there Tuesday. Coming down Buffalo bayou I saw numberless legs and arms, mostly of women and children, protruding from the muck. I believe there are hundreds of women and children near the mouth of the bayou. As soon as men can be found to do the work these poor victims should be looked after. Unquestionably most of them were from Galveston Island. Among other things I saw were tombstones with inscriptions in German and rusty caskets which had been beached by the waves."

The cruel elements were not content to massacre the living, but had to invade the silent homes of the unoffending dead.

No man has been busier comforting the grief-stricken people of Galveston than Dr. R. C. Buckner of the Buckner Orphan Home in Dallas county. He leaves Thursday morning for his institution with the homeless orphans of the Galveston Orphans' Home, which was wrecked by the storm. He has others besides these, and altogether he will take one hundred home with him.

What a grand old man Dr. Buckner is! I will take off my hat to him any day in the week. I have known him for years and there is not a nobler character alive. I saw him at Sherman when that city was ravished by a cyclone several years ago. He was there looking for orphans, and I know that he has always been quick to reach the scene of disaster and death. He got here Tuesday afternoon and lost no time in reaching his part of the work, and heaven knows there was none more important than that to which he assigned himself.

RESCUING DESTITUTE CHILDREN.

But the people of Texas ought to know what he has done. They have always loved the Buckner home. They know what it has done in the way of rescuing destitute children. They know that hundreds of good men and women of the State have come from that institution—men and women who have become successful in life and who honor the State and the home by their useful and upright lives. But Texas will have greater cause than ever to love and revere Dr. Buckner and his institution when it is known that he has added to his family a hundred hapless victims of the Galveston storm, making in all 400 in his entire family. The heart of this State is throbbing here now, and whoever renders a good service to Galveston will be honored by the State.

If the people of the State and the outside world can not grasp the full measure of the Galveston horror, neither can the people of Galveston themselves. The town is dazed, and self-contained people are hard to find. There is a well-organized Citizens' Committee at work in a consecutive and business manner, but the work before it is beyond the ability or power of any committee.

It will be some time before thousands will know the real nature of the disaster which has overtaken them, and the world will never know it all. Men and women walk the streets and tell each other experiences and weep together as gradually the stories of loss come out. They are hysterical, half crazy, paralyzed and utterly dejected. There has been so such death and so much ruin that they don't know which way to turn or what to do.

There has been much complaint on the part of visitors that the men don't go to work and help clear the debris from the streets. This job alone would give three thousand men a month's hard work. But a man can't work when he has before him the vision of his loved ones hurled to death in an instant and thinks of what has happened.

A man who lost a wife and children, no matter how strong he may be, can't get his mind on the necessities of this town when he thinks of his family among the seven hundred sunk in the sea last Monday or the thousand burned in trenches on the beach yesterday. If he does not become a maniac or does not commit suicide it is a wonder, if one will stop to think of it for a minute.

SHATTERED LIVES.

They will come around after a while and will do their part. Thousands of them have not slept since last Friday night and may not sleep for a week to come. Pity them, for God knows their shattered lives are enough to drive almost any of us insane if we should stop to think.

J. W. Maxwell, general superintendent of the Missouri, Kansas and Texas Railway; J. W. Allen, general freight manager of the same road, and Major G. W. Foster, of the Southwestern Telegraph and Telephone Company, got in yesterday from Texas City. Coming across the bay, Mr. Maxwell said, not less than 300 bodies were seen floating in the water, and many more were being buried on the mainland shore. This proves what many have contended from the first, that the casualties from the beginning have been understated. Under the debris of wrecked houses all over the city there is every reason to believe there are hundreds of bodies, and these must be disposed of as early as possible. In the rafts of the bay there are yet many bodies which must be looked for.

It will never be possible to get the names of all who are lost,

24

but every day makes the list more definite. It will never be possible to get an accurate estimate of victims. It is safe to say that more than 3000 bodies have been seen so far, and the Gulf and bay and the debris of the city will unquestionably bring many more to view. If Mr. Lewis, of Dallas, has not over-estimated the number he observed in Buffalo bayou, that stream may largely swell the total. How many have been buried beneath the shifting sand of the beach, will probably remain a secret forever.

It is touching to witness the sympathy of the nation with Galveston. As the means of communication are improved, the people here are getting a definite idea of what it means to stir the sympathies of mankind. It seems that the country has for the time forgotten its politics and its curious interest in the broad affairs of the world to weep over this stricken city. It is said a touch of pity makes the world akin, and Galveston is compassed about by the throbbing heart of mankind.

HAS REACHED A CRISIS.

It is well that it so, for this town has reached a crisis in its life when this sustaining influence is needed. It is not suprising that many surviving victims of the storm are about to succumb to despair. God knows the burden of anguish which oppresses every heart here is calculated to breed despair. The duty of the hour, however, is too plain to be disregarded. This island must be restored to its former beauty and greatness in all the arts and industries of civilization, and it is fortunate that some of the citizens here realize this. They are going to encourage the others and there is no reason to believe that there will be failure.

It required more than half a century to build up what the storm destroyed in twelve hours, but it will not require but a fraction of that period to restore the city. As Chicago rallied from the great fire, so Galveston must and will arise from the ruins of this hour. The wharves, which are the foundation of the city's commercial establishment, will be rebuilt and the traffic will come as of yore.

CHAPTER XIX.

Thousands Died in their Efforts to Save Others—Houses and Human Beings Floating on the Tide—An Army of Orphans—Greatest Catastrophe in Our History.

"WHEN did you first realize that you were in danger?" That, ordinarily, would seem to be a foolish question to put to a man who had escaped death as it rode on the storm, and yet it was not a foolish question, but the natural one. For the Galveston people had for years argued out the question of the danger attending the living on the island. True, Indianola, awful even now in memory, stood out as an alarm to those who live down by the sea. True, there had been storms and storms in Galveston. True, their were people on the great mainland who contended that wind and water would bring disaster to Galveston whenever the two acted in concert and from the right direction.

But the answer to the Indianola alarm was that the situation of that unfortunate town exposed it to a storm fury ; that it was a fair mark ; that it was almost level with the water and all that. The fact that there had been storms and storms at Galveston only confirmed the people in their security. For as each had passed away without carrying any great number of lives with them, why should not this do the same ?

As to the people on the mainland who had prophesied disaster, why, they were merely timid and ignorant people. Therefore the question "when did you realize that you were in danger" was a reasonable one. And the answer was the same in nearly every case. There might have been a difference as to the moment when these people, penned like rats in a cage, first felt the terror of impending death, but invariably the answer was that the storm was almost at its height before the realization came. In many cases only the falling houses brought the realization.

One little girl at a grocery store out on avenue P, from which street to the Gulf, the storm swept the island like a broom, answered me : "Mother and my eight little brothers and sisters were upstairs, and I went down to see what the water was doing in the store. You see we live upstairs over the store. My papa is dead a long time ago. When I went down my brother went with me and the water was half way up the counter. But that didn't scare us, because we have seen high water and heard the winds before. Well, we went back and in a few minutes we were down again.

"Then the counter was floating. Brother said not to tell mother, but I did. Then we saw a house tumble down and we heard people crying. We got scared then and me and mamma prayed. We prayed that one of us would not be drowned if the little children were not drowned, because one of us would have to be their mother."

The maternal love was uppermost. But the love of that little girl for her little brothers and sisters, as she told me the story in her simple way, passeth in greatness all understanding.

"I FELT THAT THE END HAD COME."

"When did you think you were in real danger?" I asked of a merchant.

"Not until Ritter's house went down and I saw the waters rapidly climbing the walls. We had passed through the terrible storm of 1875, and had lived. Since then the island has been raised five feet or more. Why should we not have felt easy? But when the wind and waves began to show their fury, when I saw these extra five or more feet covered by a raging torrent which raced hither and thither, I felt that the end had come. Up the waters came about the fence—up they came and covered the hedge. Up they came and knocked at the door.

"Yet I still thought the end would be reached. We had been told that the height of the storm would be at 9 o'clock. At 5 and 6 and 7 the waters continued to climb and the winds to take on new strength. At the last hour they were at the door. What must come, then, at 9? My heart fell then. I had peered out of the window and saw the dreadful enemy assault the house. Then agonized people were heard. It was dark and the spray sped in sheets. Yet it was light enough to see now and then. People in boats and wading came along. Their houses were gone. Mine rocked like a cradle, and I felt the end had come." Thus said another man : "What were your feelings ? " " Nothing but that of complete resignation. I have read much in books of the tableaux of the past appearing to the human mind on the eve of man's dissolution. In no instance have I found that the survivors of this terrible thing remembered the past. Some were frightened and simply shrieked and laid hold of anything that would relieve them from the embraces of the water. Some were frightened and prayed for mercy. Some were frightened into dumb resignation, partaking of dumb indifference."

NOBLE DEEDS IN TIME OF DISASTER.

In all great catastrophes I have yet to know of one that some special act of selfishness and brutality did not occur. There is hardly a great wreck recorded in which is not depicted the brute who pushed women from boats or from spars. In all I have heard of the thousands of incidents connected with this storm, not an instance of that selfishness which would cause one person to deprive another of his means of escape has occurred. Thousands of instances of devotion of husband to wife, of wife to husband, of child to parent and parent to child can be mentioned.

One poor woman with her child and her father was cast out into the raging waters. They were separated. Both were in drift and both believed they went out in the Gulf and returned. The mother was finally cast upon the drift, and there she was pounded by the waves and debris until she pulled into a house against which the drift had lodged. During all that frightful ride she held to her 8-months-old babe, and when she was on the drift pile she lay upon her infant and covered it with her body, that it might escape the blows of the planks. She came out of the ordeal cut and maimed. But the infant had not a scratch.

Another man took his wife from one house to another by swimming until he had occupied three. Each fell in its turn, and then he took to the waves.   They were separated and each, as the persons above mentioned, believed they were carried to sea. Strange to say, after three hours in the water he heard her call, and finally rescued her.

It is not necessary to go on and recite these instances, for there were thousands, each showing that in time of danger at least the best sentiments in man's nature are aroused.   It can be safely guessed that one-half of those who perished, died in their effort to aid others.   The trite expression of "man's inhumanity to man" has no place in all that may be written or spoken of this great tragedy.

DIRECTION OF THE STORM.

It is not a. all remarkable that of all the statements in regard to the details of this storm no two persons can be found who agree on the direction of the wind and the currents.   All agree that the most terrible blows which the town received came from the point of the compass which may be spoken of as between northeast and east.   There are those who declare that first the wind was almost from the north.   Then it veered till it was almost east, and then settled down to its herculean efforts from a point between the two; and yet there are others who say that it came from all directions at different times and prove it by the loss of windows in their houses.

These waves came in from the Gulf.   They filled the bay. The water chased across the island, met the waves and then it seems there was a battle between the two elements.   For the currents ran criss-cross.   They went down one street, up another street and across lots.   They seized a house here and placed it there.   They seized a house there and placed it here.   Men were carried to sea.   Men were carried down the island.   Men were carried across the bay by it.   No chart can be even dreamed of their peculiarities.   The wind lashed the water and it fled.   That was all there was in it, and it fled in every direction, carrying on its bosom a shrieking people.   It carried too, houses whole, houses in halves, houses in kindling wood.

The winds dipped and seized the debris and hurled it on. The air was filled with missiles of every kind. The water held them and threw them from wave to wave. The winds grasped them as they were thrown and hurled them further. Stoves, bath tubs, sewing machines, slates from roofs—these were as light in the hand of the two giants, wind and water, now in their fury, as the common match would be in the hand of the strong man.

From the northeast it is generally conceded the storm came. Galveston island runs nearly east and west. So it will be seen that it had a clean sweep from end to end of it. The streets are numbered across the island. They are lettered as they run with the island, east and west. For instance, the street running east and west nearest the bay is A street. Then there is B, and so on toward the Gulf. P and Q streets may be said to be two-thirds across the island, that is to say, they are three-quarters of a mile from the bay and a quarter of a mile from the Gulf. This is not an accurate statement and is only given to illustrate. Between Q street and the Gulf were hundreds and hundreds of houses. While many were fine mansions, the great majority of them were the houses of the poor.

HAMMERED INTO SHAPELESS MASSES.

Coming down the island from the east, the storm struck these habitations.

It was in this area, east and west, from one end of the town to the other, it did its worst. The large houses were overthrown. Where they fell they were hammered into shapeless masses. The small ones were taken up. A man can take two eggs and mash them against each other. The waters took the remnants and pushed them forward. One street of buildings would go down. That would be next to the Gulf. The timbers were hurled against another street. It would go down. The debris of the two would attack the third. The three would attack the fourth, and thus on till Q street was reached. Here the mass lodged.

It is said by some, though I know nothing of it, that about it is the back-bone, or high part of the island. The great mass

of matter became heavy.   It must have dragged upon the ground
as the water here could have only been five to seven feet deep.
But this would not have stopped it, had the last street to be
assaulted, Q street or Q½ street, not interposed.   The houses here
were rather large and strong.   This battering ram made by the
winds and worked both by the winds and the water, met with
resistance from the houses and was impeded by its own weight,
which dragged it on the bottom.   Its efforts at destruction became
more and more feeble.   The houses stood, though wrecked.   The
debris climbed to the very eaves.

But the more that came, the heavier the mass became.   And
lo ! the very assailant became the defender !   For, piling higher
and higher—piling higher and higher by the addition of houses
lately splintered, by the addition of everything from a piano to a
child's whistle, there was a wall built against the great waves
which rolled in from the Gulf, and thereby the territory lying
between the bulwark and the bay, was protected to some extent.
True, the casual observer will think as he looks even up and down
the main streets of the town, that very little protection was given.

A BULWARK OF DEAD PEOPLE.

But few lives were lost, in comparison, in this district, and
while the stores were flooded and houses toppled over by the winds
and undermined by the water, yet that bulwark made of dead
people and all they had struggled for and owned in this life, kept
back the savage waves from the Gulf and saved the rest of the
town.   Looking at this wall, from which, as I write, come the
odors of decomposition, climbing it, as this correspondent has
done, he is sure in his mind that if it had not been formed not as
many people of Galveston Island would have escaped as on
that day when Pompeii was shut out from the eyes of the world
by the veil of ashes.

These are speculations.   In years to come men may be able
to talk of this greatest of catastrophes in the cool, deliberate way
which will admit of reasonable hypotheses as to the causes of the
results, but they cannot do it now.   The wind blew from the east.

The currents were criss-cross. My God, it was awful. And that is as far as you can get with any of those left. For they know no more. They know that the wind blew. They know the waves rolled. They know, or most of them do, that they lost dear ones, and that is all. The hydrographer of the future may tell us all.

But as far as such people of North Texas, as I am, they will leave it to him. He may know the currents and the winds, and tell to the satisfaction. But he will never tell of these horrors. I cannot in the present. I may not be able to do it in the future. When the story of the funeral pyres and the burials at sea, and the reasons for both, are explained—when the pictures are given of the rescued, hunting for the dead—then indeed if all are drawn as they are—natural and unstained—another monstrosity in newspaper life will have arisen.

GALVESTON SAFE NOW.

No man—scientist or mere citizen—is authority upon the wondrous winds and ties that reduced the island of Galveston to an incomprehensible pot pourri of devastation. All is guess work, behind which there is neither science nor common sense. As far as a deliberate proposition evolved by a fair measure of judgment in which there enters as little of egotism as is possible with human beings, I would rather trust the guesser than the scientist.

As I begin the story at nightfall, the lightning is illuminating the bank of clouds massed over the Gulf horizon. For the past half hour I have looked upon the flashes, and those around me wondered if it were to come again. The "it," of course, means the visitation of last Saturday night. They look anxiously around as the streaks of gold and silver illumine the sky at quick intervals.

My friends are those who went through the awful experience of the cataclysm. I know as well as mortal man can know anything that this island is no longer a target for the elements. I know that a target like this devastated island could no longer invite the shafts of the elements, even if the elements were endowed with human or divine intelligence. And I know in the simple faith of humanity that the God who "plants his footsteps in the sea and rides upon the storm" would reach out with his omnipotent arm and throttle the agencies of nature if they should again aggravate wind and wave to vent their wrath upon these desolate shores.

I know that if the sorrows of this community, what remains of it, have thrilled humanity, they must have touched the well-springs of divine mercy and sympathy, and that the helpless victims who have survived the tragedy of this moment may feel safe from another attack from the remorselessness of the storm.

LIGHTNING FLASHES IN DARKNESS.

Galveston, stricken and bleeding, is safe from the wrath of all powers, human or divine. The vivid lightnings may cleave the sleepless waves of the sea and the thunders may play at will among the fantastic clouds in the sky. Galveston, soothed and compassed by the tenderness of mankind, is veiled in the folds of heaven's mercy, and the shrieking tempest is now but a whisper from the sky, the angry wave but the gentle falling of tears from above the stars.

It is so hard to write the story or a chapter of it without feeling the power that appalls human intelligence, just as it is hard to disassociate overwhelming sorrow from that broad sympathy which we do not understand, but which never fails to nestle close to human misery. Call it what you may, it is part of human life, and its presence comes when disaster overwhelms to bring humanity in the presence of God.

Who can dispute this in the presence of the all-pervading mystery of the storm? Who can laugh to scorn the sympathy whose manifestations have already reached the widows and orphans, whose desolate lives now find comfort from the realms above? This is not a matter of appealing to emotion. I have before me this minute four rings. The man who brings them tells me that they were taken from rigid fingers, among the 700 who on last Monday were sunk to rest amid the borderless

fathoms of the sea.   He says they may be the means of identification of three lost ones.   No; there can be no identification;
but who can tell the tender secrets which these circlets pledged?
Identification is impossible deep down among the mysteries of
the sea.

The tragedy grows greater every moment. The romances
dead to the world, the grief lost beneath the wave or carried to
the vapors above the earth, the aching hearts soothed by lasting
peace, the tired souls in the arms of endless rest, the ambitions
stilled by the calm which banishes the anguish of life's dreary
struggle—it matters not what these rings may bring to mind—
we are yet confronted with the loss of the thousands who shall
never again press these wave-kissed shores.   The sentiment of
this people is, God rest every one who sleeps beneath the wave,
and gather to everlasting peace the ashes of all whose funeral
pyres were built of these shattered homes.

A DAY OF ANGUISH.

It has been a day of anguish like all the days of this week
have been.   There has been no cessation of tear-stained faces
appearing here and there to tell of the lost.   And it is a wonder
if the end of this sad divulgence will ever come.   A motherless
boy or a fatherless girl, a now childless mother or father, or whatever it may be, they still come to tell of their woe, and the stolid
men who glide over the water or who search the shore, still bring
in the swollen and unrecognizable victims of the storm.   It will
end some day, and agonizing hearts may rest the painful throbbings of this hour.

It matters not how great the numbers of the dead, they are
numerous enough to shock the sympathies of the world, and they
are gone forever.   But we fear to look upon the sea, lest some
heartless wave shall bring to view the cold, stark form of somebody whom somebody loved.   The victims are still growing into
larger thousands, and the bereft are still coming in to tell of
losses.   It is a continued story of anguish and death, such as
Texas has never known before and will never know again.

It is needless to repeat the sad discoveries which every day brings forth. It is said that every wave of the sea has its tragedy, and it seems to be true here. In Galveston it has ceased to be anxiety for the dead, but concern for the living. The supreme disaster, with its overwhelming tale of death and destruction, has now abated to lively anxiety for the salvation of the living.

Men are at work clearing the streets of piles of timber and refuse. Men are beginning to realize that the living must be cared for. It is now the supreme duty. There is much work to be done, and it is being done. Women and children are being hurried out of the city just as rapidly as the limited facilities of transportation will permit. The authorities and committees are rational and idleness is no longer permitted. There is an element with an abundance of vital energy, who intend to save the town, and the town is being saved.

WORK RAPIDLY PUSHED.

Burying the dead, feeding the destitute, cleaning the city and repairing wrecks of all characters is under fair headway and will be pushed as rapidly as men can be found to do the work. The great utilities of the city are being repaired to a state of usefulness, men are in demand, and workers are coming to engage in the duty of restoration. Life is beginning to supersede death, and there is apparent everywhere a desire to save the city and rebuild it. Before another week has passed, the listlessness of mourning people will have been changed into a lively interest in life, and as this becomes so, Galveston will begin to realize just what the world expects of her.

Colonel W. L. Moody reached Galveston on Friday night, returning from New York. He was in New York when the news of the storm reached there and he immediately started for home.

He had determined before he reached here that he would rebuild everything he had which had been damaged by the storm, and he was hoping that telegraphic communication would be restored so that the work of relieving the distress might be rendered more efficient and so that people might wire for the material necessary to repair and rebuild their houses.

When asked for a statement as to his intentions, he said :

"I was in New York when the news of the storm came, and intended to start for home the last of this week, but immediately changed my plans and left for Galveston at once. The people of this country have responded generously, liberally, to the cry for assistance ; the disaster is appalling and appeals to the feelings and sympathy of mankind. And the country has responded liberally, as I said, even before they knew or appreciated the extent of the ruin and its consequences.

"The first news we received was very mild compared with what followed. Galveston was cut off from communication with the world, and the story of the storm was but partially told. The further along I got on my journey home, the fuller became the information in regard to the storm and we learned more and more of the greatness of the disaster. The fact that the world responded so freely to the first appeal is gratifying and inspires us with confidence in humanity. Those who have suffered from the storm will be cared for by a generous and sympathetic public. The prompt and generous aid is a beautiful thing.

DAMAGE WILL BE REPAIRED.

"What of the future? Galveston will be rebuilt ; it will be stronger and better than ever before. On my way home I stated that I would restore my property, whatever the damage might be, as quickly as money and men would do it, if I was the only man to take that course ; and I furthermore said that I believe I knew and understood what the feeling of the business community of Galveston was in this respect and that I had voiced it.

"At Texas City I met a woman from Kansas City. She was demoralized by what she had passed through and seen and she declared that Galveston would never be rebuilt ; that no one would be foolish enough to again build in a place which had been so storm swept.

"Answering her, I said that she did not know what she was

talking about; that Galveston would be rebuilt because it was necessary to have a city here; that if the storm had swept the island bare of every human habitation and every structure and had left it as barren as it was before civilized man set foot upon it, still men would come here and build a city, because a port was demanded at this place. 'And why should we not restore our city?' I asked. 'It has been visited by the severest storm on record. As it has withstood that storm, partially, why should we hesitate to rebuild? Why should we consider it less safe than another place? Can you conceive that another such a storm is more likely to strike at that exact spot again in a thousand years? Can you tell me any spot on earth, on hill or dale, on mountain or plain, on which you can guarantee me any immunities? If so, I would like to go there. If I were in the accident insurance business, I would rather insure a man against storm in Galveston than to insure a man in New York against accident on the railroads. You are now on your way to Kansas City. Do you know that you will reach there safely? Do you know that you may not be pitched into some river and drowned, or being only half drowned be burned to death?'

WILL BUILD BETTER THAN BEFORE.

"I slept at my home last night with as great a sense of security and safety as I ever have felt during my residence in this city," Colonel Moody continued. "There may be some people who will leave here, but there will be enough people left here who will rebuild their properties and go ahead with the city to form the nucleus for its future growth. We will build better than before, and the city will be better and stronger and safer than ever.

"The railroads are leading off with this better construction; they will build a double track steel bridge. Every man who builds in this city hereafter will build better and stronger than before, and the weaker structures will be weeded out. We will have better building regulations, and men will not be permitted, if they would, to construct faulty buildings.

"Some people may say, 'Oh, Moody can afford to make this talk ; he is planted down here and can not get away.' But let me tell you I could get away very easily if I wanted to. The greater portion of what I hope I own is not in Galveston, but is scattered throughout the State. It is in the hands of merchants throughout Texas to whom we have made advances on cotton. I could get away very easily if I had any desire to do so ; in fact, I believe I could liquidate and get out of town about as easily as any man in it.

"So far as our business and property are concerned, the bank is running along with unimpaired facilities. I have had an architect at work all day preparing for the immediate restoration of the bank building, the compress buildings and my other property. The compress machinery is intact, and we will be pressing cotton again within a week. Some of the partition walls in the cotton warehouses were blown out, but we will have a force of men at work immediately and will have them rebuilt before it is realized. And the walls will be better than they were before, because they were originally constructed by contract, while I am now having them rebuilt myself by day's work.

MOST MIRACULOUS ESCAPE.

"The people of Texas have not lost confidence in Galveston and have not manifested a disposition to quit the city. In to-day's mail we received bills of lading for three hundred bales of cotton shipped to us since the storm."

The most miraculous escape from the storm reached one of the newspapers in a roundabout way. An employe of the paper was coming to work when he overheard a few words passing between a couple of men talking on the street. He heard enough to elicit his interest and made inquiries. One of the men told him that an old German, whose name he did not know, had been picked out of the debris at Sherman square Saturday evening after having laid there a week.

People going by heard a sound which seemed to them like a groan. They stopped to listen and the groan was repeated. They hastily pulled off the debris and there found the old man still alive. It was understood that he was immediately taken to the home or friends at Tenth and Mechanic streets for care and treatment.

This story is the most remarkable instance of preservation of life recorded. The man must have gone through at least a portion of the storm to have been caught in the drift. He must have been above the water line at that point or he would have drowned. Why his groans were not heard before is not understood, unless it be that he laid unconscious until shortly before he was found. What a tenacity of life the man must have had to lie there for a week without food or water buried beneath all that debris.

Pete Brophey, clerk of the corporation court, is lying in a room at the Tremont Hotel suffering from injuries received in the storm. The story he tells of his miraculous escape, like the many others, wonderful, yet terrible, is also one of sorrow, as he lost his aged parents in the storm.

HE TOOK THE AWFUL RISK.

When the storm began to get so ferocious he became frightened. In the evening, just after dark, securing a boat, he started out with his parents to a Mr. Cleveland's, a neighbor's house, it being large and the most substantial in the neighborhood. At that time the water was rising rapidly and was being lashed into a perfect fury by the terrific wind. It was a terrible thing to start out in the water under such conditions, but he saw that their house would not stand long, so he took the awful risk. The boat was a small affair, and with three people in it, it was overloaded ; nevertheless, with great daring he succeeded in getting his mother and father into it, the former being 62 years of age and the latter 66. It was a terrific risk, but he had to take it. After getting his parents into the boat he started out to his neighbor's house.

The waters were rushing like mad down the street, and whipped the boat around as if it were but a straw. Added to the terrible force of the waters was the terrific wind. They were get ting along all right, notwithstanding this, and were making for the house below them, when, just ahead, he saw a man and woman and several children making for the boat. When it came near enough they grasped its sides and begged to be taken in.

It was indeed a trying situation. There he was, with his aged parents with him in a boat already overloaded, with the wind blowing almost a hundred miles an hour and carrying all before it, with the waves dashing everything to pieces and hurling the timbers of the houses against whatever might be in the way, with a force that only the most vivid imagination can picture. It was a terrible ordeal, but like the man that he is, he could not leave those begging parents and crying children without making at least an effort to save them. So, after great difficulty, the woman and children got aboard, and the perilous journey to what they hoped would be a haven of refuge was again begun, or rather it had been going on all the time, as the boat was being carried down on the crest of the waves with frightful velocity.

THE BOAT CAPSIZED.

When almost abreast of the house the boat capsized. Then again Brophey showed his bravery and that he was through and through a hero. Instead of striking out alone for the house he thought of his parents and the drowning family. After much difficulty, after having gone under time and time again in his frantic efforts to save his loved ones and the destitute family, he at last succeeded in getting them into the house.

That place they found filled to overflowing with refugees like themselves. The house was creaking and trembling under the terrible force of the water and wind, and Brophey saw that it would be but a little while before it, too, would have to succumb. So he braced himself in a door and waited for the inevitable. It was but a little while till it came. The house went down and all with it except Brophey, who found himself on top of the water in a gurgling and seething mass of timbers, roofs and other debris. He crawled up on one roof only to have another one thrown like a blanket over him.

25

Thus he struggled for two hours in what was an enormous raft of several hundred broken up houses, going before the wind, being churned together in a huge caldron by the waters. Whole roofs and sides of houses were bobbing, striking, sinking, turning over and moving together like chips in a huge whirlpool. Words can not describe that awful scene. In it all Brophey and hundreds of others were struggling for their lives almost all in vain. Dead bodies of women and children who had succumbed to the inevitable in the early part of the storm, and men and women whom the waters had not yet killed, but were playing with like a cat does a mouse before hurling them into the beyond, were carried hither and thither.

DODGING TIMBERS IN THE WATER.

Thus Brophey struggled, several times giving up and letting himself go down, but rising each time with a determination to fight until the bitter end, although terrible odds were against him. After having been in this mighty whirlpool for almost an hour, dodging huge timbers, crawling on roofs and sides of houses, being sucked under with them, he saw a house standing. With almost a last effort, he struggled and fought his way to a window of the house. There were ready hands to pull him through the window.

This haven which saved his life, together with a number of others, belonged to a negro and is situated near Thirty-seventh street. It was filled with negro refugees, and it is, indeed, to their credit that they struggled with such heroism to save Brophey and several others who drifted by.

Getting into the house, he threw himself on the floor, more dead than alive, and there remained until after the storm, when he was taken by friends to the Tremont Hotel, where he has become convalescent.

One of the interesting features of the story of his terrible struggle is his unintentional rescue of a dog. Early in his mad career in that most awful caldron he ran across a dog. From that time until his rescue it stayed with him, and would not be pushed off, and at last succeeded in crawling into the window after him. He is going to send for the dog, and declares that never while he is living will it want for a rug to sleep on and a bone to eat.

A. C. Fonda, chief clerk in the Santa Fe general freight office, at Galveston, had a fearful experience during the storm. He said that on Saturday afternoon, when it became apparent that the flood was going to be very high, that he went down to his home to remove the furniture from the lower floors to the upper, never dreaming that the effects of the storm would be more than a flooding of the first floors of residences. His family being away in California, fortunately for them, he worked alone and had about removed everything when the water got so high that he could not escape from the house.

FLOATED IN A TANK.

He had noted a large zinc-lined wooden tank on the upper floor, used for holding water, and which he thought might be used for a boat, when suddenly the crash came and he knew no more for possibly an hour. He recovered consciousness to find himself floating in the tank on the surging waters, bruised, bleeding and almost drowned. He managed to escape to higher ground in a short while and crawled into a deserted house, where he spent a night of horror, suffering from his injuries and momentarily expecting death. As soon as daylight came he sought surgical assistance, and then saw the awful results of the hurricane's work. Mr. Fonda is bruised all over, and has a deep wound on the back of his head, but no bones were broken and he is able to be at work.

E. F. Adams, chief clerk in the Santa Fe passenger department, at Galveston, is also a flood sufferer, but happily his family are in St. Louis at present, and his residence, being at Alvin, only suffered slight damage. He said that he and fifty-two others occupied the Santa Fe general offices on the night of the storm, and, in his opinion, very few of them, if any, realized the awfulness of the disaster until next day, as the sheet-iron roof on the train shed became loose early in the evening, and the tremendous noise it made in flopping up and down prevented them from hearing the crash of falling buildings, or, perhaps, the screams of drowning human beings during the night.

It was only when they came out next morning, Mr. Adams said, that he realized what the storm meant to thousands in the fated city. Almost the first object that met his eyes was the corpse of a child lying on the sidewalk, which staggered him, and with the sickening sights afterward presented to his view, gave him a shock whose gruesomeness it will take a lifetime to efface.

TERRIBLE EXPERIENCE OF A SURVIVOR.

A letter to a newspaper furnishes the following account of the terrible experiences of one of the survivors :

"I came home from my work Saturday evening about 4 o'clock, with Lewis Fisher. I left Lewis on Tremont street and avenue O, where the water was three feet deep. He said he was going out to help his people, and told me good-bye. So I started for home to see how my folks were. When I got home I found my folks all there, and the water was then five feet deep. I lived one block from the beach. I began to take them out. Our front steps had already washed away. I took them to S. Smith's house on Seventeenth and O, a big two-story house, thinking it would be safe.

"But it began to grow worse, so I took my father, sister and two smaller brothers on Nineteenth and O, in Mrs. Carlstedt's house, where there were some thirty people. I told my father to take care of the children, and started back for my mother and brother. On my way I met my friend, Gus Smith, of Nineteenth and O, and he told me that he would go with me and help me get my mother and brother.

"It took us an hour to swim one block, and when we got to the house it had already been washed into the street, and my little brother had been washed outside and was drowning, but I got him in time and took him back inside. Smith and I went inside and there we found a colored family and the Armour family, all asking us to take them away, but it was too late, as the water was then eight feet deep. Finally, the whole top of the house blew off and the water was pouring in, and all the people began to pray.

"The house was twenty-five feet high, and the waves went clean over it. Finally the whole thing fell in, and I grabbed my mother around the waist and Smith took my brother, and down we went. It was two minutes before we had a raft and were on Eighteenth street and O. There were twenty-eight in the house, and all we could save were seven people, as it was so dark that you could see no one. We got one little negro by the name of Albert of the negro family. We stayed out on the raft all night, without a stitch of clothes on, and the rain was something awful. It felt like some one was shooting buck shot at us from a distance.

CAPTURED SOME BLANKETS.

"About 2 o'clock in the morning we caught two trunks and broke them open, and it looked like a god-send to us, as both were full of blankets. We took these blankets and covered the women and children, or else I believe they would have frozen to death. About 5 o'clock in the morning I got up and started in search of my father and sister and other two brothers, and the first thing I did when I got off the raft was to step on a dead body.

"I then went a few steps further and found Mrs. A. C. Bell, of Eighteenth and O, and Mrs. Junker, of O, between Sixteenth and Seventeenth streets, both dead. We had come from Seventeenth and Beach to Nineteenth and N. Right across the street was Mr. Sewall's house, and I went over there to search for the rest of my folks and found them there all right, so I went back and got my mother and brother off the debris, and brought them all together once more.

"We have lost everything we owned and can't find a piece of the house or a button off any one's clothes, but I still have my front door key. My folks are cut up pretty much, and so am I about the feet, but I am going to stay here and try and make Galveston what it has been. In the house on Seventeenth and O is where Mrs. Armour and her five children were drowned."

Another letter says :

" I, together with many others, was a passenger on the Houston relief train last Tuesday, and among the number there was one who should háve special mention. This was Miss Lillian Bleike. I am informed she is the daughter of W. T. Bleike, a travelling salesman. This young lady was at Brenham when the news of the storm was reported, and as everything on earth near and dear to her was on the doomed island, she embarked upon the first train out.

" Ladies were not permitted upon this train. However, nothing daunted, she boarded the relief train at Houston, and through the kindness of those in charge, was permitted to go. At Lamarque, all had to foot it, and also to assist in clearing the debris. This, too, she would have done, but was not allowed to do so, and, like a good soldier, footed it through mud and slush to Virginia Point, boating it to the city, determined to learn the fate of the loved and dear ones. I have since learned her family was saved, and what a happy reunion this must have been. For pluck and courage, the adventures of this young lady stand among the few. '

CHAPTER XX.

The Storm's Murderous Fury—People Stunned by the Staggering Blow—Heroic Measures to Avert Pestilence— Thrilling Story of the Ursuline Convent.

WHILE the story of Galveston's woe can never be told, yet tne demand naturally should be that as much shall be told as the human mind is capable of telling. The man does not live now, and the man never lived who could draw the picture in all its horrible details. The greatest of poets sang of the destruction of Troy. Tacitus, and later other historians, have told of the deeds of the madman Nero. The contests between Marius and Sulla have filled pages through all time. The destruction of Pompeii has been vividly described by novelists and historians.

The French revolution, with its September and August massacres, its ravages, and its other fiendish details, have been in the hands of Carlyle and a score of French writers; the Gordon riots have been described by Dickens—but never a poet or historian or novelist has drawn anything near as shocking a picture of any event in the past as this stern and frightful reality.

Nearly every event of the past which has shocked humanity came about through contests between men. But men tire and men, however bitter, at last will abate their anger. In this case it was helpless humanity on the one side. In this case it was terrible nature in all its fury and strength on the other. There could be no appeal for mercy, because the winds have no ears. There was no resistance, because the arms of the waters were those of a giant demon. There were appeals, but they were directed above the storm. There were struggles, but they were simply those of the drowning. Those who survived were incoherent to a great degree.

The wind shrieked; it did not whistle as winds do. They all agree on that. The air was filled with spray, a blinding spray which affected the nostrils and throat and begat an inordinate thirst. It was dark. Yet it was light. They all agree on that.

391

Was there a moon? No one saw it. Yet even late at night they could see the clouds in the sky. The light, they say was a silvery one—a sort of sheen—a strange, and yet to all a fearful kind of light. Only one person ventured an explanation. She said the air was filled with the finest spray, and that this was phosphorescent. There is something in this idea.

HOUSE ROCKED LIKE A CRADLE.

Did the wind blow straight away or come in gusts? Here they differ again. One man told me that his house rocked as a cradle rocked by a mother getting her half-sleeping child to sleep. Dr. Fly described how it blew in a way to be understood. He was in the Tremont Hotel, a brick structure. He said that while it blew hard all the time gusts would come every few seconds and the wind took the strong building in its teeth then and shook it like a terrier would shake a rat.

There is sitting out on the mainland, not far from Texas City, a dredger which was employed about the wharves at Galveston. This vessel is a mile and a half or two miles from the water now. One of the men aboard told me that the boat was anchored with a steel rope. The Kendall Castle, a large iron steamer, dragged her anchor across this steel rope and cut it as a thread.

" On my word," said the man who told me this, " the moment the steel rope was cut the dredger seemed lifted in the air, and it appeared scarcely a minute till she was where she is now."

The vessel had been carried for miles in that short period. And there is nothing unreasonable in the story. The wind gauge at the office of the Weather Bureau showed eighty-seven miles an hour when it went out of business. They believe it blew 100 miles an hour after that. The people, before their houses fell about their ears, nailed up their window shutters and doors because no door latch and no windowpane ever made could stand the strength of the wind. Every one knew that once the wind entered the house, that moment the walls would be blown in every direction. No one fought against the water. It was the wind they put their feeble efforts against.

It will be remembered that the storm began to become serious early in the afternoon, and hence no one had undressed for bed when the climax came. The female survivors, or at least those who were upon the waters, came out naked. I asked a lady whether it was the waves or the flying timbers that did it. She said it was the wind. " Why, on the raft with me and my baby was a colored woman. The raft seemed to me to be the ceiling of a house because it was white. We had to lie as flat on it as we could without placing our faces in the water. The colored woman became tired and raised in a half-sitting posture. The moment she did it the wind stripped her of every stich of clothing."

CLOTHES TORN TO SHREDS.

The men, too, were deprived in a great measure of their clothes, but not to the extent of the women. Their clothes were torn from them now and then by the wreckage, but nearly all the corpses had on some garment. The reason of this was probably that the women's apparel was of weaker texture. People ask why the people did not move when the storm came from unsafe houses to safe houses. The answer is twofold. In the first place, death was on them before they realized their danger. The Galveston mind had for years been firmly convinced that Galveston Island and Galveston houses could weather any storm.

An illustration of this confidence is in order. A woman who lived at one of the numerous corner groceries said the water was almost to her neck before she left her place. She waded to the house of a near neighbor, where many of the people in the locality had assembled, because all thought it a perfectly safe house, as it proved itself to be. Here, she said, they chatted and even joked as the building rocked in the hands of the storm. When the people saw that their lives were in danger, it was then too late to try for other houses. They remained where they were till the buildings either fell and parts were being torn away and they were assured that they would soon fall.

The air was filled with every conceivable missile. Great beams and sleepers of houses went through the air like arrows.

Slates from the roofs hurtled over the heads. One of these would have cut off the head of a man as easily as a guillotine. There are thousands of mangled and wounded people in the town. One poor fellow was picked up alive at Texas City. He was cut in fifty places on his body. The tendons of his arms and legs were exposed. Others were hacked as if they had been laid down and scored as cooks score their meats. One-half the dead, perhaps, were relieved of their agony through these missiles of the storm.

CRUSHED BY A PIECE OF TIMBER.

One poor woman was carrying her child and its head was crushed by a piece of timber. It did not even whimper, yet she carried the dead infant at her breast for three long hours before it was torn from her grasp. When one sees the debris piled twenty feet high, in many places on the backbone of the island—that is, along Q street, running east and west—and when one sees the broad prairies for miles and miles covered with the wreckage that came from Galveston across the bay, the wonder with him will be that anything out on the waters that fearful night escaped to look, not tell, the story of that fearful night. For few can tell it; all look it.

Something of the strength of the winds and waves can be known when it is stated that along the beach at Texas cities I saw dead turtles even. Fish floated dead in the bay. They may have come from some wrecked fishing smack, and I am inclined to take this view of it, but there they were, covering a large space with their dead bodies. There were thousands of rats floating about. I saw even dead snakes along the shores. The chickens which lined the beach along the mainland were entirely denuded of their feathers. Not a buzzard or bird was to be seen. Not a mosquito was heard. The wind had carried all winged things away.

Down in some parts of the débris the planks and beams and sills of houses had been thrown together with such force that they were driven into each other and made as solid a mass as the most skilled workmen could join two pieces of timber. The foreman of one of the working gangs said it was impossible to romove certain portions of the mass except by clipping it away with axes or by burning it. If such a wind had struck Dallas or any other town in the State, it would not have lasted a moment.

Another thing I have been asked by the people of the interior was why the resort to the ocean as a burial ground was had, and why burning was afterward resorted to. When day broke after. that night of horror, the people could not realize the immensity of their woe. It required but a short time for them to know it. The first on the streets were the first greeted by the corpses.

They fled hither and thither, wringing their hands. Others stood still and stared in a dumb way. Some cooler citizens suggested that the bells be rung and the people assembled to grapple with the situation. And lo, there was not a bell in town to sound the alarm. It was suggested that the steam whistles be blown. And lo, there was not a whistle with steam to give it note on all the island. Then they went up and down the streets, crying, "Fall in, people; for God's sake, fall in." They got a few people together in this way. As they had gone about, more corpses appeared.

THE NUMBER GROWS LARGER.

What should be done with them? Strange to say, the suggestion was made that inquests must be held on the bodies and the law complied with. But the corpses began to grow larger in number. Inquests now were no longer discussed. Those who could work began to gather the dead bodies and carry them to the undertaker shops. There was confusion, but all were doing their best. The purpose now was to place the dead in coffins. But the number increased. The idea was abandoned because, simply, it could not be done. Seven hundred putrid bodies were piled up in the building. Something must be done.

Then it was suggested that they be taken to the sea. The substitute was offered that they be burned. But where burn the latter? It could be done on the beach where the debris was, but how get there? Every street running across the island to the beach was blocked. The substitute suggestion was abandoned.

But how get the bodies to the sea? Then it was that the law was laid aside.

Martial law was declared in fact, whether according to law or not. Men armed themselves and went on the streets in posses. They captured negro men and forced them to take hold of the bodies. Whisky was poured into them—argument was made to them. They were nauseated with the work, but more whisky was poured into them. They piled the bodies on floats and drays and every kind of vehicle and thus took them to the wharf.

A GHASTLY SPECTACLE.

Here they were placed on barges. The poor living creatures, wild with liquor, beastialized by it, because they could not have done it, embarked with the putrifying cargo. The white men retched and vomited. The negroes did the same. Yet more work had to be done and now they pleaded for whisky to dull them more for their horrible work. It was given them. No man in all the world can tell of the horrors of this trip. Those who were not wild shrunk in agony from it. Those who were mad stumbled over the corpses and laid with them in drunken stupor—but beyond the jetties the cargo was tossed into the sea.

It is claimed that they were sunk with weights. This may be partly true. This disposition of the corpses was found impracticable. The work was too slow. The sea would give up its dead. As time passed the difficulty of transporting the bodies became greater. Then the burning began. The corpses wherever found were burned on the spot. If the fire might be dangerous they were pulled to an open space.

Where several were found in close proximity they were placed together for the final act. Kerosene was poured over them. Planks, lumber, anything combustible were placed upon them and the torch applied. The incineration was never complete enough to completely destroy the bones. But the flesh, breeding a pestilence, was gone. Many were buried. But the graves were only deep enough to receive the bloated bodies. The sand was full of water. Graves could be dug no deeper than as mentioned.

A shudder will go through the world when some one properly tells of how the beloved ones found their last resting-place. For it is horrible to think of disposing of human corpses in this way. But what could be done? What else? Nothing—absolutely nothing, except what was done. The dead threatened the living. Even if the living had desired to flee from the dead, which they did not, they could not have done so—but on an island were the living and the dead. There were no vessels to run from the island to the mainland. There were no railroads or bridges. The hot sun beat down and quickly decomposed the bodies. The bruised and maimed could not work. What could be done? Nothing but what was done. 'Twas a sad and horrible thing, but it was charity for the dead to do it, and preservation to the living to do it.

It is utterly unreasonable for one to think that the people of Galveston and the workers in the cause of cleaning can proceed rapidly. Not only is it a task, but it is a task which has conditions existing which are new to the people engaged in the work, and they cannot work with the energy which is their wont.

FULL LIST CANNOT BE KNOWN.

As to the dead, as stated before, how the full list will be ever known is hard to say. There are places in the city where for blocks and blocks not a house remains, and no one can give an instance of having seen a resident of the locality since the fury of the storm was spent. Whole families were swept out to sea, and the survivors of the calamity are too busy with their own and the work which must be done to remember whom they knew when the Island City was in its prime.

Another point in the matter of the dead is that there were many visitors in the city at the time whose names have never been reported either in the list of the living or of the dead. Possibly few people knew they were here, and in the confusion incident to the days following the storm those who were cognizant of the presence of these visiters have been too busy to think of the stranger in the land.

It is true that a clew to missing people is gained by the inquiries of anxious friends or relatives, and these queries are answered either "dead" or "alive." But remember that in every city in the country there are a certain number of people who are unknown beyond the limits of their own home.

In this class also can be included many colored people. Colored people always know each other, but it is in many instances that they know nothing of surnames. There are servants whose names are not known beyond Mary or Liza or by whatever appellation they are addressed, and it is possible that a great many of these have been lost, increasing the number of dead, but never getting upon the roll of those who were so suddenly swept away.

STORY OF URSULINE.

The Ursuline Convent and Academy, in charge of the Sisters of St. Angeli, proved a haven of refuge for nearly 1000 homeless and storm-driven unfortunates. The stories of this one night within the convent walls read like the wildest dream of a novelist, but the half can never be told. Every man, woman and child who was brought to the convent or drifted there on the raging torrent could tell of an experience that would be well worth its publication.

The convent, with its many associate buildings, cottages, etc., occupies four blocks of ground extending from Avenues N to O, and Rosenberg avenue to Twenty-seventh street. The grounds are, or rather were, surrounded by a ten-foot brick wall that has withstood the severest storms in Galveston's history up to the destructive hurricane that swept the island last Saturday night. This wall is now a crumbled mass of brick with the exception of a few small portions that stand like marking pillars to show where the property line should be.

No one was refused admittance to the sheltering institution on this night of nights. Negroes and whites were taken in without question, and the asylum thrown open to all who sought its protecting wings. Angels of mercy went through the army of sufferers whispering words of cheer, offering what scant clothing could be found in this house of charity and calmly admonishing the terror-stricken creatures to have faith in God and say that His holy will be done.

In contrast with this quiet, saintly and loving spirit of the nuns, the hundred or more negroes grew wild as the storm raged, and shouted and sang in their camp-meeting style until the nerves of the other refugees were shattered and a panic seemed imminent. It was then that Mother Superioress Joseph rang the chapel bell and caused a hush of the pandemonium. When quiet had been restored the Mother addressed the negroes and told them that it was no time nor place for such scenes; that if they wanted to pray they should do so from their hearts, and that the creator of all things would hear their offerings above the roar of the hurricane which raged with increased fury as she spoke to the awe-stricken assemblage.

A SOLEMN CEREMONY.

The negroes listened attentively, and when the saintly woman told them that all those who wished to be baptized or resign themselves to God might do so, nearly every one of them asked that the sacrament be administered.

The panic had been precipitated by the falling of the north wall or that section of the building in which the negroes had sought refuge. Order and silent prayer were brought about by this noble woman's sweet determination and great presence of mind.

Families that had been separated by this merciless and devastating conflict of the elements were united by the cruel waters of the gulf tossing them into this haven of refuge. What scenes, what heart-bleeding pictures these unions presented as the half-dead, mangled and bruised wretches were rescued and dragged from the raging waters by the more fortunate members of their own family, mourned as victims of the storm.

The academy was to have opened for the fall session on Tuesday, and forty-two boarding scholars from all parts of the State had arrived at the convent preparatory to resuming their studies on that day. The community of nuns comprises forty sisters and they, too, were there administering cheer and deeds of mercy to the sufferers, many of whom were more dead than alive when brought into the shelter. Early in the storm when people dragged themselves or swam to the convent and asked for protection an attempt was made to keep a register of the unfortunates.

Their register reached nearly a hundred names and then the storm-driven humans began to arrive at the shelter in crowds of twenty and thirty. They were taken in through the windows and some were dragged through five feet of water into the basement, which long since had been abandoned, by ropes from treetops and snatched from roofs and other wreckage as it was hurled in the maddening torrents through the convent yards.

LIVING TO TAKE PLACES OF THE DEAD.

Within this religious home and in cells of the nuns four babies came into this world. Four mothers who had braved the treacherous elements and were snatched from the jaws of tragic death lay on cots in the nuns' cells and four little innocents came into this world of sorrow where the world looked the blackest. Truly it could not be said that the quartette of precious ones first saw the light of day in the cell of a nun on this eventful night. It was the darkest and most terrible night in the lives of their mothers, and yet the mingled sadness and joy attending the birth of these angels was beyond the power of man to describe.

Mother Joseph, in speaking of the incidents of the night within the convent walls, said she believed it was the first time in the history of the world that a baby had been born in a nun's cell in a convent. And they were christened, for no one expected to live to see the light of day, and it was voted that these jewels should not leave the world they had just entered without baptism. Regardless of the religious belief of the parents, a house dedicated to God and charity had afforded shelter to the storm-victim mothers, and they felt in their hearts that the good sisters should administer the baptism, which is administered in time of great danger, the presence of clergymen not being required.

The names of the mothers and the children could not be learned, with the exception of Mrs. William Henry Heldeman, who was one of the mothers, and whose new-born baby was christened William Henry. The experiences of this mother, if they could be reduced to words, would read like the wildest fiction. Only a chapter was learned, as told by Mother Joseph. Mrs. Heldeman was thrown on the mercies of the storm when her home went down and was swept away. The family had been separated when they started to abandon their home to the greed of the battling storm.

When Mrs. Heldeman was carried away on the roof of a wrecked cottage she lost all trace of the other nembers of the family, but never lost faith and courage. The roof struck some obstruction, and the next instant Mrs. Heldeman was hurled from her improvised raft and landed in a trunk which was rocked on the surging waters. Crampled up in the trunk, the poor woman was protected to a limited extent and was afforded much warmth. On went the trunk, tossed high on the treacherous sea, bumping against driftwood, until the crude bark was hurled against the Ursuline Convent walls and was hauled into the building.

CLEARING THE STREETS.

The following report of the situation at Galveston bears date of September 17th.: The work of clearing the streets of debris and wreckage is progressing steadily and with systematic rapidity. The military authorities have gradually perfected the system and divided the labors so that there is comparatively no interruption or delay in the gigantic undertaking.

To-day the reports filed at General Scurry's headquarters up to 9 o'clock to-night reported the recovery and disposition of but forty-five bodies. A reporter, who made the rounds of about twenty gangs in charge of removing debris, noted the finding of 130 bodies of men, women and children and this report is known to be incomplete for the day's work.

City Health Officer Wilkinson stated that he estimated that 40 per cent. of the debris of every description had been removed. from the streets; that 95 per cent. of the dead bodies had been disposed of, and that 95 per cent. of the carcasses of animals had been removed from the city. But as the work of removing debris goes

26

on more bodies are being unearthed every hour. There is still an immense amount of work to be done in this respect and in some quarters hardly an impression has been made in the mountains of wreckage piled up fifteen and twenty feet high.

Still the gruesome work of recovering the dead from the gigantic mass of debris that lines the south side of what remains of the city goes on. Yesterday 107 bodies were recovered and cremated. Among them was a mother with a baby tightly clasped to her breast. As the body of the mother was moved the body of the baby rolled off. In this imperative necessity of the dispatch of the dead tragic scenes are witnessed that move the stoutest hearts.

THE INDESCRIBABLE SUNDAY SERVICES.

The body of Major W. T. Levy, United States Immigrant Agent of this district, was among the number. He made a gallant struggle to save his wife and three children. All were lost, and the bodies of the wife and children have not been recovered. They are still among the uninterred dead, and when found will be disposed of as the father and husband has been.

What pen can describe the religious service on Sunday? Houses of worship ruined, congregations scattered and in despair, yet all those who survived gathered in impromptu temples and in sorrow and grief prayed for loved ones gone, and in humble thanksgiving offered up their hearts for their own preservation. The scene at the little chapel in St. Mary's University was pitiful in the extreme, the Sacred Heart Church lying in ruins, the Jesuit fathers threw open their private chapel to those who formerly worshipped in this once magnificent church. Within this meagre little chapel none could for a moment lose sight of what now existed here; many of those who received the communion from the priests' hands know no home other than this same building; children came to this sacrifice of the mass bare-footed and hatless, even their expressions showed the awe struck feeling which shrouded all.

At the low mass no sermon was preached, no word spoken, all prayer was in silence, nothing but the words of the mass was heard, as each heart poured forth in feeling deep and still their thanksgiving. The environments there each told the sad, sad story. On the lower floor of this chapel were the destitute waiting for the food supply to be given them, this in itself the saddest picture the miseries of life can sketch. On the same floor with the chapel are the priests' rooms, now the hospital wards, everywhere the sick being tended by skillful hands, looked wistfully at the passer-by. Thus in this one corner of the university, the whole effect of the tragedy is enacted; the hungry, the homeless, the ill, and above all these earthly miseries, the kneeling before the throne of God in submission and prayer.

A GLORIOUS RECORD.

There has yet to come to light any tale of brutality; those who spent the night of the storm battling the waves never witnessed a selfish act; this in itself is a glorious record to hallow the event. Man after man secure in his own house, hearing the cry for help plunged out in the fury to rescue the helpless ones; oftentimes this was attended with loss of life to the rescuer. There was no question of kin or color that awful night, the ties of a common sorrow united all, and not only was man with his intellect and strength the courageous ones; children who could have been rescued would not be taken from their loving ones, and as for the mothers who sought death with their little ones such tales as these are as manifold as the waves of the sea.

Nor were the humbler animals forgotten, many instances are known where men wading waist deep in water holding their wives and children above the water, found hands somewhere for the household dog. One young lady, a society girl, when forced to abandon her home gave no thought to silken finery and jewels, but waded in water nearly to her shoulders holding fast in her arms a large sized sky-terrier. Nor was this devotion only from man to animal, it was equal if only all were known.

One dog, we call him " Hero," as there is none to tell us otherwise, is truly a hero worthy the Legion of Honor. This four-footed hero is a small-sized Newfoundland, and in the storm he was cast adrift on Seventh and Broadway, with his master, an old gentleman about seventy years of age. Around Hero's neck is a stout black collar; to this the old gentleman clung. Hero did the rest, he swam pulling along his old master from Seventh to Fourteenth streets, where they found a house standing with veranda piled with debris but intact, and into a sheltered corner of this the dog dragged the man for safety. Both were alive, the old gentleman was much bruised, but his mind was active, and his only grief was for the loss of his wife and daughter, for save the dog he had no one.

A DOG'S DEVOTION.

Kind hands did for him all that could be done, and while feeble and heart-broken he appeared to suffer no pain. The dog never left him there, the two throughout that fateful Sunday clung together. Toward 3 o'clock in the afternoon the old man, still sitting in a rocking-chair, covered in blankets, no dry bed being available, appeared drowsy. This was only natural from fatigue and age, but when the head gently bent forward it was the sleep of death. However, such a gentle passing away of the soul could not be termed by such a harsh name; it was more a caress, in which the transition of the soul was wafted from the body.

The dog all these hours had nestled close to the old man's feet under the blanket, never sleeping, but guarding carefully the master. When the feet became cold, then the four-footed hero scented trouble. He tried to lie on them with his body. This not answering, he licked the cold feet; still no warmth. Then he sprang into the rocking-chair in which the corpse sat, carefully covered in sheets, tried to warm the body by covering it as much as possible with his own shaggy hair. By force the dog had to be taken away and locked up, for in his instinct he scented something wrong with the old man and strove to make things right by supplying the warmth of his own body. Such scenes as this old man's beautiful death and the dog's deep devotion are among the sublime lessons.

Photographers are hourly taking views of the ruins. However, there is a picture about the debris which demands a sketch to itself. The Sacred Heart Church before the storm had in the right aisle, near the altar, erected to the mother of Christ, a large crucifix affixed to a pillar. Now all the sides of this church are demolished save where this crucifix in this pillar stands and the crucifix untouched. It is a sight not to be forgotten to see this image of the Man of Sorrows looking down upon the ruin everywhere.

THE WORST EXPERIENCES.

Naturally one would say that the living through the experience of the storm was the worst part of the catastrophe, but those who had their families here but were themselves away affirm that the suspense and anxiety they underwent to learn the fate of their loved ones could not have been worse. Mr. Frank Gresham shows this. He was at Cornell College when the news that Galveston had been swept off the earth reached him. At first these reports seemed exaggeration, but when the truth became known the Galvestonian became panic-stricken. Mr. Gresham tried to communicate with his family, but as no word was received, his fears grew worse.

Deeming it not a time for thinking, but action, he came south immediately. En route he said the fast trains which make no stops would wait two or three hours for Galveston people, and trains having passengers for this city had the right of way over all lines. The sight of this panic-stricken crowd, eager to reach home or hear of friends and family was pitiful indeed.

At St. Louis one lady, already in heavy mourning, was greeted with a telegram saying her entire family had been washed away, and thus it was all along the road. Several ladies personally known to Mr. Gresham were on the train, but all were in tears from nervousness and anxiety. Words of recognition were hardly exchanged; it was a case where the heart was too full for utterance.

Two Galvestonians were on the Mallory steamer from New York which came in Saturday, after having been abroad since June. The news of Galveston's disaster did not reach the boat till they touched Key West. Up to this time all was joy on board, but when the news was received the vessel seemed to drag until this port could be reached. The passengers tried to wire from Key West to some one in Houston for information, but were greeted with the information that there were thousands ahead of them and no word could be received.

THE RESPONSE FOR RELIEF.

Thus the suspense had to be borne till the pilot reached the boat, and at this junction only the confirmation of their worst fears were realized. Only the passengers who were Galvestonians, all of whom agreed to work upon their arrival, were allowed to come in; the others were sent to Texas City, from which place they reached their various homes. The papers show how letters, telegrams and cables are daily coming in by thousands; also how the whole world has responded to the cry for help. Even the actors in New York, Philadelphia and all the large cities gave performances for the benefit of the sufferers.

One lady writes to a newspaper as follows: " While so many deeds of heroism shown during this late storm are being told I deem it one of my greatest privileges to be able to mention the names of Mr. Clark Fisher, Mr. Sam Robertson and Mr. Clarence Anglen, who, by their daring and courage, so heroically saved my family of six ladies with their large raft on East Avenue I, during the fiercest part of the storm. We had drifted with our house until it had become dismembered and then were thrown upon the mercy of the waves and strong current. These young gentlemen all cleverly proved by their coolness and bravery what was in them."

Another lady writes : " September 8, at about 4 o'clock, things began to be alarming at my place, at Seventeenth and O, and houses were leaving before that. I hoped my little home was an ark. It proved to be until the water began to pour wildly into the windows. I and an old man named Inco, who rented a rear room from me, got over the stair-casing and climbed until our heads were at the ceiling. He said to me: ' We die here together ; good bye.'

"At the same moment the house separated. I climbed over the door through the transom and on to the roof, thence from one timber to another, always keeping to the top. A dog always kept by me and caused me a great struggle. It was about Twentieth street and O½ that something hit my head, which seemed either to give me courage or ease. I remember laying my head down on the raft and felt indifferent.

"About 4 o'clock the next morning I rejoiced to see where the gulf and island separated. I was resting not extremely uncomfortable at the top of drifts of a two-story house at Twenty-fifth and beach. Some Italians came along, looked unconcernedly at me. They were hunting someone and went on. I still hallooed until I heard Mr. Beekman, who, with assistance, took me to a house. They could find nothing to cover me, but gave me whisky.

"Then came Mr. Womack, who left nothing undone to make me safe. He carried me over lumber on a board, with blanket and pillows, to his rooming house. From there I was taken to the Sealy Hospital, with the two blankets and pillows."

THE AWFUL STORY.

The following from the columns of a well-known journal has a mournful interest:

"In Galveston there is mourning; in the city by the sea there is sobbing and tears. When the young of us have grown old, when they, in their turn, are grand'thers, when a century of years has drifted past as sea-wreck drifts will the legend of Galveston be told and retold again, and white-faced children, clinging to the granddames' robes, will listen to the story of how the storm-god came in rage, and how the gulf, beaten by his thong, rushed in and did his bidding. They will hear the awful story that will never die, the tale of how the tempest and the tide slew men as pestilence slays; slew praying women and prattling babes as Herod slew the boy-children twenty centuries ago; will hear of how the sea, that once calmed at the Maker's word, made war on the orphan's home, as if he who said 'Suffer little children to come unto me,' had repented of his bargain.

" Men strive for the art of remembering—lo, now we beg that some great magician may teach us how to forget. To forget the horror of it all ; and the sobbing and the prayers. To forget the wail of the mother bereft of her young, and women's prayers that came echoing back from the flinty sky. To forget the death struggles of the legion of the dead, and the cries of ' Mamma ! Mamma !' as the screaming little ones were sucked into the throat of the tide. To forget that the sweet-voiced nuns bound the charity orphans together in lots and committed them to the care of God—to forget that the reaper came with the storm in his heart and the salt spray in his beard and gathered them by sheaves. Do not talk of consolation—there is none. Try to forget. Muffle your clamoring church bells—their noisy songs blend illy with the screams of despairing mothers beating their breasts and calling to their dead. To-day your prayers are useless, and the solemn organ's mellow tide can be freighted only with a requiem for the lost. O, for the sadness of it all; and the sobbing and the tears; for the cries of women and the thunder of the tide; for the shouting of men and the burials in the sea.

LABORERS' HEROIC WORK.

Under date of the 18th the condition of the city was stated to be as follows :

Slowly but surely the streets are assuming a decent appearance, and in a few days all evidence of the storm on the streets of the business district will have been removed. A large force of men are working systematically, and the beneficial result is shown in every quarter. The greatest amount of wreckage is piled high along the beach and for several blocks inland, where hundreds of homes fell victims to the rush of waters and devastating hurricane that swept that portion of the city bare. The amount of débris in the district extending from the extreme eastern end of the island to the western city limits, and even beyond that point, is incalculable, and the manner in which the storm packed this long ridge of wreckage challenges the heroic efforts of the army of laborers engaged in its removal.

But great progress has been made and is being made. The work cannot be described in words, even as the devastation wrought by the awful storm defies description. One must visit the scene and note the progress of the work in order to gain an intelligent idea of what it was and what is being done.

MORE VICTIMS EVERY HOUR.

As the force of wreckers make inroads into the mountains of débris the bodies of more victims are unearthed every hour. And the end is not yet. A most conservative estimate of the dead and missing is enough to prove that the wreckage yet undisturbed will reveal several hundred more dead who perished in the storm. There is no doubt that at least 200 or 300, perhaps many more, bodies were carried to sea, and that the number of bodies recovered and to be recovered and accounted for will fall short of the actual number of creatures who were hurled into eternity while the storm raged.

The record kept shows that ninety-eight bodies were reported as having been dug from the ruins yesterday. But it is known that this record is not a complete list of the bodies found and disposed of. For the first three days after the storm bodies were found by the score and disposed of by the parties finding them. Some of these persons kept a sort of record. Others, acting upon the impulse of the moment and what they deemed their duty, stopped in their search along the beach to bury the poor unfortunates whom they found in and about the ruins and debris.

Several important orders were issued from military headquarters, Brigadier-General Scurry commanding. The most important, perhaps, to the general public was an order which decrees that heroic measures are necessary for the preservation of the health of the community. It is ordered that all persons occupying houses within one block of debris which is presumed to contain dead bodies will have to vacate the premises temporarily.

This step has been taken by the military authorities in charge of the city after deliberate consideration and consultation with the Board of Health and the general committee charged with looking after the general welfare of the citizens. Camps will be established and comfortable quarters provided for all those who will be subjected to this ruling, and ample notice will be served upon the tenants of such houses. It is not compulsory that all such persons must accept tent accommodations, as it will be discretionary with them to move into some other house or other premises away from the forbidden district.

ADVISED TO LEAVE THE CITY.

In this regard it may be well to call attention to the advice given early in the present military régime that all those who can leave the city should do so; especially does this apply to women and children. A month away from the scenes of the calamity would prove beneficial to their general health, and would greatly aid in facilitating the work of cleaning the city and putting it in a thorough sanitary condition. A man who knows his family is enjoying good health away from Galveston can do better work at home under existing conditions. Should any of his family be taken sick here at home, he would necessarily be compelled to give them his time and attention, and this would greatly interfere with the progress of the good work so laudably commenced.

Another important order issued was one which establishes a cattle corral, where idle cattle and horses will be cared for and fed and used in public service if the emergency requires. There are a large number of unclaimed and strayed stock running at large about the city. A number of cows have been picked up by people who out of compassion for the suffering beasts fed and cared for them. Several cases have been reported where families leaving the city after the storm turned their stock and horses loose on the streets, or, strictly speaking, who in their haste to leave the city, failed to collect their stock which had strayed away during the storm.

The work under the direction of the Health Department is pushed with vigor. All the departments are working systematically and doing all that is possible under the circumstances. As fast as disinfectants arrive they are being distributed over the city, and large quantities are arriving daily. Over a carload were taken from the wharves yesterday and sent to the Health Department's supply depot, and almost as much was taken from that place and distributed over the city. As fast as it can be done the city is being placed in a thoroughly sanitary condition. Much was done yesterday in the way of removing debris and disposing of animal remains.

The sick and wounded are receiving the best of treatment, and the facilities are such now that any one needing medical treatment can have it by letting the fact be known. Besides the other hospitals and medical relief stations already in service, the marine hospital and refugee camp was opened up yesterday afternoon and is in shape to care for a large number of patients. A number of those able to travel have been taken from the hospitals and sent in the revenue cutter and by other means of transportation to Houston and other relief stations on the mainland. In all the outlook from a health standpoint is very encouraging.

ANXIOUS ABOUT THE CITY'S HEALTH.

The Auxiliary Board of Health met at the usual time and place on the 18th with almost all the Board present. President Wilkinson called the meeting to order, and after it had been decided to waive the regular order of business and dispense with the reading of the minutes and the reports from the committees, Dr. Trueheart offered the following resolution and moved that it be adopted :

"Be it resolved by the Board of Health and the Auxiliary Health Board of the city of Galveston, General Thomas Scurry in command, concurring, that the surgeon in charge of each and every hospital, permanent or temporary, and all camps and one and all of the medical relief stations for the care of the sick and wounded within the corporate limits, are hereby instructed and empowered to proceed without delay to thoroughly cleanse, disinfect and place in as perfect sanitary condition as practicable their respective hospitals, stations or camps and the premises thereof for the care of the wounded and sick, and they are hereby authorized to send in requisitions to the proper department for such disinfections, etc., as may be required, and empowered to secure the services, by impressment or otherwise, of such labor, implements or vehicles as may be found necessary to fully carry out this order.   This is to be done without delay."

The resolution was adopted and arrangements were made to carry it into immediate effect.

RESTORATION OF GALVESTON.

An intelligent and well-posted citizen, writing to the leading journal of the city, expressed the following sentiments:

"The restoration of Galveston is a question which does not alone interest the people of the stricken city, but all Texas as well. The discussion now going on is not confined to Galveston, but is on the lips of every public-spirited citizen of the State.   The preponderance of opinion among the people of the interior is that the city will be rebuilt or restored upon a scale of magnificence and stability far superior to anything it has ever known.   There are some, however, who express the opinion that it would be worse than a waste of energy, enterprise and money to do so, for the reason that it is liable to be swept away at any time.   This opinion is fallacious in the extreme.

"We are not prepared to give precise historical data in support of the assertion, but crossing the limits of the circle in which only exact information is contained, and invading the circle in which conclusions are only reached by a system of reasoning, it can be quite confidently asserted that the island of Galveston has been standing since the waters of the flood receded from the earth, and quite likely from the foundation of the world, and though it has been swept by a thousand storms, tossed by a thousand tidal waves and deluged a thousand times by rains, it still stands securely where the Almighty Creator placed it a million and perhaps a billion years ago.

"To successfully maintain the assertion that the island will be ultimately swept away, it is necessary, first, to prove the assertion that the storm, or tidal wave, that will do the work will be a thousand times more furious than any the world has heretofore known. Any attempt to support either proposition is absurd. It is admitted, however, that the assertion that the island has been standing since the flood, or is a part of the original creation, is a theory, and worth no more than any other theory started from a proper predicate, but Galveston island has been known for more than 400 years, and has a fairly well-authenticated history since 1542. In 1541 De Soto is said to have landed on the Texas coast near the island, established a base of operations and penetrated the interior as far as the present site of the town of San Marcos.

"After his death a part of his exploring force settled on Galveston island in 1542, and constructed some kind of fortifications to protect themselves from the Indians and Spanish pirates or freebooters. This was 358 years ago. This undisputed historical fact proves beyond question that the Spanish pirates and the American Indians were acquainted with the island before De Soto's men established themselves. Just how long is not known, but a knowledge of the island strip may be contemporaneous with the existence of the aborigines of America that were here during the explorations of the Norsemen, who made several voyages in the ninth century, 1000 years ago. In 1585, while La Salle was cruising around in the Gulf of Mexico, he mentions having lost a man in the Maligu (Brazos) River, and it is therefore very probable that he touched at Galveston island.

A MATTER OF HISTORY.

"In 1715, Governor Casparlo Awaya established the Orquisaco mission on Galveston bay and made a thorough exploration of the island. In 1816 the Mexican envoy to the United States, General Herrera, and Commodore Ansy took formal possession of Galveston island in the name of the Mexican republic, and from that time until now the history of the island is a connected, well-authenticated story, and as much is known of its climate, soil, products, temperature, rainfall, wind storms, etc., as any part of Texas. At that time the island was much lower than now, much of it a mere marsh, entirely unprotected by improvements, and a thousand times more liable to be swept by storms than now, and still it stood, and still stands.

"When Commodore Ansy abandoned the island, Lafitte succeeded him in possession and held it until 1821. Lafitte's description of its topography agrees with Commodore Ansy's in every essential, and both state much of the area was marshy and low-lying, and unfit for settlement. Is there any man who will assert that during the past eighty-eight years the altitude and stability of the island has not been constantly improved or increased? If such is the case, and truth forbids its denial, the conclusion is unavoidable that Galveston island may be crossed by howling tornadoes every week, but it is just as secure as any part of Texas from destruction.

MANY DESTRUCTIVE AGENCIES.

"In the excitement and for the moment men forget that there is any other element or power, except water, that destroy towns, when in fact the cities of the interior have suffered more destruction from cyclones and storms than all the towns on the Texas coast from Sabine Pass to Brazos Santiago. Fort Worth is as liable to destruction as Galveston. In fact insecure residences in every section of the country is a harvest for fires, floods or cyclones, as was demonstrated in Chicago, Boston, New York, 'Cisco, Sherman, Plano and scores of cities and towns in texas as well as other states during the past decade.

"In the present deplorable disaster in Galveston the lamentable loss of life was brought about, not from its hazardous or insecure location, but largely on account of the unstable character of the buildings. True, some fine structures were demolished, but such was also the case in Brenham, Hempstead, Houston and Alvin. In Brenham 100 houses were blown to pieces; of these a half dozen were substantially built. Eye-witnesses state that about the same proportions hold good in Galveston and about the same conditions prevail.

"Nearly every island city on earth, in its early life, has suffered just as Galveston has suffered. People attracted by business opportunities would rush in, and rush up cheap, insecure and temporary residences, only to be devoured by the flame or swept from the earth by the first blast. New York, Liverpool, Edinburg and other coast cities suffered in this way, and learned lessons from such sad experiences that made them prosperous, stable and great. So will Galveston.

" Many who passed through the recent storm will leave, but commerce knows no such thing as an insurmountable obstacle. The commerce of the West demands the port; Galveston will be rebuilt, by new people largely, seeking and embracing the business opportunities offered. Lots will be staked out, houses more substantial in structure erected. The whole Atlantic Ocean might roll over New York and it would roll off again, leaving the city unscathed. Manhattan island originally was no more secure than Galveston island, and Galveston island in time will be rendered just as safe as Manhattan is to-day."

CHAPTER XXI.

Unparalleled Bombardment of Waves—Wonderful Courage Shown by the Survivors—Letter From Clara Barton.

A VISITOR to Galveston thus gives his impressions on the 12th day after the great flood :

" For two days after the great catastrophe, the people of the city of Galveston were stunned. They seem to be dazed. It is a remarkable thing that there were no signs of outward grief in the way of tears and groans to mark the misery that raged in the breasts of the people. Only when some person who was thought to have been dead, appeared to a relative living who had mourned for him or her, were there any tears. There was a callousness about all this that attracted the attention of those who had just come to the unfortunate place. There was a stoicism in it. But it was unexplainable. It indicated no lack of appreciation of what had occurred.

"It demonstrated no lack of affection for those who had gone. Nature, generous in this instance, came to their relief in a way and made them dull to the seriousness of what had occurred, to an extent which prevented them from becoming maniacs. For, if the grief which comes to a mortal when he loses a dead one, had come to this whole community, the island would have been filled with raving maniacs. In case of individual losses, there is always some one near to give consolation. Had the grief came to the whole island, there could have been no consolation, for every soul on it had lost in some way that which was dear to it.

" 'The case is just like the afterthoughts of those who have participated in a great battle,' said an old soldier to me. 'If a popular man was lost on the picket line, there were tears for him, but when the time came for all to be mowed down, the horror of it dulled the sensibilities of those who survived.'

"I was talking to an estimable and bright woman on the
416

subject.   She had lost members of her family, though not immediate ones.   She said to me : ' I study myself and am overcome
at myself.   I know what has happened.   I know the losses.   I
have lost some of the members of my family, though they are
not blood kin.   I have lost the dearest friends of my life.   And
yet I have not shed a tear.   My eyes are hot.   I would give anything to cry, but it looks as if the fountains were dried.   I am
ashamed of my seeming indifference to this horrible thing and
the loss of those who were so dear to me.   But I cannot cry.   I
know that I suffer, but it looks so cruel to sit here with dry eyes
and without any other evidence of the deep sorrow that fills my
bosom.'

"I talked to one man and asked him how many people he
had lost.   He had saved his daughter and her child.   All the
rest, amounting to three souls, were gone.   But they were dry.
He spoke in a low voice, but it did not tremble.   He was agonized—I saw that—but his mind was unable to grasp the true
meaning of his loss, and when he had finished he asked if I had
a match about me.

THE SAME BELL.

"Up to Thursday night there had been no sleep in the city.
True, exhausted nature had thrown men and women and children
on their beds and they had closed their eyes and the physical
strain had been to some degree relieved, but the mental strain
was still at the breaking point.   One man said that on Thursday
morning he was awakened by the convent bell summoning the
living to mass.   It was the same bell that had rung or tinkled in
the tone since the day of the storm.

"He bounded from his bed a new man.   He was hopeless the
day before.   He had seriously thought of abandoning his house,
which he believed beyond repair, but when he looked at it on
Thursday morning it did not look so badly.   He resolved to fight
it out.   He went and found others like himself—resolved to fight
it out.

"Thursday night's sleep made the people a new people.
27

The difference in their look and deportment from that of the day before was observed by everyone. The streets were filled with them, when on the day before the streets were silent of all except those who had the horrible work of taking care of the dead on their shoulders. Now women could be seen talking to women. They met on the corners in the residence portion of the town and told their adventures. The men began to discuss the future. By 10 o'clock the town was up and buoyant. The effect of that one night's sleep was marvelous. There was no longer any talk of abandoning the town. Galveston should be greater than Galveston had ever been. That was on the lips of everyone.

GALVESTON SAFER THAN EVER.

"On Friday I would not have given $10 for the place. On Thursday I would have given more for a lot than I would have given before the deluge and storm. Why? Because the pluck of the people came out through that night of rest. Galveston should be greater than it had ever been. That is what they said. Galveston was safer than before by the island's weathering such a storm. That is what they said, too. They began to talk of their own pluck. We have stood so much, but the world will say that we stood it well. If we can do as we have done in such a trial, what can not we do in the battle of life? Galveston shall be rebuilt.

"Galveston shall be the greatest of towns. Hurrah for Galveston! Thus they talked and went about their work of throwing up breastworks against disease by cleaning the town. Thousands of the people, negroes as well as whites, went about the work of burning the dead and cleaning away the debris. They asked nothing about wages, even those who had no property They had begun the fight. It was evident that they intended to keep it up. The cold, calculating speculator would have had something to study over if he had seen these people as I saw them the day after their one night's rest. Well, there was nothing wild in their determination. The island has not a break in it.

"There is a story of millions of feet being torn from it and cast into the sea. This story may be true if applied to some part of the island which I did not visit. But where I went it is not true. There was erosion. That was to be expected. Erosion would have come from a far less storm than this. I have seen a common "rise" on the Ohio River carry away more dirt than this storm carried from Galveston Island into the Gulf. The people of the interior know where the old Beach Hotel stood.

"They know where the chimney of that house was built. They know how far it was from the beach. They will understand the work of erosion. I stated that the brick of that chimney is not in the water. The piling on which the hotel was built are in some places in the water. In fact, according to my observation, the erosion at this point has not been above 300 feet. I went to the east end of the town and to the west end of it. The destruction of the island is no greater anywhere that I saw than at the the location of the hotel mentioned.

PREDICTIONS OF DISASTER.

"For years and years people have said that when the right kind of storm came the island would sink under it or be washed away like a house of cards in a flood. It was supposed that the great currents which would rush across the island would dig bayous as deep as the bay. These would grow in width, and finally the great island would be cut into small ones, if it did not disappear beneath the waves. But the result of this greatest storm on record? Why, there is not, as far as I could hear, and I made inquiries, a single excavation made from the Gulf to the bay or the bay to the Gulf. The island stands there in all things, except in the matter of the erosion mentioned, as stable and firm as it has ever been since man knew it. That is enough. The foundation is there. Man can do most any thing with a proper foundation.

"The only need now is stable and the right kind of houses. The old houses seem to have stood the shock better than the new ones. The reason of this is apparent. The old ones were built with an eye to storms. The new ones were built in book times. One young fellow told me that his house, the one in which he was born, had stood the storm of 1875 and every storm since that time without a quiver.

"'And it would have stood this one had it not been for one thing,' he said. 'That thing was the outward flow of the tide when the storm was over. The water rushed back to the sea like a torrent. It fell over a foot and a half in fifteen minutes, and as it went out it swept many a house from its foundations.' This flow, running like a torrent, swept across the island, and yet there was not left a single evidence in the way of excavations of its going.

"FOUNDED ON A ROCK."

"Attention was attracted to the house of Mr. J. H. Hawley, the brother of Congressman Hawley. He bought the property from an engineer who lived in Galveston some time about the flood of '96. He said he would build him a house which would stand. He placed the foundations on an iron fence two feet in the ground. This foundation was of brick. In this foundation he placed the railing of the iron fence running up three feet. At the top he placed filagree brick work. His house was braced well and the timbers were heavy and well put together. The storm did not phase it.

"The fence acted as a barrier to timbers from the houses which had been destroyed. It kept away the battering rams with which the waves assaulted all places. When the night's horrors were at an end the house stood intact. Even the cistern, which was on piling, stood the test and was uninjured. Now the Galveston people begin to consider the question of whether much was not their fault in that their structures were not of the kind that should have been built, when storms were sure to come.

"It is just such things as this that give them hope. As I have said, I despaired of the town when I walked among the dead bodies and saw the destruction on every side. But like the rest I got over this depression. I caught the infection of the new life when it came. I know that I speak the truth when I say that the life in Galveston now is capable of upbuilding the town, and building it better in every way than it ever was. Millions of dollars are invested in enterprises in the town. The men who have lost thousands, not to say millions, will not permit the rest to go without a struggle.

"The railroads running into the place and depending on the thirty feet of deep water, which is said now to exist in the channel, for export of the freight, will not agree to abandon the port, the only one of such depth for thousands of miles. Cotton factors in all the world, who look to this port for their supplies, will not abandon it. The monetary interest in the city of itself would save it even if the people were not so full of heart as they are. But above this, the poor people and the working classes have no where else to go. With many of them, it is too late in life to begin it anew. It is too late for them to build up acquaintances again. They have lost their houses, but the lots on which the houses were located are there.

EXTRAORDINARY PUBLIC CHARITY.

"Subscriptions to the amount of perhaps $2,000,000 have poured in for their relief. The well-to-do Galvestonian is determined that this relief shall go to those who are poor, that they may to some extent repair their fortunes. The rich themselves will build. In a month from now every man in the place will have all the labor he can perform. Every person will be busy. The work of up-building will in some measure rub out the recollection of the horrors of the storm. The Huntington estate will continue its work. Bridges of the very first class will span the waters between the island and the mainland. If great corporations can risk their money, as they are determined to do, why shall not a poor man risk his labor to build another house on the lot he owned?

"Why, even behind the business and necessitous phases of the matter, there rises a sentiment among the people. That sentiment is that we will show the world the stuff that Galveston people are made of. Galveston is all right. The storm could not kill her, though it wounded her to the death almost. There is pluck there. There is pride there. There is money there. And, above all, there are recollections there for the Galvestonian, and he will not be downed by wind and wave. Mark that."

Galveston, Tex., Sept. 18.—It would be somewhat difficult just now to give an answer to the question : " What is new in the situation at Galveston ?" The situation has resolved itself into a routine of hard and systematic work which presents no features of special or startling interest, and which will, in the end, have the effect of showing what a stricken people can accomplish in the face of a fearful calamity if they go about their work in the proper manner.

Generally speaking, conditions are improved at every point. The various committees continue to carry out the tasks they have in hand, and on all sides progress which would not have been thought possible is being made. Business concerns are resuming business or making every possible effort toward that end. Wherever possible, buildings are being repaired, at least to an extent which will protect their contents from the elements. Roofs are being replaced with temporary shields against the wind and rain, panes of glass are being placed in the frames which were destroyed by the storm, and stores are being cleaned out and the damaged goods they contain exposed to the sun and wind in order to dry them and thus minimize the damage done.

RAIN ADDS TO THE SUFFERING.

Early this morning there was a sharp shower of rain—the first since the storm—which, while it lasted but a few minutes, showed how absolutely necessary it is to get the buildings of the town in something like their normal condition as soon as possible. In the Tremont Hotel, the roof over a part of which is the office, came in in many places—through parts of the roof itself, through the broken skylight and through the empty window panes. Out in the residence portion of the town the rainfall undoubtedly caused at least a great amount of discomfort, for hundreds of houses which were not absolutely uninhabitable during the prevalence of fair weather were drenched and deluged, and the weary and heartsick people they sheltered were rendered all the more miserable.

It must be understood in this connection that while the work of repairing and making proof against the elements the building of the city is a very important feature of the situation, the matter of cleaning up the debris and disposing of the dead bodies therein is paramount on account of the danger which might result to the public health were this work not done as rapidly as possible.

Right here it should be said that, all reports to the contrary notwithstanding, there is at present practically no likelihood whatever that anything like an epidemic will result from the presence of decomposing bodies and the deposits made by the water during the storm. This is perhaps a broad statement, but it is one which backed by all of the eminent medical authorities of the city, who are certainly in a position to know if any one is.

DISINFECTING THE CITY.

Satisfactory progress is being made in the work of removing the offending matter, and a large amount of disinfectants of various sorts is being used where it will do the most good. The fear of an epidemic is one which has probably caused a great deal of uneasiness among the people who have friends and relatives still in the city, but from the standpoint of a layman, who has formed his opinion largely from investigation and from physicians who are interested in the work of caring for the health of the city, it may be stated, without any reservations whatever that the possibility of the prevalence in the future of any malignant disease is very remote indeed. Those interested may well set their fears on this score at rest.

The progress that has been made in securing a correct list of the dead is something wonderful, considering all the circumstances. Debris is being removed in all parts of the town and many more bodies were burned to-day. There are places here, however, which the workers have been unable to reach. Unless he goes into the mass of debris he can not imagine a condition equal to that which exists. There are places where the wreckage is piled so high and is in such an entangled mass that the workers will have great difficulty in getting it cleared away. There are some places where timber enough is stacked in a confused heap which is of quantity sufficient to stock a good-sized lumber yard. Houses have been torn limb from limb, as it were, and from beneath the unexplored depths of these places more bodies will be found.

Dr. J. Wilkes O'Neill, of Philadelphia, Secretary of the Associate Society of the Red Cross, received a letter from President Clara Barton, dated Galveston, September 19, in which she says :

CLARA BARTON'S LETTER.

'The conditions here are as much as you will gather from what you have read. Like some other fields that we have visited, it does not admit of exaggeration. One can scarcely imagine how it could have been worse, and yet one sees the city full of people left alive ; but when we think of the hundreds, and it may be even thousands, lying buried and decaying in great heaps of debris stretched for miles along the edge of what was once a town, it is hard to conjecture anything worse.

"Supplies are coming in from all sides. Of course, disinfectants were the first thought, to protect the living against the dead. All that can be done by the purification of fire is being done, the pyres of human sacrifice are burning day and night. I have never had any fears of an epidemic. We have in all our experience, you will remember, never known an epidemic to follow a flood. There will, I believe, be no pestilence here.

"There is a portion of the town containing business houses, which, while being terribly damaged, stood upright, and stores with their valuable contents were entirely submerged. The streets are filled with elegant goods, drying off, and it will be most reasonable charity to buy these of the merchants at the prices put on them—which are scarcely half—in preference to using first those that are sent, until these dealers are relieved in a measure.

"Every accommodation which the city can afford was placed at our disposal. A large ware-house is being fitted to-day ready to receive the carloads of goods on the way. Every official, from the highest to the least, calls to know what the Red Cross needs, and how it can be served. The grateful confidence with which they approach us, or even speak the name, makes one humble, filled with the fear that we will fail to justify the fullness of the confidence and hope that is offered.

"There seems to be an unusually large number of children with no one to care for them or who knows them. There are five or six hundred of these, it is stated, gathered in the houses of the poor, overburdened with their own wants, and yet cannot see another child suffer. We will help them as far as possible, gather them in, and the world will give them homes. It requires great calamities to show how generous and great are the hearts of the people of the land.

GUARDING AGAINST FUTURE DESTRUCTION.

"This city will be built up again, probably finer than before —and it was a fine city always—but I hope never without a protection from the storms. It is criminal to allow people perfectly unsuspecting to settle themselves and live on territory, however beautiful, that is morally certain at some evil moment of destruction. If Galveston is worth the possession that it is and has been to our country, it is worth its protection ; therefore we shall see that it shall not fail to implore of the government that it give work to its men and security to its inhabitants by a sea wall, which shall render it almost safe."

On September 20th we find this tragic recital :

"The storm has claimed another victim, and another soul that passed through that night of nights has gone to its reward. In chronicling the death of Miss Clara Olsen, another pathetic chapter is added to the thrilling tale of horrors which will never be told in its entirety. Miss Olsen, who was a graduate of the Ursuline Academy, and a most estimable young lady, lived with her aged mother on Twenty-seventh street, near the Ursuline

Convent.   When the storm rose to its height, and their humble
home succumbed to the destructive elements, mother and daughter
were thrown out into the surging waters.

"With one hand firmly grasping her mother, the young lady
bravely struggled against the wind and sea.   At last the branches
of a large tree were sighted above the raging torrent, and mother
and daughter exerted their fast failing energies to reach the
luring tree top.   As the two weary creatures neared the haven,
the daughter reached with one hand to grab a swaying branch.
She missed it and was carried backward by the wind.   Another
attempt and she secured a hold, but her mother had been torn
from her embrace by the sea, and was swept to her death beneath
the waters.

LODGED IN A LARGE OAK.

"In the early hours of the morning a rescuing party found
the almost lifeless form of the young lady resting in the tangled
branches of the large oak.   She was carried to the home of
friends and recovered from the shock.   But the thoughts of her
mother's tragic death, and the strange feeling that she was
responsible for it, weighed heavily on her heart and mind.   The
haunted thoughts racked her brain and slowly undermined her
failing health until the end came, when the broken-hearted and
weary spirit responded to death's sweet sleep. 'Mother's in
heaven and I'll soon be with her,' were the last words whispered
by the girl."

The work of clearing the streets and the city in general progresses with surprising rapidity and systematic thoroughness.
Street after street is being cleared up and the wreckage being
stacked away.   In accordance with an order from military headquarters, a new plan has been inaugurated in removing debris.
Instead of removing the debris and throwing it to one side to
remove the dead, it is ordered that the ridge of wreckage along
the beach be separated into two piles.   The first pile removed is
to be stacked out near the beach, where it can be fired and consumed.   The bodies found are to be disposed of on pyres placed

at convenient intervals between the two piles of debris. The second pile will be fired separately.

Military law has had a wonderful effect in placing the operations of all classes of work under one head, and the work of this general headquarters has won the highest commendation from the good citizens. Every ward has its supervisor, who reports daily all work done in his respective ward, files complaints, makes suggestions, and, in fact, keeps the general headquarters informed on all matters pertaining to the management of his district.

The ward supervisor has in charge a number of foremen, who in turn are in charge of gangs of workmen numbering from ten to twenty men. General Scurry holds the ward chairmen responsible for their districts, and the chairmen hold their foremen accountable for the actions of their gangs of laborers. Every department and branch of public service is under control of Brigadier General Scurry, who is ably assisted by Adjutant General McCaleb, Assistant Adjutant Reid and a score or more of efficient clerks and stenographers. At headquarters is a busy place. There all complaints, all reports, all requisitions and all operations of the military force of over 200 soldiers are filed and made note of.

FLOOD OF TELEGRAMS.

Every class of work has its corps of officers and clerks and every communication or record is carefully filed in the proper place. Hundreds of telegraphic messages are received and answered every day. Orders are promulgated and duplicate copies distributed around the city and a thousand and one matters must be attended to and all of them require prompt action and attention.

General McCaleb, who is in touch with the pulse of the community by reason of his office and who is familiar with the detailed operations of the military department, stated that Galveston was recovering amazingly from the calamity, and that it could be stated as a fact that in three or four days the city will have resumed normal conditions.

"This department has accomplished a great deal, and to the several hundred men who have devoted their time and attention to the city's welfare too much credit cannot be given," said he. "It is astonishing to note the spirit of the people of Galveston and the manner in which they go about the work of restoring the city. We have had no serious trouble either in having to impress men into service or in keeping the lawless element under control. Considering the condition of affairs, the city has been unusually orderly and very few arrests have been made of a serious nature. I have tried but five cases since the establishment of martial law, and that tells the story of how the law is being respected."

A MARVEL OF BRIDGE BUILDING.

The construction of the bridge across Galveston bay has been a marvel of hustling, and the dispatch with which it has been done reflects the indomitable energy, good judgment and skill of the men who had it in charge. The work was not started on the bridge until Thursday of last week, because the material could not be gotten to the place, but when it was started Vice President Barr and General Superintendent Nixon said : "We will run trains into Galveston next Thursday." Not many people expected that they could make good the promise, and almost everybody said they would be satisfied if the trains came within a fortnight. But the men who directed the work said that trains would cross on Thursday, and they stuck to it.

No work was ever beset by such difficulties as the work of restoring the tracks on the island and the mainland and the building of the bridge. The men on the track had to bury dead humans and animals, strewn by the hundreds over the prairies. They toiled in mud and water under a blazing sun. They had to remove hundreds of wrecked cars and twisted and tangled steel rails. They worked in the stench of dead flesh and the horrible odor of rotting grain and other wreckage. They built the track over a wreck-strewn prairie torn by the angry sea. It was difficult to get supplies to them and difficult also to get material.

The men who rebuilt the bridge worked the first day without

dinner. It was difficult to get boats light enough in draft to bring provisions or materials or pile drivers to Virginia Point. When the boarding camp was pitched it stood in a new made cemetery, where hundreds of victims of the storm lay unidentified, unshrouded and uncoffined.

For the first four days after construction was commenced, the bridge timbers were rafted down Highland bayou and West bay, a distance of seven miles, to Virginia Point. When the track on the mainland had been restored to Virginia Point, the delivery of material by rail began. The storm swept away most of the pile drivers around Galveston. One marine driver was sent out and put to work on Sunday closing the gaps aggregating about 1000 feet of trestlework, where the piling had been carried away. The next day another marine driver was sent out, and Assistant Engineer Boschke, of the Southern Pacific, built two skid drivers and sent them out to the work.

GETTING THE TRACKS READY.

When a reporter was at the island end of the bridge, at 9.30 o'clock yesterday morning, the Santa Fe track at the island had just been completed. The steel laying gang on the bridge was about a mile from shore, with the stringer gangs about half that distance away. The caps were laid up all the way to the shore. The Santa Fe has some pretty rough tracks for a short distance this side of the bridge, but the track through the west yards is in good condition and in fair condition the rest of the way in.

The Galveston, Houston and Henderson Railroad completed its island track to a connection with the Santa Fe at the bridge yesterday forenoon, and the Southern Pacific folks expected to complete their track last night. The Southern Pacific track is in very good condition. It has been rebuilt under the direction of Mr. E. K. Nichols, the agent of the company at this point. Nearly all the material used was gathered up from the prairie, some of it having been washed several hundred feet away. The work was delayed by a large number of wrecked cars. There was no wrecking outfit to be had in the city, and it was necessary to remove the wreckage by slow processes.

The Southern Pacific had about 200 cars in its west yard loaded with grain, cotton and merchandise. The yard was terribly swept and many of the cars wrecked, some of them being washed nearly a quarter of a mile away. The new double-track railroad of the Southern Pacific, near the bay shore, was torn to pieces.

Bradstreet's weekly report commented on the great calamity as follows :

"Galveston was flooded by one of the tropical storms which from time to time vex the southern coast, and as the result of its ravages, thousands of people have been killed, many more have been made homeless, and the city has been reduced to a condition which has led some people of a pessimistic turn to despair of its future. Views of this kind, however, do not take sufficient account of the energy of the American people or of the efforts which will be put forth to save to the commerce of the world one of its great ports.

SUPERIOR TO THE CALAMITY.

"It may take some time for Galveston to recover from the shock and the horror of its late visitation, the most destructive in its effects that has darkened the annals of the United States, but the pride and energy of its people may be counted upon to rise superior to even this calamity. Meanwhile the spirit of helpfulness and charity that has made the people of the United States conspicuous among those of all the world may be counted upon to aid in healing the wounds made by this signal disaster, so that, before long, after the succor most immediately and imperatively demanded has been furnished, the great Gulf port may be once more rebuilt and made to contribute as it has done in the past to the extension of the trade of the country, for whose commerce it has furnished a conspicuous outlet. Earnestly desirous of contributing to such a result, Bradstreet's will be glad to forward to the proper relief committees any subscriptions which its readers may deem proper to confide to it for the aid of the distressed city and its inhabitants."

St. Mary's Infirmary was the refuge where over a thousand of lives were saved from a cruel death, which the terrible storm seemed so anxious to administer, and if it had not almost ceased to be at a premium on account of so many displays of that most noble virtue, the heroism displayed at and around that institution that afternoon and night would be something remarkable. Men worked with five boats all of that afternnon, never tiring in their heroic efforts in bringing women and children from their frail dwellings to this haven of safety, and when these poor frightened people arrived they were still heroically dealt with by the Sisters of Charity.

ONSLAUGHTS OF THE STORM.

Of all those who took refuge there only two lost their lives, and those were in an outbuilding where some fifty-two had taken refuge. While the main building, where most of the people were, shook and trembled under the awful onslaughts made on it by the wind and water, and although the water kept coming up into that building until it stood three and a half feet deep on the lower floor, the building stood the shock bravely and not a life was lost in it.

Only those who were there and heard the terrible noises that the wind and water made in their mission of destruction, and only those who felt the building tremble and saw the houses around the place torn down and washed away, can realize the fearfulness of that evening and night. But during it all the Sisters were there, forgetting their own personal danger in quieting the fears of those who had come to them for refuge. It was indeed a hardened man that did not there that night ask his Creator for protection.

It was early in the afternoon that the refugees began to come. They came first from the flats east of the building, which is lower than the ground around and to the west of the Infirmary, the water rising there first. Then, as the storm kept increasing and the water rising, they began to come from the houses all around.

They waded in first, but it was not long before it was too deep and turbulent for that. It was then boatloads began to arrive, and it was in this way that the boats were brought there which afterward were the means by which so many others were saved.

No sooner would a cargo of precious lives be left at the door than the boat would be snatched away by ready hands and taken out to pick up another load. This was continued all the afternoon and up until it became so dark the men could not see which way to go after they had procured a load of frightened people. At first it was a comparatively easy thing to push the boats about and collect people, but along in the afternoon the wind had so increased and the water became so agitated that it was with the greatest danger this was done.

THE MEN STUCK TO THEIR WORK.

Notwithstanding this great danger and the hard task of handling the boats, the men stuck to it manfully. Not once did they stop for even a breathing spell. They realized the terrible danger that was before those who had not found a stable refuge, and stood to the work heroically. Many times were the boats almost swamped, and many times did the occupants and those who were pushing come within an ace of drowning, but looking death in the face and defying the wind and waters to do their worst, they kept at their mission of salvation until blinded by the darkness. Even before they made their last loads houses were beginning to go down, maiming and drowning their inmates.

After the men had shown the heroism born in them, it was the turn of the women to show their mettle, and they did it, every one of them. The Sisters forgot the great danger of instant death and went about comforting and trying to ease the fears of the many who had come to their institution seeking safety. But even they shuddered with fear when they saw the house formerly occupied by the patients from the Santa Fe road, go down, burying the refugees whom they knew to be in the building, go down, not onto the ground, but into a boiling, seething mass of water—that water which seemed to vie with the wind in its destruction.

Then when the water kept rising and the wind increasing in velocity, until it seemed that nothing could stand before it, it was, indeed, a time to be afraid. This condition continued for several hours, which seemed days to those whose hope was in its abatement, until about midnight the waters began to subside and the wind to decrease in velocity.

It was not until between 3 and 4 o'clock in the morning, however, that the water had gone down enough to allow any one to venture out. When the water had receded enough for one to go outside, it was found that the Santa Fe wing of the hospital, which was a frame building, was a mass of wreckage and had washed over against the rear of the Infirmary building proper. Knowing that there were refugees in the building when it went down, there was fear for their safety.

IMPRISONED IN THE WRECKAGE.

At once men began a search and found the frightened and maimed refugees imprisoned down among the wreckage. The work of getting them out was begun. All were found to be alive except two, a child and a crippled woman named Mary Sweeny. Although the survivors were alive, they were horribly cut up and wounded, which was proof of the terrible night they had spent and of their awful experience.

Then daylight came to present a picture such as none had ever seen and none ever cares again to cast his eyes upon. The clean sweep of the waters and their horrible destruction was in full view, and to add to the awfulness of the picture, the water had left several bodies of its victims at the door of the Infirmary. The people then left, not to go to their homes, but to go to where their homes had been. Many returned on account of having no place to go, and for days stopped at the Infirmary, their wants being administered to by the good Sisters. Since then, that institution has been, as well as a hospital where the injured have been attended to, a house of refuge where those made destitute and homeless by the storm have stayed.

Martial law, which had been declared, was suspended at the
28

earliest moment consistent with the peace and safety of the city, as will be seen by the following :

"Headquarters Office, Galveston, Texas, September 20.— Hon. Walter C. Jones, Mayor of Galveston, Texas—Sir : "I have the honor to report that, in my opinion, the conditions upon which you based your proclamation declaring martial law in Galveston, have rapidly changed. Order has been restored, the energies of the city have been directed into the proper channels, and the moment is opportune for a return to civil processes.

"I would respectfully ask that you prepare to resume the functions of civil government within twenty-four hours.

"Such troops of the Texas volunteer guard as may be necessary will be retained here while needed to aid the civil authorities in maintaining order. Very respectfully, your obedient servant,

"THOMAS S. SCURRY,

"Brig. Gen. Commanding City Forces."

CITY GOVERNMENT THE SAME.

As far as the general public is concerned, there is to be no radical change in the general government of the city. The change means a shifting of the powers that govern from the military to the civil process, but the good work inaugurated and expedited under the able and efficient direction of General Scurry will be continued and hastened to an early completion. General Scurry and his military command will remain in the city, and will be continued in service for police and guard duty as heretofore, except that they will act under the direction of the civil authorities.

The resumption of civil control of the affairs of the city will remove the bars to traffic into and out of the city so far as good citizens are concerned, but certain restrictions will be maintained to keep out persons not wanted in this community. With the military force and the increased police department and sheriff's department there will be enough men to guard all the gateways to the city and patrol the streets of the city.

Mayor Jones and General Scurry desire it to be clearly understood that the lawless element will be shown no quarter. Mayor Jones has instructed General Scurry that he wants law and order maintained at any cost and that the military command shall be backed in their work.

From to-day noon it will not be necessary for persons desiring to leave the city to secure passes, nor will it be necessary for persons desiring to come to Galveston to secure passports. However, all gateways will be guarded and suspicious characters will be subject to scrutiny and examination before being allowed to enter the city.

The sporting element, including gamblers and others of the sporting fraternity, will not be allowed to come to Galveston, and if found here their immediate deportation will follow their conviction. Drunkenness will not be tolerated and all arrests upon this charge will be prosecuted to the severest extent of the law. On this score Mayor Jones and General Scurry are most emphatic and they seek to impress the people most firmly in this regard.

SALOONS CANNOT OPEN.

" I want it distinctly understood that the suspension of martial law does not mean that the saloons may open up," said Mayor Jones yesterday. " I desire 'The News' to announce that the saloons must remain closed until further orders and that no back or side door business will be permitted. The saloons were not closed under martial law, but were closed by my order before martial law was proclaimed. The proclamation closing them, therefore, holds good and will not be revoked until I am satisfied that it can be done with safety. Although martial law will be raised to-morrow, General Scurry is going to remain with me and assist me as he has so admirably done during the past ten days."

The citizens of Galveston were not in a position to look after the affairs of the city government under the circumstances. It was a public calamity that befell the city and every citizen had his burden of sorrow to bear. There is no gainsaying the fact that the establishment of martial law was the best course to be pursued under existing circumstances and the beneficial results are plainly manifest on every hand. Public spirited citizens volunteered their services and men who held back were promptly impressed into public service for their own as well as the good of every person living in Galveston.

Organization of this vast army of workers was perfected, departments were instituted to conduct the different classes of labor, and under strict military discipline order was restored. The clearing of the streets, burial of the dead, caring for the living and providing for the restoration of the city was commenced in earnest under military supervision and urged to most flattering success. There are few who regret the institution of martial law, but there are many who would deplore the removal of the military forces.

General Scurry, who has won the commendation and heartfelt thanks of this community, is a man of few words. He says he tried to do his duty and he is glad that the people of Galveston appreciate the fact. He says he was never treated more kindly and he feels that the citizens were alive to the fact that what he did was for their own good and the good of Galveston.

PLACE AND ORDER OUT OF CHAOS.

Mayor Jones stated to a " News " reporter yesterday that the people of Galveston are obligated to General Scurry for the way he has conducted the affairs of the city in this hour of peril. He has brought peace and order out of chaos and with a remarkable display of executive ability he has brought sunshine from darkness and gloom. Without the slightest friction, without disturbance of any consequence, and without aid or advice from anyone, he has wrought wonders and restored the city to normal conditions.

As the work of removing the debris progresses more dead are found buried beneath the ruins. There are no official records at hand of the bodies found, and it is probable that the record will never be completed. It is known that there are many bodies found and disposed of by volunteer parties who failed to make a detailed report of the work. It is also known that there were many dead swept to sea and to mainland. Only those found on the island and on Pelican are accounted for. Even those on the mainland were not recorded. Some of them were from Galveston and some were from that section.

Several hundred of these bodies were disposed of by relief parties coming into Galveston on the first relief trains which came near the bay shore after the storm. The trains could not get to the bridge nor to Virginia Point, and the relief parties put in their time burying the dead. No record was kept of this work.

It is not known how many bodies are still in the ruins. It is known that there are many dead buried beneath the debris yet undisturbed. There is absolutely no way of estimating with any degree of accuracy how many unfortunates remain in their death prisons beneath the mountains of wreckage yet to be released. It is believed by some that many surprises await the removal of all the wreckage.

LAST TRAIN OVER THE BRIDGE.

Mr. J. T. Grimes, of near Brandon, has a fine farm and is a substantial and reliable citizen highly esteemed and respected. He was in Galveston during the hurricane and related a remarkable experience. He said :

"I left here Friday and got there Saturday evening. The storm was on when we got there. Our train was the last that went over the bridge before it went down. The water was then rising rapidly and nearly over the tracks. The conductor asked if any one had ever seen it that high before. Nobody had. A carload of cattle that followed us on the bridge went down with the bridge."

" How came you to go to Galveston ? " asked the reporter.

Mr. Grimes hesitated, as if considering, then said : "Well, sir, it was this way : I was sitting on the gallery with a baby in my arms—the child of that man standing there, whose wife cooks for me. Suddenly it was just like some one came to me and told me to go to Galveston. It came so powerfully I sprang up and handed the baby to its mother and told her I must go, and ordered my clothes prepared for the trip. In two hours I was on the way."

"Did you have any idea what you were summoned to Galveston for?"

"No; only I knew there was some disaster threatening my children. I did not know what it was, but I could not refrain from going."

Asked further about the trip to Galveston, he said the passengers got into the depot, but he never saw or heard of any of the train crew, and he thought they all must have perished. "I got a negro to show me the way to where my daughter, Mrs. Chilton, lived. The water was then all over the city and rising rapidly. When we got to Eighth street, my son-in-law here, Stufflebram, called out to me across the street. He had seen and recognized me. I went over and we started on. There was a lot of timber and driftwood floating, and some people along the way were pulling all of it in the houses they could get.

HOUSE WASHED TO FRAGMENTS.

"We had to push it apart to get through in places, and some of them laughed and said push it to them, and I did so, and they began hauling it in. Nobody thought how serious it was, but looked on it as merely high water. A little later all those buildings along there were destroyed and all the people there drowned. Stufflebram had taken his wife up to Chilton's and Clarkson also, because it was a litle higher ground there. We finally reached it, on Twenty-second street, just opposite Harmony Hall. We were all in the house together when Prof. Smith sent word over from Harmony Hall that we had better get out at once.

"We went to the hall, and the last of the party had hardly cleared the sidewalk when a large brick building gave way and mashed Chilton's house to fragments. We staid in Harmony Hall until the cyclone ceased, though it looked once as if the hall would go when the roof blew off. It was the awfulest time I ever saw. My daughters and their families were saved, and I am truly thankful for it. They said at Galveston that we were the only family in the city who all got away alive. It must have been providential.

"We left there Thursday and went to Houston, where we were nicely treated. I never saw such charitable people and I just love Houston. Charity was a mile high there. They fed us and clothed our children and paid our fare to Hillsboro. The railroads, too, were nice, and did all and more for us than one could expect. I never saw or heard of such a time as we experienced at Galveston. Nobody can tell it as it was. It is impossible. For two days we didn't think of eating. The dead people floating, the ruins all about us, destroyed all sense of hunger. It wasn't the water that killed, death seemed to be in the atmosphere, there was so much electricity and such furious winds. It is awful, even to think of."

CHAPTER XXII.

Galveston Storm Stories—Fierce Battles With Surging Waves—Vivid Accounts from Fortunate Survivors—A City of Sorrow.

A RESIDENT of the stricken city gave the following graphic narrative of his experiences, which help to make up the dark picture of Galveston's agony and desolation :

"Some people asked, 'How did you feel when your house went down in the storm?' It is a question easier asked than answered. I was among the few who lost their houses early in the storm and before darkness set in. Up to fifteen minutes or less before the house went down I had hopes that it might survive the storm. For three hours before it went I watched the waters patiently, mostly from the south windows, but of course had the restlessness natural to people who are waiting for a great crisis in the lives of themselves or those dear to them. To sit perfectly still under the circumstances was impossible.

"A few moment's rest by a south window was followed by an uncontrollable desire to go to some other part of the house to see how matters were looking. Wandering from one point to another, the round of the house was made, and once more I found myself back of the south windows to watch the waters from the main danger point. I do not think that I or any of my family could have been called excited. There was a restless, uneasy feeling among us all, but actually no fear. When my wife left the house she fully expected to return to it when the storm was over. My boys were with her and my little girl, and for probably half an hour I was alone.

"During that time I was partly engaged in keeping the north and east doors closed. The wind blew them open several times, but did not break the hinges. When one was blown open torrents of rain poured in, and I remember thinking of the task the women would have in drying the floors and disposing of articles

440

that had suffered from the water. From this it can be judged that even at that time I was not looking for a total wreck. How did I feel? I was not excited. I was not in fear of my life. It seemed to me that what I regretted was the property loss and the struggle I would have to repair damages.

"But a total loss—a sweeping away of everything I had in the world—was not thought of. In fact, it is hard to realize now, a week after the storm. The mind cannot rest all the time on one's loss, and at times it seems when I want something at my house all I have to do is to go out and get it. My good wife last night caught herself the same way. Speaking of the need of a shirt for Sunday, she asked : 'What do you want to buy a shirt for, when you have three or four—oh, I forgot ; they were lost in the storm.' We have been housed safely, and it has seemed more like a visit than a total loss of property to her, except when she has felt the need of something that was carried away in the storm.

THE OLD FAMILY BIBLE.

As time passes and we begin to realize that all is gone, there is a desire to find something, even if it is of no value, when the wreckage is cleared away. My wife expressed the wish that the family Bible might be found, be it ever so dirty and torn. It contained records that could be nowhere else secured, and if a new one is purchased and the records again written, it must be entirely from memory.

"But though we lost all, we were among those families where no life was sacrificed in the storm, and in that respect were more fortunate than some of our neighbors and many of our friends. The number of broken families in Galveston seems innumerable. As one walks the streets he meets friends of whom he had never thought, and the first greeting is 'Did you save all your family?' An affirmative answer brings out the remark, 'You are lucky ; many have lost not only all their worldly goods but their families.'"

"In many instances the reply is that your friend has saved his family but has lost his other relatives. It seems that there is scarcely an individual in the city who has not lost some relative. Where the loss is not positive it is believed to have occurred, because no news of the supposed dead ones has been received.

"Tales of rescues and narrow escapes continue to come to light, but to record them all would require the work of hours in writing up and fill the paper full to the brim with this class of matter alone.

"The stores and groceries are again getting down to business, but they are badly handicapped by damaged stock, more especially the dry goods and clothing stores. A complete overhauling of these establishments has been necessary and the separation and sorting out and drying of damaged goods is not yet complete. Those which have fully opened for business are crowded with customers, and in some instances it is still necessary to keep the crowds out, letting in only a few customers at a time.

HARD WORKED CLERKS.

"The clerks are a hard worked set of people just at the present time. With the changes in overhauling the stock they have not yet become acquainted with the exact location of articles called for, and it requires a search to find them. This naturally retards the quick execution of business, and throws additional labor on those waiting on the customers. But order is rapidly being evoked out of the chaos existing after the storm, and in the course of time things will be moving along with their old-time uniformity.

"The street forces have got fairly to work on the business streets, and they are rapidly assuming a more passable condition. Drays are hauling away the trash, and in the course of a week or so the worst evidence of the storm will be removed. The damaged buildings will take longer to repair, but the streets will present more of the old-time aspect than for the past week.

"Work on the pile of wreckage back from the beach is progressing, and now and then one hears of bodies taken from the ruins, clearly showing that the full extent of the loss of life has not yet been realized.

"In this storm the usual conditions have been reversed. Whereas, in wrecks by wind, water or rail, first reports greatly magnify the loss of life, while in the present case it seems that the estimate of lives lost is increasing rather than diminishing as each day passes. While the total will never be known, it will be far above the early estimates.

"The relief system is fairly in operation, and it is now claimed that no one need go hungry except able-bodied men who refuse to labor. But it should be understood that those desiring relief should go to the different ward headquarters, or send some one. The committees and heads of departments have no facilities for forwarding goods to the destitute in the various portions of the city. Their time is taken up with procuring and distributing supplies from the various headquarters.

REASONS FOR BURNING RUINS.

"Suggestions have been made to burn the pile of lumber of all kinds in the rafts, but this seems both impracticable and unadvisable. If it can be preserved, every stick and board will be of use hereafter. The only reasons for burning the rafts given are that it will cremate the bodies of the dead known to be in some and supposed to be in almost all of them. Sickness resulting from the decaying bodies is predicted if this is not done. But if it is attempted more loss of life is likely to occur from it than will result from sickness arising from putrid bodies.

"Once let the fire demon get hold of the immense masses of lumber and the remaining portion of the city may be wiped out. No one who has seen a conflagration in a city can doubt that all the fire apparatus in Texas would be ineffectual to stop the march of the flames to the bay in case of a strong south wind. Many houses, partially wrecked, are in the piles, and many household goods belonging to people who have lost all may be recovered. Disinfect the rafts as far as possible, and remove the lumber. Preserve it as far as can be done conveniently. It will be needed for building temporary homes for the destitute.

"We have thousands of homeless people in the city, and while free transportation is offered to those who wish to go, there are many who have no friends to go to. These people must be cared for. Some are now crowded in the homes of friends, and others are located in the large buildings in the business district. All are only temporarily provided for. Something must be done to house them, at least temporarily, when cold weather approaches. It would be well to issue permits for temporary buildings to be erected from the debris of wrecked homes, without regard to the fire rules of the city as they now stand, but with the distinct proviso that they should be removed after a certain date. I am no advocate of ramshackle shanties as permanent buildings in the city, in any part of it, but I appreciate the fact that we are facing an emergency that requires prompt action to prevent severe suffering in the near future.

A CHARITABLE PEOPLE.

"Galveston's people have not in the past turned their faces against the suffering poor, and I do not think they will do so in the future. While strong, substantial buildings should be required in permanent structures, there is no reason why the wreckage should not be used in erecting temporary shelter for the homeless. Lumber promises to be a scarce article when once the resumption of building is begun, and every board, rafter and scantling on the pile of wreckage should be saved.

"There is valuable wreckage strewn through the rafts. There are desks and trunks that may contain papers of value to the owners but valueless to others. These should be placed aside and saved for identification by their owners. Articles of personal apparel may some time be of use in settling the estates of the dead. Wills may be found stowed away in frail desks that by some chance may have escaped total wreckage in the storm. Jewelry and personal ornaments are not unlikely to be found in places where least expected. People fleeing from wrecked houses do not stop to search in trunks for jewel boxes. Many of them doubtless remain in the mass of chaos-like wreckage and may be recovered as the piles are cleared away.

"In a walk over the flats on Friday I turned off the water—or rather turned the faucets so as to prevent the water running out—wherever I saw a water pipe, and I would suggest that others seeing water pipes should do the same thing. The waterworks employes are doubtless looking after these pipes as far as practical, but where so large a district is covered as in the late storm it is almost impossible to find all of them. Water is the prime necessity at this time, and every pipe turned off saves that much water when the works once start up."

Mr. David H. Hall, city electrician, completed a thorough canvass of the condition of affairs regarding the electric plant of the city. He said it was like awakening from a nightmare to get around and hustle to repair the appalling losses and destruction of property. Speaking after his canvass of the city and inspection of the city's electric light plant, Mr. Hall said :

PREPARING TO LIGHT THE CITY.

"While the damage to the municipal electric light plant is very extensive, there is a great deal of salvage and nothing to interfere with an early resumption of operations. Temporary sheds will be erected at once over the engines and dynamos and they will be soon put in condition for service. The principal mains, on Market street and Ball avenue, I find to be intact. The engines can be operated as soon as the steam pipes and the breaching to the boilers can be repaired. We will have the business district between avenue A and Church street, Twentieth street and Rosenberg avenue, lighted within a week or ten days. This is about the earliest date that we deem it safe to turn on the current owing to the amount of debris in the streets, the large number of men engaged in saving property and the menace to life and property that an electric current might prove to be.

"One circuit in the business district will be completed in two days. The entire lighting service in that territory embracing Tenth street to Thirty-seventh street, avenues A to avenues K and L, can be restored and in operation within sixty days. The lighting service for the public buildings will be reinstalled as soon as the buildings are put in condition to receive the wiring. I have received such generous and noble offers of assistance from strong financial quarters in the north that we will be able to secure all the material necessary to restore the plant and system at our own terms and have as long as the city wants to pay for same. The most regrettable and deplorable feature to me is the loss of fifteen of my employes and their families.

"I am not inclined to give up or lose courage or heart, and I feel like the old king at the siege of Megara, who is reported to have said when taken prisoner: 'My palace has fallen about my head, my city is in flames, my state ravaged by my enemies, my wife and children I know not where; no cloak to shield me from cold, but I have lost nothing. I have my intellect, my faith, my courage and my loyalty. These can not be taken from me, and, having them, I have lost nothing.'

OVERCOMING DISASTERS.

"Despite our tremendous losses, we can save much and make good much if we have not lost our heart and courage. Galveston will be restored; if not by us, by sturdier men who are equal to the task. I was living in Chicago at the time of the great fire in 1871. Many men, and some of them of apparent good judgment, declared that Chicago would never be restored; would never rise from the ashes. Within one year there was a better Chicago than ever before. Four years ago I went through the track of the St. Louis cyclone, and the same was said of that city. Now there is nothing to be seen there but scars of that awful storm.

"The same will be with Galveston. In three or four years, or less, Galveston will be as great, if indeed not greater, than she was before the storm, if the people are true to themselves. It is surprising what can be done where willing and cheerful hearts go to work and work in the right way. Galveston citizens are not only hopeful but determined that the city shall be resurrected, as it were, and when that spirit animates us enough is said."

"Did you ever feel the thrilling experience of being on a ship as she was just in the act of sinking?" said a sunburnt sailor to a citizen. He was one of the survivors of the ill-fated dredge boat which sank near Texas City.

"The night of the terrible hurricane at Galveston," he continued, "it was predicted by several of us on board the dredge boat that a destructive storm was approaching, and it was deemed best to put out all anchors. We had no more than done so when the wind veered to the southeast. We had not put out all of the anchors any too soon, for of all the high winds and waves, those that lashed our boat were the worst I have ever seen.

"I have been in many a shipwreck, and realized that it was only a short time before I would be in another world, for I felt the boat dragging her anchors and drifting inland at a terrific speed. We were then some eight or ten miles from shore.

BOAT PASSING OVER TREE TOPS.

"It seemed to me only fifteen or twenty minutes before the fury of the storm struck us. I saw our boat passing over tree tops. I knew we were then approaching the bay shore, and possessing that knowledge as to when to leave a sinking ship, I procured some fifteen life preservers and gave one each to the crew, and told each man how to put them on and to follow me to the upper deck, and be ready to dive off when I gave the word.

"They were all frightened nearly to death, and only two succeeded in getting their life preservers on and reaching the top deck with me. When the fearful moment came for man to battle with the winds and water, I gave command to jump. In an instant three of us made a plunge into an immense breaker, which carried us high into the air.

"I looked back and could see nothing of the boat that I had just abandoned. I have been informed that she went ashore about a mile and a half west of Texas City. If the other ten poor souls were saved, I have not heard of them.

"Do you know there is something thrilling and exciting about being shipwrecked when you are near the shores. I presume a man feels the same that a parachute man does when he gets near the ground in his downward flight. If his parachute works all right he is safe. With a sailor he must first adjust his life preserver and try to avoid the rocks and trees."

Mr. E. W. Dorris, of Houston, was one of the relief party that helped to bury the dead as they washed ashore from Galveston. At daybreak he was unable to secure a boat of any kind to cross, but he and two others constructed a raft of some loose planks and started across the bay, reaching the draw of the Galveston, Houston and Henderson bridge. They were unable to go any further or cross the channel, the party being entirely exhausted, and after signaling distress for more than an hour, the tramp ship grounded at the wagon road bridge, in the middle of the bay, finally sent a lifeboat to the rescue of the party, taking them ashore to the Galveston side. Mr. Dorris states that the party saw no less than 600 dead bodies between the bridge and the Santa Fe depot.

GLARED AT THE THRONG.

He stood on the corner of Main and Congress streets in a half dazed condition. He glared at the great throng that was passing, some on business bent while others were seeking the latest news and hunting their relatives. He did not observe that he was being watched, nor would he have cared, for the expression upon his face showed him to be a man of great determination to be brave under the greatest misfortune of his life. You could trace in his every action a man in great sorrow.

But he had to show his emotion and give vent to his feelings, which so long he tried to smother ; mechanically he raised his hand and covered his face in order to hide his grief. As he took his hands down he wiped both eyes, which had been flowing with tears. At this juncture he was approached by a citizen who, in kind tones, asked him of his solicitations and grief.

He said : "I am trying to be strong both in mind and body, but I cannot suppress my feelings in this public thoroughfare. Yes sir, I am suffering, mourning for the dead ; my wife and

sweet baby are among those who have gone to the great beyond."

"How did it occur and how did you escape?"

"Six weeks ago I kissed her (my wife) and my darling baby
good-bye and took the first train for an interior town, where I had
secured employment. By correspondence it was arranged between
us that she was to come to me on Monday. The storm occurred
Saturdy night and she and the baby were drowned.

"Were the corpses found?" was asked.

"Yes. She had the baby clasped in her arms. She was
found within fifty feet of where our once happy home stood. She
was given as decent a burial as circumstances would permit. I am
sorry, but I cannot talk any further upon this subject, as my grief
knows no bounds."

THE USUAL QUESTIONS.

After uttering the last sentence he pulled his hat down over
his eyes and he passed into the crowded throng that was headed
down the street. He looked around and said:

"There are hundreds of cases that are similar to mine, the
result of this great hurricane."

"Was your father, mother, brother, sister, son or daughter
or other relatives saved from the Galveston horror?" are questions that are frequently heard asked as friends meet and greet
each other in Houston.

"Yes," said a gentleman speaking to another, who asked him
if his son was safe. "I have just returned from Galveston with
him. You would hardly recognize him, though, bruised, battered
and bleeding, with a bandage around his head and his arm in a
sling. These wounds were not caused by trying to save himself,
but others. He was boarding with some life-long friends of our
family who had been extremely kind to him. When the storm
was at it height and danger appeared on every hand and it was
deemed advisable to abandon their home to its fate, Charlie was
the sole protector of two lone women. He took the elder one first
and carried her to a place of safety, after being washed about
29

by the water and debris of trees and buildings for an hour or more

"When the storm was raging in its greatest fury he returned to the home of his friend for the young lady. Reaching her he was surprised to find the water nearly five feet deep all around the place, and the house careened over, nearly ready to fall. With his arm tightly clasped into hers they started for the high ground. The Gulf was now raging in all its madness; billows were piling many feet into the air, and each billow seemed to vie with the other as to which could raise its head the higher, and do the greatest destruction.

"Sometimes Charlie and his precious, helpless burden would be entirely submerged for some time. At other times they would be lifted off their feet and carried a distance of fifteen or twenty feet. After regaining their equilibrium they would again forge forward to meet the elements, of danger of life and limb. Each wave had cunningly hidden beneath its sprays missiles of death, such as pieces of planks, house tops, buggies, wagons, pianos and other articles too numerous to mention. It kept these two wearied and exhausted creatures nearly all the time dodging and escaping those death missiles.

PIANO TOSSING IN THE WATER.

"When they had nearly reached a place of safety they noticed a larger wave than usual coming. Charlie saw upon its crest an upright piano being tossed about as though it were a feather. Would it miss them? was the question that flashed into both of their minds.

"Onward it came, with its ivory keys, showing it was once a messenger of joy and happiness, but it was now a messenger of death, for with one mighty bound it went straight up into the air upon the foaming and frothy water and plunged straight down at Charlie and his fair companion. He saw that he had to make one more death struggle in an instant. He threw himself in front of his lone midnight charge and placed her arms around his body and told her to hold on to him with all her strength.

"The supreme moment was over—the piano had been thwarted in its effort to crush them, but in the struggle Charlie found that he had been torn loose from his lady friend, who had been swallowed up by the raging wave. He at once began a search by feeling and diving for her. Not a flash of lightning, nor the glimmer of an arc light was visible, for, like the life of this dear creature who was engulfed by the torrent waters, they had gone out.

"At this juncture a remarkable thing happened. He had decided to dive once more. He did so, and grasped the hand of what he thought to be his missing friend. He was overjoyed, but upon bringing her to the surface he found that it was not her, but another.

"The waters had increased so in depth by this time that it was impossible for him to attempt to wade, and about this time a house top came along and he crawled upon it. While drifting about on it, he picked up four boys from 6 to 12 years of age. His frail craft finally drifted to a place of safety, where he and his young companions were rescued."

ATTRACTED NO ATTENTION.

So many are the stories, so harrowing the details, and so miraculous the escapes that for the present the experiences of different persons on the night of the storm in Houston attracted no attention; in fact, if a person wished to tell of his experience in Houston that night he could scarcely find an interested listener.

Nevertheless, Mr. Fred. Chadly, who lives near the Arkansas Pass depot, came as near losing his life that fatal night as did any who passed through its fury in the city of Galveston and escaped. Mr. Chadly left the Capitol Hotel for home about 10 o'clock, not realizing the intensity of the storm.

After an hour's fighting the strong wind and rain and dodging falling trees and flying debris of all kinds, he arrived at his house only to find the front door impregnably barricaded by a large fallen tree. Nothing daunted, however, Mr. Chadly immediately proceeded to make his way around to the back of the house and gain an entrance there.

He was walking in a crouching position with his head bent down so that the wind would not strike him squarely in the face, and was not looking ahead, therefore the large cypress cistern, as it tottered on its foundation preparatory to being blown down, escaped his notice until he was too late to dodge it. The cistern was blown over, turning twice in rapid succession, falling top downward directly over Mr. Chadly.

The cistern was about one-third full of water, but as Mr. Chadly was already thoroughly wet, the water made very little difference, as it soon ran out. Mr. Chadly called loudly for help, but owing to the pandemonium caused by the hurricane, no one heard him. The next morning the carpenter came to fix the cistern, and after raising it discovered Mr. Chadly, who was nearly smothered to death.

HOUSE ROLLED MANY YARDS.

One of the experiences of the storm was that of Miss Reine Stanton of Houston, who, with her father and a younger sister, were camping on her farm two and a half miles from Letitia. The house rolled for a distance of 200 yards and then collapsed. The girls were rescued several hours later in an unconscious condition, but, though quite seriously injured, they may recover. All the buildings on the place were wrecked.

"You have often heard that men are fond of the 'jug,'" said one of the refugees. "Well, I am fond of two jugs, for they are the cause of my being here to-day. I owned a little shanty on the west end of Galveston Island, and, like many others who lived there, I thought and argued that we were not in the storm center, and had seen the water come up near my shanty many times before and recede. This time it not only came up to my little home, but into it. After waiting patiently for it to go down, it kept climbing higher and higher into it. It dawned upon me all of a sudden that all means of escape had been cut off.

"I looked around for something that would bear my weight

upon the water. I saw in the corner of my house two two-gallon jugs. I took them and securely fastened a stopper in each and got a piece of rope and then fastened them to my body by passing the rope around under my arms, and securely tying them to each other. I then went out on the gallery and when the crash came I dove off into the maddening waters. I suppose that I was carried about twenty miles down the island and thence back, God knows how far, and inland about eight miles. When I became conscious it was nearly daylight Monday morning. I walked here, where I have some friends, and have been recuperating.

"Yes, I believe in jugs, at least for life saving purposes only."

An amusing incident occurred at the International and Great Northern depot. One of the ladies' relief corps from the North was highly indignant and pitched into Superintendent Trice because sleepers were not attached to the train going down to Texas City.

WANTED PALACE CARS.

"We've rode in those Pullmans all the way from New York, and it's a shame and outrage that you intend making us ride in a day coach now. We want those sleepers to live in." She was wrathy, but when the colonel informed her that before the party got out at Galveston they'd have to walk on dead bodies, wade through slush and slime and have a tough time generally she'd think a day coach was a palace, she said no more. It is evident that some of the "relief corps" consider the trip a pleasure jaunt. When they have been in Galveston a few days they will probably change their minds.

"First reports of storm damage are always rather exaggerated," remarked a gentleman of the Arcola plantation. "At first everything looks as though it were completely wrecked, but after the calm comes and the work of straightening up begins it is astonishing to see how little property really is damaged. We had considerable damage on our place. The cabins blew down and the convict house was unroofed. When this occurred we turned all the convicts out on the prairie and the next morning all of them voluntarily reported for duty except six, and they worked like trojans assisting in the work of cleaning up. The cane crop suffered considerably, but is by no means a loss. It is recuperating nicely. Very little corn was lost, because most of it was gathered."

Mr. Fred. Erickson, who returned from Galveston, says he saw a lady, who was drowned among the many others on a burial barge, who had on a fine watch, diamond earrings, several diamond finger rings; besides, he noticed that she wore gold clasp garters with her name upon them.

He asked the party in charge why these valuables were not removed and the garters removed as a means of identification, and he was told that they were not allowed to remove anything from the bodies, no matter how valuable and how it might aid in future identification.

JEWELS ON THE DEAD.

He noticed a woman floating in the water, and he and a policeman turned her over, and attached to her bosom was a very fine gold watch with her name upon it. He called the policeman's attention to the importance of securing the watch for future identification, and was given the same information.

Mrs. John P. Smart returned from Galveston on board the steamer "Lawrence," along with about 400 women and children. Mrs. Smart had been in Galveston for some three weeks, and came away on the first trip made by the "Lawrence." She said of her experience during the storm :

"At 3 o'clock Saturday afternoon, in spite of the efforts of the lady of the house to persuade us all to remain at home, we set out for a place of safety, the Atlanta Hotel. The water was then three feet deep on avenue P. On the way to the hotel I saw three women drowned. They were making their way down the street and were blown down by the wind and lost. We left the house none too soon. After the storm not a trace of it could be found.

"The wind was then blowing at the rate of about sixty miles

an hour. At 11 o'clock, when the wind was at its height, the water around the Atlanta Hotel was nine feet deep and the building shook terribly. As the windows were blown in, the men stopped them up again with doors. But when the worst was over and the house still stood, we found that not one of all those who had crowded there for refuge was lost.

"The sight on Sunday morning defies description. One could not look in any direction without seeing scores of human bodies. One building in the west end, in which between 400 and 500 had taken shelter, went down and every human being in it was lost. Not a house was left along the beach. On the bay shore I saw three men on horseback dead. Horses and riders, with reins gripped as if to ride through the peril at any cost, had passed over the river.

MAJORITY KILLED OUTRIGHT.

"There were a number injured, but the overwhelming majority were killed outright. The injured were taken care of at the Sealy and St. Mary's hospitals, both of which were injured, but not totally destroyed. There are doctors enough in Galveston, but medical supplies are needed.

"One pitiful incident came under my observation. Mrs. Baldwin clung to a raft for twelve hours, from six o'clock Saturday night until six Sunday morning, holding a child, a baby two years old, in her arms. The baby begged her to save its dog, a beautiful St. Bernard, too. Of course this was impossible. The baby was killed in its mother's arms by flying debris and the dog was saved.

"The horror of that Sunday morning I shall never forget; white, ghastly corpses turning up their faces to the light, or clinging to a child or loved one, their twisted, agonized faces, showing the anguish of that last unequal struggle against death, were everywhere. One woman I saw holding fast to two bags of silver, as if to say : 'Better die than be a beggar.' Nearly all the west end people were lost. Those who sought safety in large houses had but the grim consolation of dying in company, for the whole of that portion of the city was destroyed. The work of rescue began as soon as the storm abated. But the crowd of survivors on the street Sunday morning was pitiably small. They seemed to me scarce 10,000. Clad in next to nothing, bathing suits and the like, the sun brought them only the sight of dead relatives and friends—some starvation.

"There was no food and no water. For two days I tasted no water and food was scarce indeed. The city, as soon as soldiers could be gotten, was put under the strictest martial law, under protest of Mayor Jones and Chief of Police Ketchum. These officials desired to enforce the law by civil authority. Fully seventy-five men have been killed for looting the dead and refusing to halt when ordered. Every house has to be guarded lest thieves break in them and steal.

OCEAN GIVING UP ITS DEAD.

"The 'Lawrence' which at first was under the control of the relief committee and charged nothing for passage, now exacts $2 per capita to Texas City. Besides this, there are three boats in the service. The only way to get away from Galveston is to go by boat to Texas City, where there are about 1000 women and children and almost no accommodations.

"The bodies have been all cleared away from the central portion of the town and there is a continual stream of corpse laden floats, drays, etc., to the barges. The west end has been set on fire, as the mass of wreckage there makes recovery impossible. But the beach is lined with bodies yet. Every day they wash up upon the sand. Old ocean is giving up its dead.

"The women and children will probably be compelled to leave. They are badly in need of clothes and avow that they want no rags but nice new clothes, 'to avoid epidemic.' I attribute the terrible loss of life," concluded Mrs. Smart, "to the fact that the people trusted Galveston too much, and clung too long to a failing hope. This has often appeared to be a strange trait of human nature."

A correspondent furnishes the following account of a well-known family :

" One of the saddest cases which has come to light is that of the Jalonick brothers of Dallas. No man is better known than Isaac Jalonick, of Dallas, who was so long the secretary of the Texas rating bureau, and he and his brothers have hosts of friends all over the State. There were three of them, George, Ed and Isaac. The family of Ed Jalonick, consisting of his wife, son and daughter, the children being young, came to Galveston several weeks ago to spend the latter part of the summer on the Gulf coast. They had taken a house on the southern part of the island, west of the Denver resurvey.

ONE OF THE SADDEST CASES.

" It was far removed from the city, and was in a section which was so badly storm swept that not a house remains. Mr. Jalonick came last week to take his family home, but the bad weather interfered and the trip home was postponed. Saturday the storm came, and when the two brothers, George and Ike, in Dallas, heard of the disaster they came here at once, to ascertain the condition of their brother and his family. They went to the former home and but a vacant spot met their anxious search for the house which had sheltered their loved ones. They decided to make a search among the dead on the island, in the hope that they could find the bodies and give them decent burial.

"For three days they were on the hunt. Mounted and accompanied by a team, with burial boxes, they moved across the island in every direction, examining every body they found. During their journey they viewed not less than 150 corpses. Now and again they had found him or her whom they sought. Here it would be a piece of clothing, there a feature, and again the form, but each time only disappointment repaid them for the task of love, devotion and duty they had undertaken. It was an anxious search with hope deferred.

" They had no idea that they would be successful, but so anxious were they to have their relatives given decent burial, so strong was the desire to prevent them being in an unmarked grave, or consigned to the deep, or perhaps cremated with hundreds of others, that they decided to continue until every chance of a success was lost. Thursday at noon they were successful. They had searched for six miles west, and two to two and a half miles across, when suddenly Isaac recognized a shirt worn by a body which he found.

IDENTIFIED BY LAUNDRY MARK.

"It was a blue garment, one the brother had worn when with one of these brothers who was searching, and its color and cut brought to mind days when he and the lost one were together in happiness and in health. They investigated and turning back the collar they found the initials of their lost brother, as the garment had been marked by the laundry. This removed all doubt, and the body was put into a box and prepared for burial. It had badly decomposed, having laid for five days where the waves cast it, beneath the warm rays of a summer sun, and exposed to the elements of the night. With the helpers they succeeded in gathering it tenderly into the confines of a rough box.

" 'They dug out a grave a few feet deep,
And there in earth's arms they laid him to sleep.'

"They did not abandon the search because of finding one body, but continued it further on, and at 3 P. M. they found the boy. The little fellow was not far from his father, showing that the two had remained together as long as life remained in the parent. He was identified beyond all doubt. He was laid by the father. The two graves were marked, and it is the intention of the surviving brothers to have the bodies removed to the family lot in Dallas as soon as conditions justify. They will continue the search for the body of Mrs. Ed Jalonick and the little girl."

It is at a time like the occasion of the Galveston storm when real heroes are made, when individuals become men of the hour, and when the true manhood of a man is made known to his fellows. The silent, modest, quiet man of every day life has never the credit that is his due, because he does not seek the notoriety which is necessary. There are men praised by the people of the United States because they were on a boat at Santiago or Manilla, or followed a commander up a hill at San Juan; by Great Britain because he was of Modder river, Ladysmith, or possibly Pretoria; and by other countries because of distinguished bravery in battle.

They were men who had been schooled to danger, who had gone into the fight, with the one idea in mind, to kill and be killed for the honor of the flag they followed. They went into the conflict believing that it meant death or honors of war, and their heroism was of a character qualified by the conditions leading up to it. Not so with the men who passed through the flood of last Saturday and enrolled their names upon the tablet of fame. There are many instances, but they can not all be told. They were frequent during the terrible times of that day. One of these has already been told, that of the act of the boy of George Walker, of Austin, a little fellow not yet in his teens, who, by his heroic act, saved his aunt, who was all but drowned.

GALLANT WORK OF FIRE DEPARTMENT.

But one has not been told. The people of the west end of the city speak in the highest praise of the boys of No. 6 fire station, which is located on Broadway, near Thirty-seventh street. When the water was very high, they secured their horses in the basement of the Broadway school building, tying high their heads so that they would be saved, and they were all brought out alive. The men then worked manfully for those about them; man after man, woman after woman, with many children were brought out of the water by these men of the fire-fighting force, and taken to the large school building opposite their station. They saved many people. There were 1200 people in this building at one time, and every one of them was saved.

Mrs. Frank Nichols, her daughter and little Miss Selkirk were down the island at their summer home, and Mrs. Nichols tells of the bravery of Captain White of the "Wasp." The "Wasp" saved Captain Andrews and family of the life saving station. The sails blew away and the boat capsized with all on board, but the mast broke in the water and she righted herself. She drifted all night and landed in the bayou near the Nichols place Sunday morning with all safe.

The son of Mrs. Nichols got a horse in Galveston at 2 o'clock and managed to get to them, saving their lives. Their home was wrecked, but the young man built a rude shanty of the wreckage on the shore and they secured enough food in the ruins of their home to give the people on the "Wasp" a Sunday dinner. Mr. Nichols was in town. His home was completely wrecked and the clothes were torn from his back by the wind and wreckage. He is a little disfigured, but still able to be about.

MAN CARRIED THIRTY MILES.

Mr. A. A. Van Alstyne had a large quantity of provisions, such as rice, canned goods, etc., stored with him. He and his family escaped unhurt, and every since have been using their house as a basis of supplies for the needy in their immediate neighborhood.

Mr. Henry R. Decie, who lives eight and one-half miles down Galveston island, was in Houston, and reports that he was at his home when the storm began, but took his wife and children to the house of Mr. Willie Raine, a close neighbor. After reaching there he says the water, with one bound, raised four or five feet which took the house off the blocks.

" My wife and I were sitting on the foot of one of the beds at that time, which was 6 o'clock. We felt the house quiver, and my wife threw her arms around my neck and kissed me and said, 'Good-bye, we are gone.'

"Just then the house crushed in and we struggled hard to get out. My baby boy was in my arms a corpse, having been killed by a falling timber. Another wave came and swept the overhanging house off my head. I looked around and discovered that my wife was gone and the remaining part of the house was drifting apart. Catching a piece of scantling I was carried thirty miles across the bay, landing near the mouth of Cow bayou."

CHAPTER XXIII

Heroic Incidents—Arrival of Relief Trains—Hospitals for the Injured—Loud Call for Skilled Labor.

A LADY correspondent who went from Houston to view the wreck of Galveston reported as follows :

"We are only just beginning to find out what this awful calamity has been to the people in this vicinity. The first shock is wearing off, the long lists of dead and missing are getting to be an old story now, and the sick and suffering are crawling into our places of refuge. Some of them have been sleeping on the open prairies ever since the storm, most of them, in fact, men with broken arms and legs, sick women and ailing children.

"They crawl out of the wreck of their homes and lie down on the bare ground to die. Our relief corps are finding them and bringing them in as fast as they can. Dr. Johnson and his party came in from the Galveston district and reported that they found over 5,000 people and attended medically about 200 patients.

"While we were standing at the door of the hospital talking things over a man rode up on horseback. He threw his arms up to attract our attention.

"'Is this the relief hospital?' he said.

"Dr. Johnson told him that it was."

"'Ive come in from the Brazos bottoms," he said. 'The folks there are starving. There is not a pound of flour left and the children are crying for milk. There are so many sick people there that we don't know what to do. Can you send some one down?'

"Dr. Johnson had not slept for twenty-four hours. He had not had time to get a full meal for thirty-six hours. He was worn out and travel stained, but he heard what the man told him.

"'All right,' he said. He picked up his coat, put on his hat and turned to his assistants. 'Come on, boys,' he said. 'Let us go down and get the cars into shape. We'll get down to your place, my man, just as fast as the Lord will let us.'

"The man on horseback leaned over his saddle and tried to speak. Something in his face frightened me, I called to two doctors. They ran out and caught him. He was in a dead faint. When we had brought him to he laughed sheepishly. 'I don't know what's the matter with me,' he said. 'Ain't never been taken this way before.' The doctors looked at each other and smiled, but the nurses' eyes were full of tears. The man had not tasted food for thirty-six hours, and he had ridden fifty miles in the broiling sun of Texas. Dr. Crossway and his men are down the island relieving the sick and burying the dead.

HOSPITAL OVERCROWDED.

"'Alkali Ike,' they call Dr. Crossway, that is because he is tall and rawboned and comes from Texas himself. If a man gets a nickname in this part of the world you know that he is loved. The women and children who came from the district where 'Alkali Ike' is working know his name and their eyes fill with grateful tears at the mention of it. The hospital at Galveston is well named. The corps is effectively organized and we hear from there that they are doing splendid work. Our own hospital here in Houston is in ship-shape condition.

"We have built a partition or two, put up temporary quarters for a dressing room for the nurses and doctors. The great ice boxes are filled and the range, which burned wood, has been replaced with a gas range to keep the heat down as much as possible.

"There is a little railing just back of the great wide door of the hospital where the entrance to the theater used to be and there the relieving nurse sits with her assistants. The bookkeeper has her desk there and the man who answers inquirers is standing there.

"This is no ordinary hospital work. People come crowding to the doors, and nearly all night they come. Some of them are hungry, some of them are sick, some of them are hunting for missing friends, and some are merely curious. Some are neighbors who come to offer help, some are women bringing delicacies to offer to the sick. It takes the entire time of three persons to attend to this crowd of visitors intelligently.

"We are keeping records of every case entered at the hospital. The name and age and final disposition of the case. These names and the facts concerning them are kept on the books for reference, so that people are easily identified, and so that any one who has contributed to the fund can investigate and find out just exactly what became of the money he gave. It is hard to pick out a case in the hospital which does not deserve special attention. A man was brought in with three broken ribs. They were broken the night of the storm, he having been working ever since burying the dead.

"A young man was carried to the hospital on a stretcher late last night who was wandering up and down the island for the past three days trying to find the body of his young wife. He found and buried over forty bodies which had been overlooked by the burying committee, but he did not find his wife. He is lying out at the hospital now in a stupor.

SUFFERING UNTOLD AGONY.

"A boy of twelve was brought in who has been suffering untold agony from an injury to his eye for four days. He has not had a soul to help or to speak to him, and all he has had to eat in that time was a handful of crackers. A woman came in at 11 o'clock last night. She had a baby in her arms and three children hanging to her skirts. None of them had tasted food for nearly three days.

"A young girl was brought in by one of the outside corps at 9 o'clock last night. The relief corps found her huddled up in an empty freight car, laughing and singing to amuse herself. The doctors say food and care is all she needs to restore her to reason. Three-fourths of the people who come in are mentally dull. The physicians say with proper care that most of them can be cured."

One of the many touching incidents of the storm occurred at

Houston on the 18th. Mrs. R. Qualtrough and Mrs. Will Glass were at the International and Great Northern depot Monday intent on the relief of any who needed, when they saw a little woman with a baby of about eight months in her arms. The mother was weeping bitterly, so the two kindhearted friends went up to see what was the matter. The stranger said she had just arrived from New Orleans to find Galveston shut off from the world, and her husband, mother and sister were there, and she feared they were all lost. Mrs. Glass finally prevailed over the little woman to go home with her, where she could care for her.

Tuesday Mrs. Qualtrough was busy at the market house helping to distribute the clothing and food to the sufferers, when her son came to her and told her there was a man from Galveston in the room, and he wished she would go to him. The man, who was bruised and beaten in his fight with waves, was in great distress. He wanted to get to New Orleans, but had no money, his wife and child were there, and he had to tell her that her mother and sisters were drowned.

WOMAN DRIFTED NEARLY THREE DAYS.

An instinct told Mrs. Qualtrough the truth. She asked what was the size and complexion of his wife, and how old was the baby. Looking at her strangely, the man described exactly the woman and child found at the International and Great Northern station. " I believe your wife is here," was the extraordinary comment on his story. Calling to Mrs. Ward, the fish merchant, Mrs. Qualtrough asked her to take the man to Mrs. Glass' home, and the husband and wife met. It was a pitiful scene, for while she had got her husband back, the poor woman learned of the loss of mother and sisters.

A woman was brought into Houston who was two days and a night drifting about in Galveston bay, bringing with her a parrot which she had held above the waters all that time. The parrot and a bag of money was all she had left.

Mr. A. C. Fonda, a patient at the Houston infirmary, was a clerk in the Gulf, Colorado and Santa Fe freight office at Galveston, and lived on Broadway. He tells a tale of his experience which is miraculous. He remained in his house until it was blown down, and then, in some miraculous manner, he was blown into a large cypress cistern which was about half full of water. After being in the cistern for about an hour a kind of twister struck it and blew all the water out, but left him. When the cistern was relieved of the water it rose and was finally washed out on the Gulf, where it remained until Monday morning, when the wind and tide brought it back to Galveston and its occupant was rescued in a thoroughly exhausted condition.

Beaumont, Texas, September 14.—Mr. A. Zwirn, one of the Beaumonters who left for Galveston on a freight train Monday afternoon, returned yesterday after having spent fourteen hours in the stricken city. Mr. Zwirn reached Galveston Tuesday evening, having succeeded in getting across the bay on a small sailboat. He went to the Island City to search for friends and found a greater portion of them alive.

FIRST CITY TO GIVE ASSISTANCE.

Mr. Zwirn says Beaumont was the first city to get assistance into Galveston. He was present at a meeting of Galveston citizens when it was announced that a boat with ice and water from Beaumont had arrived, and he says the fervent thanks which went up from the gathering and the tribute one of the men paid to the Queen of the Neches made him feel proud of his residence here.

"It was, however, not the fault of Houston," said Mr. Zwirn, "that the Bayou City did not get supplies to the Island City quicker. The train on which I came to the end of the railroad track had several cars of provisions, ice, etc., and many more were standing on the tracks when we arrived. The trouble was the absence of transportation across the bay to Galveston. There were many boats, but the owners found it more profitable to carry passengers from $1 per head up than to transport supplies. I can not describe the joy with which the boat from Beaumont was received. It not only contained that which the sufferers needed

30

badly, but it was evidence that there was communication with the outside world, and revived the spirits of many who had become despondent."

Under the rules and regulations prescribed by the military laws governing the city, the work of clearing the streets, disposing of the dead and cleaning the city in general have progressed very favorably. The plans mapped out by the military department brought the operations down to a system. Where there is order and system much can be accomplished, and this was most clearly demonstrated by the reports of one day's labors in this field. Nearly three thousand men were organized in gangs and squads of from ten to twenty-five, working under the direction of foremen, supervised by ward superintendents, started out early in the morning and worked faithfully until dark. The detailed results of their labors were not to be had, but enough was shown by the reports to demonstrate the value of organization.

THE ARMY OF WORKERS.

All foremen were ordered to report daily at military headquarters, where a large force of clerks were kept busy chronicling the amount of debris removed, the number of dead bodies disposed of, etc. Another force under command of Adjutant-General McCaleb was kept busy printing orders issued for the guidance of the work, laws governing the protection of property and the lives of citizens, etc.

The militia was placed on guard duty in all parts of the city and the city police and sheriff's department are co-operating with the military authorities, which is supreme in control of the city.

While the power is invested in the military authorities, Brigadier-General Scurry, commanding, Adjutant-General Hunt McCaleb directs that men may be impressed into service in cleaning the streets and performing other labors incumbent upon the department, it is gratifying to know that very few men had to be impressed into service. Some few held back under one pretense and another, but when given to understand that they would be compelled to work they invariably joined the army of laborers.

The beach and the western part of the city presented the picture of about one hundred or more pyres where human bodies and the carcasses of dead animals were disposed of by fire. Separate pyres were designated for human bodies and animal carcasses and the work progressed rapidly. The gruesome task was heartrending and many able-bodied men succumbed to the terrible ordeal. The bodies recovered yesterday and those still buried beneath the debris are in an advanced state of decomposition and utterly beyond recognition or identification unless by the clothing or some ornament worn by the dead. Ninety-five per cent. of the bodies recovered are naked.

The hurricane, aided materially by the action of the raging torrents, invariably stripped the victims of all vestige of clothing or other articles that might lead to identification. Another remarkable fact, which shows the force of the storm in packing the wreckage and debris in high mounds, is seen in the amount of water held by the wreckage.

MILES OF WRECKAGE.

Six days of sunshine and seven nights of cool Gulf breezes have failed to draw the water held by the wreckage which, jammed into water-tight ridges, formed tanks to hold the salt water which inundated the city. While the ground all around these ridges is dry and hard, the removal of the top ridge disclosed several feet of water. At least 20 per cent. of the bodies recovered yesterday from the wreckage were taken out of water.

A reporter who attempted to make a circuit of the rescuing parties working on the beach and throughout the western part of the city, noted the finding of 123 and the discovery of at least twenty more bodies, which were so hemmed in by wreckage that it was impossible to get them out. It is impossible to estimate the number of dead buried beneath the miles of wreckage.

When the forces started out yesterday morning it was thought by many that the greater number of dead had been removed from the prisons built by the storm. The work had not progressed far before the workmen began to dig into ruins where bodies were found. During the hasty tour of the reporter he witnessed the finding of ten bodies between Tremont and Thirty-first streets along the ridge of wreckage which marks the path of the storm from the east to the west on the beach and extending inland from three to seven blocks.

The most important journal in Texas, the "Galveston News," commented as follows :

"The 'News' desires to repeat what it has already said to its now unhappy people on Galveston Island. The sorrows of the past few days are overwhelming, and we all feel them and will continue to feel them so long as we live. It could not be expected that our friends and relatives and loved ones should be so suddenly torn from us without leaving scars from which those in the ranks of maturity can never recover.

FORTITUDE OF SURVIVORS.

"But it is all in the past now. We cannot recall our dead thousands. Wherever they sleep, beneath the tireless waves or under the arching skies, we will love their memories and recall as long as we live the unspeakable and mysterious tragedy which destroyed them. But it must be remembered that we have more than 30,000 living, and many of these are children too young to have their lives and energies paralyzed by the disaster which has overtaken us.

"Our homes must be rebuilt, our schools repaired, and the natural advantages of the port must sooner or later receive our earnest attention. We have loved Galveston too long and too well to desert her in the hour of misfortune. Our distress and destitution are going to be relieved, for a sympathizing country is already providing for temporary needs. This people are too proud and self-reliant, however, to lose spirit and fail of duty. In the very darkness of the moment there is light ahead, and we must look to the light ahead. Even in the midst of our dead and our ruins light appears.

"The railroads are bending every effort to repair the bridges and place us once more in commercial communication with the mainland; the telegraph companies, putting their heavy losses behind them, are restoring their wires as fast as men can do it; the telephone company is doing likewise, and the wharf companies are similarly engaged. As the 'News' understands it, the Southern Pacific Company proposes to double its force to complete the improvement which was so damaged by the storm.

"The waterworks will soon be restored, the street railway repaired, and all the other elements of a metropolitan life placed in working order. The ships will come into the harbor for traffic and get it, and that traffic will afford employment to thousands. If the people will take heart, they will soon find that all has not been lost, and, moreover, much is to be saved. If we lost 5000 people, there are more than 30,000 to be provided for; if we have lost $15,000,000 in property, we still have that much to save and restore.

REBUILDING GALVESTON.

"There is much to hope for and to strive for, and we must hope and strive to save ourselves and meet the expectations of the world. The 'News' received a telegram last night from a great New York paper inquiring if Galveston would rebuild. The answer was sent back that Galveston did not intend to succumb to her crushing misfortune, but would again resume her place as the great port of the Gulf. This is the duty of the people here, and the 'News' expects in good time to see all the energies of the people concentrated upon the great work of recuperation and restoration. Will this expectation meet disappointment? Knowing this people for nearly sixty years, the 'News' answers, No."

Colonel John D. Rogers was at Toronto, Ont., when the big storm swept Galveston. He and Colonel D. C. Giddings, of Brenham, have gone North together for a vacation every summer for several years past, and this year they picked Toronto as the place of recreation. As soon as the news of the storm reached them they started for Texas, and Colonel Rogers arrived on Friday, the 14th.

To a gentleman who called on him and asked for an expression of his views as to the future, and his intentions as to the various properties he is interested in, Colonel Rogers talked most hopefully and confidently :

"So far as property losses are concerned," said he, "I suspect I have lost about as heavily as any men in Galveston in proportion to the property I own here. But this constitutes no reason why I should be discouraged. I felt that way even before I reached Galveston. Colonel Giddings, from the newspaper accounts of the storm, doubted somewhat that Galveston would come again. But I told him Galveston was bound to be restored. I told him I didn't believe the wharves were gone ; no man who knows anything of the construction of wharves could have believed that story. I told him that the maintenance of Galveston as a port for the west was imperatively necessary, and that if the people of Galveston laid down and got off the island, other people would come here and build up a city.

RESUMING BUSINESS.

"A week in Galveston has made me still more confident that I was right in my conclusion. The work done during the past week has been wonderful, and within another week, I believe, every kind of business will be going on as before. We are again ready to receive cotton, and I have instructed our shippers to send it in. Before this business season is over we will be doing as much business as ever before, and before twelve months have passed our buildings will be restored.

"I know that croakers will say that this cannot be done, but the croaker will never rise in any country. I don't believe in croakers. I believe with "The News," that this storm has indisputably proven that the island will not wash away. If that storm, the severest in the history of the world, did not wash the island away, nothing ever will eliminate it from the map. And it is not conceivable that another storm of that severity will ever strike again in this spot. The flood of the Brazos river, in last July, was unprecedented.

"There had never been such a flood before, and there had never been an overflow of that river in the month of July in all the history of the State. Again, the previous rises of the river had been gradual, but in July, 1899, the river rose two and a half feet in one night. All of that was very unusual, and it is improbable that it will ever be repeated. The storm at Galveston was likewise very unusual. The waters came from the bay and Gulf simultaneously, and met on the island. They did not go up Buffalo bayou, as they did in 1875, when lives were lost at Lynchburg.

"A great deal of the loss of life has been due to flimsiness of many houses put up here in recent years for rent. The lesson which Galveston has received is a terrible one, but it will lead to safer and better buildings. It is true that some good buildings were wrecked by the jamming of wreckage from flimsy buildings, but the fact that we have many buildings standing unharmed, proves that we can build enduring structures.

GREAT DETERMINATION.

"I have given my attention since coming home to the restoration of the Gulf City compress and other property in which I am interested. We are going right ahead, with greater determination, to increase our business and to build up the city."

"I am glad to see you alive" is the greeting with which a Galvestonian now meets his fellow-citizen on the rubbish blocked streets of the once proud city by the Texas coast. Those who have not been here can not realize what it is to a man to meet a friend alive, or to find a relative who since Saturday has been missing from the huddled few remaining who are gathered in some desolated, wrecked and wind torn building, which but a week ago was a happy home of happy people.

When a drama has finished, the curtain falls, and as the orchestra plays some popular air the audience makes its way to the street, talking for a few moments of the characters and the scenes, but shutting out from mind, with the falling of the curtain, the happiness and the pain which was depicted by moving characters who but represented a story of man's imaginative mind. Not so with this.

No curtain can be drawn and the stage remains ever before them. They have it now as a desolate picture to gaze upon, and they will have it forever, wander where they will upon this earth's surface. No curtain can force it from the mind, and no effort can efface it from the tablets of memory. Many of the actors in this great drama are not here. Some of them yet remain, and their stories are stranger than fiction which Jules Verne or Dumas have written.

Amid the smoke of battle, when men meet men in armed conflict, and thousands fall beneath the leaden hail, there is time taken to make a trench and consign to a resting place the bodies of the fallen thousands, and the chaplain has his moment to ask a merciful God to receive His own. Not so with this. No trench can be made for those people who have been found where the angry waters threw them up, where the falling timbers caught them, or where they are floating on the waters of a waved lashed shore.

QUICK WORK NEEDED.

They are disposed of, not as humanity would direct, or as sentiment dictates, but as necessity demands, and it is not with the accompaniment of a clergyman's prayer, or the simple words of the man of the cloth, that "God has given and God has taken away, blessed be the name of the Lord ; earth to earth, dust to dust and ashes to ashes." Bodies have been consigned to that element which destroyed the vitality of the material—the water and the waves which came from the storm tossed Gulf of Mexico to invade the portion of land which nature set aside for the habitation of man.

This could not be continued for long. The conception of man's mind, which first suggested this disposition, proved to be wise judgment in the first emergency, but nature's laws prevented a continuance of the plan, and it became necessary to turn to a quicker and more convenient method, as the decomposition which fast began a destruction of the mortal, rendered handling impos sible. Cremation was then resorted to, and without the facilities of science to assist, the destruction of the remains was affected by using burning debris, upon the places where the corpses were found.

Humanity may think this is terrible and sentiment may revolt at this story, but that humanity and that sentiment is not to be found in Galveston. Here the people have thrown aside custom and formalities, all men are equal and that equality extends throughout the whole city. No custom of dress, no formality of appearance and no false modesty enters into one's mind. Men and women cover their nakedness with what they can procure from neighbors, from friends or from the relief committee or what perchance was saved from the wreckage of their own homes, and they proceed with the work of looking after their own, their friends and their neighbors, as necessity demands. All people are neighbors here and all have a common interest.

NEW CHART OF BAY NEEDED.

A phenomenal thing has occurred in the bay. There are now bars there which have never before been seen. They are across from the Twenty-fifth street wharf and from the Twentieth street wharf. There may be others, but these two long ridges of sand have been noticed by the observing men who know the bay front as well as they know anything, and it is possible that when the water is sounded quite a number of these will be found in various places. It may require a new chart of the bay to determine the damage, and until this is done the greatest care must be exercised in moving about the harbor.

Those who live away from here will have an idea of the wreckage when it is stated that within an area bounded by Thirteenth street on the west, the end of the island on the east, the Gulf on the south and Broadway on the north, there is not a standing house. Between Broadway and Postoffice street and between Thirteenth street and the end of the island there is not a house standing. In the territory south of avenue K and east

Tremont street all the way to the Denver resurvey there is not a house standing. There are other portions of the city which are in a similar condition, but it is impossible to tell them now.

The Sealy hospital was first reported as having been blown away, but it survived the storm in a most remarkable manner, notwithstanding the fact that it is situated where the raging waters were the highest. With the exception of broken window panes, a damaged ceiling and a good drenching of a number of the rooms, with their contents, it is virtually unharmed. The nurses' home, which stood opposite the infirmary and was used in conjunction with it, was completely demolished, but with no loss of life.

There was no loss of life among the regular inmates of the hospitals. A number died during the storm, but they had been brought in in a dying condition.

CLOTHED ONE THOUSAND.

One thing developed by the storm that has not been commented upon is the manner in which the so-called "society men" have taken hold of things. They have worked like Trojans, every one of them, and have proven that the wearing of good and fashionably cut garments is no evidence of lack of manhood. Some of the first to go out in charge of gangs of men clearing away the debris and burying the bodies were the young fellows one meets at cotillions and fashionable functions. To-day their fair skins are cracked and burned with sun and wind, their hands blistered and burned, and their clothes covered with mud and slime. They glory in their young manhood, and are not one bit ashamed to go about with their colarless negligee shirt open at the neck, or their sleeves rolled up. Some of them have not shaved since the storm, and look more like subjects for charity than many who apply for relief.

One young man, who probably clothed one thousand people in two days, is going around in a very much soiled, borrowed shirt. His home was destroyed, and all the clothes he saved he had on his back at the time. He has not had time to buy new clothing, although he has probably clothed one thousand people. He would as soon have stolen as to have taken one of the nice clean shirts he was giving away. Besides, it never occurred to him.

Mr. J. Martin, one of the refugees at Houston, who passed through the storm at Galveston all right, save a gash in the head, a black eye, a mashed nose, and a sprained arm and leg, says that on the night of the storm he sought shelter in six different houses. As the last of these houses in turn succumbed to the force of the hurricane, Mr. Martin was plunged into the dark and angry waters, amid its splintering ruins. Numerous times, he said, falling timbers would knock him unconscious for a few moments, and after regaining his senses he would be so full of water, so exhausted and weak from his desperate exertions and loss of blood, that he felt like giving up all hope and allowing the water to draw him under and relieve him of his sufferings.

FOR A MOTHER'S LOVE.

He says he saw other men who were physically stronger than he do that very thing. Still he would not give up and he struggled on. He had no wife or child to live for—there was just one person in the world whom he fondly loved, and that was his mother. Every time, he says, that he decided to let himself go down beneath the water and drown his mother's face would appear before his vision. Clearly and distinctly he could see the look of reproach in her eyes at his threatened weakness, and each time this vision would spur him to greater effort, and he would battle on until he reached another place of safety.

Finally, when the storm had spent its fury and he crawled into a place of safety, he drifted into unconsciousness and remained in that condition until late Sunday evening. Mr. Martin says that his mother lives in New York and he knew she was safe, but says had it not been for the image of her face which constantly appeared before him he certainly would never have lived to tell his experience.

There are no better hearted people in the world than the Americans. Not a case of genuine suffering or honest and unavoidable misfortune need ever go long without generous assistance in any part of the United States, if only the people know that it is a proper case for their sympathy. And this is true whether the misfortune be an individual and private or a public calamity.

The papers in all parts of the country, without exception, called the attention of their readers to the destructiveness of the hurricane in Texas, expressed their profound sympathy with the sufferers and urged instant relief measures. There never was a more general manifestation of popular solicitude, or a readier or more widespread response to an appeal for assistance.

And yet this is the American rule in such cases. The humblest and the highest give and give quickly. Nothing is too good for the unfortunate when it is known that their misfortune could not be warded off and that they are left utterly helpless.

It makes us love our country better when we find it has such a people within its borders. We regain the confidence in mankind which may have been shattered in sordid every day business. We feel that down in the heart, the good impulses remain, and that only something a little out of the ordinary is necessary to reveal (to slightly paraphrase Goldsmith) that

> To relieve the wretched is our pride,
> And e'en our failings lead to virtue's side.

CHAPTER XXIV.

One Hero Rescues Over Two Hundred—Traveler Caught in the Rush of Water—Report of a Government Official—How the Great Storm Started.

THERE are many people who are composed of the material that constitutes a hero, but the majority pass through the time allotted to them on earth without having the opportunity of demonstrating the fact to the world. On the night that the awful catastrophe visited the city of Galveston few were those who had not this opportunity presented to them.

Of course there were some who failed to develop this quality. The every effort of these was directed with the one supreme purpose of self preservation. Others there were who devoted their services unreservedly to the helpless and in consequence their names will never be forgotten by those whom they preserved from a watery grave.

Some of the deeds of this nobler class will never be known—not even after the relentless sea gives up all its dead. There is one name, however, which will be recorded and preserved in the memory of some as long as that never to be forgotten night of the hurricane at Galveston is remembered by the sons of men. That name will be taught by mothers to their children in the age to come as the name of one possessed of undying courage and heroism.

The name is that of Zachery Scott, a young medical student who was at St. Mary's Infirmary at Galveston on the fateful night. Alone and single-handed Mr. Scott rescued over 200 souls from the very jaws of death. St. Mary's Infirmary is composed of a large brick building and several wooden structures, and the latter were entirely destroyed by the fury of the wind and the water. In the wooden buildings were nearly 200 patients who were too sick and weak to battle against the elements and the raging storm,

477

besides a score of the sisters who were at the time acting as nurses.

When the water began to rise, Mr. Scott, who was in the brick building, went over to where these patients were quartered and soon returned, through water waist deep, with one in his arms. Over 200 times he performed this feat, although before the task was completed the water between the two buildings was over six feet in depth.

Back and forth, during all the stormy night, he went and every time he returned another soul was saved from a dreadful fate. When the storm was at its height, the debris was flying in all directions, the resistless waters carrying people on to destruction and when he was weak and weary from his exertions, the inmates of the brick building begged him not to attempt the feat again. But still, with a dauntless courage born of devotion, he never faltered in his duty, and every person in the doomed building was taken to a place of safety. Such courage, devotion and heroism deserves a place side by side with that of the greatest heroes who ever lived.

A MARVELLOUS ESCAPE.

Harry Van Eaton, a well known traveling salesman for Tenison Bros., Dallas, was in the midst of the disaster, but saved his life in a marvellous manner.

"It was the worst trial of my life," he said with a shudder. "I shall never forget its horrors. I arrived in Galveston Saturday morning and immediately went to the beach with a party of us and for a while had a good time in bathing. But the waves soon became furious and we were notified by the life saving crew 'to get out of the water as there was danger coming.'

"Luckily we obeyed their command, for when we had dressed, the waves were enormous. We had to wade waist deep in water before we reached the Tremont Hotel. The wind kept increasing and at this stage of the game I began to realize something awful was going to happen.

" At eight o'clock that night the wind must have been going

a hundred mile an hour gait and it was about this time that the roof of the hotel gave away and the sky-light fell in on the thousand or more people who were there. I walked through three or four feet of water to reach the front door.

" There was a regular mill-race rushing past the door and I was caught in it, but by God's help and by expert swimming I managed to reach the mainland.

" It was a terrible experience ; whirling by me were hundreds of bodies, more than I dared to count, crushed and mangled between timbers and debris. Men, women and children sinking, floating and dashing on, many to an instant death. I also passed many dead horses and cattle. How it all ended, that I reached safety, I hardly know ; but I kept my presence of mind and by God's help was saved."

PERILS OF A RELIEF TRAIN.

One of the passengers on the first relief train that went out of Houston on Saturday evening, during the prevalence of the storm, to bring the people in from La Porte and Seabrook, gives the following description of the trip :

" Little did we know what trials were before us as we started out for La Porte and Seabrook at 8 o'clock on that fatal Saturday night. But we did know our loved ones were in danger, and with a brave volunteer crew in charge of the train, and trusting to the good God above to care for us, we started, hoping for the best.

" The first obstacle that impeded our progress was a pine tree of about two feet in diameter across the track. This was soon cut in two and we journeyed along, the wind almost blowing the train off the track. We had gone only a few miles further when we collided with two box cars that had been blown from the switch to the main track.

"After a considerable delay we started again, engine crippled, and everybody wet as water could make them. At Pasadena we took on board several men, ladies and children, who had been standing waist deep in water for several hours. Soon Deep Water was reached. Here two ladies got off and were carried to the residence of Mr. W. E. Jones. The train had just started again when the depot blew away, part of it against our train, breaking the windows and blinds of the coach and throwing glass all over us. Luckily no one was hurt.

"We had now been three hours coming twelve miles, and we all began to grow more uneasy. It was at this point where we first felt or knew what a storm we were in. The coaches rocked like cradles, windows blew in, and it seemed that we would be blown away ourselves. After two hours more we reached East La Porte. There most of our companions left us to look for their people. It did not seem that anyone could live in that storm— the wind must have been blowing 100 miles an hour. But our friends knew that they were needed at their homes, and they launched out. Some to be blown back to us, only to try it over again ; others to be blown in the mud and water.

DIFFICULTIES OF A TRAIN.

"After a considerable delay the train started on. At West La Porte we found the depot blown across our way. All went to work cutting and moving timbers, and with the assistance of the wind, we soon had the track clear. We now had but one more serious place to get across before we could get to Seabrook. At last we reached it, and were in a few minutes across Taylor's bayou, which we found to be a half mile wide and the waves four feet high. This bayou, in ordinary weather, is about fifty feet wide. On reaching Seabrook we found the depot full of refugees, houses all gone, water over everything. Some of the families of our companions on the way were lost, never to be seen alive again.

"Here we started out to work in earnest and it was only a very short time before we had everyone that was without a home on board. By this time the train crew had fires in the coaches and and we served coffee, cheese and bread to the hungry ones, and made them as comfortable as possible. We still had lots of work to do, though, and we were looking for it when a man appeared on the scene, reporting Judge Tod's barn had blown down on two ladies and several children. We went to work to get them out, and after three hours' work we rescued all alive except the mother. She probably could have saved herself, but she gave up her life for the children. She was found in a position leaning over them protecting them.

"Finally day came and we could now see what damage the storm had done. Mr. Hamilton's house was the only one left in the flats, and most of the houses on the ridge were blown to pieces. It was a miracle that more lives were not lost.

"We gathered up everyone who wanted to come and left for Houston at 9:30 A. M. Sunday, and arrived at Houston about 12 o'clock; our journey lasting eighteen hours, was over. The gentlemen on the train who had families at La Porte and Seabrook are under lasting obligations to the Southern Pacific officials and especially to the train crew. No braver crew ever went out with a train, and we wish to tender them our earnest and sincere thanks. Courage and manly conduct have always been lauded by the world, and no men ever stood more nobly to duty on battle grounds than did these men who ran the relief train in the full fury of the storm to the search for the wave-tossed people of La Porte and Seabrook."

As showing the immediate demand for laborers, the following advertisement inserted in the "Houston Post," will be of interest :

WANTED AT GALVESTON IMMEDIATELY.

"24 plasterers, $4.50 per day and board paid; 30 bricklayers, $5.50 per day and board paid ; 25 tinners, $3.50 per day and board paid ; 100 laborers, $2.00 per day and board paid."

The old saying that it is an ill wind that blows good to no one is illustrated in this advertisement. Probably never before in any Texas city were workmen offered wages so high.

Colonel Walter Hudnall, the representative of the Treasury Department of the Government, who was sent from San Antonio to Galveston, to investigate the conditions and report completed his work.

Colonel Hudnall spent several days in the stricken city. He

31

came prepared for the worst, but when he saw what actually had occurred, he threw up his hands in amazement. No man, in his opinion, can form an estimate of the loss of life and property from the reports which have been sent out, and the extent of the devastation is beyond the grasp of human reason. He has made a canvass of the city mounted; he has visited every place which a man could on a horse, and he has made a complete investigation of the conditions as they exist.

He knew Galveston as she was before being struck by the storm, and he knows her as she is to-day. In his report to the Treasury Department, he will say that no man can estimate the property loss in the city, and that it is his opinion that any one attempting to make such an estimate will miss it by $10,000,000; the idea of making any estimate of property loss appears to him ridiculous.

MAYOR JONES' STATEMENT AND APPEAL.

Of the loss of life, Colonel Hudnall believes that it will be between 6000 and 8000, and he will so report. He will say that he does not believe that it is possible for it to be less than 6000 lives, and he would not be surprised should it be 8000. He calls attention to the fact that in places there are from forty to sixty solid squares of ground swept clean as a parlor floor, as far as standing buildings are concerned. Colonel Hudnall does not believe disease will result if the proper sanitary precautions are taken, and this is being done as fast as the laborers can distribute the quicklime and carbolic acid.

As he was leaving he was asked regarding his idea of the future of Galveston. He said : " If the expression of the people who live here is to be my guide in forming an opinion I will say that Galveston will be rebuilt and will be a prosperous city. There is no doubt that the property owners expect to go to work repairing the damage as far as they can.

"There has been a great deal said about martial law," continued the colonel. " The city is yet under the control of the mayor, and civil law is in force. The soldiers are being used simply to enforce the civil law and to maintain a discipline which is necessary under the disturbed conditions. The soldiers do not work a hardship on any one."

A statement and an appeal addressed to the American people, signed by Mayor Jones and members of the Relief Committee, and endorsed by Governor Sayres, was issued September 25th. It set forth in detail the extent of the disaster which overtook the city, in part as follows :

"Seventeen days after the storm at Galveston it is still impossible to accurately estimate the loss of life and property. It is known that the dead in the city will number at least one sixth of the census population. The island and adjacent mainland will add perhaps 2000 to this number. Actual property damage is incalculable in precise terms, but we have the individual losses, and losses in public property, such as paving, water works, schools, hospitals, churches, etc., which will easily amount to $30,000,000. This estimate takes no account of the direct and indirect injury to business. Along the beach front upwards of 2600 houses, by actual map count, were totally destroyed. Moreover, we estimate that 97 ½ per cent. of the remaining houses throughout the city were damaged in greater or less degree. In fact none entirely escaped."

CONFRONTED BY A GREATER PROBLEM.

Grateful thanks are extended for the help received, and the address continues : "But a greater and a graver work confronts us. Some kinds of homes, be they ever so humble, must be provided for the 10,000 people now huddled in ruined houses, public places and improvised camps, to the end that they may not become paupers, but may speedily set up their households wherein repose all that is best and noblest in American life. We believe that the well to do and the charitable people of this nation will not be contented to merely appease hunger and bind up bruises, but will in very large measure and with more far reaching effect contribute to the restoration of this people to a plane of self support and self respect. It is for this purpose that we make this further appeal."

Miss Clara Barton also endorsed the appeal, saying : "Could the people of our generous country see as I have seen in its dreadful reality the desolation and the destruction of homes by thousands, the overwhelming bereavement in the loss of near and dear ones, and the utter helplessness that confronts those remaining, the appeal of Mayor Jones for continued help would meet with such a response as no other calamity has ever known."

REVIEWING THE SITUATION.

Reviewing the situation in Galveston, a correspondent communicates the following : "On Sunday following the storm all saloons were closed by order of the Mayor. On the following Sunday several saloonists began selling liquor on the quiet. They were arrested and taken before Adjutant General Scurry, who warned them they must not repeat the offense. A prominent saloon man was arrested for disobeying the order and was put to work in a street cleaning gang. Dr. Donaldson, chief surgeon of one of the relief corps, says it will not be necessary for the outside surgeons to remain here longer than two or three days more. He has written an article for a medical journal commenting upon the comparatively small number of seriously wounded and sick persons. He explains the absence of a large number of seriously vounded persons by saying that most of those so wounded were drowned, but says it is surprising that more people, especially women and children, did not get sick from such trying experiences.

"Efforts are being made to open the public schools on October 1, the date set before the storm for their opening. Three of the school buildings can be made usable at slight cost and it is planned to hold two sessions a day.

"The estimated losses to the life insurance companies at Galveston are about $500,000. Most of those who carried old line life policies escaped. The fraternal orders will lose quite heavily.

"The Gulf Port Trading Company addressed a letter to General Manager Polk of the Gulf, Colorado and Santa Fe railway, advising him that strenuous efforts were being made to divert business from Galveston to other ports on representation that Galveston would be unable to take care of the shipments. He was asked to say whether his line would issue domestic and foreign bills of lading for export shipments through Galveston. Colonel Polk replied that the representations were entirely false; that it is expected to have rail communication open to Galveston very soon and to begin the delivery of local and export freight here Friday morning the 21st; that orders have already been issued to superintendents to let Galveston freight come forward and lthat agents have been authorized to accept freight for Galveston and sign domestic and foreign bills of lading as usual.

A PECULIAR CONDITION.

"The wheat in elevator 'A' is being turned over and put in shape to deliver to vessels. There were about 1000 cars of wheat on track here and most of these show a peculiar condition on inspection. It appears that in nearly all of them there is a foot of wheat on the bottom to which the water rose. It was salt water and the wheat caked so hard that the 'tryer' used by the inspector will not penetrate it. The grain above this water line appears not to have been damaged. The good grain was being transferred by hand to other cars and that on the bottom will probably go to distilleries or some other places. A number of grain exporters, in fact, all who do business through this port, have written letters of sympathy aud express themselves as having confidence in the ability of the Galveston people to care for their wheat in the best manner.

"Hanna & Leonard's new elevator has started. It was about completed before the storm, little damaged during the storm, and has been completed since the storm in order to handle the grain and put such as is out of condition into condition for export.

" A census bureau has been established and placed in operation. A mortuary bureau has also been opened where relatives and friends make oath of the known death of persons lost in the storm. These bureaus will greatly assist in securing an accurate estimate of the loss of life. The clearing of debris in the streets proper has progressed and the spirit of rehabilitating the city is seen in every business. The military forces are accomplishing wonders, and the prediction is made that Galveston will assume normal conditions in a week. Resumption of trade in every channel is apparent. But five arrests and court martial trials is the record for the past week (the second after the flood) since General Scurry assumed control of the city.

"Insurance Inspector J. G. Youens has begun to go over the town to make a detailed report of the houses destroyed. Up to date he has covered the district bounded on the north by East Broadway, on the east and south by the Gulf, and on the west by Fourteenth street. In these forty-five blocks he found destroyed an average of sixteen houses to the block. The fire insurance companies are arranging to refund a pro rata on policies on houses and furniture where the same have been entirely destroyed by the hurricane, and the holders thereof want them cancelled."

DR. YOUNG'S GRAPHIC STORY.

The following very interesting account of the beginning of the great Galveston storm and graphic story of his experience was prepared by Dr. S. O. Young :

" Tuesday morning, September 4, I was standing near the signal service officer who makes the weather bureau map each day for the Cotton Exchange. This is simply a large blackboard on which is painted a map of the United States. Wherever the bureau has a signal station the readings of the barometer, thermometer, direction and force of the wind and rainfall are recorded on this map, different colors of chalk being used to indicate each.

" When the observation at Key West was recorded I saw that the barometer was low, that the wind was from the northeast, and the map as a whole showed pretty plainly cyclonic disturbances to the south or southeast of Key West. There was a region of high barometer over Pennsylvania and New York, shading gradually down to Key West and presumably far to the south of that point, while there was another region of high barometer over Colorado, with a comparatively low barometer between the two, all shading toward low the further south the records were made.

" I remarked to the observer who was making the map that the Key West record, backed by the map as a whole, showed pretty plainly that there was a cyclone forming. He agreed with me, but said his office had received no notice of anything of the kind. Wednesday afternoon the tide in the Gulf was high and the water was rough, though there was no wind to cause the disturbance. Thursday afternoon the tide was again high and the water very rough, while the atmosphere had that peculiar hazy appearance that generally precedes a storm, though not to a marked degree.

" The wind was from the north, and during the night was rather brisk. Friday the wind was from the north, and as night came on it increased in violence. The tide was very high and the Gulf very rough, though as a rule with a north wind the tide is low and the Gulf as smooth as the bay. I was then confident that a cyclone was approaching us and accounted for the high tide by assuming that the storm was moving toward the northwest or against the Gulf stream, thus piling up the water in the Gulf.

KNEW CYCLONE WAS COMING.

" For my own satisfaction, and at the request of my friends, I constructed a chart, outlining roughly the origin, development and probable course of the cyclone. From the Key West observation and the map of Tuesday I assumed that the center of disturbance was originally somewhere south of Cuba ; that it moved to the northwest as cyclones always do at first, and that the storm had developed into a cyclone in the neighborhood of Yucatan ; would move to the northwest and strike somewhere near the mouth of the Mississippi, going thence to the northeast and passing into the Atlantic ocean off the New England coast. The error I made was in placing its course too far east.

" My residence was within two blocks of the beach, so I had ample opportunity to observe the Gulf. Friday night there was a strong wind from the north, and Saturday morning, about 6 o'clock, I went to the beach. I saw that the tide was high, but that it had fallen again and was then at a stand. While I was out there the tide began to rise again, and soon washed up to and over the street railway track near the Olympia. I was certain then we were going to have a cyclone, and so soon as I could get to town I telegraphed to my wife, who, with my children, was on a Southern Pacific train coming from the West, to stop in San Antonio. I told her that a great storm was on us, but not to say anything about it and not to feel anxious about me.

"By 12 o'clock the wind had increased in violence to between 40 and 50 miles an hour, blowing from the north, and the water, both in the bay and Gulf, was very high and still rising. At 1 o'clock I visited the wharf front. The wind had shifted a point or two to the east of north, and was over fifty miles an hour. The bay water was over the wharves and was slowly encroaching on the Strand. All low places were completely inundated.

LARGE BUILDINGS FLOATED PAST.

"From the bay I went to the Gulf side, and found the tide very high and the water very rough. At 2 o'clock I concluded to go home and look after things there. My residence was on the northeast corner of avenue P½ and Bath avenue. As both P½ and Bath avenues were low at that point, my sidewalk had been curbed up about four feet and the whole lot raised four or five feet above the level of the street. When I got home I found about two feet of water on my lot. I sat on my front gallery and watched the water. It rose gradually until the third step was under water, when it apparently stopped rising and for over an hour remained stationary.

"My house, a large two-story frame building, stood on brick pillars about four feet high, so I had no fear of the water coming into the house. I dismissed a negro boy I had with me, went inside and proceeded to secure the windows and doors, and to make everything ship-shape before dark, for I felt pretty sure the electric lights would all be knocked out.

"At 4 o'clock the water was two feet deep on my ground

floor, and was rising gradually. The wind had hauled further to the east and was blowing at a terrific rate. I moved my chair near the window and watched the water as it flowed down avenue P½ to the west at a terrific rate, carrying wretched shanties, boxes, barrels, wooden cisterns and everything else that fell in its power. The flow was almost exactly from east to west, just as the streets run, for a box or barrel that passed my house, in the middle of the street, kept the same position as far as I could see it.

"Between 5 and 6 o'clock the wind became almost due east and increased in violence. The debris fairly flew past, so rapid had the tide become. At twenty minutes to 6 o'clock (I am exact because I noticed my large clock had stopped, and wound it up and set it by my watch) there was a marked increase in the violence of the wind. I went to a west window to watch a fence I had been using as a marker on the tide, and while I was looking, I saw the tide suddenly rise fully four feet at one bound. In a few minutes several houses on the south side of P½, between Twenty-fifth and Twenty-sixth, went to pieces and floated away, and the debris from a number of large buildings began to float past from the east.

THE ROAR WAS AWFUL.

"It was then getting dark very rapidly. I turned on my lamps, but, as I had anticipated, there was no electricity. I had found a candle and lit that, then I thought I had best save it, so I blew it out, got a comfortable arm-chair and made myself as comfortable as possible. Being entirely alone, with no responsibility on me, I felt satisfied and very complacent, for I was fool enough not to be the least afraid of wind or water.

"About 7.30 o'clock I heard heavy thumping against the east side of my house, and concluded it was downstairs in one of the lower bed rooms. I lit the candle and went to the stairs, and found the water was very nearly up to the top of them. I put the candle down, went to the front door and opened it. In a second I was blown back into the hall. I eased myself along the east side, caught the door knob, then the side of the door on the gallery and drew myself out far enough to catch hold of a blind, and, clinging with both hands, I drew myself out on the gallery and stood there. The scene was the grandest I ever witnessed. It was impossible to face the wind, which had now increased to fully 100 miles an hour, and drove sheets of spray and rain, which were blinding.

"The roar was something awful. I could see to the right and to the left, and, so far as I could see, only my house and that of my next door neighbor, Mr. Youens, were left standing. All the others were gone, and we were left practically out in the Gulf of Mexico. About two minutes after I got on the gallery, I saw Mr. Youens' house begin to move forward. It turned partly around and then seemed to hang as if suspended. Suddenly the wind switched to the south by east, and increased in violence. Mr. Youens' house rose like a huge steamboat, was swept back and suddenly disappeared. I knew that he had his family with him, his wife, son and two daughters, and my feelings were indescribable as I saw them go.

POSTS BLOWN AWAY LIKE STRAWS.

"The new position of the wind and its increased violence caused a sudden rise in the water, and at one bound it reached my second-story and poured in my door, which was exactly thirty-one feet above the level of the street. The wind again increased. It did not come in gusts, but was more like the steady downpour of Niagara than anything I can think of. One of the front posts on my gallery blew out, split my head open and mashed my shoulder badly. I was knocked insensible for a moment, but pulled myself together and hung on.

"The constant shaking and jarring had loosened the front door facing, and I saw I could tear it loose from the top when the crash came, so I kept hold of it all the time. I had outlined a plan of campaign from the first and carried it out to the letter. The other posts and railing of the gallery blew away like straws. The top of the gallery was lifted up and disappeared over the top of the house.   The gallery floated away, and, with one foot inside the door, I was left hanging against the front of the house.   It was an easy thing to stay there, for the wind held me as firmly as if I had been screwed to he thouse.

"It is hard to believe, but still it is true.   A little after 8 o'clock the wind actually increased in violence.   I am confident I do not exaggerate one bit when I say it was blowing fully 125 miles an hour.   I could see into the hall, and saw a beautiful phenomenon when the wind was at its height.   Whether from phosphorescence of the sea water or from electricity generated by the high wind, I can't say, but, from whatever cause it was, the drops of rain became luminous as they struck the wall, and it looked like a display of miniature fireworks.   The luminous particles were about the size of a pin head, though one ball about half as large as a boy's marble, formed on the door facing and slowly slipped down into the water.

WIND AT 125 MILES AN HOUR.

" The wind at 125 miles an hour is something awful.   I could neither hear nor see when it was at its height and it was difficult to breathe.   I am nearly six feet in height and estimating the surface of my body exposed to the wind at five square feet, my body sustained at that time a pressure of 390 pounds.   I began to think my house would never go.   The wind acted as if it thought so, too, for it got harder and harder and harder until finally I felt the house yielding.   I took a firm hold of my door facing, placed both feet against the house, exerted my full strength,   tore the facing loose and as the house went kicked myself as far away from it as possible, so as to avoid sunken debris rising to the surface.

"The house rose out of the water several feet, was caught by the wind and whisped away like a railway train and I was left in perfect security, free from all floating timber or debris, to follow more slowly.   The surface of the water was almost flat.   The wind beat it down so that there was not even the suspicion of a wave.

"The current impelled by the wind was terrific. Almost before I had felt I had fairly started I was over the Gartenverein, four blocks away. The next moment I was at the corner of the convent. Here I got in a big whirlpool and caught up with a lot of debris. I was carried round and round until I lost my bearings completely and was then floated off (as I found afterwards) to the northwest, finally landing in the middle of the street at Thirty-fourth and M½, or fifteen blocks from where I started.

"It was very dark, but I could see the tops of some houses barely above the water ; could see others totally wrecked and others half submerged. I knew it was not so very late and as I could not see a light or hear a human soul I concluded that the whole of that part of the town had been destroyed and that I was the only survivor. For eight hours I clung to my board, which had found a good resting place, and during the whole time I did not hear a human voice except that of a woman in the distance calling for help.

NEARLY FROZEN TO DEATH.

" The wind beat the rain on me and nearly froze me to death. I was never so cold in my life. I think I had at least a dozen good hard chills before the water fell sufficiently for me to wade to a house half a block away, a little elevated cottage of two rooms in which fifteen or twenty colored people, who forgot their own misery when they saw me bareheaded, covered with blood and shaking with cold. They pulled me in out of the rain, wrapped some half dry clothes about my shoulders to get warmth in my body and for the moment forgot their own misery.

"When daylight came two of the men piloted me to town, where I met a friend whose room had escaped destruction. He took me there, sent for a doctor, had my wounds dressed and by 9 o'clock I was myself again and barring weakness from loss of blood was as well as ever.

"In conclusion, I desire to say this of the storm. In my opinion it began south of Cuba, developed fully near Yucatan, came to the northwest, landed west of Galveston, its center pass ing south of Galveston between 6 and 7 o'clock Saturday evening, and that it was from 200 to 300 miles in diameter. It passed to the northeast, going out of the United States over the great lakes through Canada and died out in the far North Atlantic. I have seen absolutely no report of this storm, but this is my con. clusion from my observation."

Said a citizen of Galveston : "It is not all tears in Galveston, not all sorrow. Hearts bowed down with grief are not heavy all the time, and there are smiles and good cheer and hearty hand shakes with it all. Here is a sample of the conversation :

" 'Hello, Bill, I'm glad to see you alive !'

" 'Same to you, old man,' as they join hands in hearty clasp.

" 'How 'bout your family ?'

" 'All safe, thank God.'

" 'I lost my little one, but the rest are safe. How's your home ?

" 'Gone : knocked into kindling wood, but that don't matter, as I saved my wife and children after a hard struggle.'

TEARS IN MANY EYES.

"And the two pass on, the one light hearted, the other a smile glistening in his tear dimmed eye, both glad for what was left them. I saw a telegram to a Galveston woman from a sister in Houston with whom she had hardly been on speaking terms for years. It read :

" 'Are you safe ? Do you want any money ? Come up to Houston and live with us.'

"Is there necessity of comment ? I saw neighbors who had been quarreling and saying spiteful things about each other for months, riding down the street in the same buggy, the most loving chums in the world. I saw rival candidates for the same political office catch hold of opposite ends of the same log, and with a 'heave ho !' toss it up out of the way of wagons and pedestrians, each doing the work for humanity's sake.

"Social distinction is wiped out. I heard the banker tell his story of the storm to his stableman with as much vim and gusto as though hobnobbing with his heaviest depositor.   White and colored stopped to make inquiries of each other and shake hands. I saw a blind mendicant, a continual object of charity, on the corner of Twenty-first and Market, and heard of hundreds upon hundreds of great, strong, useful men who went down with the flood.   Life is stranger than fiction, but it does seem an ironical providence that saves the halt and the maimed and takes away the useful."

Police Officer W. H. Plummer is the happy possesser of a four-oared boat which he has christened " Cyclone Rescue," in honor of its work in the storm.   The boat is constructed on the pattern of what is known as an Eastern pod, such as is used by the lobster fishermen of Maine.   The boat was built to withstand the rough seas, and was so constructed with two air-tight compartments as to be used as a lifeboat.   This boat, with lashed oars, was kept by Officer Plummer in his yard, corner of Seventh and Church streets, one of the first districts to suffer from the invasion of the destructive Gulf on the fatal day of the storm.

GRAND WORK OF RESCUE.

When Captain Plummer went home to dinner on that day the Gulf was rising very rapidly and the storm gave indications of greater severity.   Having spent many years at sea, Captain Plummer called his two sons, who are sailors, and the three men launched the boat and started rescuing families in the neighborhood, taking them to St. Mary's Infirmary.   From noon until late that night the good boat and its faithful crew braved the terrific storm and are credited with having saved two hundred lives.   On the last trip that night, with Captain Plummer almost helpless from exhaustion and his sons fast succumbing to the terrible battle of the day, the boat suffered a slight mishap.   She was struck by a piece of wreckage driven with great force into her side.   But the boat held the water and landed her crew safely at the Infirmary.

Once, during the height of the storm, the boat, with seven on board, was capsized, but the experienced seamen soon had her righted and baled, and all on board were saved. Captain Plummer lost his home and everything but the scant clothes on his back, but he says he wouldn't part with the "Cyclone Rescue" for its weight in gold.

Some who were out in the water from the time the houses first began to go down drifted but a few hundred feet, while others were carried miles by the water. So it was with Miss Anna Delz, a 16-year old girl, who lived out in the west end near the beach. She drifted a distance of over eighteen miles, landing not far from Texas City. She passed the bay bridge and hung for some time on one of the piling, then catching a piece of driftwood, continued her perilous journey, landing not far from her aunt's house on the mainland.

STORY OF A PERILOUS TRIP.

She tells the story of her trip on the crest of the waves as follows :

"It was about 2 o'clock in the afternoon when I first realized that the storm was increasing. Together with a girl-friend who was in the house, I packed my mother's trunk and carried all of the household goods that I could and piled them in the second story to keep them from being washed away by the water, which was rapidly rising. During this time the wind had been increasing in velocity all of the time.

"At about 4 o'clock my mother and sister, who is 13 years of age, were taken to a place of refuge by a friend. A girl friend and myself were left, thinking that we would be safe, but it was not over an hour after that when the house went down. It went with a crash, and myself, together with the others in the house were thrown out into the furious waters. I caught onto a tree and stayed there for a little while, but was dashed off and sank under the water several times. While hanging on to the tree a roof came along, on which there were about twenty people, mostly women and children. I got on with them and stayed there for some time, seeing my companions in distress being washed off one by one, until at last there were only a young girl and myself left.   Soon she went, and I was left alone to battle with the waves. Soon I caught a piece of driftwood and I think I floated out into the Gulf.   Then the wind changed and I began going the other way.   I was tossed out into the bay at last, having passed during this time many people floating on drift of all kinds, and people struggling in the water trying to save themselves.

"I drifted thus for a long time, coming after a while to where the railroad bridges crossed the bay.   I caught hold of one of the piling and stayed there for a time trying to rest.   During the night my clothes had been entirely torn from my body and I was in a horrible plight.   After having stayed there a little longer, I caught a piece of drift and turned loose and drifted with the tide. At last I drifted to a pile of lumber, and finding that the water was not deep there, I fell on top of the lumber.   I was so exhausted by the terrible ride that I had taken that I immediately went to sleep.

"About daylight I awakened and found myself in a strange place.   I walked to a house some distance from there, and on inquiring, found that I was at Lamarque.   Remembering that I had an aunt living at that place, I found her house, which was also almost a ruin.   This aunt took me in charge and I stayed there until I heard from my father, and then came back to Galveston."

CHAPTER XXV

Storms of Great Violence Around Galveston—Wrecked Cities and Vast Destruction of Property— Appalling Sacrifice of Life.

A CLOSE observer and correspondent who is familiar with every part of Texas and is capable of sizing up the situation, writes as follows concerning the disaster which has left Galveston a scene of death and ruin:

"At first glance it would seem that the population of Galveston had been endowed by a thoughtlessness which invites the calamities it has suffered. Three times in twenty-five years storms of great violence have swept over the island on which it occupies a position exposed to every energy of the elements, and on the two occasions whose history is complete the survivors rebuilt their city, as they probably will do again, and the storm broke upon it, as most likely it will once more, with death and destruction in its blast.

"Apart from the deep sympathy which one feels for the people the situation may awaken a philosophic inquiry whose consideration is of less importance than the interest the subject awakens and which is reinforced by parallel cases in the history of disaster since the world began, and I propose to show in a few great cases how the citizens of Galveston are only repeating history when, even as they gather their dead, they plan a new city whose foundation shall be enduring and which shall stand defiant and permanent, a triumph of man over antagonistic nature and a civic crown of glory to their efforts. It is no ignoble purpose.

THE DYKES OF HOLLAND.

"The sturdy Dutchmen who threw their dykes across the sea, the Sicilians who terraced Aetna's lava sides with vineyards, the people of San Francisco who rebuilt their city when it was cast down by earthquakes until at last they found a structural design that would resist the seismic influence that hold the Pacific coast in tremulous expectation ; Chicago that has risen twice from ashes to finer and more secure architectural proportions, and Calcutta, whose existence has been marked by three beginnings, are all expressions of the same splendid pertinacity with which the people of Galveston are already animated and from which will certainly appear a new and grander Gulf city offering to the menaces of nature a richer challenge.

A GREAT BREAKWATER.

" It was no accidental selection that caused Galveston to be built as it was upon a low island whose approach from the sea offered no harbor to ships and to whose low, sandy shores the products of the State of which she is the metropolis came only by artificial and difficult channels. The sweeping curves of the Gulf of Mexico reach its northern apex at or near this point, and it is there that the ships seeking the nearest approach to the cotton fields of Texas came, while the bay itself is as nearly as possible the average centre of industrial life in the State. The bay was never a harbor. To those who are familiar with the Jersey coast the situation of Galveston is easily presented.

"Just as part of the land has reached out into the sea and swinging around in different directions the points came in touch and raised a breakwater which, gathering sand and pebbles, became the beach at distances of four to ten miles from the mainland, leaving interior bays, with shallow inlets connecting them with the ocean, Galveston island was formed.

THE SWIRLING TIDES OF THE GULF.

" If the visitor to Barnegat or even to the Inlet end of the island at Atlantic, will recall how a narrow channel of tidal water reaches back to the sedge fringed bays that extend from Sea Girt to Cape May, and quadruple the width of those interior waters, he will have a fair idea of the position and surroundings of Galveston. Across Galveston Bay the railroads make their approach over eight to fifteen miles of tracks supported by piling.

" The waters of the bay are indeed navigable and through its shallows the moderate tides of the gulf swirl out channels, which the small draft boats of Buffalo Bayou paddle and sail just as the wood and oyster schooners and yachts move up Great Little Egg Harbor Bay on the Jersey coast. In fact, the situation of Galveston is not unlike that of Atlantic City, except that the sandy island on which it is built is lower and its front is to the south instead of to the east.

"Of course there is no well or spring water and the potable supply comes from the house roofs, which are carefully built to gather as much rain as possible, to be stored in cemented cisterns for use. As to the harbor itself for sea-going ships there is, in fact, none. Only the open gulf pushed at this point furthest into the shore, but in a sweep so grand that there are no headlands whatever. The water shoals slowly from the sea and ships of the draft of eighteen feet or more come in to take the first parts of their loads in the shallower water from lighters and move out from time to time until, when down to the load line, they are sometimes six or seven miles from land.

TRYING TO MAKE A HAVEN.

"Great efforts have been made to give Galveston a harbor commensurate with her commercial enterprise, and in some ways success has attended these efforts. Long spurs of breakwater were built out on the principles of the Boca harbor at Buenos Ayres, with a view to enclosing an artificial haven for ships, but the prevalent southerly winds, the currents which they engender and the ceaseless tides have made this work one of great difficulty. A further obstacle has been the shifting, sandy bottom, whose permeable formation reaches down many feet before it rests upon clay or rock.

"The city itself is built chiefly of wood and on the lines of architecture adopted for coolness in tropical climates. That is to say, with vast doorways and windows, cutting out as much of the framework as possible and yet leave enough of support for a roof. This structural form permits the whole house to be opened for the passage of every breeze, but at the cost of stability.

"At intervals and particularly when the spring or high tides prevail, and when the southerly winds bank up the waters of the northern gulf, the streets of the city are flooded, the sewers deliver themselves the wrong way and the uncertain foundations of the city are weakened and prepared for the fall which follows close upon the weather conditions when they are intensified.

THE CITY A PREY TO THE STORM.

"We have now the situation of Galveston fairly before us, and can understand how it easily succumbed to the violence of the late storm. It is true that the cyclone was of a potentiality' which might have razed a more firmly built city, but probably in no other city in this country could it have caused such complete devastation.

"In twenty-five years the city of Galveston and the coast line of Texas have had three visitations of tropical hurricanes, bearing death and destruction in their blasts. Every year about the equinoctial season storms of greater or less fury occur and never, on account of the fragile materials and loose methods of building, have they failed of doing damage, but these three occupy thrones of mark above all others. In September, 1875, the coast of Texas, from the mouth of the Rio Grande to the Sabine Pass, was swept by a cyclone that followed with its central zone the curve of the the coast, the wind varying at different times in its journey to southeast to southwest.

"The town of Indianola was blotted out of the world in an hour. Not half a dozen of its 1,200 inhabitants escaped, and the sea swept away the island on which it stood, and its site has no other mark than that which the waves rolling over it can offer. There were not enough of people to ask for help. And as there was no longer a place to rebuild, the little remnant moved elsewhere. The storm swept over Galveston, raising a tidal wave that changed in its impetuous flow the whole shape of the island. From the western end nearly two miles of land was cut off and carried around to the north side. The city was unroofed, houses toppled and fell, the water flowed in resistless currents along the levees, floating off to sea thousands of bales of cotton and destroying in its wild swirls the contents of stores and houses and many lives. The number never will be known but estimates place it at 800. For a week telegraphic communication was cut off.

SPILES WRENCHED FROM THEIR PLACES.

" It was my fortune to be in Texas as a correspondent at the time and on the day of the storm at Houston, some sixty miles away, built at the head of Buffalo Bayou, and I was ordered to the wrecked city. At that time there was only one railroad, the Houston and Galveston, and it was utterly destroyed for over thirty miles of its length. The top structure on the spiling across Galveston Bay was, of course, swept away, but it was a remarkable fact as showing the violence of the storm that about one of every three of the great spiles, 50 to 55 feet long and driven down 25 to 30 feet in the sand, was wrenched from its place and swept away.

" Others had resisted, but were twisted and split by the fury of wind and waves. Two small boats, stern wheelers, drawing from 28 to 30 inches of water, built on the Mississippi steamboat model of ancient times, with a cabin over the cargo and engine deck, a texas or officers' cabin on top of that, and a glass wheel house on top of that—more fragile things you could not imagine— were moored at the mouth of the bayou, where the sluggish stream enters the bay.

" Strange to say these escaped with the loss of their smokestacks, and were available to send aid, which was not lacking, to the desolate city. It was impossible to transport the quantities of food and clothing that poured in from the North, and more rotted and was lost on the levee at Houston than reached the distressed inhabitants of Galveston.

" That part of the city which was not blown down was imbedded in sand. The Strand, a street in Galveston, whose name is now familiar to the world by reason of the awful scenes that so recently have been witnessed there, was four feet deep in sand, and the Tremont, Cosmopolitan and Great Southern Hotels were filled with sand and hotel was kept on their second floors.

AROSE LIKE A PHOENIX.

"But the city, although cast down, was not discouraged. It began to rebuild itself, and by Christmas of that year almost every trace of the awful calamity had disappeared. The question naturally arises why a population which had received such an awful warning of its exposed condition should not abandon what in a military term would be called an untenable position. The answer is obvious. They had something left there. Even the island, although distorted and out of shape, was still there and theirs, and they had nothing elsewhere, nor means to go to another place.

"So, with hopeful philosophy they rebuilt their city, restored its commerce and, encouraged with such empty precepts as ' Better luck next time,' ' Lightning never strikes twice in the same place,' went forward to meet their next blow, in 1893, when another hurricane visited them. It was not so terrible in its effect, but differed only in degree. The late severe storm gives further emphatic warning, more terrible and heart-breaking in its losses of life and vaster in its destruction of property. But they will, of course, rebuild their city and seek to establish protective barriers of breakwaters and seawalls to maintain it in existence. In all likelihood they will succeed, for the history of these efforts is of final security after trial and loss, and the firm resolution of man rises over every obstacle.

ASLEEP OVER A VOLCANO.

"Perhaps the persistency of the people who dwell on the slopes at the foot of Mount Vesuvius offers the most striking illustration of disregard of danger against which no human provision can be made. With a volcano boiling on the verge of eruptions that are forever imminent they pasture their flocks and press their grapes, careless of the menace which familiarity has taught them to despise. The whole kingdom of Naples is marked by the same disregard of natural and uncontrollable danger. The statement is accepted by the encyclopedias that in seventy-five years — from 1783 to 1857—the kingdom lost 111,000 inhabitants by the effects of earthquakes.   About 1,500 a year in a population of less than 5,000,000.

The city of Lisbon sits smiling and prosperous on the north bank of the Tagus, and its inhabitants still point with pride to scarred earth dating from the earthquake in which 40,000 lives were lost.   Charleston, S. C., is rebuilt.   Johnstown, Pa., is restored to its prosperous industry.   The Japanese still go their flowery way in Jeddo, where in one great shock 200,000 lives are said to have been lost—which figure is even approximately the greatest disaster the world has ever known.   St. Thomas, in the West Indies; Port Royal, Jamaica; Cape Haytien, in Santo Domingo, with a tribute of 45,000 lives within the memory of men yet living, and the spice island of Krakatoa. are still peopled despite the black danger signal of the death which constantly waves over them.

MYRIAD LIVES LOST IN GREAT DISASTERS.

" If you will refer to the statistical sources of information you will find that in one hundred and fifty years, a mere moment in the life of this world and its races, and add up the round thousands only and leave out the hundreds of lives which are charged to lesser lists the sum will reach 1,563,000 souls in the thirty-seven most important earthquake, volcanic eruptions, hurricanes and inundations that have visited the earth.   It is, of course, impossible to give any sort of guess as to the accuracy of the estimates of the loss of life.

"Even in Johnstown it is not certainly known to this day within 2,000 persons how many were lost.   The identified dead numbered 2,228.   The best informed and conservative estimates place the figure at 3,500, and others reach 5,000, while published reports, which ought to be authoritative, calmly name the death list at 9,000.   It is the same at Galveston, where the number is so variously stated that no reliance can be placed upon any numerical report beyond the fact that anywhere between 1,000 and 3,000 lives have been lost. If this, then, is the waywardness of figures in cases where not only the population is known, but in communities where the associations of commerce and social life has been such that the survivors can count the missing and recognize such of the dead as may be found, how wild must be the estimate placed upon such cataclysms as that in Southeastern Bengal and the Niegen Islands, where on October 31, 1876, in a cyclone, 215,000 people are said to have perished.

CARELESS ABOUT ALL DANGER.

" But even there, where such a loss would imply the sacrifice of one in every four persons inhabiting the territory so awfully stricken, the people still pursue their daily avocations, toil and rest, love, hate, mourn and die with the composure and ease of mind that prevail in Philadelphia or New York, where no shadow of storm is known to hover and where no devastating earthquake or fiery volcano lurks for victims. But, of course, these awful figures have very little relation to the actual losses. In the storm in Bengal Sir Richard Temple, who had charge of the crown relief, did not find that 20,000 lives were lost and that probably not more than 10,000 died of the famine which the loss of the crops insured. In the potato famine in Ireland, in 1846 and 1847, the loss of life was named at 120,000 by those who charged the whole business to English misrule and was named at from 8,000 to 20,000 by the royal commissioners entrusted with the distribution of the £10,-000,000 of Parliamentary grant for the relief of the famished land.

LAWS REGULATING STORMS.

" So the loss in battles always begins to be told in numbers that occasionally would require more than the combined forces of the two armies to supply. The first reports of Shiloh or Pittsburg Landing, in the early days of the Civil War, is a case in point. Had we fought on at the rate given then the country would not have had a male person in its population a year before the date of Appomattox. So that we can hope every day will reduce the number, although it cannot lessen the horror otherwise, of the visitation the death angel has made in the Lone Star State.

" It is interesting to study the law of storms which take on such a rythmical obedience as it would seem to appear at given places and times. In this case the weather bureau was accurately alert to the approaching disturbance. Four days before its arrival on the coast its formation in the Caribbean Sea was noted and its probable course northward chartered and proclaimed as a danger to the Atlantic States. The meteorological phenomenon was correctly defined and watched in its development until on Thursday night it reached the Florida coast and struck a rude blow at Tampa. Up to this moment the weather office had made no mistake and its predictions lifted its utterance to the domain of verified prophecy.

FREAKS OF THE HURRICANE.

" Then the behavior of the storm with reference to its movements becomes almost fantastic. It was as if its controlling spirit had received a notice of the warning that had preceded it and the preparations of commerce to defend itself from its attacks. Therefore it made a feint demonstration upon the Atlantic Ocean, and suddenly turning fairly about in its course flew westward out of barometric supervision to seek a more vulnerable spot. Galveston was open to it, and sweeping across the gulf, from which no herald of warning could hasten in advance, it struck the Texas coast on Saturday and went howling with demoniac fury over the Mississippi plateau, across the lakes and down the St. Lawrence Valley out to sea again, to be chilled to death in the frigid air currents of the polar seas.

" When the West India Islands and the ports of Mexico are equipped with weather observing stations from which prompt and frequent reports shall be made, no storm can draw nigh on shores to effect a surprise. Commerce can in a measure protect itself, but ill-built cities and crops must at intervals suffer. The lesson of the last one is of warning, but how to profit by it outruns prevision that seeks absolute security. There can be no such thing, ' for as the pestilence walketh in darkness and destruction wasteth at noon still a thousand shall fall and ten thousand at thy right hand, for the hand of man cannot stay the tempest.' This is according to all human experience."

To have saved and then to have lost is if anything harder to bear than to have lost at first. It was thus with Mr. William H. Irvin, who succeeded in saving his wife and all but one of his children from the death which the elements were so anxious to administer, but afterwards lost his wife, who succumbed to the injuries she received that night.

The story of Irvin and his family's escape is like those of others who succeeded in getting out alive. It is simply marvelous, and their coming out with their lives can only be credited to that supreme power which is even mightier than the winds and sea. While he did all that any human could in saving his loved ones, yet his efforts were naught in that mighty battle of the elements.

GREAT DARING SHOWN.

In point of detail his story corresponds with the many others that are told of that night, but it is one of great daring also, one in which quick action and a trust in Divine Providence played an important part. Irvin was living with his happy family in a little story and a half cottage near the corner of Nineteenth street and Avenue O½ before the storm, but now all of that happy home is gone, and two of that happy family are no more.

It was early in the afternoon that the water began rising out there, but it was not until later, when all chance of getting out and coming to town to a place of safety was gone, did they become frightened. The house, though small was strongly built, and it was this that caused several of the neighbors who were living in frail houses to come to the Irvin home for refuge. They were Mrs. Crowley, two sons and a daughter, and Miss Aldridge. Along in the afternoon they became thoroughly frightened by the waters, which were rapidly rising, and the wind which was increasing in velocity every minute.

And well they might, for at that time the house was beginning to groan under the fierce onslaughts of the wind and the water. They stayed downstairs until the water had creeped up into the house, coming up and up until it drove them to the stairs. Then it drove them up step by step. They were frightened, yes, but never did the dreadful picture of what did happen present itself to even their terror-stricken minds. No imagination was then able to make a picture like the one in reality.

They were thus driven up into the attic by the waters and terrorized by the wind until after dark. Then, as if to follow out the idea that whom the gods wish to destroy they first make mad, the wind added to their fright and almost crazed them by carrying before it to their ears the frantic appeals for help from those who were already in the storm's clutches and were soon to become its victims. The houses around them went, nothing being able to stand against the mighty force of the wind and waves. Then it was that their house began to creak and groan louder than ever, until at last Irvin and his fellows in distress felt that it was going the next minute, and if they did not get out then they never would.

EIGHT CHILDREN THROWN OUT OF WINDOW.

So, having no time for a second thought, he picked up one o those eight children, whose life was part of his and who made his life worth living, and with a prayer tossed him out of the window, to alight on what he did not know, if to alight on anything. But he thought, and wisely, as circumstances proved, that they would have a better chance in the open than in a falling house. He risked their falling into that turbulent sea and sinking, never to come up, to leaving them in the building to be maimed by flying timbers and killed by the falling house.

Thus he threw out all of the eight, then came his wife, then the others who had come to him for refuge. He did not know what the fate of each of the former was when he threw out another, but trusted to Divine Providence, and not in vain. For as he threw the first out a shed in the rear of the house, as if with heroic instinct, washed against the building directly under the window, and there it stayed for a few seconds, catching each member of the family as he or she fell, even waiting for him.

The rest of Irvin's story is that of a continual fight to keep his family from being blown and washed off of the raft that Providence had given him. This fight lasted for hours and their perilous position was made even greater by the flying timbers and pieces of slate which the wind would seem to take such delight in hurling at them. It was a battle between providence and the elements to see which should claim the family for its own, and not until nearly three o'clock did the wind and water cease in their efforts to add the Irvin family to their long list of victims. The elements were recompensed by taking one of the eight children and injuring the wife so that she would later become one of their dead.

At about three o'clock the next morning Irvin found himself and family, except the little one who had been lost, several blocks from where he had formerly lived, and mixed up in the debris. At daylight he succeeded in getting his wife and children out and brought them to the business part of the town.

THE MOST REMARKABLE EXPERIENCE.

As soon as possible he sent the children to relatives in Houston. In the meantime his wife had been taken to the Sealy hospital suffering from the injuries she had received during the storm. At this time he realized that he was hurt also and went to the temporary hospital at the Custom House, where he stayed for several days under treatment. It was while he was there that the last sad chapter was added to his story. While there confined to his bed, his wife died in the Sealy hospital, and he had to lie at the Custom House without getting a last look at the woman whom he loved, while strangers were burying her body. Of his neighbors who took refuge with him all were saved except the little daughter of Mr. Crowley.

IMPRISONED BY THE STORM.

Thrilling Experience of Colonel Anderson, the Fort Point Lighthouse Keeper and His Wife—In the Face of Death the Light Was Put Up—Isolated for Days in the Wrecked House Without Supplies.

THE government reservation of several hundred acres situated at the extreme eastern end of Galveston island met the full force of the storm of September 8th. Unprotected from any side the destructive hurricane and relentless gulf swept the historic spot and the massive concrete fortifications crumbled like so much papier mache. The substantial, double iron-braced barrack buildings and quarters were battered into kindling wood and not a stick stands to mark the place where thirteen buildings stood. Situated within the United States government reservation were the quarantine officers' home and headquarters; the torpedo casemate, torpedo cable-tank, torpedo warehouse, engineers' store rooms and wharf leading to the cable tank and casemate.

These structures were located on the bay shore in the northwestern corner of the immense reservation. Following the jetty as it extended eastward and curved to the south were the United States life saving station and the Fort Point light house, each about two hundred yards apart. At the northeastern point of the island are the two rapid-fire batteries pointing over the jetty and commanding the channel in the bay between the two jetties. Around on the eastern and southeastern edge of the point are the 10-inch rifle battery and the 12-inch mortar battery, about 500 yards apart. In the centre of the reservation were grouped the barrack buildings. These buildings were built about eighteen months ago and afforded accommodations for a one-battery post.

The government was raising this reservation by filling in the site about ten feet above mean low tide. The quarters had not been occupied, having been built on piling, high in the air, to allow for the filling which was being distributed in the shape of sand pumped from the bay by the government dredge boat. The detail of twelve men from battery O which cared for the batteries at Fort San Jacinto, which was the new name given to the historic "Fort Point" of early Texas days, occupied quarters in temporary structures erected in the rear of the 10-inch battery.

Before the storm Fort San Jacinto was a most inviting and attractive place. The immense reservation east of the fence, which marked the western boundary, extending across the island from bay to gulf, was a most picturesque section of the island. When the storm had finished its merciless onslaught, Fort San Jacinto and its government structures presented a picture of terrible ruin. The costly coast fortifications, which had been constructed to withstand the attacking powers of the navies of the world, were silenced and rendered helpless by the combined batteries of the wind and sea.

The life saving station, where Captain Edward Haines and nine of his brave comrades stood ready to render succor to the storm-driven wretches, was picked up with its load of boats, beach apparatus and other life saving paraphernalia and crushed like a match box. Only four or five of the long pilings mark the site of the station house. Mrs. Haines, wife of Captain Haines, and one of the crew met their death at the station when the building collapsed.

WATERS OF BAY AND GULF MEET.

The south jetty, which marked the northern and eastern boundaries of the reservation, pointed its long line of rail-capped rocks five feet above the tide before the storm. But when the northeast gale backed the waters of the bay against the stone wall and the storm swelled the bay out of its banks, the water rose above the jetty and swept like a millrace to meet the waters of the gulf, which came running in from the southeast. This was early in the afternoon, and as the hurricane increased in velocity and the gulf roared out its warning, the terrible work of destruction commenced. The reservation was inundated and the force of the mighty waters quickly dug channels beneath the fortifications.

Then the wind and gulf joined forces and the great coast defenses succumbed to the attack and were washed from their foundations and half buried in the grave dug by the waters of the gulf. The immense concrete and rock structures toppled like toy houses as the greedy waters plowed channel after channel in the quicksand upon which the batteries stood. With the wooden structures, the barracks and warehouses, the wind made quick work, and the wreckage was shot through the rapids and carried to sea.

As the waters on their reservation rose higher and higher and the fortifications sank from view the lighthouse stood alone in the high sea which made the gulf and bay one. In this structure two human souls watched the storm gods at work and waited for their time. There was no hope of escape. The steel bridge leading from the top of the jetty to the lighthouse had been twisted by the wind and carried away; the lifeboat which hung from davits beneath the house had been snatched from its position and smashed against the iron supports, and the water carried off the splintered remnants.

Night came and the lamp in the tower, as though defying the hellish work of the raging elements, cast its mellow rays of light upon the scene of devastation and death which Night had just covered with its mantle. That human hands should dare to illuminate the appalling scene of tragedy must have enraged the murderous elements, and the storm batteries were turned on the tower. For an hour or more the attack continued with increasing vengeful power, and then—the light went out. Satisfied, perhaps, that the last defender of the reservation had been silenced the warring elements abandoned their fierce attack and entered the city to finish their destruction.

With the dawning of day an aged couple, who had faced many dangers in life's stormy sea together, came out on the gallery of the lighthouse and, standing arm in arm, viewed the funeral procession in the bay. They had survived the night, and while they stood there high above the water in silent thanksgiving for their safe deliverance, they saw the ebbing tide carrying its dead to sea. Out through the jetties the long cortege moved swiftly, with the angel of death piloting the craft of human corpses.

RISES TO A HEIGHT OF SIXTY FEET.

Fort Point lighthouse is situated two miles from the city. It is a six-sided iron structure rising above the water to a height of about sixty feet. It stands about 300 feet south of the jetty, and the water up to the time of the storm was never over two feet in depth around the house. At times it was dry, but usually only a few inches of water played around the iron screw piles, which were screwed into the sand about eighteen feet, and upon which the iron superstructure is supported. The metal framework supporting the lighthouse proper and the light tower rises about thirty-five feet from the base.

Then comes the living apartments of the keeper, Colonel C. A. Anderson, and his wife. On top is the light tower, a six-sided glass house, with iron framework. A gallery encircles the living apartments, and another the light tower. About ten feet beneath the living apartments and about twenty-five feet above the base a wooden platform served the dual purpose of basement and back yard to the isolated habitation. On this platform two large tanks furnished fresh water for the household, a shed held the wood supply and another shed was used as a storehouse for a several months' supply of kerosene oil for the light.

From the jetty a steel bridge led to the lighthouse, and from the bridge a stairway extended to the basement and living apartments. In the rear an iron ladder leading from the gallery of the keeper's home communicated with the "back yard" and basement, and also with the boat house and a platform extending from the rear of the structure to the bridge in front.

When the wind had subsided and the sea receded the naked metal frame supporting the house was all that was left of the lower structure. Wrapped around the iron pillars and braces were steel railroad tracks, which the wind and sea had wrenched from the jetty railroad and twisted around the lighthouse supports. The bridge had fallen an easy victim to the storm, and the water supply, wood, oil, lifeboat and stairway were torn from their fastenings and carried to sea. The jetty, with its huge rocks, weighing tons, had suffered many a breach, and a large opening was in front of the lighthouse. Through this break the waters of the gulf and bay rushed like a mill race, and a new channel connecting the bay and gulf was cut in a night. The isolation of the lighthouse was most complete.

STORM HOWLS A DEATH WARNING.

Colonel Anderson is seventy-three years of age and his wife some years his junior. No human mind can picture their experiences on that night of nights. Words are inadquate to convey an idea of the feelings of this devoted couple while the storm cried out its death warning and these two mortals prepared for the end which they were so sure was at hand. To attempt to leave the home would have been madness itself, but this thought was not for a moment entertained. The colonel would never desert his post, and his consort was happy to be near that they may both go to their death together.

Four rooms and a bath room comprised the home of the keeper, and the many friends of the family speak of the place as "Mamma Anderson's doll house." Not because the apartments are small, for they are comparatively good sized rooms, but because they were the cosiest and prettiest furnished rooms to be found, perhaps, on the whole island. Every nook and corner reflected the exquisite handiwork of the c r housewife who made this home an emporium of fancy needle work, embroidery, dainty laces and other rich and beautiful decorations and ornaments in which she justly took great pride.

The affectionate couple addressed each other in the endearing terms of "Mama" and "Papa," and their home far beyond the city is truly "home, sweet home."

Early in the afternoon of the storm Captain Haines and his brave crew from the life saving station manned the life boat and started to go to the lighthouse to bring the keeper and his wife to town. But even at that early hour no boat could live in the gale and raging sea that was threatening the destruction of the whole island. The wall of rock, called the jetty, would not permit any boat approaching within several hundred feet of the sharp-pointed line of stone extending five miles to sea. But, as Mrs. Anderson said in relating the incident to a *News* reporter who visited the stricken home two weeks after the storm: "It was a noble act for Captain Haines to attempt to rescue us, but it would have resulted in a useless risk, because Papa would not have left the lighthouse while it stood and I would never leave without him."

PREPARED FOR THE WORST.

Two hours after Captain Haines' attempt, the life saving station collapsed and Mrs. Haines, the nearest neighbor of the lighthouse keeper's family, and one of the crew were killed. As the shades of night began to fall the destruction in and about the Point was about complete, and the keeper of the light and his faithful companion withdrew to prepare themselves for the worst. From the sleeping room of Colonel Anderson a stairway, winding around a steel post, which extends from the top of the light tower through the center of the entire structure, and fastened to a screw pile in the sand bed, leads to the light tower.

Promptly at the usual hour the keeper who, for five years, has watched and cared for the light, made his way to the tower with his brass kerosene lamp and placed it within the strong, magnifying circular lens. The linen curtains which shade the glass enclosure during the day were drawn aside and the bright light shed its rays out into the gloom, and storm-tossed vessels in port were able to get their bearings.

The water rose higher and higher and the storm waves sent their spray over the top of the tower. The hurricane increased in violence and the slate from the roof of the keeper's home was picked off piece by piece by the wind. An hour passed, and the keeper had made frequent journeys to the tower to see that the light was burning. He went up again, but had hardly reached the landing through the small opening in the floor, when one of the large panes of thick glass on the northeast side was smashed by flying slate. The light was extinguished and a piece of glass struck the aged keeper in the head and face. The opening

33

in the lens faced the broken window pane and it was useless to relight the lamp. Stunned by the blow, and bleeding from the wounds in his head and face, the old man made his way down the stairs where his wife waited and watched for his return. "Mama" quickly dressed the wounds, and then the aged couple went into the parlor and in silence waited for the end.

Above the howling tempest the agonizing grinding of the jetty railroad iron on the metal supports of the lighthouse struck terror to the hearts of the anxious watchers imprisoned above. The slate roof suffered severely and the rain pouring in from above added to the pitiful experience of the night.

IN DANGER OF STARVATION.

This is just the plain story of what happened on that fateful night, but the sufferings of the next few days were even greater to the keeper and his wife. There were no provisions in the house and the supply of vegetables, fuel and fresh water in the "basement" had been washed away. The water around the house even after the tide went out was over ten feet deep. The life boat had been stolen by the storm, and not even a plank to serve as a raft was to be found on the premises. Having weathered the terrible storm they were apparently left to starve to death. The shipping in the harbor had suffered and no boats were to be seen in the channel. The flag of distress hoisted on the gallery was not responded to, and no small boat could enter through the breach in the jetty; it was too dangerous. Alone and forgotten. Who thought of the lighthouse and the two mortals imprisoned there by the storm and isolated by fate?

Three days passed and the scant supply of three or four cans of soup and fruit had long since been exhausted. On the third day a voice was heard calling from below and Mrs. Anderson recognized her son, C. D. Anderson, Jr., a boy of 16 years, swimming in the water from the jetty to the lighthouse. He had for three days been trying to get to his father and mother, having been up the bay with a surveying party when the storm struck the island. Dr. Mayfield, the quarantine officer, had brought him in his boat from town.

Young Anderson was fearful of the fate of his parents and he made his way to them as soon as possible. In a small bundle which he managed to save while he swam the stream, he carried some nourishment, but he had not contemplated that he would find his mother and father suffering for food and water. The boy returned to town and notified the authorities to send food and fresh water to the water-bound keeper and his wife, but the request was not complied with. The city was weighted with sorrow and every man was burdened with grave responsibilities. No boats were running out in that direction.

Ten days wore away and the situation had become critical with the noble keeper and his wife when the Arbutus, the light-house tender, came into port, and passing the light house saw the signal of distress flying from the prison-home. That day a supply of food and two small casks of tainted water were delivered at the light house. It was not the food that the family was accustomed to—it was simply hard tack and salt meat, which is supplied as rations to the crews of vessels. The government does not furnish supplies to its light house keepers, and Colonel Anderson's home always boasted of the goodies served at meal time at his own expense.

THE COLONEL A NOTED CHARACTER.

Two weeks after the storm the situation had been somewhat improved, but the fresh water supply had been exhausted and when a News reporter visited the home Colonel Anderson and his wife were praying for rain that they might catch a supply of heaven's dew in a tub which had been placed under the spout from the roof. The light house tender Arbutus had sent a man who repaired the damaged light tower, but the aged couple were left to their own resources to get water and food. The reporter, who had been able to reach the light house through the kindness of Assistant Engineer Wilcox of the United States engineering office, brought back to town another communication asking that food and water be sent out to the light house.

Colonel C. D. Anderson is quite a noted character and is well known as a man who figured conspicuously and gallantly in the civil war, and also in public office since the war. He is a native of South Carolina, a graduate of West Point and held a commission in the United States army before the civil war. He received his appointment as second lieutenant in the Fourth artillery from Texas on June 26, 1856, was made first lieutenant July 6, 1859, and on April 1, 1861, resigned his commission and came south to join the army of the confederacy. He was appointed to a captaincy and distinguished himself and rose rapidly to the rank of Colonel and was given command of the Twenty-first Alabama infantry.

He was in command of Fort Gaines and his gallant defense of that fort won the admiration of Admiral Farragut, who returned Colonel Anderson's sword which was delivered to the admiral at the surrender of the fort. Colonel Anderson has the sword in his possession and prides it as a gift from his friends when he came south and joined the confederate army.

The blade of the sword bears the following inscription which Admiral Farragut had engraved on the weapon before its return to its owner :

"Returned to Colonel C. D. Anderson by Admiral Farragut for his gallant defense of Fort Gaines, April 8, 1864."

The sword was carried by Colonel Anderson in the battle of Shiloh and through many other battles and historical occurrences in the long struggle between the north and the south.

After the war the colonel, who is a civil engineer of note, held several prominent positions under the government in river and harbor engineering, and finally came to Texas where he has resided for many years. He engaged in railroad construction and built many miles of Texas roads. He served two terms as city engineer of Austin and then came to Galveston. The new custom house in this city stands as a monument to the engineering skill of the aged keeper of Fort Point lighthouse, whose life history reads like a romance. Mrs. Anderson comes from a family closely associated with the history of this country, and the department of justice building in Washington was her father's home and the house where Colonel Anderson, then a gallant young army officer, claimed her as his bride.